CW01024692

# OUTBACK
## *Heart*

# OUTBACK
## *Heart*

## Joanne van Os

**BANTAM**
SYDNEY • AUCKLAND • TORONTO • NEW YORK • LONDON

Aboriginal readers: Please note that in the picture sections of this book are photographs of people who may now be deceased.

OUTBACK HEART
A BANTAM BOOK

First published in Australia and New Zealand in 2005
by Bantam

National Library of Australia
Cataloguing-in-Publication Entry

van Os, Joanne.
Outback heart.

ISBN 1 86325 502 8.

1. van Os, Joanne. 2. Ansell, Rod. 3. Women – Northern Territory – Biography. 4. Country life – Northern Territory. 5. Northern Territory – Rural conditions. I. Title.

920.72099429

Transworld Publishers,
a division of Random House Australia Pty Ltd
20 Alfred Street, Milsons Point, NSW 2061
http://www.randomhouse.com.au

Random House New Zealand Limited
18 Poland Road, Glenfield, Auckland

Transworld Publishers,
a division of The Random House Group Ltd
61-63 Uxbridge Road, Ealing, London W5 5SA

Random House Inc
1745 Broadway, New York, New York 10036

Map designed by Anna Warren
Typeset by Midland Typesetters, Maryborough, Victoria
Printed and bound by Griffin Press, Netley, South Australia

10 9 8 7 6 5 4 3 2 1

*For Callum and Shaun*

'Some people hear the howl of the wolf at night and understand its voice. They are unable to stay in the safe places of the world, and seek out its soul in spite of how dangerous that can be. Sometimes that search is for the wild and remote places of the world. Sometimes it is for the wild and remote places of the human spirit, perhaps an even more dangerous journey.'

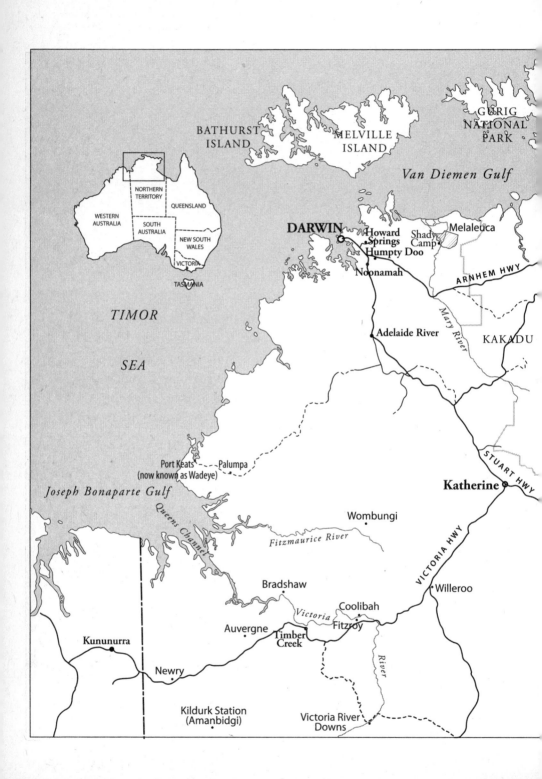

BATHURST
ISLAND

MELVILLE
ISLAND

GURIG
NATIONAL
PARK

*Van Diemen Gulf*

NORTHERN
TERRITORY

QUEENSLAND

WESTERN
AUSTRALIA

SOUTH
AUSTRALIA

NEW SOUTH
WALES

VICTORIA

TASMANIA

**DARWIN**

Howard
Springs
Humpty Doo

Shady
Camp

Melaleuca

Noonamah

ARNHEM HWY

*TIMOR*

*SEA*

Adelaide River

*Mary River*

KAKADU

Port Keats ---- Palumpa
(now known as Wadeye)

*Joseph Bonaparte Gulf*

*Queens Channel*

STUART HWY

**Katherine**

Wombungi

*Fitzmaurice River*

VICTORIA HWY

Bradshaw

Willeroo

*Victoria*

Coolibah

Auvergne

Fitzroy

Kununurra

**Timber
Creek**

*River*

Newry

Kildurk Station
(Amanbidgi)

Victoria River
Downs

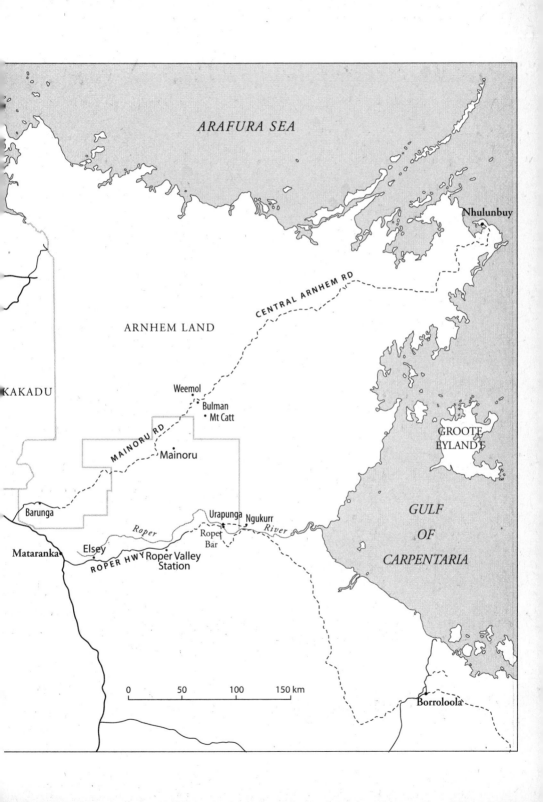

ARAFURA SEA

Nhulunbuy

CENTRAL ARNHEM RD

ARNHEM LAND

KAKADU

Weemol

Bulman
Mt Catt

GROOTE
EYLANDT

MAINORU RD

Mainoru

GULF

Barunga

OF

Urapunga Ngukurr
Roper                    River

CARPENTARIA

Roper
Bar

Mataranka

Elsey

ROPER HWY Roper Valley
Station

0      50      100      150 km

Borroloola

# Contents

# Prologue

3 August 1999. The two policemen had been on duty since 3.30 am. There had been no sign of the madman who had been shooting up houses in the area a few hours earlier. Now it was past 9 am, and the sun was doing its best work. The heat haze was already warping the view north up the highway to Darwin. White striped bitumen, khaki olive bush and red dirt shimmered and wavered into the distance. South of the roadblock a long line of road trains, cars and caravans grew impatient and irritated as they slowly roasted in the relentless heat.

Sergeant Glen Huitson and his partner, Constable Jamie O'Brien, had been roused from their beds in Adelaide River in the dead of night after shots had been fired at residents in the Darwin rural area, about 60 kilometres south of Darwin. They were ordered to set up a roadblock at the intersection of the Stuart Highway and Old Bynoe Road, less than a kilometre from the northern roadblock at Kentish Road, stopping all traffic from moving through the area. The Tactical Response Group had been searching most of the night without any result, and it now seemed unlikely that the gunman would still be hanging around in broad daylight.

A couple of locals, waiting to get to work, wandered over to chat with the officers. Jonathon Anthonyszz leant against the bonnet of the squad car, and Anthony Hobden squatted nearby, talking to the officers. It had been a long night, but now in broad daylight, it seemed like there wasn't much to worry about.

The first shot spun Anthonyszz off the bonnet and onto the ground. The policemen snatched up their weapons and returned fire, just before the gunman's second shot tore through a gap in Huitson's ballistic vest, and dropped him to the road. O'Brien kept up a hail of shots in the direction of the armed man who he could just make out across the road.

The TRG squad ran for their vehicles as soon as they heard the gunfire. The two vehicles swerved to stop a few hundred metres away from the roadblock, and one clipped the other and rolled. The crash attracted the gunman's attention, and he rose up onto one knee from his position in the grass, and swung his rifle around at the men scrambling from the rear of the wrecked troop carrier. Constable O'Brien suddenly had a clear shot, and took it, and the gunman fell.

It was the end of several things. It was the end of the life of a fine young policeman, a man with a young family who was loved and respected in the small community of Adelaide River where he lived and worked. It was the end of the Crocodile Dundee story, according to the media. And it was the end of Rod Ansell, also a man with a family who loved him, and who had once been a national hero, a reflection of what Australia liked most about itself. Now he lay dead on the side of a road in the outback, his face in the dirt, his blood seeping into the hot ground, his body torn and blasted with shotgun pellets.

This is the story of my life with Rod Ansell, who had first captured the imagination of Australians when he survived for two months in 1977 on a remote river in the far north. Our relationship spanned twenty-two years, first as lovers, then spouses, parents, business partners and finally as divorcees.

How does someone go from being a person whose extraordinary story of survival in the wild inspired so many people to a psychotic, drug-crazed gunman who shot four people, killing one of them – a police officer – before being killed himself? It was the question asked by a lot of people when Rod died, and I am attempting to answer it here, or at least to shed some reasonable light on it. It may help people understand what happened to a man who could have been anything, and who had so much to offer, but who got lost along the way.

Maybe he was a captive of his dreams and fantasies, maybe he had some fatal flaw that no one could see or circumvent. He took a young girl from the suburbs of Melbourne to the outreaches of her existence, and made her life the most exhilarating, terrifying and awesome experience, in his own quest to find out what life was all about. What he didn't understand, and didn't learn, was that you don't have to destroy life, or the people you love, to find that out.

This is a story of love, and how the people we love can have devastating effects on us that bear little resemblance to the effects of love. It's a story about survival in more ways than one.

# 1

# My Father's Genes

Mum blames it on the family loo. When people ask her why her eldest daughter lives so far away, she points to the toilet. She hung a huge map of Australia in there one day, with the throwaway line that while we were attending to business, we may as well learn some geography. I used to study that map, and in particular the far north coast. There were no roads, but there were little towns. Miles and miles of apparently nothing. How did people live in that part of the world? The first chance I got, I was going to go and find out.

My father, Martin van Os, had emigrated from Holland in 1952, on board one of the Liberty ships, the *Waterman*. Third youngest of nine children, he was born in 1929 in Veghel, a small village in the south of Holland, where he spent his adolescent years under German occupation during World War II. He hated the cold, the snow and the dampness of his home country, and often told people that as soon as he was old enough he was going somewhere warm. The Dutch army thoughtfully sent him to do his national service in the hot latitudes of the West Indies, where he thrived in the heat and the strangeness of islands filled with donkeys and cactus. He had a way with words, and filled in any spare time there writing letters and love poems for his fellow soldiers to send back to their sweethearts. His older sister Anne had married and emigrated to Australia, so the choice of where to go after he left the army was simple. Australia was booming in the fifties, there was plenty of work for a qualified carpenter, and it was definitely warm. His brother-in-law met him when he landed in Melbourne in

November 1952, and Martin stepped off the ship and onto the back of a motorbike to ride to Eildon Weir where a job was waiting for him. The following year he went to work at Kwinana in Western Australia, returning to Melbourne to spend Christmas with his sister's family.

In January 1954 Martin boarded the *Stratheden* at Port Melbourne to sail back to Perth. Coming out of his cabin the first night on board, he bumped into a young lady with 'the most beautiful smile'. Therese O'Sullivan had joined the ship in Sydney and was also bound for Western Australia, where she was going to work as a governess for her sister Peg Pennington on her sheep station. Just two nights later Martin asked Therese to marry him. After a courtship conducted for several months over country phone lines with the neighbours listening in and offering advice, they returned to Therese's family home in Sydney where they were married in December 1954.

Therese had grown up in a noisy, busy household, the ninth of twelve children. The youngest of six girls, in the middle of her six brothers, she was born at the Nepean Dam west of Wollongong in New South Wales in 1931, where her father Thomas O'Sullivan was working. The family moved to Sydney not long afterwards, and in 1944 Thomas died, leaving my grandmother to raise a large family on her own, with nearly half of them still at school. It was a year for tragedy, because her eldest son, also named Thomas, was killed fighting in New Guinea just seven months later. For the last three and a half years of the war, her daughter Catherine, who was a nun in New Guinea, had been held in a prisoner of war camp by the Japanese with the rest of her convent. The nuns had refused to leave when the war came to their part of the world, instead staying in Rabaul to nurse the Allied wounded. My grandmother May O'Sullivan was made of some pretty tough stuff. In spite of everything she managed to keep her family together under extremely difficult circumstances, and lived to see most of her forty-seven grandchildren before she died at the age of seventy-five.

By 1958, my parents had three children. I was born in October 1955, Peter in 1957, and Robert one year to the day later in 1958. We had lived with my grandmother and her three youngest sons so far, which helped my parents get on their feet, but there was more work for a carpenter in Melbourne, and land was cheaper there than it was in Sydney. And it must have been getting a bit cosy with all of us under one roof, even though it was a big house.

Mum must have missed her family terribly when we moved to Melbourne. However, with three children by the time I was twenty-seven months old, she probably didn't have a lot of space to think about it. Two more daughters followed, Leonie in 1960 and Pauline in 1966. Our new neighbourhood had a lot of young families, and Mum soon got to know the other mothers in the street, most of whom have remained friends for the last forty-five years. It was a great network of women who supported each other through various crises, celebrated every happy event, looked after each other's children, and of course provided me and my siblings with a whole lot of playmates.

Ringwood was 26 kilometres from the city, and the outer limit of eastern suburbia at the time. Maidstone Street was just a dirt road, and the countryside surrounding us was a combination of paddocks and uncleared bush, paradise for energetic kids. Our childhood was typical of suburban Australia in the early sixties. Every house in our street seemed to be full of kids. We roamed the bush with them, and played in each other's backyards. Dad built us amazing cubbyhouses which he kept improving as the years went on, and constructed all kinds of playground equipment in our backyard.

Looking at the safety-conscious designs of today, Dad's were a litigation looking for a courtroom, but every kid in the street thought we were the luckiest in the world. The merry-go-round was a smooth-barked log mounted on a centre pivot, with a seat at each end, the centrepoint greased well so it spun as fast as we could push it. A large and heavy wooden rocker could hold six or eight kids, and be rocked to within a gasp of disaster. And look out if your toes got in the way . . . We had ropes hanging out of the trees to swing on, parallel bars nailed up between them (which someone would regularly fall off while hanging upside down), swings and a big heavy seesaw. There were bumps and scrapes but no one ever seriously hurt themselves.

Building billycarts was a major obsession. Peter, Robby and I messed around with apple crates and pram wheels, but Dad's billycarts were the envy of the neighbourhood. One in particular was an ancient push/pull chain-driven affair, which Dad modified and rebuilt until it looked like Fred Flintstone's car. The hill in our street was steep enough to get up some speed, and once this billycart got going, there was no steering it, let alone stopping. Dad was a wizard with anything timber, but mechanics were not really his field. There were no brakes, apart from a length of wood he fixed to the back, with the instruction to push it back as hard as you could so it dug in the ground and slowed you down. We worked out pretty soon that this was the quickest way to capsize the cart . . . Permanently scabbed knees and elbows were just a normal part of life.

Dad had come to Australia looking for the outback and better weather. Melbourne certainly wasn't the outback, but at least the weather was warmer than Holland. He made up for the tameness of the suburbs by taking us kids into the bush, anywhere he couldn't see houses and telegraph poles, at every opportunity. He'd walk the legs off us, exclaiming all the way about the smells, and the sounds of water far off, and hidden lyrebirds, singing songs at the top of his lungs, and somehow never losing any of us.

When I was eleven we bought our first car, and began going on camping holidays for three weeks every Christmas. Two or three other families usually came with us, which meant that there were around fifteen children to entertain each other. Mum loved the beach, so we mostly headed for the coast, or somewhere with water. Three weeks with five children in a tent – it was no mean feat for my city-raised mother and, being Victoria, that sometimes meant five children in a *wet* tent. We were all given our jobs, and once breakfast and clothes washing were finished, Mum would head for the beach with an umbrella and a stack of books. It was the only time of the year when she really could relax.

We grew up surrounded by a wonderful multicultural blend of people. The huge wave of immigration to Australia after the war meant that my classmates right through school were a mix of Italian, Polish, Latvian, Dutch, British, Irish, Hungarian and Yugoslav migrants. I never heard anyone called a wog or a dago at school, but woe betide you if you were caught out in the street in your uniform passing the state school. There was no racism that I ever saw, but there were plenty of religious wars between the kids who went to Our Lady's Catholic primary school, and the kids from Ringwood State School.

'Catholic frogs, sitting on a log!' was responded to with 'Proddy dogs, sitting in a bog!'

Aquinas Girls College, Ringwood, opened the year that I began secondary school. One hot summer morning in 1967, ninety little girls lined up in rows on a freshly gravelled yard in front of a building so new you could smell the paint. Our uniforms didn't arrive for another six weeks, so we were an oddly colourful lot for a Catholic girls' college. There were just three first forms to start with, and each year a little more construction happened, so that by the time we reached sixth form, the college was complete. I made a group of friends in that first year who have remained my friends ever since, and I had some excellent teachers. Two who made a lasting impression on me were Sister Helen Reed, a St Joseph nun with a brilliance for teaching English literature, and a Dominican nun, Sister Gabrielle Kelly, our very young principal, who had a skill in dealing with students that belied her own youth. The school was unusual in that it was staffed by nuns from five different orders, as well as lay teachers. It also wasn't bound by years of tradition and patronage, so I think we students unconsciously absorbed the idea that there was more than one way to do just about anything.

My adolescence and teenage years were fairly serene – I think my parents got off lightly. I was a very late starter where boys were concerned, not actually having a real boyfriend until I'd left school. My girlfriends and I were more interested in doing things together, like horse riding, hiking, writing plays and performing them, and hanging out together talking.

I was seventeen when I completed Year 12 in 1972. I had no clear idea of what I wanted to do with my life. All I knew for sure was that I didn't want a 'boring office job'. I found myself a job as a laboratory technician in lieu of taking up a place at university, and for the next three years worked with the Marine Pollution Studies Group (MPSG), part of the Victorian Fisheries and Wildlife Department. The lab was near the industrial part of the city, in ancient buildings in South Melbourne overlooking the muddy brown Yarra River at the bottom end of Flinders Street. I worked with Dr Graeme Arnott, studying zooplankton, gathering population data for Westernport Bay, and establishing tolerance levels for various toxic heavy metals.

It was interesting work, and I felt that I was doing something useful.

By the beginning of my third year at MPSG I was ready for a change of direction. For the past year I had been going out with a young man who also worked there, and we became engaged. John was an active outdoors person, and as well as teaching me to scuba dive, he shared my love of hiking and camping. He was my first serious boyfriend, and I had believed I was in love up to that point. After weeks of dreadful uncertainty I realised I wasn't ready to marry anyone, and feeling like a traitor I broke the engagement. I was nineteen years old and at a crossroads in my life, unhappy where I was, but uncertain where to go next.

At Mass one Sunday that winter the priest asked if families could billet some young Aboriginal boys coming to see the bright lights of Melbourne for the first time, from their home in the Northern Territory. My family took in two of them. I was intrigued by these boys. They were about fourteen years old, spoke a little halting English, and had the blackest skin I had ever seen. I knew nothing about Aboriginal people. I had always assumed – if I thought about it at all – that there were few, if any, full-blood Aboriginals left in Australia. I thought I had grown up in a multicultural environment, but here was a completely alien culture in my own country, and I barely knew anything about it.

At a barbecue during their stay, I talked with Father John Shallvey, the priest who accompanied the boys, about Port Keats, and about the people who lived there. At the time my best friend Sabrina Lethbridge and I were thinking about making a long working trip around Australia, and I wondered if it was possible to call in and visit a place like Port Keats.

'You should come and work with us for a year,' he said enthusiastically. 'We have lots of young people who come and help us run the mission.'

'But I'm not a nurse or a teacher,' I answered, *and I'm certainly not a missionary,* I thought privately. I had a strong Catholic faith, and had been an active part of the youth groups in our parish, but I wasn't an evangelist.

'Oh, there's lots of things that need doing there,' said Father Shallvey. 'I'll let you know!'

In the meantime, a new marine biologist came to work at MPSG, a red-headed Englishman called Dave Kay. We began going out with each other, although I made it clear that I was planning to leave Melbourne at the end of the year. Dave bought himself a Mini Moke, and I would devise weekend trips into the bush via the most obscure dirt roads I could find. He introduced me to politics and widened my view of the world in general. He didn't share my religious beliefs in any way, but he was respectful of them, and apart from intellectual jousting over contentious issues, never tried to change the way I thought. Dave could definitely take credit for improving my music tastes, though – he thought I listened to far too much Joan Baez.

The newspapers were running lots of stories about the rebuilding of Darwin after the devastation of Cyclone Tracy in December 1974. Tracy had almost wiped the town off the map, destroying over 10 000 houses and killing at least sixty people. The reconstruction of Darwin kicked off a boom that wouldn't stop for twenty years. I read everything I could about this place that I'd never considered before, now that there was a vague possibility I might go there. But it wasn't the building activity that caught my attention, it was the photos of people in shorts and sarongs. In July. It was freezing in Melbourne that winter, and Darwin seemed like another country altogether – a much warmer one. My father's genes were showing through.

About October, Father Shallvey's letter arrived with an offer of a job as the radio operator and assistant to the mission superintendent. Experience didn't seem to be a prerequisite. By now Sabrina and I were planning a trip overseas, and as I had saved most of the money I would need, I decided I could afford to take the low wage offered by the mission, and still be able to have enough to make the trip. A year sounded pretty good. I would finish my job at Fisheries and Wildlife in January, and head north soon after that. Mum was expecting her sixth child, due in May 1976. I planned to start at Port Keats in early February, and come home for a week or two in May to help with the new arrival.

As the first of the family to leave home, my parents watched me go with some trepidation. Mum was satisfied it would be safe because I was going to be living on a Catholic mission. Dad worried about me being speared by wild Aborigines, but agreed that being run over by a truck in Flinders Street was a lot more likely. If anything, he wished he was the one heading north to the wilderness.

I took my leave of Dave with bittersweet confusion. Our relationship had grown over the last few months, and I was hesitant about going away now. I was in love with him, but I knew it wasn't enough to stop me from following my plans. I felt sad on the plane as I left, but also elated at knowing I was at the beginning of a new stage of my life. I was twenty years old.

# 2

# Lying Down with the Ants

Darwin was hot and humid in February 1976. The plane landed during a lull in the storms, and I stepped onto the steaming tarmac, amazed that air this hot and damp was still breathable. It wasn't a pretty town, and it looked strangely bare and barren, not at all like the tropical paradise I'd expected. Cyclone Tracy had destroyed many of the trees, and left the town exposed to the fierce glare of the sun. It was utilitarian, stripped to the basics, and didn't look very inviting.

The clean-up after the cyclone had been completed in record time, and one year later there wasn't a lot left to show of the terrible destruction, apart from the missing greenery, and houses with only the pillars and floorboards left standing. Driving through the suburbs, I'd come across the remains of houses wrapped in tarpaulins and cobbled together with wire and corrugated iron sheets, sporting signs such as 'We still live here – KEEP OUT!' and 'OCCUPIED – Piss Off!' The buildings in the city itself were uninspiring and ugly, except for the Darwin Hotel, which was evocative of the kind of tropical outpost I'd expected to find. It had high ceilings and dim cool rooms, with palms and bamboo fittings, and old fashioned punkahs gently stirring the air. Just the place for a gin and tonic and Somerset Maugham, except the bar was usually full of blokes drinking beer.

At first I didn't like Darwin much. Apart from being an ugly town, it seemed as if it wasn't sure what it was. It was both suburban and frontier at the same time. People worked in office jobs, shopped in supermarkets, and sent their children to school. And they drank beer like there was no tomorrow, went fishing for monster barramundi in rivers full of legendary crocodiles, and considered themselves a different breed from 'southerners'. A person's worth seemed to be reflected by how long they had been in Darwin, and the main topics of conversation invariably included a defensive tirade about how much better life was 'up here' than it was in the benighted 'down south'.

A couple of days before I was to leave for Port Keats, I went shopping for food supplies to take with me. Woolworths was the biggest store in the city, in a prime position on the corner of Smith and Knuckey Streets. What I remember most were the long empty shelves, with the odd, sad looking tin of something no one wanted. There were scurrying cockroaches, and the packets of rice were alive with weevils, but no one seemed to object.

'Three dollars for a cabbage?' They were only about thirty cents in Melbourne in 1976. Three dollars seemed incredible.

The checkout girl looked at me boredly. 'They have to come in by plane, and freight costs a lot.'

'How come there's no food on the shelves?'

She rolled her eyes heavenwards, and fixed me with a glare that dared me to complain about it. 'It's the *wet* season.'

'Oh. Right.'

I was clearly a typically ignorant southerner who just expected things to be the same as at home. I didn't dare ask about the weevils. I discovered later that the roads were in fact closed for longer than usual, slowing the road freight and causing shortages of some items. Fresh vegetables and fruit were always more expensive due to the costs of air freight.

What I very soon came to love about Darwin was the tolerance of oddity it had – and still has. At a party the drunk in the sarong quoting Shakespeare and falling into the pool could be a plumber, or a Supreme Court judge. Homeless itinerants wandering the main streets were given a kind of legend status by the rest of the town, like Walking Tommy. He was very tall, very thin, and had long white whiskers and hair. He would be seen in the city centre one day, and miles out of town the next, always walking with a strange faraway look in his eyes.

The chef at one restaurant I went to emerged from his kitchen waving a cleaver, demanding to know 'Who's whingeing about the fuckin' food?', and went round the tables tasting bits off people's plates. No one complained, or even seemed to think it was unusual. There appeared to be a total absence of the conventions and rules of Melbourne. This was underlined by the numbers of young people compared to the older generation. It was like the kids had taken over the town. It was full of young labourers, young lawyers, young teachers, young entrepreneurs, all jostling and sparring to make their mark in a place that was more likely to let them than the southern capitals.

People laughed louder, drank more, played harder and had a complete contempt for pretentiousness. There seemed to be a concentration of the most iconic Australian characteristics – broad accents, with sentences usually including 'big mobs' and ending in 'ay?', a devotion to yarn-spinning that was almost religious, a casual approach to the most serious topics and an attitude of getting on with the real job, and not worrying about the p's and q's. 'This place is an open-air lunatic asylum', I wrote to a friend. 'There are people walking around here who'd be locked up in Melbourne. It's wonderful!'

People dressed differently from their southern counterparts. Suits were non-existent, and ties rarely seen. If someone turned up in a shirt and long trousers, his mates would either assume he'd been to a funeral, or ask him, 'How'd you go in court?' There was a kind of uniform for the male office worker, which was a (largely unflattering) ensemble of short-sleeved nylon shirt, tailored shorts, and long socks and shoes. The avant-garde wore sandals with their socks. Men wore their hair long, and sported sideburns. On weekends this dress was generally swapped for the ubiquitous 'stubby' shorts, and a singlet or T-shirt and thongs. Dressing up meant a better kind of T-shirt. Women dressed much more casually than in Melbourne. Dresses were short in the fashion of the seventies, and pretty much straight cotton shifts. They were cool, anyway. I didn't see a pair of stockings for years.

Casual dress was *very* casual. Sarongs knotted across breasts, terry-towelling shorts and 'boob tubes', shorts and tops and thongs. Fashion was much more relaxed than in Melbourne. *People* were much more relaxed. Doors were rarely locked, windows usually louvred to let in the breezes, assisted by whirring overhead fans, and refrigerators large to hold the necessary quantities of cold beer. Visitors always seemed to be welcomed whether expected or not, and pressed to share a drink or a meal. Generosity was the word that characterised Darwin. Almost everyone I met showed the same open generosity, whether it was just sharing a beer, or offering a place to sleep for a night, or a few months if need be.

Several years after I moved north, my parents came to Darwin to visit for the first time. We were about 30 kilometres out of the city when my car suddenly spluttered and died. I pulled off the highway and raised the bonnet, while Dad hovered beside me, presumably looking for any wooden bits he could fix. We had only just started to check the obvious things when a ute pulled off the road in front of us and two men got out. Without a word to Dad or me, one hopped in the driver's seat, and the other proceeded to fiddle with bits of engine, and after about ten minutes they got it going again. They nodded briefly, said, 'She's right,' and took off in their ute.

Dad stared down the road after them. 'Does that often happen up here?'

'Yes,' I said. 'It does.'

Sixteen inches of rain had closed the Port Keats airstrip the day before I was due to fly there, and it was a week before I finally arrived to start my new job, and my new life. Port Keats was bright green, and bright red. The vegetation was almost too green to be real, and the rest of the picture was red – sticky red mud. No one would get in or out by road until at least May. I was well and truly isolated, geographically at least. I didn't mind at all. The further the plane travelled from civilisation, the more my excitement and anticipation increased. This was as far from 'anywhere' that I had ever been, and I couldn't wait to find out what life here would be like.

Port Keats was the last settlement on the western coast of the Northern Territory. It was close to the West Australian border, on the Joseph Bonaparte Gulf, a few kilometres up the aptly named Sandfly Creek, about 60 kilometres north of the Fitzmaurice River mouth. You could get there by light aircraft from Darwin in an hour, or else spend eleven hours driving over incredibly bad roads. The surrounding country was generally dry open forest, with some spectacular red cliffs edging the coast and a table-topped mountain nearby. It must have been good country to find a living in, because it was supporting seven Aboriginal tribes when the Missionaries of the Sacred Heart started a mission there at the request of the government, in 1936. Then the people settled around the little outpost, stopped warring with each other, more or less, and became Christians. There were thirty-five Europeans when I arrived in February 1976, and about a thousand Aboriginals.

I moved into a house with two other girls, both teachers. Julie Carr, also from Melbourne, was the same age as me, and Christine Steer was a 25-year-old graduate from Sydney. The other four young women lived in the single girls' house, a large brick building nearby, and adjacent to that was the single men's quarters. Married couples had their own houses, while the nuns and priests lived in their convent and presbytery, both very old, corrugated iron buildings. There was a small hospital, run by Sister Moira and her staff, and a bakery operated by the indefatigable Sister Frederick, who also cooked for the priests, nuns and the single men, and provided our daily morning tea at the Old Presbytery. The school catered for about two hundred and fifty children, up to Year 7. The Aboriginal people lived in four main areas, according to their clans. Their houses were mostly corrugated iron sheds in various stages of disrepair, although there were some European style houses as well. There were dogs everywhere, and lots of rubbish. Third World stuff to a girl from the suburbs.

But in 1976, Port Keats was a wonderful place. There was no alcohol in the community then. The community was peaceful and seemed to manage a happy blend of traditional ways and Catholicism. During the week the place bustled with energy and purpose. Most able people seemed to be employed one way or another, in the hospital, shop, bakery, housing project, or working for the council. At nights I would go to sleep listening to the sound of clap sticks and didgeridoos down in the camps. On weekends we would often go out camping and hunting with local families, looking for goanna, magpie geese, fish and turtle. Everyone travelled in the back of 4WD utes – kids, dogs, old grandmothers, a hessian bag full of some protesting future dinner, all jostling together. We'd eat the food caught during the day, with hot damper and golden syrup, drink lots of sweet black tea boiled in empty flour drums, and sleep under the stars listening to soft voices speaking in Murinbata, the main language spoken at Port Keats. It was like travelling in a foreign country, with friendly foreigners who were pleased to show us their home, and attempt to teach us their language.

The first weekend I was there Lesley Rourke, who had been at Port Keats for a couple of years already, invited me and my house mate Christine to come for a walk with her and some old women to Ardan-itchi, a place on the coast about 7 kilometres away. We were going hunting for mangrove crabs. I was left completely in awe of those old women. We sloshed through swamps, crossed a deep billabong on an underwater log, climbed through mangrove trees, and those old ladies never slowed down. They scampered around the mangrove roots and up the trees like they were teenagers compared to Christine and me, who constantly needed to be helped out of the deep mud. At one point they started giggling nervously and pointing at what looked to me like big wide drag marks between some trees. Christine and I were stuck in the mud again, up to mid thigh in the sticky grey stuff. Lesley interpreted and said, 'They say this is a crocodile slide, and they think you two had better go and wait back with the kids in case it's still around.'

I think they just got tired of pulling us out of the mud. We were shepherded from the swamp to where the children waited by a shallow sandy creek. The kids were pleased to have someone else to talk to, and we sat around chatting for a while. One of them, a little girl called Janet, said she was going to lay down and have a sleep.

'What, on the ground? What about the ants and things!' said Christine, looking horrified.

Janet grinned and closed her eyes. 'I don't care, I'm a black man!' she said.

So we laid down with the ants and went to sleep too.

The women came back with hessian bags full of mud crabs, and proceeded to cook them in the coals of the fire we had kept going. I don't think I've had mud crab so delicious ever again. They weren't boiled, just knifed, buried in the hot coals, and left to cook slowly in their own juices.

The trip back was a bit more interesting. It was dark before we were halfway home, and I realised with a sinking feeling that we still hadn't crossed the deep billabong, the one with the underwater log we had to balance on. It was so dark we could barely see each other in the gloom. One of the women gathered handfuls of dried pandanus leaves, tied them together with a bit of a vine, and set it alight. Now we could see where we were going, and soon came to the deep billabong. The one with the underwater bridge. Thoughts of crocodiles came back to me. The water reflected the burning torchlight and looked black and sinister. I was tired, sunburnt, bitten by a million mosquitoes and sandflies, covered in scratches and welts, and plastered with mud from the swamp. I looked at the old women, who just picked up the littlest kids and proceeded to cross, feeling their way forward with their feet. I decided there and then that if I survived this, I was going to just love this place.

My job gave me a bird's eye view of the Territory. In 1976 there was no telephone network outside of the major towns. Some stations and settlements had the radio-telephone, but Port Keats' only means of communication was by telegrams, which were transmitted over a two-way radio system, called 'Victor Juliet Yankee Outpost Radio Darwin'. Or just VJY for short. Contact with the outside world was in brief short code, because every word cost money. My job was to send and transmit messages over VJY several times a day, send weather reports, and assist the mission administrator. I also had to maintain contact with mission headquarters in Darwin, which operated on a different frequency, and had its own network with the other missions, which were Bathurst Island, Garden Point on Melville Island, and Daly River. Occasionally we would hear from the even more remote Kalumburu Mission over in the very north of Western Australia.

In 1976, I was hearing messages coming in static bursts from a little island to the northwest called Timor. The transmissions would come and go, depending on the weather, and the telegrams dictated to VJY were often hundreds of lines long. Because it sounded so unusual and so desperate, I copied down what I could overhear of the messages, but I didn't keep them, something I regret today. They were a plea to the Australian government and the Australian people for help. This was just after the invasion of Timor by Indonesia, and the start of a long war for the people of East Timor. Those telegrams also made me aware just how close we were to the rest of the world up here, and that people were dying just a few hundred miles away from us. Being the radio operator was often fascinating, because it was virtually a ringside seat to life in the bush. Every communication was by telegram, and just like the orders for spare parts or groceries, the more poignant moments of daily life had to be reduced to abrupt, brief lines spelt out across the static. I could only imagine what it must be like to be far away from your family, copying down a telegram informing you of the death of someone you loved. Several years later, VJY was able to facilitate calls directly between a telephone and a radio receiver, but for now it was limited to telegrams.

Football – Australian Rules football – was a passion with the local people. Teams were divided up by clans, and the games were basically transformations of generations-old-rivalries. Every weekend during the season the whole town would be down at the 'oval', barracking and cheering on their warriors over possession of the pigskin. Sometimes passions ran particularly high, and on those days, Father John Shallvey, the umpire, would have his motorbike waiting for him at the edge of the grounds. As soon as the final siren went, he would race for his bike, leap aboard, and gun his way through the crowd before the supporters of the losing side came after him.

I loved being there so much that by the end of the first year, I didn't want to leave. I was only just starting to feel as if I belonged, and not like an awkward outsider any more. I had been adopted by an elderly couple, Mary Tchembing and her husband Joseph, and by now I knew most of the people I saw. Like so many white people who go to live in Aboriginal communities, by the time I had been there a few months, I knew exactly what was wrong with the way things were, and exactly how to fix it. By the end of that first year, I understood that I knew very little at all, and had none of the answers. But what I had gained was a real respect for Aboriginal people, and for many of the nuns in particular who had devoted years of their lives to this community. This was in spite of my growing doubts about the Catholic Church as a whole. Most of the Europeans at Port Keats were there because they wanted to help, not to convert and evangelise, but to assist the

Aboriginal people to learn how to manage in our overwhelming culture. I was told when I started that my job was to teach myself out of a job. Like most of the white employees at Port Keats, I had an Aboriginal assistant, a young woman named Francesca, who I was training to be able to take over my role.

So I happily stayed for another year. Julie and Christine, my house-mates, were also staying for a second year, as were most of the other young single people who had started the previous January.

Halfway through 1977, I set off on my long awaited overseas trip. Sabrina was already there, working in Wales and giving me itchy feet with her descriptions of the country and the people. Dave, my English boyfriend from Melbourne, and I met in London, hired a car and made the most wonderful exploration of England for the next month. After the harshness and the stark isolation of the bush around Port Keats, the gentle green hills, winding hedgerows and thousand-year-old churches of England were overwhelming. I felt like I couldn't take it all in. We meandered from London to Land's End in the far west of Cornwall following the old smugglers' coast, north to the breathtaking beauty of the Lakes District, across to the bleak Yorkshire Dales, minus Heathcliff, and down to Norfolk in the east, before meeting up with Sabrina in London. After Dave returned to Australia, Sabrina and I hitchhiked our way around Scotland and the Outer Hebrides, found our way to as many folk festivals as we could manage back in England, and finished up in Holland, where we visited my father's family in Veghel. While we were staying there, Dave sent me a news clipping from the Melbourne papers, a front page story about a man who had been found on a remote river in the Northern Territory by Luke McCall. Dave had met Luke when he visited me at Port Keats the previous Christmas, and knew I'd be interested to read this story about him.

The photo was grainy and indistinct, but I recognised Luke and Rupert, lined up with two other Aboriginal men and a slight bearded man who scowled at the camera, his hands shoved into the pockets of his denim jacket.

'Well, that would've been a nine day wonder in Port Keats,' I said to Sabrina. 'The Palumpa blokes on the front page of the paper!'

# 3

# Six Weeks in the Wilderness

**November 1977**

The office door opened, and a figure was framed in the intense bright light. I glanced up and squinted against the glare at a slight, slim figure in a big hat. There was a boy standing there, a very handsome, blond haired, blue eyed boy. He was dressed in blue jeans, a blue shirt, high heeled riding boots, and a big brown hat which he took off as he came into the room. He looked about seventeen, and was frowning slightly at me, as if he had important things on his mind.

'Hi. Can I help you?' I said. I guessed straight away who he was. I'd heard that the young man whom Luke McCall had found marooned on a nearby river a few months before, was coming here this week, and no one else in Port Keats, except for the Aboriginal ringers from neighbouring Palumpa Station, dressed like this. He looked a lot younger than the papers had said he was.

'Yeah, g'day. Rod Ansell,' he said, extending his hand and shaking mine with a firm, confident grip. 'Ah, Luke asked me to give Joanne a message. He said to look for the prettiest girl in Port Keats, so I guess I've found the right one.'

I blushed and laughed. He grinned a bit then, a flash of brilliant, even white teeth in a lean brown face. He had the smoothest, softest looking skin, with lightly curling sideburns giving him a very country and western look. His hair was cut longish, but above his collar, and was a tousled, sun bleached blond. Small neat ears set close to his head and an almost perfect straight nose completed the picture. The only thing that jarred was a soft moustache, underlining the fact that he didn't look old enough to shave every day. He still looked very serious though, and I was reminded of an earnest youngster trying hard to impress an elder. It made me feel very worldly wise and all of my incredibly ancient twenty-two years.

'Well, maybe you have. I'm the only Joanne here, anyway. How is Luke?'

'He's fine. Said to tell you he'll be sending in some beef in a few days.' He had the most intense blue gaze I had ever seen. His eyes crinkled at the corners and seemed to be smiling even when his mouth wasn't.

'That's great – tell him thanks a lot.'

Rod nodded, looked serious again, said he'd see me later, and disappeared out the door.

Sometime in July, about four months earlier, Rod Ansell had been discovered stranded on the banks of one of the loneliest rivers in Australia – the Fitzmaurice – by Luke McCall, the white manager of Palumpa Station, and its Aboriginal owners, Rupert Wodidj, Raphael Thardim and Christopher Wodidj. The men were walking their packhorses through the remotest part of their station, looking for cattle in an area they hadn't been in for thirty years. Rod, camped on the other side of the river, heard the packhorse bells and paddled his dinghy across the river and raced after them, giving Luke the shock of his life.

Rod had set out on a fishing trip early in May 1977, from Kununurra, a little town near the Northern Territory border in the far north of Western Australia. He drove to the Victoria River, leaving his vehicle on the river bank hidden in the bush, and motored down the river in an 18 foot boat, towing a smaller dinghy. He was headed to the mouth of the river, where he had heard there was good fishing. He had two eight-week-old, bull terrier-cross pups, a few camping supplies, enough food and fresh water for a few days, and rolled inside his swag was a rifle, ammunition, knife, sharpening stone and steel.

Just before dark, something overturned the larger boat, tossing him, his dogs and all his gear into the murky, dangerous waters of Queens Channel. The dinghy was still afloat, attached to the half-submerged boat, and Rod managed to scramble into it, rescuing the pups and his swag, and one oar. The turning tide swept everything else rapidly out of reach. He tried to pull up the bigger boat but it was hopeless, and he had to cut it free or be pulled down himself. He spent the night battling to stay afloat as a strong wind had picked up and the open water of the Channel hammered the little dinghy with 3-metre waves. Daylight brought the realisation that he had been carried a long way north, some 20 kilometres across the Channel, with little hope of getting back again and into the Victoria River, where it was nearly 50 kilometres to his Toyota and safety. The fresh water and food were all gone.

This part of the world is about as remote as you can get in northern Australia. From the air it is an artist's palette of greens and greys, delicate traceries of almost black channels winding amongst glistening greys and greens of mud flat and mangrove. The brown plumes of silt washed out of the river mouths that empty into the Joseph Bonaparte Gulf testify to the force of the water flow. Tides are immense, ranging 9 metres between high and low water, dragging the water forward and back in terrifying haste, carving out new channels and erasing old ones at every turn. Magnificent, awesome, even serenely beautiful from above, at sea level it is dangerous, terrifying and vast. Rod was in a tiny dinghy, with one oar, at the mercy of the wind and current. The nearest habitation, Legune Station, 30 or 40 kilometres south, was a tiny pinprick on the map, in country he'd never seen. Too easy to miss the station by a few miles and wander deeper into the wilderness, assuming he could find enough fresh water along the way to stay alive. Port Keats, an Aboriginal mission of 1000 people about 80 kilometres due north, was too far away.

Going back to the Victoria River was not an option, so he decided to take his chances with the smaller, faster Fitzmaurice. A couple of months earlier he had been in the manager's office at Kimberley Research Station where he worked, being reprimanded by the boss for some misdemeanor. There was a large map on the wall behind his angry employer, so he weathered the storm by studying it intently, nodding occasionally and looking contrite. He remembered the general area well enough to know there was an inlet behind the low islands he could see to the north, and that the Fitzmaurice flowed into it. He hoped that he'd find fresh water sooner upstream, as the tidal push wouldn't intrude so far up a narrow channel. Two long nights later, having battled whirlpools, white water rapids, and the ferocious tides, he reached water fresh enough to drink, and knew he was going to make it.

For the next two months, Rod Ansell lived off the land. Sounds like a walk in the park, 'living off the land'. Like all you have to do is get up in the morning and pick some fruit for breakfast, catch a rabbit for lunch, pick a few berries for variety. He had to work hard for every mouthful of food, walk a long way to find it every day, and hope he didn't injure himself in the process. The country is tough, and food sparse to a non-Indigenous eye. However, Rod had a few things on his side. He could track and hunt, he had a rifle and a knife, and he was resourceful. Above all, he was young and fit, and quite in his element, even if usually he would have brought some tucker with him.

What helped him survive was his upbringing. He had learnt old-fashioned bush skills from his father George Ansell, and his maternal uncle, Les Hair, who in turn had been taught by old bushmen in their own youth. Rod could shoot with astonishing accuracy, skin and butcher an animal, and pretty much 'make do' with whatever was to hand. Because of their training, he felt completely at ease in the bush. Being marooned as he found himself on the Fitzmaurice wasn't frightening, it was just not what he'd planned.

So here he was, stuck on a remote river, miles from any settlements, and no one knew where he was. Moreover, no one was going to start missing him for about three months, as he had told friends in Kununurra he'd be away for at least two.

Rod thought there may have been a small chance that a stock camp from Bradshaw Station might turn up, as part of its mustering program. He was on the southern side of the river and, as far as he knew, that was Bradshaw country. So far he hadn't seen any branded stock, but time would tell. If nothing else happened, his general plan was to walk out once the rains came, five months later in October at the earliest, when finding water wouldn't be such a problem. Assuming he survived that long.

'If I lasted the rest of the Dry, I planned to walk out, overland to the Victoria once it started raining,' he told me one night shortly after we'd met. 'Then I'd follow the river till I came to Timber Creek, or maybe Bradshaw Station homestead.' He shrugged. 'But I probably wouldn't have lasted that long. All I had to do was break a leg, or get an infection, and I would've been cactus. I was running out of bullets, and if I couldn't hunt, I would've starved to death.'

He didn't starve to death. Cattle were plentiful along the river, mostly old scrub bulls, but the feed was good and the cattle were in good condition. A fat cow wandered down to the river the very first day, and Rod snatched up his rifle and shot her immediately. This probably saved his life as much as anything else, because he was in no condition to go hunting. He was exhausted after three days and nights in the dinghy, weak from hunger, and his feet were painful and tender from being immersed in water for so long. He tore into the meat, eating it raw, sharing it with the pups. Raw meat was fine, but fire was what he needed now, to cook the meat, but also to be able to attract attention if a plane came within sight. He started a fire by using the gunpowder and the primer out of a bullet and kept it going for the next two months.

A few days later he tallied up the resources he had on hand. They weren't much: his swag, a rifle and twenty-seven rounds of ammunition, and a leather roll containing a skinning knife, a boning knife, a stone and steel. Two leather swag straps, one with a hobble chain swivel. Part of a roll of fencing wire. Two shirts, one pair of shorts, jeans and a jacket. Three empty tins. A belt. No boots or hat.

On the fifth or sixth day, Rod made a greenhide rope, something else he had learnt from his father. He shot a young cow, and carefully skinned the hide in one whole piece. Back at the camp, he spread the hide out on the ground, sloshed some water over it and, beginning from a hole in the centre, cut a strip of hide in a spiral going outwards, until he had the length he wanted:

A two strand rope was all I needed. There were two trees the right distance apart close to the camp and the doubled-up strip stretched between them nicely. It had to be twisted, so I cut the swivel chain off the swag strap, and used that at one end, and made a ring out of wire at the other. Once both ends were tied to the trees with more wire, it was just a matter of using the steel stuck through the swivel to rotate it, twisting the two strands tighter and tighter together until the greenhide was stretched taut between the two trees. It would slacken off after a while, and needed tightening up several times, but in the end it would be a good strong rope. It would come in handy if I sprained an ankle or broke a leg and couldn't hunt, or if I lost the gun and ran out of ammunition. I could use it to trap a beast.

From *To Fight the Wild*

He constructed a platform out of branches in the low fork of a tree and packed it with leaves and bundles of dry grass. It made a soft base for his swag, and got him up off the ground to sleep at night, mainly because it was warmer on the platform than sleeping on the ground.

To keep sane, Rod set himself jobs such as drying meat from the cattle he shot for food, training the pups, making a spear, writing poetry in his head, exploring the country, and finding food such as fruits, yams, and once some wild honey.

One day he paddled upstream in the dinghy and climbed to the top of the gorge on the Palumpa side of the river. From there he could see the river snaking to the coast, disappearing in a haze to the west. Upstream, it vanished into rainforest, which gave way to hard looking country. Gazing around, he realised he was in a virtual oasis, with rough, parched country surrounding him on all sides. He could see for a good 30 kilometres in every direction, and there was nothing but wilderness. He realised then that the possibility of a stock camp turning up was very unlikely. He hadn't seen a single beast with a brand or a tipped horn, apart from one old bull, so he knew that the country wasn't mustered.

By the sixth week, Rod was beginning to falter. Once a light plane droned overhead in the distance, but not near enough to see him or his smoke signals. Cramps were starting to be a problem, and his stamina was fading. Cattle were getting harder to find, and his supply of ammunition was running low. He began to worry about getting out, and how long it might take him. One morning he heard a metallic banging noise, and raced down to the river thinking it might have been a boat. It was only an empty 44-gallon drum floating upstream on the incoming tide. This evidence of civilisation depressed him even more. He knew there would be no rescue party out looking for him. Even if his Toyota was found on the Victoria River, no one would think to search the Fitzmaurice. It would just be assumed he had drowned in the Victoria on his fishing trip.

He woke up a few mornings later feeling depressed and unwell. It was late, but he needed to go hunting again, and he sat sharpening his knives in preparation. Then he heard the sound of horse bells across the river. Once he realised what it was he was hearing, he jumped into the dinghy, paddled across the river, and raced like a madman after the movement he could see not too far in front of him.

> . . . just up ahead, I saw a hat. Just a big dark hat above the tall grass. And raced for that. Gave another shout, a bit of a cooee . . . and got a cooee back. The hat sort of spun around and waited as I pushed my way through the grass towards it.
>
> And there was this bloke, riding a mule. A whitefellow, dressed in black, with a blue bandanna scarf, his hat pushed back a bit, white hair and beard, and his mouth open.
>
> I said: 'G'day.'
>
> He said 'Where'd you come from, how'd you get here?'
>
> From *To Fight the Wild*

Luke McCall's strongest memory of Rod at that point was of a quiet, serious young man, with no arrogance about him. He was clearly embarrassed to be in need of help, Luke said, like any good bushman would be. Unlike Rod, Luke seriously doubted that Rod would have been able to walk out when the rains came: 'Even if he lasted that long – and he was pretty weak by the time we came across him – he didn't know the country. He'd never worked on the station, didn't know where the water was, or the homestead. He wouldn't have lasted too long once he left the river . . .'

The trip back to Palumpa Station took six days, and in some ways was harder than the whole two months on the river. There was no spare saddle, so Rod rode bareback. Luke put him on a horse called Old Cooney, with a folded blanket to sit on, and gave him a spare hat out of his own swag. The two little pups, Bouncer and Cindy, trotted along in the shade of the horses' bellies. Rod became ill with the change of diet, and at one point Luke and Rupert considered leaving him in the care of one man while the others rode back to the station for help. He tried to shoot a bull, to make a bag from the scrotum for Rupert, but started to feel dizzy facing the beast in the middle of a bare plain, and was nearly gored before he brought the bull down with his last bullet. As he said in the book he collaborated on with Rachel Percy, *To Fight the Wild*, 'To survive everything else, get rescued, and then get clobbered by a bull out on the flat would have been a bit hard.'

They arrived back at Palumpa, where Rod had his first 'normal' meal in nearly two months, and reacquainted himself with the inside of a house. Visitors from Port Keats happened to be there at the time, and one of them – Alan Lawler – took a photo of Luke, Rupert, Raphael and Christopher with the gaunt, bearded stranger they had brought in from the bush.

Every paper in the country ran the story, many on the front page, on Saturday, 6 August 1977, and it struck a chord in the population. Most Australians live in the city. Where we were once a nation travelling on the sheep's back, and working the land, by 1977 we had become largely urbanised and quite separate from the bush. Our cities hug the coast, and our outback is rapidly bleeding dry as its people move away for a myriad of reasons, mostly economic. But here, on this particular Saturday morning, was a story about the Australia we truly, secretly believed was us. A young man who had survived in the wilderness, away from shopping malls and timetables and tax returns, reminded us that there were still places beyond the reach of drudgery and the everyday. It was a romantic story, full of all the right props – survival, danger, wild animals, wild country, life and death. And it was right here at our own back door. One of us. We could still cut it.

I did see Rod Ansell again. The day after we had first met in my office, Alan Lawler, the man who had taken the photo of Rod back in July and sent it to the *Northern Territory News*, called by.

'You've got a dinner invitation,' he said with a gleam in his eye. 'Rod Ansell's coming to dinner at my place on Friday night, and he asked if he could invite you. You have quite an ardent admirer there,' and he went off chuckling to himself.

I was intrigued to be invited to dinner by someone I had met for just two minutes, but even more so when Alan called by again on Friday morning.

'About that dinner tonight. Something has come up, and I can't do it now. Rod's coming in from Palumpa tonight but I can't get a message to him. Do you think you could do me a really big favour and have him over at your place for dinner?'

I agreed, not suspecting for a moment that this was all a plot cooked up between Rod and Alan.

# 4

# Hooked

Rod turned up at my place on Friday afternoon in clean white moleskins, blue shirt and RM Williams riding boots. He looked different, and I realised he'd shaved off the funny moustache. He looked even more handsome. He sat in my office for an hour or so while I worked, until I offered to take him out for a look around the mission while I delivered some telegrams. I was surprised to find this apparently shy country boy had a sharp sense of humour, and a broad interest in life in general. He told me he had a photographic memory.

'What, your life is just a series of pictures in your mind, so you never forget a face, that kind of thing?' I wasn't sure whether to believe him or not.

'Kind of. I just remember everything I've read, basically. I can read a poem tonight, and repeat it back to you word for word tomorrow.'

'That must be great – I wish I'd had that when I was sitting exams at school.'

He frowned a bit, and said ruefully, 'It's a mixed blessing. You also don't forget anything.'

I wondered how that could be a problem.

'Well, it's fine remembering the good things, how you felt, and so on. But I remember everything as if it happened yesterday, with the same intensity. And that's not so great, if you're remembering fear or anger or sadness – it's like experiencing it all over again.'

He was quiet for a moment, but then laughed a little and said: 'Have you heard this one before?' and proceeded to reel out a long Banjo Paterson epic.

We had so much in common – a love of the bush, a fascination with the natural world, a love of reading and of bush poetry, and talking about ideas. I found myself feeling more and more relaxed and comfortable with this man, who in turn seemed to be very interested in me, and in who I was. By dinnertime that evening, I felt like he was almost an old friend.

Julie and Christine shared the meal with us, and peppered him with questions about his time on the river. 'Didn't you go a bit crazy, not having anyone to talk to?' asked Christine.

'Yeah – most people think I still am,' he answered, dazzling us with a brilliant white smile and a look that said he was anything but crazy. 'I talked to the dogs a lot. I reckoned as long as they didn't start answering back I was okay.'

'But how did you know what to do? I mean, if we were stuck out in the bush like that, we wouldn't have a clue about what to eat, or which way to go. Most people would just lay down and die.'

'Well, if you got lost in Sydney, and you'd never been there before, you wouldn't panic, or think you were going to die, ay? You'd know where to find a feed and a drink if you had to, and you'd know what else you had to do to look after yourself. It's the same with me in the bush. Just because it's a piece of country I hadn't been in before didn't make me panic. I still knew how to look after myself in it, even if I hadn't exactly planned to be there. I've been in the bush all my life,' he said. 'It's a case of learn quick or die young. I learned a lot from my old man, and I had my gun and knives, so as far as I was concerned, it was more like a change of plan rather than a total disaster.'

He gave me another smile and focused on his food again, and then Julie said, 'This is a great time to bring this up, but did you really drink blood?'

Rod nodded. 'Had to. I was getting really bad cramps, because I wasn't getting enough salt. It was stopping me from hunting, so the next time I shot a killer, I caught handfuls of the blood when I cut its throat to bleed it, and tried to drink as much as I could.'

'Oh, gross!' Julie screwed up her face and laughed. 'That's me dead. I couldn't do that if my life depended on it!'

'Yeah, it was pretty disgusting. I don't think it worked, either.' He grinned again. He had a very engaging smile.

He ate sparingly, cutting small portions, moving food around on his plate, not actually eating very much. When Christine commented on how skinny he was, and that he should eat some more, he told us his stomach had shrunk, and that he couldn't eat much. In fact, he said, a nurse had told him that he probably wouldn't get back to his normal weight for about five years.

After dinner, Julie and Christine left us to ourselves. I made tea and we retired to the living room chairs. I was becoming more and more attracted to this young man. He had a way of making me feel like the sole focus of his interest, even when he was talking to someone else. It was very intoxicating. But what was more intoxicating for me was that we had so much to talk about. We were still deep in conversation when my house mates returned a few hours later. More tea. More talking. He could discuss philosophy and dreams, science and psychology, argue about politics and Aboriginals and religion. There seemed to be so many layers to him. He told me about his relationship with the bush:

> I live in it, and I become a part of it, not an intrusion into it. Not many people can live like that, without electricity, fridges, soft beds. So I like to be in it on my own. And when I'm in the bush alone, all the things my father taught me are what count the most. Those old blokes knew what they were on about. They had a connection with the land that most people have lost now. It's civilisation that alienates people from the land. We used to be hunters, and to do that you have to live with the land, you have to be *of* the land, you know? Once we started planting crops, building houses, we changed, forgot how to look after ourselves, became these soft creatures who were afraid of anything outside the village fence . . .

When I asked him what his philosophy of life was, he said, 'I guess it would be following my own road, and not someone else's. Being good to people as much as possible, doing no harm, I guess, and making the most of the quiet spots along the way. Like this one.'

We smiled at each. There was a genuine recognition, an understanding, that meeting someone you could talk with so easily, about so much, was a rare find.

I was describing the high plains country of Victoria to him, enthusiastic about my favourite place in the whole world, around

Mt Feathertop, and Mt Hotham. Trying to make him understand what it was like, I said, 'It's hard and dangerous and beautiful, but it's kind to cattle – they run fat and shiny up there in the summer.'

He stared at me for a moment, and smiled. 'You know, don't you?'

I wasn't sure what he meant. I probably should have asked him to explain, but it was such a poetic moment I let it pass. I wanted him to think I was as in tune with my environment as he was with his. I also wanted to keep that blue gaze resting on me, and to feel this incredible empathy, as long as possible.

A little while later I was talking about the time I had spent in Europe that year. I got up to find a photograph I wanted to show him. We looked at it together for a while, till I noticed he was staring at me and not the picture. I put the book down on the bench and said, awkwardly, 'Um, what?'

'I was just wondering if I could kiss you,' he murmured.

I'd had two previous boyfriends, and each time the relationships were slow to progress. It took weeks or months of dating and getting to know each other before we became lovers, until I really felt I was in love, that we had something special. With Rod, I suddenly understood what 'falling' in love meant. I had spent about six hours with this man, and I felt as if I'd known him all my life. It was such a strong, over-whelming feeling, and such a sure one, that I had absolutely no doubts at all when the kiss turned into passionate lovemaking. Afterwards, we kept talking, and talking, and talking.

Daylight surprised me with the conversation still firing. We wandered down to the barge landing as the sun came up, dodging the camp dogs that came out to bark at us. The rising sun behind our backs cast long shadows across the water of the creek, throwing into relief the crab holes and the strange little mudskippers that skittered across the glistening grey mangrove mud. I'd had no sleep whatsoever, but I felt elated and energised.

Rod was working at Kildurk Station at the time, a cattle property about 250 kilometres due south of Port Keats. Before flying back there a few hours later, he extracted a promise from me to come and see him there before I left for Melbourne. My two years at Port Keats were at an end, and it was time for me to go back to the 'real' world, although

I had no clear plans for the future, apart from vague ideas about doing a social work degree. With only three weeks to go, I didn't think it was likely that I'd get to Kildurk, but a couple of days later a telegram came from Rod, telling me he'd be in Kununurra at the weekend, and could I come and stay with him. I expressed some doubts to Christine about whether I should go. Now that I was no longer being dazzled by his smiles, I thought perhaps I had imagined the whole thing, that I was just being a trifle giddy. Christine looked at me like I was a complete idiot: 'If I'd been walking into walls all week the way you have, this place wouldn't keep me here for two minutes! What have you got to lose? If you like him that much, just go!'

We spent four wonderful days together at a pretty piece of land along the Ord River diversion dam that some mates of Rod's were squatting on. It was about a twenty minute drive from Kununurra, a little town some sixty kilometres over the border in Western Australia. I have a memory of green lawns running down to the water, but I doubt that it was lawn in the usual sense of the word. I don't know who nicknamed it Bundaberg Downs, but it wasn't an understatement if the name was a reference to the amounts of Queensland rum consumed by the blokes who lived there. They were my introduction to the white bush community of the Top End. I felt like I had discovered a whole underground culture I didn't know existed. Until then, my experience in the Northern Territory had been of city people living in a remote place, with Luke McCall and the Aboriginal stockmen as the sole representatives of the pastoral industry. Davo, Rick, Stretch and Kenny, amongst others, opened up a world I had no idea existed, where people spent their working hours on horseback, slept in swags most of the year, cooked over campfires and lived hard. They were complete larrikins.

It was impossible to tell how old they were. To me they all seemed to be in their forties, but I think they were much younger. They were weathered and creased by the sun, and had hard calloused hands. They smoked and drank too much, and laughed at anything, usually some misfortune that had happened to either a mate or themselves.

A discussion about religion arose one evening, because a visitor from town was a religious woman, and was stating her belief in the efficacy of prayer.

'Pray?' said Rick. 'Of course I pray.'

'Really?' said the woman. 'That's wonderful!'

'Yeah,' said Rick. 'Every day I wake up and say, *Jesus* Christ – it's morning!'

They worked hard and partied hard. After one particularly long and boozy night, I was making some breakfast when one of them came into the little flywired donga that served as a kitchen, and prepared his own. He shook some cornflakes into a bowl, poured a liberal amount of rum over them, looked at my muesli and yoghurt, and said 'That stuff'll kill ya.'

They had a small generator to provide electricity when it was needed to run power tools, or the deep freezer occasionally. There was a kerosene fridge in the kitchen, and kerosene lamps lit up the donga at night. Meals were cooked on an open fire. It was quiet and peaceful most of the time, the only sounds coming from the millions of white cockatoos that periodically lifted in raucous screeching clouds from the trees along the banks. Squads of pelicans mustered fish with military precision, and scores of other water birds picked their way along the muddy shallows hunting little fish and yabbies. The place was heaven on a stick for bird watchers.

We ran out of meat, and Rod and I went out to 'get a killer'. The first time I heard this phrase I thought a psychopath was on the loose somewhere, and that the locals were mounting a posse. Fortunately I kept my mouth shut and eventually worked out what they meant. The term comes from the practice on stations of choosing an animal for slaughtering from the cattle run into the yards. The chosen beast would be left on its own in a separate yard to be killed after the other animals were gone. Although why it's called the killer instead of the killee, I don't know.

Rod saddled a couple of horses, strapped two belts around his waist, and hung a leather pouch containing some knives off his saddle. We wandered off down the track at a comfortable pace, as if the last thing on our minds was looking for a beast to kill. It didn't occur to me that he didn't have a gun until he took off after some cattle at lightning speed. 'Catch my horse for me!' he yelled as he disappeared into the scrub.

I trotted along behind until I came across his mare, and caught hold of her reins. Soon I heard him calling out, so I followed the direction of his voice till I found him leaning over a young cow, holding one of its legs high in the air as he wrapped a leather belt around it.

'Come and unstrap the other belt off my shoulders,' he said as I dismounted and tied the horses to a branch. He finished strapping both hind legs with the one belt, and I handed him the second one.

'Now while I hold her head back, you strap her front legs.' He dashed to the head of the cow and pulled her head back till the horns touched the ground.

'You're joking . . .' I said, looking at the heaving, struggling cow. I couldn't work out why she hadn't already leapt up and shaken Rod off her back legs like a tick.

'Nah, you'll be right. Just do as I tell you. It's easy. Grab one leg, cross it over the other one – that's it. Don't worry if she kicks! She can't hurt you. I'm keeping her head back so she can't get up . . .'

I followed his instructions, wrapping the belt several times around the legs above the hooves, until there was just enough belt left to hook through the buckle. I couldn't believe what I was doing.

'Hand us the boning knife – the one with the narrow blade,' he said. He held the cow's head back and cut its jugular with a swift sure motion, leaping back as it struggled and kicked. While the blood gushed out over the ground, the cow bellowed and strained against the straps, gradually quietening as its spasms weakened and finally stopped. Rod gently tapped one of its glazed eyes to check that it was dead, and proceeded to skin it.

I'd noticed that as the cow lay dying, Rod squatted beside it with a hand on its flank, patting it gently.

'Why do you do that?' I asked. 'You can hardly be comforting it!'

'It's just something I do,' he replied. 'I do it when I'm bull catching too. When I catch a bull, I've just knocked down an animal that's never been knocked down in its life. Then I'm going to stick it in a truck, and take it to a yard, and load it on a road train where it'll go to the meatworks. I'm apologising to it for doing that. Or for killing it, like now.'

This time the cow hadn't been knocked down by a vehicle. Rod had galloped along behind her, then jumped off his horse, grabbed the cow by the tail, and thrown her to the ground. He had explained to me earlier how his father, uncle and aunt did this in Queensland, to fully grown bulls, but I didn't appreciate just what that must entail until I saw this large animal heaving and panting on the ground at our feet.

He cut a pile of leafy green branches and stacked them next to the cow. As he worked, cutting deep into the twitching muscle, he explained to me what he was doing, what each cut of meat was called, and what it was for. When he'd finished, he cut another branch, gave it to me with instructions to keep the flies off the carcase, and rode back to the camp with the horses. He returned a few minutes later with a ute, and we loaded the meat onto a bed of more green branches in the back of it.

As well as the Bundaberg Downs boys, I met his good friend Clayton Bell at the Kimberley Research Station, where Rod had previously worked, and we netted mullet in the river and sat up late that night over a few bottles of wine. I also met Gavin Perry, an eccentric Englishman who grew grapefruit and limes on the banks of the Ord River, and seemed in a perpetual state of incredulity about the Australians around him.

'This bloke's a bit weird, you know,' he muttered in a loud voice when Rod introduced us. 'D'y'know he refuses to sleep in a bed, and cooks his food outside on a fire when there's a perfectly good kitchen inside this house? We go and sit at his fire and talk to him sometimes. It's a bit like visiting the old man on the mountain. Weird . . .' I liked Gavin from the start.

'Australians are odd people,' he insisted. 'Look at them! They make a virtue out of how much damage they can do to themselves – work hard in the sun, drink ten gallons of rum for dinner, have a punch-up, fall down, stagger off to work in the morning and do it all over again.' But he wouldn't live anywhere else.

I liked the fact that Rod had such unusual and interesting friends, but he told me that most people didn't like him.

'Why not?' I asked, not believing that anyone could fail to see how wonderful this man was.

'People always think I'm really young and stupid, and that's how I like it. That way they underestimate you. The downside is that I always get picked on in pubs, because I'm small. That's why I hate pubs. But –' and a grin spread over his face – 'they don't win the fights.'

He didn't smoke, and he didn't drink very much. Hated beer, would drink a little wine, but preferred Southern Comfort if he had to drink alcohol. One night at Clayton's we all drank too much. I was fascinated to see that Rod didn't appear to get drunk, in that he didn't slur words or say silly things. He just lost the use of his legs. He literally couldn't move his legs, and Clayton and I had to roll him into his swag. He didn't drink coffee either. Tea was his preferred poison and he'd have it with lots of milk and four or five spoons of sugar. He had a huge sweet tooth. Any kind of lollies were fine but green mint leaves and red raspberry jellies were his favourites, and brazil nut chocolate. Other than that, food or mealtimes weren't important to him. It was just fuel, something best got out of the way so you could get on with more important things.

Mixed up with all of this was an undercurrent of – not quite danger, but something risky, something volatile and virile. Rod seemed closer to reality than anyone I'd ever met. Like he had dispensed with the niceties and pretences of society, and dealt with life on his own terms. A lot of the stories he told me about himself reflected a willingness to push the envelope, to go over the edge, rely on wits and agility, strength and quick thinking, quite the opposite of the world I knew, where people observed social conventions and edged around each other to keep the peace. He certainly had a sudden way of waking up. If he was deeply asleep, and I woke him, he would sit bolt upright and ready to defend himself. He even warned me about it, saying that his mates knew to kick him and stand back.

Rod Ansell was perfect. He was twenty-three years old, handsome and intelligent, fit and agile in both body and mind. He was possessed of an intoxicating blend of blond, blue-eyed innocence, and an edgy, dangerous, risky recklessness. He could talk about the things I thought were important. He was full of contradictions – gentle and dangerous, a protector and a risk taker, and he was utterly charming and romantic. I was twenty-two, idealistic and naive and thought I knew it all. I didn't stand a chance.

# 5

# Reeled in and Landed

At Christmas 1977 I was back in Melbourne. It was wonderful to be home with my family after such a long absence, and to meet the new baby Danielle again, but I was distracted. The family borrowed a friend's beach house down the coast to spend New Year together, and my sister Leonie and I walked for miles along the beach talking. Well, Leonie probably did more listening, as I attempted to describe this amazing man I had met. However, I had some other things on my mind as well as Rod Ansell.

During this holiday, I told my mother I wasn't going to Mass any longer. I had been struggling with my doubts about the Catholic Church, and organised religion in general, for well over a year. I had always been a very committed and active Catholic, observing the sacraments, and being involved in youth groups and other church community activities, but my time at Port Keats had made me uncomfortable about the Church's effect on other cultures.

I had never doubted the concept of Catholic missions and missionaries operating in other countries. My mother's sister was a missionary nun, and I'd grown up with images of smiling nuns and happy natives working together to improve the lot of the locals. And I knew my aunt. She was a wonderful woman, who had achieved remarkable things, especially for young girls there. Aunty Cath was a member of the same order of nuns at Port Keats, the Daughers of Our Lady of the Sacred Heart, and had become the Mother Provincial of the order in Papua New Guinea. Going against the tide on this issue was very difficult, and as well as my own feelings, I had to deal with the sense that I was a traitor to my whole family's beliefs. However, two years at Port Keats had left me convinced that we had no right to impose our beliefs on other people, especially those who weren't generally in a position to refuse them. Mum was shocked, but accepted my decision ruefully.

I also had another formal ending. As much as I loved Dave, I was unable to make the commitment to a permanent relationship. I had realised it wasn't going to happen over the last few months, and meeting Rod Ansell had crystallised things for me. Saying goodbye was sad and difficult. I didn't even know if I was ever going to see Rod again, but I knew if I could feel so strongly about someone else, I had no business keeping Dave waiting for me to make up my mind.

A letter arrived from Rod, with a poem and some photos of himself. His older brother Malcolm was getting married in Parkes, New South Wales, where his fiancée lived, and Rod was to be his best man. He hoped he could come and see me afterwards. One morning at my parents' house there was a knock at the door, and there was Rod, denim jeans and jacket, hat, boots, swag over his shoulder, and a little white pup at his feet. You couldn't imagine a more incongruous sight in suburban Ringwood. He fixed me with a very serious stare, and said, 'G'day, girl.' Without another word, he cradled my face in his hands and kissed me like his life depended on it. If I was hooked before, now I was completely reeled in and landed.

'Who's this?' I asked, after we disentangled ourselves. The pup was sitting at our feet, looking up expectantly.

'This is Little Bull. I called him that because that's what he is, a little bull terrier, with a touch of boxer. A mate in Katherine gave him to me when I came through on my way south. He's for you.'

A bunch of flowers was probably the more usual gift a courting lover might have brought with him, but I was already well aware that Rod Ansell wasn't usual.

I led him into the kitchen where my mother and two of her sisters, my Aunty Cath, the nun, and Aunty Nell, were about to have a cup of tea.

'Mum, this is Rod Ansell.'

'Oh! I was wondering why you were at the door so long!' She shook hands with Rod, and I introduced him to my aunts. Wow, I thought, if this isn't the acid test – not only to meet the mother but some of the old aunts as well, *and* a nun! Oh well, if he survives this . . .

My family liked him from the start. He was friendly, but not over-confident. A little shy, but without making anyone feel awkward. I think he found our big noisy family dinners a bit overwhelming at first, with everyone talking and laughing at once, but he fitted in very quickly. That beautiful white smile just bowled everyone over.

'How did you manage to get the taxi driver to take a dog?' my mum asked.

'Well, I convinced him that he was only a little dog, and that he'd already been to the toilet. After a while the driver started saying things like, so you're down from the bush, huh? And you haven't been to Melbourne before? He seemed to be going down a lot of little streets and out of the way places, so I picked up the pup, and said, gee, you know this fella's never been in a motor car before. I wonder if he's getting a bit carsick? And suddenly we were back on the main road, and found your place really quickly.'

A play about one of Rod's great heroes, Breaker Morant, was being performed in the city. We took the train in early, crammed in with the morning commuters, so we could spend the whole day in town before going to the play that night. I'd persuaded Rod to leave his hat behind, but he still looked so out of place on that train, I couldn't understand why the whole carriage wasn't staring at him. He had an appointment to see a publisher in Elizabeth Street. Some of his poetry had been printed in the newspapers the year before, and Collins Publishers, he said, had asked him to show them the rest of the poems he'd composed on the river. He came back half an hour later with a smile, saying they wanted him to write another twenty or so, and they'd go ahead.

We wandered around the town, looking at the shops and the people while Rod gave a running commentary: 'Look at everyone, hurrying along, completely wrapped up in whatever they're doing. They all think they're in charge of their lives, but it's all make-believe. If the power went off, they'd all be cactus.'

'But that's how societies work, don't they? Everyone does a part of it, to keep the whole thing running – including the power – and that way it works. People have jobs, people eat, people buy and sell things to each other, people get looked after if they can't look after them-selves, and so on. It seems to work okay to me,' I said.

'But none of these people are honest, if you think about it. Someone else grows their food, brings their water, makes the clothes they wear. They live at arm's length from reality. Look how far removed city people are from the earth – the bitumen on the roads, the concrete paths, the buildings, the sheer area that's changed and covered. People wear shoes on their feet to keep from touching the ground. It's like they're afraid of the earth itself.'

He could talk like this for hours, and I listened. He had an answer for every argument, and an argument for every answer. I found it surprisingly easy to believe in this man who seemed to sit outside of everything I was familiar with, yet who could operate within it with ease. He had an overview of life that the rest of us didn't have, as if his bush background had grounded him more solidly in the world. To my twenty-two years, he seemed incredibly wise and knowing, and it was so easy for me to trust him, and to love him.

Rod stayed at our house for about a week or so, sleeping in my brothers' room. Without ever actually discussing the subject of marriage, we both seemed to understand that we would be staying together. We talked about children and what we'd be doing together that year, and it felt like the right and most natural thing in the world. We would head back to the Territory, via Rod's home town of Murgon, and take up the bullcatching contract he had waiting for him on Kildurk Station. Murgon was near Kingaroy in southeastern Queensland, about 230 kilometres northwest of Brisbane. I'd found it on a map, and it looked a long way from the city.

A few nights before we planned to leave, Rod asked to talk to my parents formally. With an almost quaint, old-fashioned manner, he explained to my parents how we felt about each other, and that we wanted to spend the rest of our lives together. We planned to go back to the Territory in a few days, and we wanted their blessing. My parents were unhappy about the prospect of us living together and not being married. Rod assured them that we were intending to get married, and that most likely I would be working either in town or in the office at the station while he was away out bush. They let themselves be satisfied with that, but I don't think deep down they really believed it.

We needed a car to get back, as Rod had hitchhiked to Ringwood. I withdrew some money from the bank, and we bought an elderly Ford Falcon sedan for $450. It had a blue unroadworthy sticker, but it was in good running order. I was a bit startled when he scraped off the sticker at home, saying, 'This old girl's fine – she'll get us all the way back, no worries. The blue sticker's only because of "technicalities". It's a good, safe car. Really! It'll be fine!' As I was to find out, Rod had little regard for the rules, and preferred to trust his own assessment of things.

We said our goodbyes to family and friends, and headed north in early February. We travelled fairly light – Rod had just a swag, and I had my backpack, a suitcase, my guitar and, of course, my little dog. On his way south at Christmas Rod had stopped off with Linnie (better known as Shorty) and Patsy Hayes at Uralla, just outside Katherine. Patsy was a famous Katherine beauty, with flashing dark eyes and waist-length black hair. She looked glamorous and exotic next to Shorty, a small, stocky, weatherbeaten bloke with a sharp, wry face. Shorty Hayes, who was definitely not pretty or glamorous, was famous for a lot of things, and one of them was his dogs.

His old bitch Minnie was legendary in that part of the country. She was as mad as a meat axe, but smart at the same time. She had put more good men up trees at Uralla than any scrub bull could lay claim to, and such was the fame of Minnie that none of them was ashamed to admit it. Fiercely devoted to her owners, she was fine if Shorty or Patsy were around, but no one got out of the car without checking first. Pups from Minnie were highly prized, particularly if the father was the equally famous Hippo. The Hippo was a big old white bull terrier cross dog, with the most lovable, affable nature imaginable. I guess his good-natured genes balanced out Minnie's mad ones in their pups to produce generally good sorts of dogs. Little Bull was out of Hippo and Minnie's last litter, and Shorty had given him to Rod.

So Little Bull was my introduction to a very important part of Rod's life. Dogs. Rod confided to me some time later that he was really relieved when I agreed to go back to the Northern Territory with him. I thought, wow, he really loves me that much. 'Yeah,' he said, 'I was sweating you might say no, because Little Bull's such a good little pup, the last of Hippo's, and I would have hated to leave him behind . . .'

Indeed, when we called in to see Shorty and Patsy on our way through a few months later, Shorty greeted Rod with a quizzical eye and a grin, and said, 'I see you got your pup back.'

We talked nonstop the whole way, about life, and the bush, and religion, and city versus country. I listened to more stories about his time in the bush, about the people he knew in the Territory. He also talked a lot about his family, especially about his father.

'We always laugh at how he works his dogs. He has great dogs. But where most people work their dogs with whistles and single commands, Dad would yell out whole sentences like, what are ya doin' over there? Get away round that mob *that* way. And the funny part was, the dogs always knew just what he wanted.'

'The old feller smokes like a chimney – never lets his pipe get cold. It sits beside his plate at dinnertime, so he can light it as soon as he's finished eating. Used to drive me and Malcolm mad. You could break a leg, or get sick, but that wouldn't stop you mustering as far as Dad was concerned. But if the old bloke lost his pipe, that was it. There we'd be, scrabbling around in the long grass trying to find it so we could get on with the muster.' George Ansell may have smoked a lot, but according to Rod, no one could handle a horse like his father.

He talked with great affection and humour about his uncle and aunt, and their four children. His mother's brother Les Hair, and his wife Nell, owned a cattle station out in central west Queensland, and managed several others over the years. There were still wild cattle and a lot of scrub out there, and the stock had to be mustered with horses and dogs, the scrub bulls thrown from horseback. Rod's family often went out to visit, where they spent holidays mustering and handling cattle. George had taught all his children to ride from a very early age, and out at the station, Rod and his brother learnt to throw bulls from a horse, starting out with little mickey bulls and young cows. Throwing bulls by the tail seemed like the craziest thing I'd ever heard when he described it to me:

You gallop your bull steady – just hard enough to keep him running ahead, but not too fast or he'll just turn around and charge you. When he starts getting puffed out – and it doesn't take long because he's a big animal who doesn't usually gallop anywhere – his stride changes, gets slower and more uneven, and saliva and mucus starts stringing from his mouth. That's when you get really close, jump off your horse and run right up behind him, and grab his tail. As soon as the bull feels that, he swings around to have a go at you, so you step to the opposite side. He swings around that way to hook at you again, and you step back the other way, only this time you pull down and sideways on his tail, and it throws him off balance. As soon as he's on the ground you have to get a belt on his hind legs, and get back on your horse real quick because a bull can still get you even with his legs tied up.

Working with cattle was all Rod had ever wanted to do, he said. He wanted to leave school at fourteen and be a drover, taking mobs of cattle on the stock routes for months at a time. His parents wouldn't hear of it, and insisted he complete his education. The arguments were furious he said, but he stayed at school, finishing Year 12 at the local high school in Murgon. He was a clever student, but drove his teachers mad because he couldn't be bothered doing the work. He was often in trouble, often in fights.

As soon as he could, he headed for the Territory, and worked on Victoria River Downs (VRD) Station as a stockman. By the time I met Rod, he had been head stockman in the Centre Camp at VRD, an AI (artificial insemination) technician working with a local vet out of Kununurra, a technical assistant at Kimberley Research Station, and a bull catcher. He had packed a lot into the years between leaving school at seventeen, and the age of twenty-three, when I first met him.

He spoke so much about his Uncle Les and Aunty Nell, and about the times he had spent with them out at Jo Jo and Collieblue Stations in Queensland, that I thought that was where he grew up. I built up an image of a totally daunting family, all crack riders leaping off horses to throw huge wild scrub bulls by the tail, hard, tough people who could all handle themselves in the bush like Rod. As a very mediocre rider who knew nothing about cattle or the bush, I felt like a lamb going to certain slaughter.

As we drew nearer to Murgon, he warned me about the reception we might get from his family. He then told me how he had been engaged to a young woman from his home town who had gone up to

Kununurra with him a couple of years earlier, and that they had broken up long before he met me. However, he said, they hadn't told their parents until they had each returned this last Christmas. His mother, he said, didn't take the news well, as she was very fond of the girlfriend. My eagerness to meet his family was tinged by a sinking apprehension.

We bought a crate of peaches at Goondiwindi. 'They love peaches, that mob,' said Rod. 'These'll help break the ice!'

I was starting to feel worried.

'It'll be okay,' he reassured me. 'We'll only be staying a few days, just to pick up the dogs, and the rest of my gear. We'll be back in the Territory in a couple of weeks.'

We arrived in Murgon a couple of hours later, and in spite of my misgivings about the horsey family, and the broken engagement, I was looking forward to meeting them. I was surprised when instead of arriving at an isolated homestead on a cattle property, we pulled into a suburban house in a small country town. Clearly I had misunderstood something along the way.

Mrs Ansell was not pleased to see us. She nodded politely at me, and glared at Rod. Mr Ansell seemed a bit awkward, as if he was quite happy to meet me, but didn't want to upset his wife. Malcolm, who had moved nearby with his new bride, seemed to find it all highly amusing, so I got the feeling that maybe things weren't as bad as they appeared. But then Malcolm had a healthy sense of humour. And to cap it all off, the peaches were terrible.

My image of a remote pastoral property where everyone rode like demons was a bit off centre. I realised that Rod was so focused on cattle as a way of life that, for him, the time spent out at Jo Jo with the Hairs *was* his life. Everything else paled into insignificance as just the mundane things done in between the trips out to the station. It must have been galling for him to have to live in a small town on a half-acre block when he desperately wanted to be working cattle, living on the land and practising the skills he was learning from his father and uncle. When he was about fourteen, his family purchased a small farm on the outskirts of Murgon. It had a house on it which they rented to a couple of elderly ladies, while George and Eve used the rest of the farm for cattle grazing. Rod was able to handle the cattle, and spent as much time there as he could working on the land, laying irrigation, ploughing, planting hay crops. It might not have been the outback or wild cattle, but it was closer to it than the inside of a classroom, and must have mollified him to some extent.

My prospective mother-in-law kept me at arm's length, pretty much. In hindsight, it was incredibly tactless of Rod to expect his mother to have the new girlfriend as a houseguest so soon after she'd learnt of his broken engagement. At the time I didn't really understand the situation I found myself in, and for a little while just felt like three-day-old fish. However, things improved and Eve and I began to get along the way we would have if the circumstances had been different.

The best way to deal with the awkward conditions at home was to get out of the house, so we spent most of the first few days down at the farm breaking in a brumby mare which had been caught on a nearby property. It was wonderful watching Rod with horses. He seemed to have a connection with them that was supernatural. When he rode, it was like watching a centaur. He melded with the horse so completely that you barely saw the movements he made to control it. Didn't move from the saddle except in a trot. Every time I saw him on a horse, I would fall in love with him all over again.

Our original plan was that we would only stay in Murgon long enough to get ourselves organised and on our way back to the Northern Territory. Rod had left his catching plant at Kildurk Station over the Wet, ready for the coming season's bullcatching. Then we received word that the contract had fallen through.

At the same time Perth film maker Richard Oxenburgh contacted Rod again. The newspaper reports on Rod's two months on the Fitzmaurice had caught the attention of Richard and his wife, writer Rachel Percy, who were interested in making a documentary recreating his experience. Rachel tracked Rod down in Kununurra and flew from Perth to meet him in August 1977. They spent several days scouting out possible filming locations, and visited Bradshaw and Palumpa Stations, talking to Dick Gill, Bradshaw's head stockman and pilot, and to Luke McCall at Palumpa. She satisfied herself that the story was real, the character was real, and that a film was quite possible. Ever since then she and Richard had been raising the finance to make the film, and Rachel had been writing the script, after taping Rod's story during her time with him.

Richard met with Rod in Brisbane. They liked each other straight away – 'Doesn't know the first thing about the bush, but he's a good bloke' was Rod's appraisal when he came home after signing a contract to play the part of himself. He also negotiated the contract to outfit the location camp, and to provide the catering for it. But that would not begin until the middle of the year, and with the loss of the Kildurk contract, we no longer had a job in the Northern Territory waiting for us. Rod used what money we had left to fly to Darwin for a week to see a lawyer friend about the broken contract, and to secure his catching equipment which was still at Kildurk. For the next few months we did what work we could, cutting logs, building yards and doing odd jobs, and gradually saved up enough money to leave.

During this time I met the rest of Rod's family, except for his sister Christine, who was living interstate. His older brother Malcolm worked as a cattle buyer for a large meatworks, and he and Rod were great mates. Malcolm was as steady as Rod was mercurial, but he understood his brother better than anyone. Where Rod was idealistic, Malcolm was pragmatic and wise, but they shared a love of horses and cattle, and a great sense of humour. Jennifer was the eldest of the four children. A lovely, tiny woman with wavy blonde hair, and a happy gentle nature, she rode like an Amazon but without any drama or ego. Jenny taught at a college in Brisbane, and was married to John Fielding, a New Zealand musician she'd met and fallen in love with in Europe a few years before. She was friendly and open in a relaxed way, understanding completely the situation I found myself in.

'You just have to give Mum and Dad a bit of time to get used to the idea that Rod's broken up with his old girlfriend,' she said. 'They really like her, and she had been around for a while. It came as a bit of a shock to them.'

I omitted to say that it had come as a bit of a shock to me too. I stayed with Jenny and John in Brisbane while Rod flew to Darwin to try and salvage something from the Kildurk contract.

I got along well with Rod's father George. He had a trucking business that kept him flat out all week, and spent every other bit of spare time at the Murgon farm, or at the family's lease in the

Black Snake ranges, where they ran a small herd of cattle. It was rugged country, exactly the kind of riding conditions both Rod and his father appeared to cherish. I spent a memorable weekend there with them, watching them chase mad cattle through impenetrable scrub down impossibly steep hillsides, and having a great time of it. I could see then what a strong bond this lifestyle had created between father and son.

My relationship with Rod's mother improved, and by the time we left I think she had accepted that I was a likely part of her son's future. Eve was an interesting and intelligent woman who liked to ask questions about life. She had a strong creative streak, and always had a new project on the go in her workshop outside the house, usually something practical like leatherwork or making things instead of buying them. She worked hard, operating a mail contract which took her out around the rural properties three times a week delivering mail, and worked on the family farm in between. As well as this, she looked after the family home in the Murgon township, until she and George finally moved down to the farm to live a few years later. Eve and I had managed to nurture the beginnings of a real affection, but I was still very happy when the day of departure for the Territory arrived, and Rod and I would be on our own again.

# 6

# Learning the Ropes

We finally left Murgon in early May 1978, packing up the old Falcon till the springs bent backwards. Rod was taking back his large tool trunk, saddles, bridles, bits of engines, a swag, and other bits and pieces, so we removed the back seat to make more room. On top of all this went four dogs: Little Bull, my pup; a runt no one wanted called Trouble; and Deaf Dog and Bouncer, who were going to be movie stars too. Bouncer had been one of the two dogs on the river with Rod, but Cindy, the other dog, now had a litter of pups, so Deaf Dog, Bouncer's father, was stepping into her role.

Dogs were such an important part of Rod's life. While we were staying at Murgon he had seven or eight dogs who lived down at the farm and kept Rod busy shooting wallabies to feed them. He had always had dogs, mostly bull terrier/boxer crosses, with gentle friendly natures. He used them for catching bulls sometimes, something else he had learned from his Uncle Les and Aunty Nell. They used them when they were mustering from horseback, but Rod took his dogs out in the catcher, chasing a bull until it tired a little, and then setting the dogs onto it. They would grab the poor bull by the nose, or whatever part of the head they could reach, and keep it occupied while Rod grabbed the tail and threw it. I loved watching him with his dogs. He would play with them as if they were human, wrestling and teasing them but never leaving them in any doubt as to who was the top dog.

Travelling with four dogs in a sedan isn't something I'd recommend, but the dogs were very well behaved. Occasionally there would be a bit of growling between Deaf Dog and Bouncer, as Bouncer was almost an adult dog, and ready to argue the rights of succession with his father. But mostly it was peaceful and quiet in the back. That is, until we got to Three Ways Roadhouse in the Northern Territory, where the Barkly and Stuart highways meet.

It was time for some dinner, so we left the dogs in the car with the windows down a bit, as it was early evening, and there was plenty of shade. About fifteen minutes later we came out to find our car all alone in the car park, and people looking at us strangely. We had only been gone a little while, but that was when old Deaf Dog decided it was time to tell Bouncer who was boss. They discussed it from the back seat into the front and back again, and there were signs of the discussion dripping from the ceiling, down the windows, seats and dash, and all over the two pups. Their chains were all tangled up, and the poor pups had been dragged back and forth in the middle, no doubt terrified that at any moment they'd be discussed by mistake.

The inside of the car looked like the scene of a Mafia hit. We looked at the car, at the people staring at us, and jumped in and drove off. Rod was swearing and cursing at the dogs, until we both started laughing so much we had to pull off the road. We drove till we found a creek, stopped and cleaned the dogs up, and the inside of the car as much as we could. It smelled like a butcher's back room for days.

Before crossing the Queensland–Northern Territory border we had stayed a few days in Mt Isa with my uncle Vince O'Sullivan and his family. Four of my mother's five brothers lived in Mt Isa then, and they are all very fond of their littlest sister, so anyone fooling around with her daughter was in for some heavy scrutiny. They had heard that Rod was a bull catcher, whatever that was, lived in the bush, and had got himself lost the year before. None of which sounded terribly promising.

We all had dinner together at Uncle Joe's house, and by the time we had reached dessert Rod had everyone fascinated. I relaxed, and watched him tell story after story, keeping everyone laughing. When the conversation became more serious, he was equally comfortable, and right in the middle of it. Then the poetry started, and our plans for an early morning departure were history. Uncle Joe was probably the hardest to please of my uncles, and the one I thought most likely to give Rod a tough time. As we left, he looked at Rod, shook his head and said, 'I just can't work you out.' But he smiled and shook his hand. Joe kissed me goodbye, and muttered, 'Seems like a pretty good bloke'.

Victoria River Downs was our last stop before Kununurra. It was once the biggest cattle station in the world, the place where Rod had first worked as a stockman in the Northern Territory, and where he discovered his great passion: bull catching. We stayed with Wayne and Karen Brown, good friends of Rod's who welcomed us into their home and gave us a bed for the night. Rod had worked for Wayne and Karen a couple of years earlier when the Browns had an outfit called 'Bullcatchers Incorporated', and the contract to catch scrub bulls on the station. I asked why scrub bulls had to be caught separately from the rest of the herd. Why weren't they mustered into the yards along with everything else? Bull catching might be exciting, but why do it that way?

The cattle stations of the Northern Territory were – and still are – vast by any standards. In 1970, for example, Victoria River Downs station was 12 400 square kilometres in size. In 2004, the largest station in the Northern Territory was Brunette Downs at 12 212 square kilometres, while Victoria River Downs now checks in at 11 800 square kilometres after selling some of its land since 1970. It's a mind-boggling concept, the idea of managing livestock on such large scales. It was impossible to muster many of the stations completely in any one year, and there were few fences. Cattle were harvested more than managed. A mustering camp would go out for weeks or months at a time, searching out the herds and running them into yards. Once behind wire they were then drafted by age or sex, the bulls, bullocks and barren cows sent to the meatworks, the cows and calves put back together, and unbranded stock earmarked, branded, and the males castrated. They would then be tailed out into paddocks, or back into the areas they had been taken from, to grow until the next time they were mustered and sent on their own trip to the abattoir.

Left alone for several years, the male to female population of the herds would become unbalanced. On a smaller farm in one of the southern states, one bull would service all the cows in his paddock. Here, in the vast reaches of the outback, a cow on heat would be serviced by every bull within range, often meaning an early death for the cow. Also, she faced possible death during calving, either from complications or from dingoes when she was most vulnerable. If they weren't mustered before they reached maturity, the male calves were not being castrated, so the result was a large number of bulls running on the properties. They presented a problem for the musterers.

It would take several days or even weeks of hard work to muster all the cattle in just one part of the station, and even then some would be missed. Basically the men would go out with a quiet mob of cows, called the 'coachers', and keep them close together. As they found little groups of scrub cattle, they would add them to the quiet herd, the calmness of the coachers soothing the newcomers into submission. But occasionally big old scrub bulls would run in with the others. They were worth a lot of money at the meatworks, being bigger and heavier than the cows, so an effort was made to keep them with the mustered cattle in spite of the trouble they could cause. A bull would walk along steadily for a while, as long as the mob happened to be going the way he wanted, but as soon as there was a change of direction, or the bull just changed his mind, he would burst out of the mob of quiet cattle and head for the hills.

In the old days the stockmen would gallop after the bull and throw it, always a risk to both man and horse. Bull catchers took this dangerous job off the stockmen. Instead of someone having to jump off a horse and grab a half tonne, sharp horned, angry bull with his bare hands, a driver in a catcher could chase a bull, roll it with the bull bar, and then strap its legs while it was pinned under a tonne of Toyota. Its horns would be tipped – the sharp ends sawn off – and the mob moved up close so that when the bull was unstrapped, it would head for the safety of the herd, and generally stay there. It was riskier for the bull, who had the chance of its legs being broken, but it was a lot safer for the men, and the horses. Rod valued the old ways, but he was no slave to them in the face of modern innovations. When he saw this technological improvement on the methods taught to him by his father and the Hairs, he didn't hesitate. Here was the adrenaline rush of tail-throwing and the thrill of a high speed chase rolled into one, with some of the danger removed.

This was all so new to me. I had been out in the stock camp at Palumpa, with Luke McCall and his men, but that was quiet and calm compared to the muster we attended the next day. I found myself in a helicopter with pilot Ian Petherick at daylight, whirling above the Victoria River Downs (VRD) treetops looking for cattle in the half-light. Mustering in a helicopter is like the scariest roller coaster ride you can imagine. The doors are off, and you're enveloped in a maelstrom of wind and sound as the machine banks and swoops and spins at high speed, backwards, forwards, up and down, until the only thing you're sure of is that you're going to be sick. Not many people last very long beside the pilot. I managed only half an hour before Ian put me down behind the mob as he pushed the cattle the rest of the way to the yards.

I also had my first ride in a bull catcher with Jim Donovan, the head stockman at VRD. A lot of scrub bulls were coming in with the mob, so the catchers went to work. If the helicopter wasn't enough excitement, the bull catcher filled in the gaps. We ripped across the paddock at high speed, following a bull as it dodged and weaved. I was shocked when Jim finally spun the wheel into the beast's side, and bowled it over, the bull bar coming to rest on its heaving flanks.

'Stay in the catcher!' he shouted as he jumped out, strap in hand.

There was no way I was going anywhere. I was shocked by the fact of the bull on the ground. I knew the process, having had it described to me several times by Rod, but actually being there and seeing it was something else. I wasn't prepared for the physical violence of it – the speed of the chase was one thing, terrifying and exciting, but ramming into a living creature, pinning it under a car, strapping its legs and then sawing off its horns as it lay stunned on the ground, blood spraying out in fierce bright plumes – that was confronting.

'Why do you have to cut off their horns?' I asked, thinking the poor bulls must have suffered enough already.

'Quiets them down, and stops them horning the other cattle,' Jim answered, spinning the wheel and heading after another bull. 'It doesn't hurt them, and gives them something to think about – makes staying in the mob look a whole lot safer.'

By the time Jim had caught another five or six bulls, my squeamishness had been replaced by exhilaration and adrenaline. After the bulls were let up into the mob, they stayed there, snorting and hooking at the others, but they could do little more than inflict bruises.

We caught up with Rod in another catcher, where he was strapping for the driver. He was in his element, surrounded by the sounds and the smells and the action he loved best.

'How are you finding it?' He looked at me a little warily, as if he expected me to demand to be taken back to Melbourne at once.

'It's fantastic! I had no idea it was so much fun!'

He grinned and gave me a quick hug. 'It'll be even better when we're doing it for ourselves.'

We finally reached Kununurra on 11 May 1978. It had taken us a while to get here, but we'd finally made it. I was ecstatic to be on our own at last, starting a new life together. At least that was how I saw it. Rod was a lot gloomier about the future. We had no money, and we needed to find a catching contract to carry us through until the Fitz-maurice filming started in July.

However, the very first thing Rod did when we arrived in the little town was to go straight to a jeweller's – the only jeweller's – shop, and buy me a gold ring. When the catching contract on Kildurk Station fell through in February, Rod had flown up to Kununurra to deal with the company managers to try and resolve the problem. While he was there, he found that everyone thought he had married 'that girl from Port Keats'. He decided that, since we were intending to get married eventually anyway, it might be useful in terms of getting contracts, or a bank loan, if he was seen as a married man, and not just a footloose ringer. It wasn't the way I had ever imagined myself 'married', but as far as I was concerned, I was already married in spirit, and wearing a ring seemed like a silent confirmation of that. So we spent $70 of our fast dwindling cash on a ring, and I became Joanne Ansell.

We may have had no money and no job, but at least we had some-where to stay. The boys were at Bundaberg Downs when we arrived, and a very drunken party was underway. As soon as we could excuse ourselves, we slipped away to where Rod's old International truck was parked under a tree. It had a stock crate on the back, half filled with gear and boxes, and we cleared some space and unrolled the swag. I lay there, amongst the truck parts and the fuel drums, looking up at the stars, listening to the raucous, drunken revelry coming from the donga, and reflected that for all intents and purposes, this was our honeymoon.

The next day we moved into the feed room at the back of the saddle shed. I found some old 20-litre drums and a wire gate, and unrolled the swag on top of them, so that we were off the floor, and made a shelf with some more drums and planks. Things started to look up.

The first thing to do was find work, and after a couple of phone calls, Rod had a meeting about a bull catching contract. He hired Stuart Skoglund to fly him to Auvergne Station to see the manager, Lloyd Fogarty. Stu had been in the Ord River area for a long time, flying crop dusters and helicopters, and is generally regarded as one of the finest helicopter musterers, if not the first. In 1968 he convinced the manager of Ivanhoe Station, near Kununurra, to let him try mustering cattle into a yard with his helicopter, and the muster was so successful that he continued, kicking off an industry that would change the standard of pastoral practices in the Northern Territory. Rod had told me many stories about Stu and his flying exploits, and he sounded like an amazing man, but unfortunately I only met him once. A week later Rod was offered a catching contract for both Auvergne and Newry Stations. Then a cheque arrived in compensation for the lost contract, and we were able to afford to go out to Kildurk and collect the catching plant Rod had left there over the wet season.

The equipment had deteriorated a bit over the Wet, so we spent the next two weeks getting it ready for work. The compensation cheque was soon gobbled up by fuel and engine parts. I learnt a lot more about mechanics than I ever wanted to know, and added a whole new category to my vocabulary, not all of it repeatable. I also learnt how to use the oxy-acetylene equipment, and to repair flat truck tyres, and to live with ingrained black stains on my hands. It seemed that everything had to be done from scratch. Rod even made up a clutch plate for the truck when the one in it broke. We had so little money that we had to do as much of the repairs as we could ourselves, and improvise our way around all kinds of mechanical problems.

Rod's good humour started to take a battering. It wasn't just the workload, and the grind of having to repair things that really should have been replaced with a new part. I became aware that he had to prove himself constantly. He was the best bull catcher, the best horseman, the best lover, the best at anything. He had no argument from me, but my approval wasn't enough. His stature in the eyes of his peers meant a lot to him, and success at this year's catching contract was crucial to him. He needed to be operating before the season was too far advanced, and the delays in repairing the gear made him irritated and cranky, and he was often frustrated and short tempered. But it didn't last for long, and we would usually finish the day's work with a swim in the river, and sometimes head into town for dinner at the little tavern where we'd remember that we were still in love with each other, and laugh about the trials of the day.

The bull catching plant consisted of a four-wheel drive Blitz truck, the old International truck, a very old and battered long wheel base Toyota with no cabin, and Rod's bull catcher. This vehicle was a short wheel base Toyota with the roof and sides taken off, and bull bars all the way around it. The radiator was on a frame up behind the seats to keep it from being horned by bulls, and to provide extra airflow for cooling. The catcher was painted bright red, where it had any bodywork to paint, and had huge wide tyres. It was Rod's pride and joy.

Once the vehicles were almost ready, the next thing was to teach me how to drive the Blitz. Somewhere along the way, Rod had acquired this old ex-army, ex-World War II, four-wheel drive truck. It had a huge ancient General Motors engine, which poked up naked into the cabin, searing the driver and anyone foolish enough to be a passenger with hot air and exhaust fumes. It was unbelievably noisy, had no suspension to speak of, no windscreen or doors, just a seat for the driver and a handhold for the foolhardy passenger. You needed both hands to change gears, and the steering was a very direct rack and pinion style, which meant that any rock or stump the wheels encountered spun the wheel in a vicious wrench. I learnt very quickly not to hook my thumbs around the steering wheel. My previous car had been a 30-year-old Renault 750, not quite as old as the Blitz, but very, very small. Four healthy teenagers could lift up my car and park it on the footpath, or other such embarrassing places. Now I was supposed to drive a huge truck?

My first lesson was in tyre changing: 'You have to be able to change your own wheels,' said Rod. 'When you're way out in the bush, you stake a few tyres, and there won't be anyone around to help you, so you have to be able to do it yourself.'

That was fair enough. I knew how to change a flat tyre on my Renault. But its wheels only weighed about 10 kilograms. The Blitz's wheels were nearly as big as me. I learned how to manoeuvre them into position with a complicated system of crowbars and tyre levers, and felt very chuffed when I did the first one by myself. Then I discovered that changing the wheels was the easy part. Removing the tyres to repair the punctures was a whole different ball game . . .

Next came driving lessons. The cabin of the Blitz was painted bright yellow, so you could find it in the bush, with a white roof to reflect the heat of the sun, and a black interior to reduce the glare. Steering was one thing, but changing gears was another all together. However, I mastered the intricacies of double declutching, a necessary procedure to change gears, and memorised the patterns of the gearbox. That was okay. On a level surface I was fine. I could steer, turn corners, and change gears like a pro. Then Rod decided to set up the two-way radio system he had bought while we were in Melbourne. This was so we could maintain radio contact when he was off catching bulls all over the flat, and I was following along picking them up. He attached the radio to the inside of the truck cabin in a safe place, and then mounted the antenna on the roof. I looked at the antenna, poking up above the truck like a flagpole, and expressed some concern about its safety up there, given the nature of the country I was to be driving through.

'Just make sure you don't drive under any low branches. It's *simple!*' Rod was becoming hot and bothered. We had just spent about three hours adjusting various bits to make the radio work, and he was getting cranky. I stopped asking questions, and hopped in the truck for a test run. All I had to do was drive around in circles a few times and change gears, test the brakes, that sort of thing. The first thing I did was drive straight under a low branch, and wiped off the antenna.

Rod was speechless, but he had to remain speechless, because just then two good friends of mine from Melbourne, Don and Adrienne Axelrad, turned up. They were on a driving holiday, and had made a special detour to come and visit us in Kununurra. It was so strange seeing people from my old life in Melbourne. Don was a biologist at the Marine Pollution Studies Group – now known as the Victorian Institute of Marine Science – and Adrienne was an accomplished artist. We had kept in touch while I'd been at Port Keats, and they were keen to see what I was now doing with myself. The rest of the day was declared a rest day, and we showed the Axelrads around the river, and relaxed. The next day was our first day catching.

Rod went out early on his own, while it was still cool, and caught four bulls, leaving them tied up in the shade. The first crack in the plan appeared when the hook on the cable which pulled the bulls up into the truck broke, and Rod had to weld up a new one before we could get going. It was now starting to warm up, and Rod was understandably getting anxious about the cattle tied up in the scrub. The hook remade, Rod set off with Don in the old long wheel base to find the four beasts, while Adrienne and I followed in the Blitz. This was when the other weakness in the plan became apparent.

I had assured Rod several times that I had a very poor sense of direction. I used to get lost in Melbourne all the time. I gave up going to town in my lunch hour when I worked there, because of the number of times I was late back to work. I'd go into Myers on one street, go round in circles for half an hour, and then leave the store on another street altogether, and head back to work in exactly the opposite direction from the one I should have been taking. Rod, on the other hand, had a sense of direction like a homing pigeon. No matter where he found himself, he unerringly knew which way was home, or which way he wanted to go. He could not believe that I could get lost so easily: 'Look, you just keep an eye on the sun, remember where it was when you left the road, and note landmarks as you go. Any fool can do it.'

I had not been able to sleep for a couple of nights worrying about how I was going to be able to accomplish all this. I had driven with Rod chasing bulls through the bush out from Kununurra. I failed to see how you were supposed to remember what the sun even looked like after you had changed direction seventeen times to avoid big boulders, steep gullies, impassable creeks and other points of interest, all the while staying upright and avoiding those low branches.

Adrienne and I got our instructions wrong and took off the wrong way, driving for about fifteen minutes in all directions. The radio wasn't working, probably because of another low branch, so I finally gave up and parked the truck in what I thought was the most central spot to wait for the others to come looking for us. As I turned off the engine, the ignition switch broke off, and I couldn't restart the truck. The Blitz had a strange bodgied-up electrical system, and if the ignition wasn't turned off, the coil would burn out, so I tried to disconnect the battery to stop that happening. No spanners or any tools in the truck. Just as I was about to run back to the camp to find some, Rod roared up in the old long wheel base looking for us, fixed the ignition with another improvisation, and hurried us after him. There was a grass fire burning, and we had to pick up all the bulls before they were caught in the flames.

We collected the first bull, who was very stirry from being tied for so long, but en route to the second I bogged the truck in a sandy creek, fortunately in the only clear spot for a long way, so we sat and choked as the fire burnt up close around us. The mood was anything but bright, as we expected to find the bulls injured or dead, and we all felt terrible at the thought. Nothing would pull the truck out. Rod took off to the camp and returned with another long wheel base Toyota and an electric winch. Still no good. Finally the old International truck was brought up, pulled the Blitz out with no effort, and we raced off to find that, miraculously, all the other bulls were okay.

It had been an amazingly bad first day, but it wasn't to be the worst. Don and Adrienne left a day later to continue their holiday, while Rod and I repaired the truck, and caught a few more bulls. The country we were working in was soft and sandy, and we had all kinds of trouble. The catcher would get bogged as it pulled the bulls up the slide into the truck, usually with an animal halfway up. The bull would then struggle and fall off the slide, or get its horns stuck in it as it was dragged up, or the catcher would stall and take fifteen minutes to restart. We were trying to operate on the barest smell of an oily rag, and with just the two of us. And one of us didn't have a clue what she was doing anyway, so that put most of the strain on Rod's shoulders.

Just a few days later the bull catcher was running badly, and I had a sprained hand from driving the truck, so we took the morning off to work on the vehicles. The old Falcon sedan was playing up as well, so Rod set me to work pulling out the spark plugs and cleaning the battery terminals to try and sort out its faults. A mate, Peter Rutherford, drove up just as Rod was about to take the catcher for a test run, so I stood chatting to him as we watched Rod disappear around the first corner of the track. There was a sort of a thump, and Peter said, 'He's rolled it.'

We jumped in his car and got to the corner just as Rod appeared out of the bush, walking towards us and holding onto his arm, otherwise looking to be all right. But then he said in a very strained voice, 'I think you better get me to the hospital, mate.'

Peter took off in a cloud of dust with Rod while I ran back to the camp, threw the battery and spark plugs in the Falcon, and caught up with them in the hospital a little while later. Rod had a badly broken collarbone, and several broken ribs. He refused to stay in hospital, so we crept home in the old car, trying to avoid the bumps and corrugations on the road without much success.

We went to look at the catcher the next day. It had crashed into a tree, bringing it down, and then flipped over a barbed wire fence landing upright on the other side without even breaking the top wire. The driver's seat was shredded by the barbs, but somehow Rod had been thrown out before that point, otherwise his injuries would have been much greater. The steering had broken, causing the crash, but the only other damage to the vehicle were broken springs and engine mounts, and a snapped weld on the bull bar. The damage to Rod's self esteem and good humour was much worse.

We'd had a bad start to our catching contract, and now we were off the road altogether. I saw it as a time to finish getting all the gear prepared, and concentrate on being ready for the filming, which now looked like being the only real money we were going to make this year. Rod became gloomier and gloomier. Normally I am good at pulling people out of black moods, but Rod affected me too, and soon I was just as despairing as him. I couldn't do anything right. He would ask me to do ridiculous things, like fix the clutch on the truck, or weld up a frame for the portable generator, and then rail at me for not being able to. There was just so much to get done, and he was unable to do anything at all for the first few weeks. The sheer pain stopped him at first, but before long he was attempting to do things he shouldn't have been, and ended up with a permanent lump on his collarbone where the break hadn't healed smoothly. I did as much as I could, but there was no getting round the fact that I had never welded anything, and that I didn't know where to *find* the clutch plate on a truck, let alone fix the damn thing.

To make matters worse, I also didn't understand the way Rod worked in this country. I had always been a very open person. If someone asked me a question, I would generally answer without even thinking about whether or not I should. Now I discovered I had to think carefully about everything I said before I said it.

This was brought home to me one evening when we went out to visit another couple, Ralph and Sadie Searle. They had a bull catching contract on the Ord River at the time, and were in town because Ralph had injured his leg. Rod had worked with the Searles in the past, and often cited the way Ralph did things as the benchmark for bull catching. He went into another room to talk to Ralph for a couple of hours, while I was left to wait in the living room with Sadie, whom I'd only met once before. She was a pleasant, friendly person, and we chatted on about nothing in particular.

When Rod and I left, he asked me, 'So what did you and Sadie talk about?'

'Oh, the usual small talk,' I said. 'She was interested in how we were getting on.' This didn't surprise me because I knew Rod had worked with the Searles before, and had a lot of respect for the way Ralph did things.

'Did she ask about the catching?'

'Um . . . she asked who was doing our carting, I remember.'

'So what did you say?'

'I told her that we hadn't used anyone at all yet because we hadn't caught a full load before your accident.'

Rod was furious. I just assumed it would be common knowledge around the place whether we'd sent any stock away or not, but Rod said it wasn't, and that he needed people to think he was doing well and getting out a lot of animals, or the contract might be jeopardised. He had been telling Ralph the exact opposite, that we'd sent away three or four loads before the interruption of his accident, and would be getting back to it soon. Now, he said, people would know that he hadn't sent off any animals yet, and that the contract wasn't being met. Up here, he went on, a man had to live by his reputation alone, and there were too many people ready to damage it if they had the chance.

I sank down in the seat of the car feeling like I'd let the side down badly, but I was also confused about how the hell I was supposed to know how to answer such questions in the first place. I didn't understand this way of life at all. I was used to being able to take people as I found them, and vice versa. I didn't expect that people were out to hurt me for no reason, or that I should have to tell lies, or at best distortions of the truth, to get by every day.

It was the first time I had seen a sign of paranoia in Rod, but I didn't recognise it as such. I just assumed that I didn't know anything about this place, and that things must be done differently here. Rod was virtually the only person I saw most of the time, so I didn't feel as if there was anyone I could talk to about it. I just became a little less forthcoming, and a little more reserved with the people I met, and didn't say much.

Rod started to talk about giving up, giving the game away. It was already mid July and he hadn't sent off an animal to the meatworks. After three weeks his collarbone and ribs still gave him a lot of pain, and clearly he couldn't do any heavy work for a while yet. Our financial situation was looking desperate. We had managed to borrow $3000 from the bank, but it was almost immediately swallowed up paying bills. The catering contract for the film would bring in about $10 000, but we didn't have the money to even get started on organising that.

However, I felt optimistic. The film was going to start soon, we had a place to live even if it was just the feed shed at Bundaberg Downs, we weren't starving, and most of all, Rod and I were together. I didn't really care what else happened, as long as we were together.

The very next day, Rachel Percy telegrammed to say that she would be arriving up from Perth in two days' time, to start preparations for the film.

# 7

# Reliving the River

The worst thing you can do in the bush – maybe the bush anywhere, but certainly in the Northern Territory – is to promote the idea that you might be more interesting than the next bloke, and draw attention to yourself. This is the country where a man is honoured for doing heroic things silently. Where blokes get gored by a wild buffalo, shove their intestines back in with their fist, stitch the wound up with a bit of horsehair and barbed wire, and shrug off assistance with 'Ah, s'only a scratch, mate.' So when it was rumoured that Rod Ansell was making a movie about the time he got himself lost on the Fitzmaurice River, the tall poppy clippers swung into action.

A lot of local people didn't believe the story was true. When the newspapers published the tale of the rescue, along with the photo taken by Alan Lawler out at Palumpa, it was weeks after Rod had actually arrived back in Kununurra. The papers ran the story as if it had only just happened, so people who knew Rod in Kununurra said, 'Bullshit, I saw him only last week! He wasn't lost in the bush – he was right here. . .' That was one problem. Rod compounded it by having the audacity to then allow someone to make a movie about it. Who did he think he was?

Rachel Percy arrived from Perth in July to do a final reconnoitre of the film locations before shooting commenced in August. She and Rod flew to Palumpa to organise the timing of Luke's arrival at the river – no small consideration given the distances the horses had to cover – and while Rachel met with Catholic Missions in Darwin to complete those arrangements, and returned to Perth, Rod and I pored over long lists of equipment and materials that would be needed on the river.

It didn't take long for word to get around about the film, and the ribbing started immediately. Much of it was just good natured, typically Australian reaction to such news. But there were also a lot of nasty jibes. As the weeks went by it was clear that many people hoped it would all fall over. I grew to hate going into shops and businesses around the town when I was getting the equipment and supplies together. It wasn't so much that people said things – it was the squinting of their eyes, and the knowing sneer, and the nodding heads, as if to say, 'We know he's just a busted-arse bull catcher pulling the wool over these dumb southerners' eyes.' But in spite of this attitude, Rod was cheerful. His depression lifted and mood swings eased, and he became positive and happy again, the man I remembered from Port Keats. Now here was something he could get his teeth into. Here were challenges he could tackle with both hands.

As well as having the starring role, Rod had contracted with Richard and Rachel to provide the catering and logistical support. We had the job of getting all the equipment and supplies for six weeks' filming to a place about 120 kilometres past where the road stopped – the 'road' being two faint wheel tracks through long grass and scrub. From our starting point in Kununurra, the only access to the Fitz-maurice was through Bradshaw Station, and the only way to Bradshaw was through Coolibah Station, about three hours' drive east of Kununurra along the Victoria Highway. Bradshaw is on the north side of the Victoria River, across the tidal flow of the river. Coolibah homestead, formerly the operational heart of Bradshaw but at this time just an outstation, was a lot further upstream, about 110 kilo-metres east of Bradshaw. Just below the homestead was a crossing where vehicles could safely ford the river in the dry season. This was the way our Blitz truck and the long wheel base would have to go in.

To save the long journey around by road, Bradshaw had a barge, which was an old tip-truck tray with several 44-gallon drums welded to it for flotation. Stores and provisions would be delivered to the barge landing about forty kilometres north of the Victoria Highway, and then ferried across the river on the barge which was towed by a dinghy and outboard motor.

In July Rod and I flew out to Bradshaw to meet the manager, Rowly Walker, and his pilot and head stockman, Dick Gill, and talk about the best way to go in. Rowly and Dick were both big men, especially Dick, who was at least 193 centimetres tall. I remember them looking at this fellow who had got himself lost on their station, this little bloke who wouldn't have been half their weight wringing wet, and the scepticism on their faces was plain as day.

In a classic bit of bush understatement, they said the road was useable: 'Yeah, there's a road in. Some blokes travelled over it recently, right to the bottom of the gorge where you're going. It's a bit rough, but you should get through okay.'

They were clearly not excited at the prospect of a film crew running around on their property, far from their supervision, and they didn't know Rod. But they agreed to let us in, and offered us accommodation at the homestead while we were setting up the camp.

When Rod took on the contract to provide the camp for the film crew, he had never been on Bradshaw Station, apart from the time he'd spent along the river, and a couple of hours at the homestead the previous August. Bradshaw was majestic in its isolation, cut off from the rest of the country by the mighty Victoria River on its southern border, and by towering ranges and brokenback country to the north. We were planning to take three vehicles and a dozen people over a road that hadn't been travelled for years, and we hadn't even checked it out for ourselves. Fortunately I was too green to realise this might be a problem.

Spreading maps out on the kitchen table Dick Gill gave Rod directions: 'You head west from Coolibah homestead, and climb the saddle of Wandoan Hill, then down into the Coolibah paddocks, up this wide pocket to the north, and then you strike the big jump up. It's a pretty difficult climb, big rocks, very rough, and it's a long way from end to end. I saw old Les Little come down it on a grader once,' he said, a wry smile creasing his face. 'The grader jumped out of gear at the top, and had no brakes. I yelled to him to bail out but he stuck with it and rode it to the bottom. I don't know how fast he was going, and how high he bounced over some of those rocks, but old Les hung in there. But you'll be right with the four-be-fours.

'From the top of the jump up you head west again to Crocodile Yard. There's a big rock bar and a drop-off into the gorge close to the south. Here you're about sixty kilometres from Coolibah. Then you go west past Larung Yard and Bosun Yard and the plains. All flat country here.' He brushed at a place on the map. 'Up ahead you'll see the Yambarran Range above Bradshaw homestead. The road up to the homestead goes along the cross-strip [of the airstrip], past the old Bradshaw house that was built early last century. There used to be a set of gallows out the front, and they weren't used to hang bullocks.' Dick paused a moment and looked up at us, and I made a mental note to find out about Bradshaw's history.

He went on: 'That's about a hundred and ten kilometres, Coolibah to Bradshaw. Leaving the homestead, you head down off the rocky ridge and across the river country – it's all coolibah trees here – past the Dome, across Gregory Creek, and close by Bradshaw's Tomb. That's it off to your left, right on the bank of the Victoria River. The Bradshaw people killed in the 1905 massacre are buried up there.' Now I understood the significance of the gallows near the old house. If Bradshaw seemed isolated to me in 1978, it must have been a faraway place in 1905.

'You follow this valley to Barramundi Spring. It gets more timbered around here, and the track runs north up this narrow pocket. About ten kilometres north of the spring you run close to a rock wall that runs north-south. At Jiminjerri Waterhole – there's a yard there too – you head west for the Koolendong Valley, a valley that runs north to the Fitzmaurice.

'Once you meet the Koolendong Valley you head north, cross over Saltwater Creek, which can be a real tough crossing, and past Revolver Yard. Right here the Koolendong is less than a kilometre wide, there's a rock rampart to the east, and rough broken country to the west. It's a straight run north from Revolver Yard to the Fitzmaurice, mainly open savannah woodland, and about another ten kilometres will bring you onto the river . . .' He rolled a smoke and lit it while Rod bent over the maps.

'Just don't get anyone killed,' admonished Dick as we were leaving. 'The paperwork's terrible.'

A fellow named Daryl had been staying at Bundaberg Downs for the past couple of months. He seemed a handy sort of bloke, and appeared to know his way around the bush, so we employed him to be camp manager at the Fitzmaurice. He also had a 4WD station wagon which we could use to transport the film crew and the camera equipment from Bradshaw into the river camp. That solved a major dilemma. We could get most of the gear across the river using the station's barge, but our vehicles weren't suitable for transporting the crew and their camera gear such a long distance. We thought we'd have to hire a couple of four-wheel-drives from Kununurra, so we were very glad to have Daryl's Landcruiser instead. It would save a lot of money and time.

Rod and Daryl went in with the first load. The Blitz truck, loaded up with all the heavy equipment for the camp, tipped over on the big jump-up, the one that old Les rode the grader down, and Rod was knocked unconscious when the truck's battery broke free and struck him on the head. Daryl was following behind in the long wheel base Toyota, and made him rest for a couple of hours before they unloaded the Blitz in order to pull it back onto its wheels.

They loaded up again, and this time got the truck to within ten kilometres of a suitable campsite on the river, and ferried the gear in with the long wheel base. Rod and Daryl flew back to Kununurra from Bradshaw, instead of taking the terrible track through Coolibah again, and Daryl immediately quit, saying he wasn't going to take his own vehicle across such a bad road. That left us with a huge problem, because it was clear that we couldn't take rented vehicles over the jump-up either.

Rachel Percy flew in, and a day or two later cameraman Bill Grimmond arrived from Perth to start filming, a big affable man who infected everyone with his enthusiasm for the project. Bill had plenty of experience working on remote locations, and his CV included the classic Australian movie 'Jedda'. As far as he was concerned, no problem was too big to get around, and even our worries with transport seemed to shrink. A few days later he and Rod were driving through the bush in Rod's catcher checking out a site for a bull catching sequence, when something flew up and hit Bill across the face, breaking both his jaws and lacerating his top lip. He was flown out to Perth that night, and a new cameraman had to be found immediately.

Rod was badly shaken, and blamed himself, although it was the kind of unavoidable accident that could have happened at any time. He was depressed and withdrawn for a few days, until Paul Tait, the new cameraman, arrived, along with the rest of the crew, and he had to start performing.

There was a bit of filming to be done in and around Kununurra. Not only did Rod suddenly have to 'act', he had to do it in front of half the town. One scene was shot at the Kununurra races. For a while no one realised who the camera was pointing at. One friend came up to Rod for a yarn, oblivious to the camera and crew nearby, chatted away for a while and then said, 'So when's this movie caper starting?'

'As a matter of fact you're starring in it right now,' answered Rod. His mate looked terrified, jammed his hat further down on his head and retreated at high speed.

Some filming was done out at Carlton Hill Station, some at Max Lamoreaux's place outside Kununurra, and at other locations around the area, such as Long Michael Plain, and Maxwell Plains. In between acting stints and finding locations for the camera, we were racing around finding the equipment we still needed for the camp, and ordering the rest of the food supplies.

The boat capsizing scene was filmed out at Bundaberg Downs. The boys were all away working, and the quiet stretch of river below the donga was perfect for the close-up action footage that was needed. It took all afternoon and lots of ingenuity to make the boat actually tip over satisfactorily, with Paul Tait in the dinghy as well, stripped down to his jocks and clutching an underwater camera.

We had just finished packing up and the crew was about ready to leave when two of the Bundaberg boys turned up. They were clutching armfuls of beer and rum, and were very drunk, and very belligerent. Rod tried to talk to them, but they lurched around, yelling and swearing, insulting the crew and knocking things over. It was a fraught, tense few minutes. Then one of them kicked over the corrugated iron windbreak we'd put up around the fireplace, and Rod said, 'That's it. Everybody, let's go.' He herded everyone into the cars, and we headed into Kununurra, left the crew at their motel, and found ourselves somewhere to stay.

At dinner that evening he tried to explain it to Rachel and Richard,

Richard having only stepped off the plane from Perth that afternoon: 'Ah, the boys have been on the piss all day. Guess they didn't like finding a mob of strangers at their place like that. I'll go back and sort it out with them tomorrow, when they've sobered up.' He tried to sound confident, but he looked bothered.

Next morning Rod went out to Bundaberg Downs to see the boys. He returned some hours later, looking so grim faced and stricken that I worried about what must have happened.

'They want us off the place. This afternoon you'll have to go out there and pack up our gear, as much of it as you can shift,' he said to me. 'I have to go off with Paul and get some more . . . ah, some more . . .' He turned away. He was quiet for a moment, and then he began to weep. He sat on the floor with his head on his knees, and just cried. His good mates, the blokes I had heard so much about, so many funny stories and so many good times, had told him to get out. It was the crucial last straw on the camel's back, and Rod fell in a heap.

All the stress of the past few months just crashed over him with this awful rejection by his mates. The stresses of trying to find work, trying to pretend he was doing well when he wasn't, getting injured, trying to do everything with no money, Bill Grimmond's accident and now being involved in shooting a film that seemed to make him even more the outsider in this town – all these things were bearable. But to have his mates turn on him like that was too much. To complicate it further, it had happened in front of the film crew, strangers to whom he felt he had to keep up the image of being the one in control. I had never seen Rod so upset. The timing was impossible – we had to be on the river in a couple of days, with a helicopter due, and now we had to find somewhere to put all the equipment we weren't taking to the river, and somewhere to stay ourselves.

We moved all our stuff off Bundaberg Downs that day, and stored it with Rod's mate Cedric in town, who was also helping us transport gear out to the Bradshaw landing in his truck. Rod couldn't do everything by himself, so he hired three blokes he found through the Social Security office in Kununurra. One was an overweight young ringer called Terry, one a long-haired, weedy looking character called Russell, and the third a middle-aged bloke called Tony. I took one look at them and felt my stomach drop a few levels. I looked at Rod.

'I know,' he muttered. 'They were all I could get. Anyone who's any good is out in a stock camp somewhere, not a dole office . . .'

The job of getting everything and everyone out to Bradshaw turned into a logistical nightmare, and in the end Richard and Rachel had to hire a helicopter to get the crew and the camera equipment to the Fitzmaurice camp site. It took several trips using Cedric's truck, a rented four-wheel-drive and our own little car, to get the rest to the barge landing and over the river. Rod's bull catcher was a problem. He didn't want to drive it around by the long road, as much for the time it would take as for the damage it might incur. So we loaded it onto the barge, balancing the back wheels on planks of wood because they wouldn't fit inside the tray. There couldn't have been more than six inches of freeboard. We waited for slack water in between the tides, and slowly towed it over, expecting that at any moment it just might sink to the bottom of the river.

We all spent the first night at Bradshaw Station, where the manager, Rowly Walker, and his head stockman/pilot, Dick Gill, seemed to have overcome their initial scepticism and suspicion of what we were trying to do, and had put on a barbecue for us. I think they were impressed that Rod had actually managed to drive a truck into the Fitzmaurice. Rod was in no doubt that they hadn't expected him to make it, and that the film idea would have been given away: 'I think that was a kind of test they didn't expect me to pass,' he said, not looking too unhappy. They were also impressed that Rod had floated his catcher across the river on their barge. They did it themselves a few months later, but we noticed that they welded a few more empty 44s on to the barge first.

Half the station's stock camp was in, and with the dozen of us added we made up a good-sized party. Someone found my guitar and when everyone had got outside of enough rum the singing started. A few more rums, and poetry reciting took the floor. Even though it was 1978, and rock bands like Led Zeppelin and Pink Floyd were far better known than Paterson or Lawson, most of the young ringers there could remember at least a few verses of a bush poem. It was a great night, especially when the station cook got drunk and gave me his secret bread recipe. When he sobered up the next morning and realised what he'd done, he came over to me, and said: 'Here, you've got my bread recipe, you may as well have the 'dourie too,' and presented me with a shiny new Bedourie oven in which to bake my bread.

Bedourie ovens are a canny invention, originating from Bedourie Station in western Queensland. Instead of packhorses, the station used camels, and the usual cast iron camp ovens could break if the packs fell from such a height. So they made camp ovens out of rolled steel, with the lid coming halfway down the sides of the base pan to keep the dust storms out. Great to cook in, more versatile than a camp oven because you could fry steak in the upturned lid, and a damn sight lighter to lug around. I still have mine. I made bread every morning. I was very grateful to the Bradshaw cook – I'd never baked bread anywhere but in a regular oven before, and my bread was perfect from day one.

Our camp was at the beginning of a steep-sided gorge of dark red rock, at the limit of the tidal reach. It was about eight kilometres upstream from the place Rod had camped the year before. His tree was just as he'd described it – the platform of branches he'd rolled his swag out on was still lashed in its fork, and the bark was splitting and swelling around the marks he'd gouged out to count the days.

The spot we stayed at was much more salubrious. It was an old cattle camp, used by wild scrub bulls, and they had worn down all the undergrowth beneath the shady trees to create a conveniently clear area for us to set up our camp. Four or five enormous ancient fig trees and wild peaches formed a big circle around a large flat-bottomed hollow, so that the camp was in shadow for most of the day. It was about 100 metres from the river. Away from camp, Rod and Daryl had built a shower with a concrete floor, close enough to the river to pump water from it into a tank up in the tree above, and a wood-fired hot water system so that the crew could have hot showers. They also dug a deep pit toilet with corrugated iron walls. We thought it was pretty flash. Portable generator, freezer, sleeping tents, camera gear tent, food store tent, and that was about it. The refrigerator had been a casualty of the Blitz roll-over on the way in, so we had to make do without it. We had a Codan HF two-way radio for communication, and sent our telegrams through the Flying Doctor base in Wyndham.

It wasn't until I had set up the cooking area under the trees that the thought of feeding all these people for six weeks on just a campfire actually hit me. Who was I kidding? I was suddenly overcome with a huge dose of nerves and doubt, and sat looking at the camp ovens and the billycans, wondering how long I would get away with this charade. I'd cooked on a fire at Bundaberg Downs, sure, but these people would expect much better meals . . . Rod turned up at that point, and came over to me. He brushed the hair off my face, kissed me and said, as if reading my mind: 'You'll be right. Want me to dig your camp oven holes for you?'

I discovered there really wasn't much you couldn't cook in a camp oven. A good supply of firewood – of the kind that burns down to coals and not just ash – is important. A long-handled shovel is next, first for digging the holes to bury the camp ovens, and secondly for lifting out the hot coals. Then a pair of fire hooks, long pieces of heavy-gauge wire bent at the ends so you can hook the wire handles of the ovens and drag them out of the heat. We ate our meals around the fire where I'd cooked them, and sat on the bags of horse cubes brought in for Luke's horses – until they were eaten out from under us. We'd forgotten about bringing in chairs.

The menu was pretty simple – curries and roasts, stews and casseroles, and the occasional barbecue when we had a fresh killer. Fish would appear on the menu too, if the crew'd had time to throw a line in between takes. Vegetables were basic – whatever would last the longest, like potatoes, carrots, onions and cabbages – but every time the helicopter was due I'd order fresh vegetables and salad. Sometimes there was dessert as well – custard and canned fruit, with plenty of brandy if it had been a hard day, or pancakes and golden syrup. I baked fruit cakes with lots of rum, bread, rolls, fruit buns, brownies, biscuits. These were always popular but my forte was definitely the bread. As long as there was plenty of freshly baked bread, everyone was happy. I had to try and make it when no one was around, or else it wouldn't even get time to cool down before it was eaten.

The film crew settled in remarkably well. We had been half expecting a bunch of Sydney prima donnas – the crew all came from New South Wales – but apart from one woman who complained about the beetles in the pit toilet – and left soon after – they were very relaxed and easy to get along with. As well as Paul Tait the cameraman, there was Roly McManus, sound recordist, and Jan Kenny, camera assistant. Rachel and Richard were the producers, although Richard wasn't on location with us all the time, coming and going as his other filming schedules allowed. Paul eventually left to meet another filming obligation, and was replaced by Keith Loone. Jan left some weeks later and was replaced by Mike Harley. Roly and Rachel remained with us the entire time.

It must have been so strange for Rod to be back at the river, in the place where he had been alone for six weeks the year before. Now he was surrounded by people, noise, and a rigorous filming schedule. I asked him several times how he felt about it, but he would shrug his shoulders and point out the list of things that had to be done. There wasn't time to reflect on anything. But he was a natural in front of the camera. He followed direction easily, anticipated problems, and caught on to the intricacies of continuity so quickly that the crew were impressed. If we had been dreading a bunch of prima donnas, they were probably expecting to work with an equally difficult first-time actor. Richard Oxenburgh admitted later that they had thought it would be a lot harder, even to the point of perhaps requiring an actor to play Rod's role. For most people, acting isn't an easy thing to do, especially if they're untrained, and portraying yourself in front of a camera is a lot more difficult again.

Rod amazed them all with his unerring sense of direction. One evening he and Richard were returning to camp from scouting a spot for the next day's shoot, when the Toyota broke down. Too tired to try and fix it in the dark, Rod suggested they walk back. It was a moonless night, and Richard had no idea which way led to home. He had no choice but to follow Rod, and they trudged on for an hour straight across country, until they walked right into camp. They were all well aware of how much they depended on him – we all did. If anything had happened to Rod out there, especially while they were filming away from the camp, they would have had a hard time finding their way back.

Luke McCall – the manager of Palumpa Station who had rescued Rod on the Fitzmaurice – was the kind of bloke you heard about long before you met him. A bit like a mirage off a desert – both the mirage and the desert are spectacular, but you're never quite sure which is real.

I had been hearing about Luke for weeks before I first met him at Port Keats in 1976.

'Luke's coming in soon!'

'You girls had better watch out when Luke McCall gets to town!'

I was expecting a combination of Paul Newman, Robert Redford and Clint Eastwood by then, and was totally unprepared for the mud-spattered, white-haired *old* bloke who showed up in my office asking for the key to the flat under the single men's quarters. I was under strict instruction never to let anyone else stay in that flat. Luke may only have come to Port Keats two or three times a year, but he paid the weekly rental on his accommodation all year long. He couldn't abide the thought of someone else staying in his flat when he wasn't there.

A couple of hours later he was resplendent in fine clothes, complete with a coloured neckerchief, his snowy hair and beard neatly brushed and his boots polished.

'Forgive me for looking so awful earlier on, lovey! Country's too wet for a motor car, and too hard on the horse this time of year, so I walk in from Palumpa.'

Palumpa was 30 miles away, and the road waist deep in places with mud and water. Luke was on his annual leave, flying off first class to the southern bright lights to stay in the best hotels and meet beautiful women. Although his hair was white, he was only about forty-five or so then, and tall, with twinkling blue eyes, a broad smile full of perfect white teeth, and a voice that was both cultured and country at the same time. He talked fast and soft, as though he didn't really want to be overheard, and entertained us for hours. Luke didn't drink alcohol, or smoke, and he believed that anyone who voluntarily chose celibacy, such as the priests at the Port Keats mission, was just plain stupid.

He loved having visitors come and stay when he was at the station, provided we observed his house rules. Fastidious almost to the point of obsession, he couldn't abide the least bit of mess. If you put a glass on a table, he would swoop down with a cloth and wipe up the ring of moisture before handing you a drink coaster with a slightly miffed air. We much preferred visiting him out at the stock camp, where we slept on the ground in swags and ate round the campfire, and there were no tables to be kept ring-free.

I've seen a lot of stock camps since then, and Luke's was in a class all its own. At the end of the day, packs would be taken off the horses and lined up neatly, stockhorses unsaddled and their backs dusted with baby powder, and the saddle gear cleaned, repaired and carefully hung up. The 'kitchen' was handled in the same fashion. Luke would spread out a tarpaulin, arrange the tins of powdered milk, sugar, tea and so on in straight rows, and set about cooking, after he had tidied himself up a bit. Nothing was thrown down haphazardly, and nothing got lost. 'Takes as much time to do it sloppily as it does to do it properly,' he would say.

It was out in the bush that you saw Luke in his element, astride his big pacer or his mule, dressed from head to toe in black, with a coloured bandanna at his neck. 'The Black Prince' they called him around the traps in western Queensland and the Territory. He said he wore black because it didn't end up looking as grubby as the jeans or moleskins favoured by most other stockmen. He ordered them from RM Williams in Queensland, who kept a special supply just for him.

Luke was something of a legend in the northwest of Queensland and the Northern Territory. He never spoke very much about his own exploits or his history, but I heard from other people in later years how he was considered a fine horseman and cattleman. He had a reputation for strength – another of his nicknames was 'The Ironman' – and he was known to use it if anyone brought grog to Palumpa, which was a dry station. The offender would simply get clobbered by Luke, and sent on his way again. It didn't happen too often – at least not with the same offender. Once would have been enough.

At Port Keats – 'in town' as Luke and the stockmen referred to it – Luke was widely respected by the Aboriginal people, and he and the stockmen were afforded hero status. All the little kids wanted to be like Luke and Big Rupert. Luke was a bit of a hero amongst the white community too. I think he just looked so different from the ordinariness of the rest of us that seeing him arrive in town was always an occasion. He didn't come to Port Keats very often, but would turn up for the occasional party or gathering if he wasn't away with the stock camp.

Palumpa operated under an unusual arrangement. It was owned by an Aboriginal board of management, and Luke was employed as station manager by the same men in his stock camp to whom he gave his orders. Rupert Wodidj – Big Rupert – was in charge, and Luke consulted with him over what had to be done with the stock and the station, and Rupert would then pass it on to the men. Luke had a good relationship with them all. He treated them with respect, as the Aboriginal stockmen did him.

It was wonderful to see Luke arrive at the Fitzmaurice with Rupert and Raphael Thardim, capable and efficient astride their horses, in their Akubras and riding boots and shirts, a million miles away from the T-shirts and shorts and caps worn by the rest of us. It had taken them a good week to get to the film shoot location, and they looked pleased to be able to pull up for a bit. Luke was wearing the same black clothes I remembered from Palumpa, although he confided to me that he had brought along his good hat, and a few extra bandannas. They also had a string of horses with them.

The fire along the northern bank had burnt what little feed there was, and they were hoping to get their part of the filming done quickly. Our fireside seats – those bags of horse cubes – were about to disappear.

Filming in such a remote location was difficult. Every day seemed to throw up a fresh obstacle. Vehicles broke down frequently, or the generator did, which was crucial for recharging the camera batteries. The river was treacherous, full of sandbars and rocks and whirlpools, sharks, stingrays and big crocodiles, and the tides were unpredictable and difficult to work with. Far more helicopter time was needed than had been allowed for. Wildfires burnt through on the Palumpa side, right up to the river, spoiling aerial shots and requiring a rewrite of the script, and threatening Luke's horses. A lot of the early shots were unusable, and pressure of time and money meant they couldn't be reshot. Communication was patchy and inefficient, and to top it off the national telephone carrier went on strike, so we couldn't even send or receive our telegrams.

Richard arrived up at the end of the second week and stayed for a fortnight. The overwhelming logistical difficulties, and the burgeoning costs, were worrying him considerably. Then we had bad news from the film editor in Sydney. The bull catching scenes looked completely uneditable, and he told Richard they'd have to be reshot. At this point Richard decided the film was too hard to make, and that instead he would make a film about the difficulties of shooting this one. Show the country in all its magnificent impossibility, and the obstacles it flung up in our path. He went into his tent for a while, then came back out and announced he was going to wrap, that everyone would be paid to the end of schedule, but that it was all over, and he disappeared back inside his tent. The evening meal was quiet and suspenseful, and nothing much was said. The next morning however, a quick radio conference with Dick Gill established that he could pick up the film rushes in Kununurra and fly them out to the camp, so a few nights later we hung up a screen, turned on the generator and watched some of the footage that had been shot earlier. The scenes *were* useable, now that the crew could see them for themselves. The relief was palpable. There were still lots of problems, especially from the fires that obscured the aerial shots with smoke, but everyone seemed more optimistic now and filming continued apace.

The only cast or crew members who never worried about anything at all were the dogs. Bouncer and Deaf Dog were, as always, completely relaxed, except when they spotted a bull. It was necessary to keep them tied up most of the time because of this, and more so because of the crocodiles in the river. They travelled everywhere with Rod, balancing in the bull catcher or on the back of the long wheel base, but the transport method they loved the most was the helicopter. Old Deaf Dog would sit in the front of the chopper with his nose pressed up against the perspex bubble, watching for bulls. As soon as he saw one he'd get so excited you'd have to hang on tightly to him before he launched himself out the door after it. They were both very friendly dogs, and brought a pleasant distraction to the camp. Deaf Dog, a white bullterrier, really was deaf. He had been kicked in the head by a bull when he was a young dog, and had lost his hearing completely. So he watched people all the time, to see what it was they wanted. Some people found it quite unnerving, to be stared at unblinkingly by a bullterrier, but Deaf Dog was the least dangerous dog you could ever meet, unless you were another dog. Even then he wasn't a huge threat, because he had very few teeth left. Bouncer was a big strong brindle dog, a bully-boxer cross with the same lovely nature as his father. The two of them were good mates ever since they had sorted out who was top dog a few months back in our car, but occasionally Deaf Dog would get sick of things and pick a fight just to remind Bouncer that he didn't know everything. We had left my dog, Little Bull, behind with friends in Kununurra.

Dick Gill flew into our camp occasionally to check that we didn't require any of that terrible paperwork. If anyone should have been starring in an outback movie, it was Dick Gill. The classic Aussie icon – tall, lean and handsome – Dick was originally from Sydney, but a passion for flying and a love of the bush sealed his fate when he came to the Territory. He would land his Cessna on a small clearing nearby and be shuttled between his plane and the camp in Rod's bull catcher. When the rest of us humble mortals went anywhere in that vehicle, we'd be crouched in the so-called passenger seat, hanging on with both hands. Dick always perched on the side bar with a leg hooked under the body, coolly rolling a smoke. Class.

There was a kind of recognition between Rod and Dick, like two wary dogs who circle each other for a while, always on the alert for any weakness or aggression on the part of the other but otherwise content to stay peaceful, if watchful. Later, when Rod and I spent some time in the Bradshaw stock camp, we got to know Dick better, and he and Rod became good mates.

Rod enjoyed the filming. It was the best of both worlds for him. He was constantly busy, earning good money, and surrounded by interesting people. And he was in his element, deep in the bush, where everyone depended on his skills and knowledge. Not only did he act for the camera, he also had daily conferences about the script, filmed himself in the bull catcher, sorted out filming logistics, provided the meat supply, repaired the vehicles and other equipment, drove the crew around, provided the transport, was the film carpenter, mechanic, and animal wrangler, sorted out continual problems with the three fellows we'd employed to help, and kept the cook happy.

He also relived the entire time he had been stranded on the river, and re-enacted everything that had happened to him. As Richard Oxenburgh said to me one morning as we watched Rod drive off with the crew to a location downriver, 'If Rod didn't actually get stuck out here, like some people think, he's gone and done every single thing he said happened anyway.'

# 8

# My First
# Mickey

Filming on the Fitzmaurice finally came to an end after five
weeks, and in late September we packed up the little camp.
Most of the crew flew back to Kununurra by helicopter with all
the film equipment, while the rest of us loaded up the gear to be trans-
ported the 130 kilometres back to Bradshaw. Roly McManus, the
soundman, drove the red catcher, followed by Terry and Tony in the
long wheel base. Rod and I brought up the rear in the old Blitz, Rod
figuring that we were the least likely to break down. The trip to the
station had been made twice more since we first came to the river, so
the track in was well enough marked for the others to follow.

The truck's gearbox seized up in the bottom of a gully and we
stopped, the silence of the bush crashing in over us after the
cacophony of the truck. We could hear the old Toyota ahead of us
getting further and further away. As the sound of the engine grew
fainter, Rod remembered that the toolbox was in the long wheel base.

He rummaged around in the cabin and found a screwdriver, a small
shifting spanner and an old butter knife, and managed to remove
the top of the gearbox, but the repair job was far too complicated for
the tools we had. It was almost too much for him. The buoyancy
of the film making, the excitement of the pace and action, had all
evaporated. The party was over, and here he was again, trying to get a
job done in this hard country with crap machinery that let him down
constantly. To make it all worse, we had run out of water, the last of
our supply having gone into the truck radiator some hours earlier.

'Fuck it,' he said in disgust. 'Fuck everything.' He unrolled the swag in the shade of a tree, and lay on it, staring into the branches. Every word I said was angrily rebuffed.

'Are we just going to stay here then?' I asked finally.

'I don't give a shit. I'd burn the fuckin' thing if I had some fuckin' matches.'

After another few minutes I said, 'Well, looks like you won't need any matches.'

A grass fire we'd passed some miles back had caught up with us, and although we were in a reasonably clear spot, it was going to get a bit uncomfortable if we stayed where we were.

Rod climbed in the truck for another look. With him driving and holding 3rd and 4th gears out of the way with the screw driver, while I jammed 2nd and reverse back with the butter knife, gear oil spraying all over us like a fountain, the truck ground its way out of the gully in first gear, flames licking at the wheels. We pulled up on some bare ground, Rod made a few more improvisations and we limped on our way.

We stopped at an old stock camp site, known as Boab Yard. Night was falling, and we decided not to trust the battery and the electrics as we still had some rough track to cross. We hadn't had a drink for about seven hours, so we were thirsty, uncomfortable, and covered in pungent gear oil. But the stars were magnificent. Rod's good humour had returned, and we lay on our swag looking at the sky through the branches of the ancient boab overhead and talked about what it was like to be thirsty.

'We're really thirsty now, but thirsty like this is fine, because we know we'll get a drink tomorrow,' he said. 'But even like this your mind starts playing tricks on you. I don't even like beer, but all I can imagine is a cold glass of it, all frosted with droplets of moisture . . . You have to concentrate on something else.' Even so, he climbed into the boab tree to see if it had any water trapped in the pocket created by its branches, but there was only the acrid smell of flying foxes.

He talked about how living in the bush, living hard, prepared you for harder things: 'If you only ever slept in a comfortable bed at the homestead, never in a swag on the ground, you'd never cope with the stuff that the country throws up at you. Like now, because we don't expect a four course meal with the best china and silver every time it's dinnertime, it's no big deal to miss out now. Or to go to sleep without a hot shower, or a change of clothes. This is real, right down to the basics, nothing in between us and the bush. It's your attitude that counts, more than anything.'

I glowed a little at the thought that I was right here, being authentic and real, even if I hadn't actually sought out this state by myself. I came back to earth the next morning.

The first water we came across when we set out again in the morning was a muddy soak, which the cattle had obviously got to before us. It was thick and murky and smelled like the cattle.

'Drink it – don't worry about the taste, it's water.' Rod frowned when I looked askance at the brown slurry in my pannikin. We filled up the water bags and the drum, and set off. Not ten minutes later we turned a corner and there before us was a beautiful crystal clear billabong.

'You knew that was there!' I yelled at him.

'Yeah, well, you need to be able to drink whatever water you find in the bush. You can't just wait for the good stuff to come along . . .'

I glared at him and jumped out of the truck. I wasn't thirsty anymore, but the sight of all that clean water was too much, and I was annoyed at being 'taught a lesson' like that. Of course I would do whatever you had to do to survive, if it came down to it. But where Rod and I differed, I was starting to realise, was that he would often choose to live by the survival method, not just when he had to.

A couple of hours later we were almost at Bradshaw Station, and in case things were going too smoothly, the front tyre of the truck suddenly exploded just three kilometres from the homestead. With no more spares left, we set out to walk the rest of the way, but old Les Little, who looked after the kitchen garden and did a bit of fencing, came along in his ute and picked us up.

Les had lived at Bradshaw Station since 1957. He was a quiet, gentlemanly old fellow, perhaps well into his seventies by then, but like many old stockmen on stations, the idea of 'retiring' never entered his head. Bradshaw had been his home for twenty years, and he was going to die there. He'd already told Dick where he wanted to be buried. He had fought in New Guinea during the war, and had been wounded by a Japanese dum-dum bullet which came out of his back in six places. After the war he turned to droving, and was a well-known boss drover, walking mobs of 1200 bullocks from the Territory into the Queensland channel country. He was employed as head stockman at Bradshaw in 1957 and remained there till he died in 1982, highly regarded by everyone who knew him. As he showed in the grader-down-the-jump-up episode, not much perturbed him. Les and Dick were looking for cattle in the Cessna one day, when Dick quietly turned off the fuel without Les noticing. A few minutes later the motor spluttered and died. As the nose of the plane dropped, the old man glanced out the window and said: 'Oh well, looks like we've got a bit of a walk.'

After another week of filming, picking up shots at Palumpa and in Kununurra, it was all over. The crew headed back to civilisation, and Rod and I returned to Bradshaw to pick up the rest of our gear. While we were there repairing the Blitz and patching tyres, Dick Gill and Rowly Walker invited us out to the stock camp, seeing that we had a perfectly good bull catcher doing nothing. Rod made a deal with them that in return for the loan of a truck to move some equipment, and a flight up to Darwin later, we would spend a week working in the stock camp.

I had something else to think about too. A couple of weeks before, Rod had suggested we should get married soon. I was in agreement, if surprised that he'd made the suggestion, but then he seemed to change his mind, saying that perhaps we didn't have to rush into it. I was in a quandary now, not knowing if he was having second thoughts about me, or just about the prospect of a wedding. I tried to get him to discuss it, but all he would say was, 'Let's talk about it later.'

While Rod and the crew were completing the last of the filming at Palumpa, Luke and I had a few moments to ourselves. We sat out on the verandah one evening waiting for the others to return and Luke asked me how things were with Rod. He may have sent Rod in to Port Keats to meet me, but I'm not sure if he had expected such an intense relationship to come out of it.

'You're pretty serious about this bloke then?'

I nodded.

'So he's a good lover?'

'Yes, he is,' I replied, 'everything's great. We're planning to get married. I'm really happy with him, Luke.'

'Well, that's good then, lovey. But just remember something. Don't trust anyone too much. It's not fair to them, and it's not fair to you.'

I just nodded, but I wish I had asked him to explain exactly what he meant. It might have made a difference. Then again, it probably wouldn't have.

Before we joined the stock camp, Rod and I had to shift two of our vehicles over to Coolibah Station from Bradshaw, which meant a frightening descent down the same steep track where Rod had tipped over the Blitz on the way in, and Dick had watched old Les Little bounce his grader all the way to the bottom. We pulled up at the top of the jump-up, and I stared at it in horror. It was basically a dry waterfall, with enormous boulders down its length. Rod descended first in the truck, and I followed in the long wheel base. I didn't trust the brakes, so I switched off the engine, and just lurched down using the clutch and the gears to slow my descent. The wheels were forced from right to left by the rocks they bounced over, and I would have broken my thumbs if Rod hadn't warned me about not hooking them through the steering wheel. I reached the bottom full of admiration for old Les in his grader. But I wished that he might have lowered the blade a few times on his way down . . .

We were leaving all our gear at Coolibah for the wet season, while we went south, but in the meantime we were going to have a bit of a 'holiday'. Dick collected us from there in the late afternoon, and we flew into the stock camp, landing on a claypan near a wire yard full of cattle. That night I lay under the stars listening to the quiet sounds of cattle, and the murmur of the night watch riding slowly around them. I realised it was my twenty-third birthday.

There is something soothing and peaceful about cattle at night. Maybe it's the unspoken contrast between how they are now, and how they could be if all hell broke loose. I always thought stockmen sang to the cattle while they walked their horses around on night watch to make them settle and sleep. But they don't – they do it to keep them awake. If all the cattle go to sleep, the slightest noise, like a branch falling, or a horse kicking a stone, can have the whole mob on its feet and rushing in a moment. The yard at Meanyu was just a temporary one, a 'bag yard', made of two strands of barbed wire and star pickets, with hessian bagging draped around to make it appear impenetrable to the cattle in it. It was holding nearly a thousand head that night.

They used an aeroplane to help with mustering at Bradshaw. Dick Gill flew a high-wing Cessna 185, which he flew like he was still in an acrobatic team. He was famous for being able to land that plane almost anywhere. Tourists at the Timber Creek Hotel were sometimes surprised by a plane landing on the highway outside and taxiing up to the pub. Dick would climb out, pick up a few cartons of cold beer, and take off again on the highway. Night time didn't stop him either, let alone the absence of runway lights and control towers. Frequently he would head back to the station just before sunset to pick up supplies, and then find his way back in the dark to the stock camp. The men would light a fire at one end of the strip – usually just a claypan or a clearing in the scrub – and down he would come.

When he was mustering, Dick took the doors off the plane so that he could see out better, and also so that he could fire a shotgun loaded with pellets at recalcitrant cattle hiding under trees or down gullies. The roar of the plane, the noise of the gun and the stinging pellets pretty quickly encouraged the most stubborn beast to move. One day the manager Rowly Walker was flying with him, firing the shotgun from the passenger seat. They had been bull catching earlier that day, and Rowly still had a bull strap belted across his chest. Whenever they came across uncooperative stock, Dick would bank the plane hard on its right side so that Rowly had a clear shot out of the doorway. Rowly would lean against the seatbelt, the shotgun braced across his lap, and drop a load of lead pellets on the beast below. What Rowly didn't notice was that after one shot, the recoil of the shotgun had unclipped his seatbelt. The next time Dick banked the plane, Rowly fell straight out the doorway. He dropped the shotgun, but managed to grab a handhold strap inside the cockpit as he fell, leaning out into space with his feet still inside but nothing else to brace himself against. Dick instinctively reached for him as he went, and grabbed the bull strap. There they were, Dick trying to keep control of a plane already on its side, and being pulled half out of it himself, and Rowly practically dangling by the grace of God and Dick's right hand. Dick couldn't let go of the controls to use both hands to pull Rowly back in, so in a moment of sheer inspiration, he banked the plane sharply to the left, and Rowly became the first person to fall *into* an areoplane.

Bradshaw combined the plane with traditional stock handling methods. A mob of coachers – quiet cattle which were used to teach, or 'coach', the wild cattle that were run in amongst them – would be tailed out on an open plain, one where the bull catchers could manoeuvre easily. Then the plane would muster the surrounding country, driving cattle out of the hills and scrub, and towards the waiting mob, always upwind of them. The men on horses stay on the far side of the mob as the new cattle run in, and the bull catchers circle, waiting for the scrub bulls to bust out, which they inevitably do. I spent a wonderful afternoon perched on a high hill overlooking the cattle and men, recording the action with Dick's old Super 8 movie camera. It looked like absolute chaos. Bull catchers screaming in all directions raising great clouds of dust, stockmen on horses galloping after breakaways, while others rode around the mob holding it together. The vehicles were pushing cattle back into the mob, or rolling breakaway bulls, while the stockmen were throwing their share of bulls from horseback. Most of the cattle stayed in the mob, choosing the safety of the herd instead of the frightening noises around it.

Moving a mob of cattle of any size can be difficult. I had helped move small groups of cattle with Rod during our stay in Queensland, but there was always a fence nearby, and the yards we were heading for no more than a few hundred metres away. Here, it was quite different. There were so many things that had to be considered. The most basic, of course, was simply knowing where you were going. It never ceased to amaze me how someone could be at one spot in the middle of a few million acres of bush, and know exactly which way to go to move 700 grumpy cows to another spot in those millions of acres, 50 miles away, with rough country, hills, creeks, thick bush and broken gullies in between. Not to mention knowing where to find water along the way.

Then there were more specific moments, such as knowing the right way to get those 700 cows across a steep creek. They're not going to wait in line and go over in tidy little pairs. If pushed too fast they will all start galloping up the other side, and keep going when they get to the top. In this case, you have to take the quiet cattle over first, so that the mad fresh cattle will see them and run straight into them when it's their turn to cross the creek.

The wind is important. Fresh cattle won't run into a mob of coachers if they can smell the men and horses. Rain livens them up and makes them stirry, while getting them overheated makes them stubborn and angry. Fresh cattle always run at the head of the mob, then when all the cattle are quietened and wearied, the old coachers get up there and lead the way.

So the man on the horse has to recognise the new bulls from the old very smartly and watch them for signs of trouble. Experienced stockmen can read a herd like a newspaper. They can see where the trouble is, where a little gang of new bulls is getting ready to bust out, or where some cows have been separated from their calves and don't want to leave them behind. It's an art developed over a century and a half of handling wild cattle. It is in the basic nature of cattle to be domesticated, and when wild cattle are put together in a mob, most of them soon learn to respond to a man on a horse, or a bull catcher. It's just the males that cause all the trouble, the independent, testosterone machines that wander over the vast unfenced reaches of outback Australia and call it their own. The scrub bulls, I mean, of course.

The day in a stock camp starts early. Everyone gets up when the cook yells 'Righto!' or 'Daylight!' even if the notion of daylight is somewhat optimistic at 4 am. The cook has been up a good while already, and calls the men when breakfast is about ready.

Cooks in the bush are a breed unto themselves. Very few of them confess to actually liking the job, and even fewer are really good at it. There's a great line in a book by Tom Ronan, where he describes bush cooks as 'Cooks, Cuckoos and Wilful Poisoners'. They were given very basic ingredients to prepare meals with, and unless they had a few skills, the men had good reason to complain about the food. I haven't met many people who really enjoy salt beef. That was just kept for times when the fresh meat and the corned meat had run out, and, there being no refrigeration, we ate salt beef a lot.

The first camp we were with on Bradshaw had a terrible cook. The men were cranky, and the cook whinged and fretted about everything.

When he was challenged about his slackness in only cooking damper and not making bread, he indignantly retorted, 'It's not damper, it's scone loaf!' Damper is a kind of bread made with flour, baking powder, salt and water or milk. Served hot, with melted butter and golden syrup dripping off it, it's great. But hard stale 'scone loaf' was no reward at the end of a difficult day's work. This fellow couldn't cook to save himself, and finally the camp revolted, and he was sacked. We teamed up with the other camp when we met at a watering point, and joined the two mobs together. Best of all, they had a real cook, old Bob Thomas.

Bob was an interesting bloke. He was about forty-five or fifty, I imagine, although from my twenty-three years he looked more like sixty. Like a pleasant old codger who was somebody's grandfather. Bob was a fencer by trade, and had been around stock camps for many years in various roles. He didn't really like cooking, he said, because the bastards always complained no matter what you did. But no one complained in this camp. Bob produced great food. He cooked mainly steak or roast beef, presented in a gravy, with boiled potatoes, peas and whatever other vegetable he could get hold of. Sometimes it was a stew or a curry, but it was always good to eat. Making a stew with salt beef was a challenge, and I'll never forget the taste of it, but Bob could make it more than edible. His bread was heavenly and, most importantly, rarely ran out. He even made the occasional dessert, like tinned fruit and custard, or a jam dumpling.

Breakfast was usually steak, gravy and bread, with plenty of hot sweet tea. At smoko, Bob would drive out to the mob with a 4-gallon billy of black tea, and a box full of hot damper, or fruit buns, or a delicious brownie – a favourite in stock camps, this was a kind of solid cake, usually flavoured with mixed spice, ginger and currants. The men were well fed, and therefore happy. I noticed this, and it became my mantra for the rest of my time out bush. No matter what else was happening, people were always well fed.

When the camp moved, Bob would set his bread dough, put it in a covered box, load up his kitchen gear into his ute, and head off for the next campsite to prepare for the next meal. He would get to catch up on his sleep in the afternoons if all was quiet, but sometimes the cook would be needed to help out at the yards, or even on a night watch if they were short handed. Bob was a man of hidden talents, and later turned to oil painting, when he eventually moved to Katherine.

I loved this life. I had no idea that this kind of stockwork still existed. If it wasn't for the roar of the bull catchers, or the soaring plane overhead, we could have been living a hundred years ago. This was Rod in his element. It was the life he loved best, the values he understood, and the rules he knew how to play by. It was such an authentic way of life. You worked as hard as your body let you. There was some kind of achievement every day, whether it was helping to yard a thousand head of wild cattle, or just managing not to get thrown off your horse that day. Food was enjoyed, simple and filling, but it was just fuel. That tiredness when you fell into your swag at nights, not even caring that you hadn't been able to wash, was the most effective sleeping pill ever made.

Early rains turned the black soil plains into quagmires and not only the bull catchers found it tough going. We spent four hours unbogging Rowly's catcher one afternoon, and turned to find that the horses, which some of the stockmen had tied to trees when they came to help, had sunk to their knees in the mud. That evening we camped in a storm beside Jackaman Creek, and spent the night watching the creek rise from a dry bed that afternoon to a torrent 20 metres wide and 5 metres deep. I remember looking out from under the dripping tarpaulin, wondering which trees we were going to climb once the creek broke its banks, but it managed to stay in its channel, just.

Our week's stint with the Bradshaw camp turned into a month, and we finished at Wombungi, right up on the headwaters of the Fitz-maurice. Here the river was just a creek you could almost leap across. I threw my first mickey bull near Wombungi. We were chasing a very undersized looking beast, and just as I was about to ask why we were bothering with such a runt, Rod said: 'You can throw this one. He's the best size to start on.'

The runt suddenly looked pretty big to me. After a great deal of hesitation I jumped out and grabbed the mickey's tail, wrapping the hairy end twice around my hand as I'd been instructed. Half my brain was saying, you idiot – *what* are you doing?! The other half was just intent on not getting the rest of me anywhere near those spiky looking horns. I managed to pull him down on my third try, and fell over his back legs to hold him down. Somehow I was able to get the strap off my shoulders and wrap it around his back legs while Rod stopped the catcher and grinned his approval. He tossed me the horn saw, and I cut the little bull's horns off. Just then Dick Gill and his mate Graeme Hockey, a Lands Department inspector, drove up, and decided this beast had to be identified for all time, so the poor little mickey bull was earmarked, castrated and dewlapped as well.

'We'll remember this fellow the next time he comes into the yards,' said Dick. I was just sorry I didn't have my camera with me to get the evidence.

It was surprising to realise how exciting it was. The adrenaline was still rushing around in me hours later. I could now understand why Rod and Dick leapt out of the catcher at every opportunity, instead of letting the bull bar do the work. There is something about pitting yourself against the odds. Against nature – against something you have no control over. You put all your faith in yourself, and in all you have learned, and you ask your body to meet the challenge. Rod did this every day, and he was completely addicted to that rush of adrenaline.

# 9

# A Sojourn Down South

Rachel Percy and Richard Oxenburgh needed Rod to come to Sydney to complete some final shots, and to do some voice-over work in the studio. They organised a hire car for us in Darwin, and as promised Dick flew us to town. Early rains had closed the highway between McKinlay and Winton in Queensland, and turned the unsealed sections into black sticky mud. We pulled up in McKinlay to refuel, and the drinkers lined up along the verandah of the pub to watch us leave.

'You won't get out of sight!' they hollered as we took off. I guess they didn't know they were talking to a bull catcher who'd just spent the previous week bogged in the Wombungi. Rod wasn't going to let a mob of beer drinkers tell him what he could or couldn't do. I hung on tight when we left the bitumen. I don't think hire cars are supposed to go places that one did.

'Is this a really dumb idea?' I said to Rod as we fishtailed up the first slope, mud and stones spraying like shrapnel behind us. 'It's not a four-wheel drive, you know . . .'

'Nah – she'll be right! Brand new car, good engine, lightweight. We'll get there. Just hit the windscreen wipers for me, I can't take my hand off the wheel . . .'

It was like that for the next 200 kilometres, apart from one lonely kilometre of bitumen through the hamlet of Kynuna. Rod wrestled the steering wheel while I flicked the wipers off and on, clearing the mud from the glass. We spent more time travelling sideways than straight, and frequently had to head bush to find a way around really bad sections. Road trains were bogged all the way along, some drivers yelling encouragement as we slewed past, others abusing us for being so reckless. We bogged down a few times, but managed to reach Winton by 10 pm that night. As we pulled into the service station, stranded drivers hurried over to us to ask if the road was open at last. They looked at the car, and us, and one bloke said, 'If this is open, I'm going back to Brisbane.'

There wasn't one square inch of the station wagon's bright red paint showing through the mud. We weren't a lot better. When we reached Murgon the next day it took hours to clean the car, and to remove the thick black mud from underneath the chassis. We left Bouncer and Deaf Dog with Rod's parents, but took Little Bull, my dog, with us to Sydney where Rachel and Richard had booked us into a hotel in the middle of Kings Cross.

It was strange seeing Rod in a city. I guess I expected him to be a bit out of his depth the way I was in his territory, and that I would be the one with the local knowledge. However, that wasn't the case at all. Rod may have been scornful of city ways, and things he perceived as soft or self indulgent, but he was no country bumpkin. I was fascinated to see him holding court with sophisticated urban dwellers at parties and during filming beaks, and they were transfixed by what he had to say. Everything he said had an aura of salt of the earth wisdom, and they couldn't get enough of it. He would pick holes in the way they lived, their disconnection with the earth, their disconnection with each other, and they would all nod and agree and lap it all up.

'You cover up the earth with concrete and bitumen, and wall yourselves off from nature with glass and steel, and only allow it in through the television. Even your air is filtered and processed through an airconditioner. There's no responsibility – you can flick a switch to turn on a light, and never have to worry about how the power gets to you. Or how the water gets to your tap. Or the meat you buy – it's all packaged up in sterile little parcels. You haven't had to hunt it, or kill it, or cut it up. The balance is all wrong, and the reason that cities are becoming unliveable is because there's no recognition of nature in them. There's not a proper exchange. It's dishonest.'

Someone made a comment about the violence and the aggression of hunting, that at least animals destined for our tables were well treated.

'Have you ever been to a meatworks?' said Rod. 'Hundreds of cattle being forced up the race into the killing pen? They're terrified! There's fear all around them, and they can smell death. They get into that box and they're just trembling until they're hit with the stun gun. And in the bush, it can be just as bad. If an animal isn't killed by a predator – and that's basically only man in this country – it will die of starvation when its teeth are too worn down to chew, or it might get bogged in mud and die slowly, having its eyes pecked out by crows, and eaten by ants before it's dead. When I shoot a beast, one minute it's eating grass, the next minute it's dead. Tell me which way you think is better . . .'

Rod was such a hit in Sydney because he was so fluent, and so quick. People expected him to be a bashful, awkward country bloke who only knew cattle, kangaroos and Slim Dusty, but he caught them off guard all the time. He was at ease wherever he was, whether it was a dinner in Paddington with a publisher, or a meeting with TV executives in the city. He knew enough science and philosophy to be able to argue with most people about most things. And he appeared to be such a mass of contradictions. He killed animals, and he wrote poetry. He got into deep philosophical discussion, and could have everyone on the floor with a dirty joke. He could behave decorously at upmarket functions, and he told stories about raucous rough gatherings at the bush pubs up north, and then got down on the floor and demonstrated the pub games.

People were intrigued by this country boy who exuded a confident urbanity when he was supposed to be overwhelmed by the bright city lights. He thrived on centre stage, and it showed in his confidence. It helped that he was so handsome, too. Increasingly, *I* felt like the fish out of water. I didn't have much to do, except tag along to meetings and parties. I was somewhat overawed by the busy capable women who worked in the film industry, who all seemed to know exactly who they were, and where they were going. The things I could talk about didn't seem terribly relevant here. It was a hard shiny world, brittle with competition and tension, and I felt like a complete foreigner.

We went out for dinner in Kings Cross one evening, and as we walked into the restaurant, Rod said to me, looking around the room, 'It'll be strange, you know, we won't be able to do this for much longer.'

'What, go out for dinner?' I asked, thinking he meant once we were back in the Northern Territory.

'No, go into restaurants and not be recognised. Once the movie comes out, life's going to be really different, people recognising me and everything.'

I thought he was joking, but looking at his face I could see he was serious. I doubted our lives would change very much at all, apart from some media attention when the film was first released, and I didn't think that one docu-drama was going to make Rod a huge star. It worried me that he might be very disappointed. 'I'm sure you'll manage it just fine. Besides, if you're out bush all the time, the fans won't be able to bother you!' I laughed, but I felt uneasy that he had such high expectations, and thought how bad he would feel if it didn't happen like that.

Rod was happy. The daily interaction with so many different and interesting people – who were all interested in him – compensated for the city environment. To keep himself in condition he joined Ernie McQuillen's gym and revived his love of boxing, sparring with heavy-weight Tony Mundine in one workout which left him with a few marks on sore muscles. The post-production work on the film was going to keep Rod in Sydney for another few weeks, so Little Bull – who had been staying with Roly McManus because his house had room for a dog – and I took the train to Melbourne to visit my family, anticipating a quiet time.

Although we had talked about getting married earlier on, Rod seemed to have grown a bit cold on the idea since then. I wasn't in any hurry to make our relationship legal myself – we were very happy with each other, and I didn't see that a wedding would change anything. So I was quite unprepared when Rod phoned one evening, chatted for a few minutes and then asked to speak to my father.

I heard Dad say: 'Oh! Well, yes, I don't see why not! Good heavens! Very nice of you to ask me!'

Dad came off the phone, looking a bit bemused, and said: 'It's Rod on the phone. He just asked me if he could marry you!'

I took the phone from him. 'Don't I get a say in this?'

'Well, what do you think? Seeing we're down here, and we might not get back for a few years, we should do it now . . .' Rod actually sounded a bit worried.

'Well, it's not the most romantic proposal I could imagine, but I suppose it'll have to do. Is "okay" good enough for you?'

We set a date for 16 December, less than three weeks away. Then I discovered that you can't just 'get married', you have to give one month and one day's notice to the Registrar of Births, Deaths and Marriages. After being told it was an absolutely immoveable law, I made an appointment to see the Registrar in the city. I told him our story, how we didn't know about the rule, how we were unlikely to be in Melbourne near my family again for a long time, and that we were heading back to the wilds of the Territory shortly.

He looked at me for a moment, and then said: 'What plans have you made for the wedding?'

'Well, we've invited the guests, made the cake, and my dress is being made . . .' I muttered, thinking how lame it sounded.

'Oh well, if you've already made the cake . . .' He smiled, and signed the forms.

Rod arrived just two days before the wedding. After handling Sydney so well, he seemed a bit less comfortable when he came to Melbourne. Maybe he was experiencing the traditional male reaction to the thought of getting married, even though it had been his idea. Perhaps after the excitement and the glitz of all the Sydney parties, we appeared a bit suburban and ordinary. It was only a few days, but he seemed cool and patronising towards my family, and easily irritated. He complained about the expense of buying a new shirt and trousers for the wedding, and acquiesced only grudgingly to my mother's insistence that he spend the night before our wedding at a family friend's house.

'Weddings are just a social sham,' he complained as we drove off to see the celebrant and finalise the arrangements. 'Presenting the bride on a plate to the groom – it's all a lot of crap.'

'Are you having second thoughts?'

'No. I want us to be married. I just hate all the carry-on.'

I wanted to agree with Rod about social shams and pointless cere-monies, because he seemed right in one sense. But I also wanted to celebrate our wedding, the public affirmation of our love for each other. I could understand why ceremonies were important, but Rod could always make me doubt what I felt, if it was different from his point of view.

In hindsight I could see he was putting up a barrier between himself and the rest of my family, but at the time I was so much in love, and so happy to be marrying this man, that I didn't look too closely. Even so, I felt an undercurrent of unease all through the days of the wedding preparation, and on the day itself. Something wasn't right. It was as if I couldn't join two important halves together. I loved my family, and I loved Rod. I had made a big effort to be accepted by his family, and I'd immersed myself in his world completely for the past year. I expected that he would make the same effort on my behalf, especially as it was only for a few days, and that he would be more friendly and enthusiastic than he was. In the end I put it down to nerves, and tiredness from the pace of activity in Sydney, but I couldn't shake the feeling that things weren't quite how I thought they should have been when you were marrying the love of your life.

We were married in the back garden of my parents' home, on 16 December 1978, with about forty family and friends present. Rod's parents couldn't make it because of the short notice, but they were pleased and excited about the wedding. My sister Leonie and my brother Peter were our witnesses and my youngest sister, three-year-old Danielle, our flower girl, who sang 'Happy Birthday' as she preceded Dad and me across the lawn to the ceremony. I wrote the words to the ceremony, and in what was to later become an irony, the words stressed the importance of keeping one's individuality within the marriage.

Rod managed to keep up a good front all the way through the service, but I vividly remember being aware of him just 'getting on with it'. He didn't believe in social conventions like marriage, but he did ask me to marry him. I took that to mean that he loved me enough to go through this ordeal for my sake.

It was only 11 pm or so when Rod said he was tired and wanted to go to bed. I was enjoying the party, but thought it wouldn't look too good if the groom went to bed and the bride didn't. At this point Mum realised that we hadn't made any plans for where Rod and I would be sleeping. No arrangements for unmarried couples to sleep together in my mother's house. Until our wedding night, Rod had slept on a spare bed in Peter and Rob's room, and I was back in my old bedroom. Mum packed us off to her and Dad's bedroom, and said they would sleep on the folding couch in the living room. About half an hour later, Dad came barging into the bedroom, sending us diving under the sheets.

'Oh very sorry, very sorry! Forgot you were in here! I just have to find that bottle of Drambuie – I promised the drunks out there that I'd give them one if they'd go home.' He looked around in the wardrobe, but couldn't find the bottle, and went out.

Five minutes later, the door opened and Dad came in again, this time with a couple of mates. Again we dived under the sheets just in time.

'Don't mind me,' he said, waving vaguely at us. 'Carry on, carry on . . . Your mother said it was in the bottom of the wardrobe . . . you couldn't hold this for me, could you?' he said, handing Rod his beer glass. He rummaged around noisily for a few minutes, gave up, and went out again.

'Do you think it's safe now?' asked Rod as we picked up where we'd left off. Just then the door burst open. I shot back under the covers, but Rod refused to budge.

'I *told* you where it was . . .' Mum was saying to Dad as she marched in ahead of him. 'Oh my goodness, he's naked!' she shrieked.

Dad stepped up onto the bed and walked up and down it searching in the top shelves of the wardrobe while Mum hovered at the door, not knowing which way to look.

'Found it!' Dad climbed down from the bed. 'Sure you wouldn't like one?' he asked us, indicating the Drambuie in his hand. I was laughing too much to reply.

'Sure you don't want to invite everyone else in as well?' said Rod with a grin.

'Are you sure?' said Dad, looking pleased. 'I'll just get th—'

Mum grabbed Dad and hauled him out of the bedroom.

We returned to Sydney a day later, and as I said goodbye to my family, Mum, Leonie and I were in tears. This time my departure northwards felt a lot more permanent. I really was leaving home. Rod had bought a truck in Sydney which he planned to take back to the Northern Territory after building a stock crate for it in Murgon. I packed our things into it while Rod did the last of the film work, and a few days later, at 2 am, when the traffic was at its thinnest, we headed out of town.

The truck broke down several times, first of all losing its brakes as we were going over the Blue Mountains. Rod managed to get it down the other side, using the gears to slow down, but more things went wrong with it, so we gave up near Lithgow and put it on the train to Murgon. We couldn't get ourselves on a train at all, or find a hire car, and we couldn't take Little Bull on a bus, so the only other choice was to charter a light plane and fly to Wondai, a little town with an airstrip, next door to Murgon. The plane was stacked with our suitcases, my guitar, wedding presents and spare parts, and of course Little Bull, who sat blissfully on top of the luggage in the back of the plane, and farted all the way to Queensland.

We were welcomed back with open arms by Rod's parents. I was relieved to find I had a friendly mother-in-law after all, and Eve Ansell and I became good friends. Rod and I spent the next month doing up the truck, and finally sold it so that we could get back to the Northern Territory. Although we had been well paid for the film and the catering, there wasn't much money left by the time we had covered the costs of wages and supplies, and repaid our bank loan.

I realised I was pregnant about two months after the wedding. Both of us wanted children, but hadn't talked about exactly when we might start a family, and now the choice was out of our hands. I felt like I was on a roller coaster ride which I had to stay on until the very end, but Rod was really happy. Eve was delighted, and brought me weak black tea and toast in bed every morning.

We bought an old station wagon in Murgon to drive back to the Territory. We had left all our gear at Coolibah when we'd finished with the stock camp, so we headed for Bradshaw Station. Once again we had very little money, and none in sight unless we could secure a contract somewhere. After all the excitement and action of movie making, everything now seemed a bit of an anticlimax. We reached the

Victoria River crossing at the end of March 1979, but our messages had gone astray and no one from Bradshaw was there to meet us. Rod fired a couple of shots in the air hoping to attract someone's attention at the homestead, but no one came. He was never good at waiting. After an hour, he said: 'I'm going to swim across and walk up to the homestead.'

I was horrified. Even the dogs were tied up so they wouldn't be tempted into the water. It was about 300 metres to the other side. 'Wouldn't it be better just to drive into Timber Creek and ring the station from there?' I said, knowing I was wasting my time.

'Nope. Be dark by the time we got back here. There's a couple of big planks of timber over there. I'm going to tie them together and push across quietly. It'll be okay.'

He got the timber ready, and then told me to get the rifle out of the car: 'Just watch me through the scope, and if you see any crocs coming at me, blow them away.'

'You realise you're in more danger of me shooting you than a croc getting you,' I said, only half joking.

'You're a better shot than that. Just keep watching the water around me. I'll be back as soon as I can.'

It took him about fifteen minutes to get across the river, but it felt like hours. I trained the scope on him the whole way across, scanning the surface of the river every few seconds for the legions of salties I was sure would appear. He dragged the planks up on the other side, waved at me, and trotted off up the bank heading for the homestead.

I put the rifle away and sat in the car. Was I a coward, I wondered, because I would rather have taken the safer route of driving back to use the phone, or was I just not prepared to take a risk which would save time and inconvenience? I did think it would be a lot more inconvenient to be grabbed by a crocodile in the middle of the Vic, though.

I was in a strange environment. It wasn't my natural place, and I was dependent on Rod to interpret it for me, because I didn't have a set of guidelines of my own that fitted. The ironic thing is, had I been on my own, I would have managed. But I had my knight in shining armour explaining it all to me, and I think I saw it as an affirmation of his love, that he was so keen to show me his world and for me to love it the way he did. I was convinced that he knew more about everything than anyone else. Rod was a natural teacher, and I was a star-struck student at his feet. So in the end I accepted that what might have been logical in the city wasn't necessarily logical out here, and that apparently desperate measures were just part of the currency in the bush.

Our good friend Gavin Perry came out to Bradshaw to spend a few days with us. Gavin and I had become good mates since Rod introduced us. We had a lot in common, not least of all feeling totally inadequate in the bush around Rod, so I had an ally in my 'embarrassing' city origins when Gavin was around. We had a similar sense of humour, especially a deep appreciation of *Monty Python*.

Gavin had first come to the Kimberley in 1974, and was working on a friend's grapefruit orchard when I met him in 1977. He had lived with Rod at various times, and was the perfect foil – the eccentric out-of-place Englishman to Rod's straight, outback Australian. Where Rod wore moleskins, riding boots and a hat, Gavin was resplendent in a colourful Hawaiian style shirt, shorts or a sarong, sandals and a battered straw hat if he wore one at all. He viewed the people and the culture around him with a sense of delighted astonishment that never seemed to wane, and which reminded me that there was always another way to look at what I was seeing. Admittedly, when it came to Rod, I was not quite so objective.

We shared a love of photography, and he encouraged me to keep recording what I was seeing around me: 'This country is quite bizarre, you know. No one will believe you if you don't take photographs. Look at bull catching! I mean, where else in the world do people *do* this stuff? Risking life and limb hurtling through the bush in these ridiculous jeeps, smashing into trees and rocks, flattening a bloody great bull and jumping out to tie it up with a belt, just to sell it to the meatworks for a couple of dollars . . .'

One day we were helping Dick Gill to take a load of fuel across the Victoria River, and Gavin came along with us. After we had spent a couple of hours wrestling 44-gallon drums of Avgas and petrol off the truck and down the river bank and through the mud, we watched as the first load was towed across the river by a little dinghy piloted by Frank Clarke, the grader driver on the station. The drums were roped together in pairs, their tops just clear of the water as they bobbed along behind the boat, which was barely making headway against the current. Sometimes the tide would turn sooner than expected, and the dinghy, fuel drums and the hapless ferryman would be washed downstream, fetching up against a little island until the tide turned again.

Gavin turned to me, shaking his head, and said: 'Where is your camera? *Why* aren't you taking photos of this? This is lunacy!'

I stared at him, not sure what he was talking about.

'You're getting too used to all this. This is not normal. This is insane! Take photos of it!'

He was right. I was trying so hard to fit in and be a 'bushie' that I wasn't seeing things objectively anymore. If the job required a total disregard for personal safety, and extreme physical discomfort, then that was how it was supposed to be, it seemed. Mind you, there usually wasn't another way to do it anyway.

Rowly Walker asked us to take one of their vehicles around the long way through Coolibah Station, as their barge wasn't operating. The vehicle in question had been left on the south side of the river, but was needed for the mustering season which was about to start. Bradshaw and Coolibah were both owned by an Israeli company, Unibeef, at that time, and the two leases were run as one property. No one had lived at Coolibah homestead since about 1970, when the station headquarters had moved to Bradshaw, which was in a better, more central location for cattle management. Occasionally the stock camp might stay in the old stone homestead when they worked in the Coolibah area, but most of the time it was empty.

We set off in the Toyota, and stopped in at Coolibah homestead to check on our Blitz truck which had been left there since the previous November. It had two flat tyres, so Rod decided to change them before we headed off to Bradshaw. He was sitting on the ground doing up the wheel nuts after putting on a new wheel, when the jack collapsed, dropping nine tons of truck on top of his foot. The truck had a terrifying lean on it, right over him, and Rod was jammed fast. He shouted out instructions, and I tried a couple of ways to get him out, none of which worked. Finally I put the truck's gears into neutral, leapt into the Toyota and drove it around to the front of the truck, and pushed it backwards off Rod's foot. He hopped around cursing and swearing for a minute, and shouted at me to bring him the shovel. For a terrible moment I thought he meant to chop off his foot with it.

'What for?' I asked, visions of him amputating his foot and tying up the stump with an old corn bag flashing in front of me. He had told me enough stories of rough bush surgery that it didn't seem too ridiculous.

'So I can use it for a crutch! Hurry up!' He was angry, probably at himself, but I was conveniently there to take the brunt. I hurried it over to him, feeling as if I were somehow to blame for the incident. I wish I'd dealt with that feeling there and then, because it was to become a pattern in our relationship, me feeling guilty about everything that went wrong, whether it had anything to do with me or not. But I wasn't to know that then.

His foot didn't seem too badly damaged. He had dug a hole under the wheel so that he didn't have to raise the jack so high, and this had protected his foot from being completely crushed, but it was definitely broken. However, Rod insisted we still had to take the Toyota through to Bradshaw. He wouldn't let me drive, because the track was overgrown and the vehicle had very bad steering, and practically no brakes. It was going to be a drive of just a couple of hours, so we weren't planning to take much stuff with us, let alone any food.

For someone who had been marooned without food, and who nearly died of thirst once before, Rod had an amazingly casual approach to what I considered vital supplies. I had a city person's respect for being stuck somewhere without food or water. Rod rarely took any with him, wherever he went. He said not to bother with any stuff because we'd be in Bradshaw that afternoon, but I tossed in a sack containing some pannikins, powdered milk and a tin of Milo. I also filled an empty 20-litre petrol drum with water in case the radiator needed it. I had been stuck with Rod on a waterless creek with an over-heated truck once before, and I wasn't about to repeat the experience. I threw in a small flask of water too, but it wasn't much.

About an hour down the 'track' we hit a big washaway in the road, obscured by long grass. We bounced across it completely out of control, and smashed into a tree. Both of us were dazed – my head had left a big crack in the windscreen, and the sights of the rifle, wedged between the front seats, had gouged a hole in my leg. Rod was badly shaken, and had banged his broken foot around. The Toyota was much worse. All the suspension bolts had snapped off, the steering was completely broken, and there was a big hole in the sump. We were seriously stuck.

I unrolled the swag, which we'd brought with us, under the shade of a tree and we sat down to wait for the people at the station to miss us. We had no food, of course, but we had water, and the powdered milk and Milo covered up the taste of petrol a little. The next morning we heard the drone of a plane, and I waved a shirt at it. Dick couldn't find anywhere close by to land, so circled a couple of times and dropped a note saying he would get the police at Timber Creek to come and pick us up. A few hours later the police arrived to rescue us, much to Rod's chagrin. But he didn't say too much about it. Neither did the police officers, thankfully.

We moved into the old stone homestead at Coolibah and started repairing the vehicles, in the hope of some work soon. There didn't seem to be anything that Rod couldn't do. If he had a welder, a set of oxy-acetylene gear and some basic tools, he could make or fix anything. Cut a stock crate in half, build a new one, straighten a chassis, customise the wrong part to become a suitable one – it didn't matter. It just needed to be done, and it generally was. As I was to learn, this was hardly an uncommon skill on cattle stations. The remote workshops and vast distances to town made it impossible for someone to nip down the street and pick up a spare part, or the right sized left-handed screwdriver. If it wasn't available at the station workshop, then you made do.

Rod was very good at making do. He once was stuck a long way from home when a water hose burst on the engine of his vehicle. No spare hoses. He had a rifle in the cab, as most station vehicles do, so he shot a wallaby, skinned the tail in one piece, and 'cobb 'n' coed' it to the engine in place of the burst hose. I learnt how to do a 'cobb 'n' co' very early on. It's a particular wire twitch, made with a doubled piece of plain fencing wire, and gets its name from the story that the Cobb and Co coaches were held together with such twitches. I don't know if the story's true, but the Territory is certainly held together in places with cobb 'n' co twitches.

Mrs Olive Quilty had built Coolibah homestead in 1943, organising her husband Tom and the Aboriginal workers. Flat, square stone from the Victoria River formed its walls, and wide verandahs all round kept the sun off them, and made the house a good 10 degrees cooler than the outside. When I was at the homestead by myself, I'd roam the verandahs looking out at the escarpment and the hazy distant horizon, and wonder what it must have been like for a woman to be here forty years before, when a trip into Katherine probably took two days instead of two hours. I wondered if I would have felt so comfortable being pregnant then. We had no electricity or running water, but by comparison I felt positively suburban.

The country around Coolibah was spectacular. Westwards from the Victoria River Crossing, the Victoria Highway passes through some of the most beautiful landscape in the Top End on its way to Kununurra. The river meanders through an ancient worn valley, crowned with crumbling breakaway ranges and flat-topped hills. In places the hills are very close to the highway, and the wet season waterfalls cascade down their sides, creating little pockets of lush growth contrasting with the dry open country in between. The further west you go, bottle trees are common, and the country becomes drier and the vegetation sparser. There is such a sense of space here.

There were plenty of scrub bulls around. I spent many nights there by myself when Rod was away seeing station managers about contracts. Night noises were plentiful, and the most common was the bellowing of the scrub bulls as they went mumbling and grumbling along on their way down to the river, like cranky old men. In the deep of night they sounded like hunting lions. Then, just when I'd relaxed, and convinced myself the noise was only an old scrub bull, one would roar out loud, like a rogue elephant about to tear down the house. They make a peculiar scream which doesn't sound anything like 'moo'.

Then there were the dingoes. They were around most nights, so we had to keep our dogs tied up and close to the house. One night I was awakened by the most amazing chorus, only a few dozen metres away. I could see at least fifteen dogs in the moonlight, sitting together and singing like a choir in a cathedral, howling their haunting, eerie music. It was the most beautiful thing. Even our dogs kept quiet.

Tourists used to call in to Coolibah on the odd occasion. The homestead had featured in the Charles Chauvel movie *Jedda*, and was known as an unofficial historic site. Occasionally travellers came by wanting to see it for themselves. One day three cars pulled up while Rod and I were there.

'Hello! Mind if we have a look at the house?'

Just as I was showing the visitors the rooms, a big king brown snake slithered out of one of the doorways. I called to Rod who was working nearby.

The tourists and I followed him gingerly down the verandah as he sprinted silently after the snake, and picked it up by the tail. Ducking out through the open door, he flicked the snake around and then brought it down like a stock whip, killing it instantly by cracking off its head. The tourists paled, and scuttled back to their cars, saying they'd seen enough of the house, thanks . . .

I could never understand how Rod could kill things like that, while professing to be such a part of the bush. I didn't like snakes, but I felt they still had their rights to survival, unless they were actually attacking me. I would brake to avoid them out on the highway. Rod would run them over as if he was performing a public duty.

Rod managed to get some work mustering at Fitzroy Station next door. The station had recently appointed a caretaker, and had no working stock camp. The owner wanted to keep operating and employed Rod to work as a contract musterer. The change in him was immediate, and he was back to the Rod I knew, energised and cheerful, and very focused. He found a couple of backpackers on a trip to Katherine, and brought them out to help, promising them food and board, and some money if we made any. We would continue to live at Coolibah, and drive across to Fitzroy each morning to work.

It was about a 15-kilometre drive from Coolibah to Fitzroy, although only about five as the crow flies. The first muster had us excited and eager to start. We didn't have a clock or a watch between all of us, so when Rod woke up during the night, he had a look outside and decided we may as well get started, in order to be over there and ready to go by sunrise. We had a quick breakfast by candlelight, and took off. The homestead was dark when we arrived, but we thought it wouldn't be long till dawn so we sat down and waited at the yards. And waited. And waited. And waited. We must have waited for four hours before it began to get light. Rod might have been able to tell the time by the sun, but he wasn't too good at it at night.

Richard Oxenburgh and Rachel Percy, the film's producers and directors, came up from Perth to visit, and brought news of the film's progress. It now had a name, and was to be called *To Fight the Wild* after the title of one of Rod's poems, which had also been set to music. In the months since we had returned to the Northern Territory, I hadn't thought about the film much at all. Even the time we'd spent in Sydney seemed a very long time ago. Rachel had been busy writing a book, also called *To Fight the Wild*, from tapes she had made interviewing Rod, and was hoping to have the book published to coincide with the film's release. They warned us that there would be a lot of publicity.

# 10

# Fitzroy Station

By the middle of 1979 we were living at Fitzroy Station. The caretaker had left, and Rod had been offered the job of manager by the station's Darwin bookkeepers. The property was foreign owned, and was in a very rundown condition. The fences and yards were barely standing, and the house wasn't a lot better. The flywired verandahs were in tatters, and half fallen down on one side. It had a bathroom, but there was only a dribble of water from the shower, although the bath and handbasin worked. However it did have some furniture and a working gas stove. A noisy diesel generator only metres from the house provided electricity, so for the first time in eighteen months we were able to have electric lights and fans for a few hours at night. To save fuel we turned the generator off at night, and didn't restart it until midday.

The station also had a radio telephone, an improvement of sorts on VJY, the outpost radio network I had used at Port Keats and the Fitzmaurice. In place of a two-way radio with a hand-piece, there was a normal-looking telephone with a transmit button on the receiver, and a red light instead of a dial or a number pad on the phone itself. And instead of waiting for your scheduled radio time to send your telegram, you could be connected to a telephone anywhere in the world by the operator, and no one else could overhear your conversation. The drawback was that there were eighteen other customers on our channel, all sharing the one line. I was to spend many hours in the office waiting for the damn red light to go out so that I could call the operator and book my calls.

We installed our fridge and freezer from the film camp, and I felt like I had a kitchen to compete with the best. We could have butter, and fresh vegetables, and cold water! There was even a hot water system, provided you chopped enough firewood to keep the fire going. We were to operate on an unusual basis, in which Rod was the manager but would muster the cattle on contract, getting our share of the meatworks value of the stock we sent away. We were to be paid wages during the wet season, when the mustering was finished. We had a place to live, and were going to be paid as well. Life was looking pretty good.

The view from the homestead was spectacular. Wandoan Hill, a great flat-topped peak, towered across the river on the Bradshaw side, and the Victoria River had carved out a deep channel for itself a few hundred metres from the house at Wandoan's base. The river banks were steep here, and the water looked deep and dark. Immense breakaway ranges and mesas lined its course, and the country became drier and even more dramatic as the river snaked its way with gigantic lazy loops for a hundred miles to the west. The country around the homestead itself was open and timbered with coolibah trees. It was a lovely place.

Fitzroy, like many cattle stations in the Northern Territory, had a camp where the Aboriginal stockmen lived with their families. An old couple, Nida and her husband Old Mick, lived down there with their little daughter, a heap of dogs and one cat. They used to work in the vegetable garden, but once Rod started mustering in earnest, Old Mick swapped his hose for a horse, and looked a lot happier. After a few weeks, he was joined by a couple of young Aboriginal boys, and the following year three more men arrived at Fitzroy with their families to work. Traditionally the stockmen were paid wages for their work, and the station supplied food staples to the camp. We could keep them supplied with food, and the stockmen with riding boots and hats, but we didn't have any money to pay wages at first. Old Mick was happy just to be able to stay at Fitzroy. At the end of that first year, we gave him our old Ford Falcon sedan as payment, and he was delighted.

Rod was finally happy again. We had a comfortable place to live, a good contract, and he could be his own boss. I think he was happy because he felt he was providing his family with a proper home. He had worried much more about how we would live once a baby came along than I did. I didn't have a pressing need to live in a 'proper' house just because we had a baby. I think I had such faith in Rod's ability and affinity with the country we were in that I was completely relaxed about however and wherever we found ourselves. As it was, I had an easy, uneventful pregnancy. I saw a doctor only about three times during the whole nine months, but occasionally the sisters from the health clinic at Timber Creek called by to see how I was going.

Rachel Percy and Richard Oxenburgh had been busy. Rachel had finished her book, and work on the movie was just about done. Our six weeks on the Fitzmaurice River with the film crew in 1978 seemed a very long time ago. In August 1979 Rod had to go down to Perth for a couple of weeks to do some publicity work, which involved television appearances, and radio and newspaper interviews. I stayed behind at Fitzroy. With only about five weeks till my baby was due, I wasn't going anywhere.

Callum Peter Ansell was born on 4 October 1979, in Katherine Hospital, the first grandchild in both the van Os and the Ansell families. A few weeks before, Dick Gill had phoned to see when I was planning to go in to have the baby. He flew over a week later, buzzed the house, and dropped a balled-up note which said: 'I'm going to town in two days' time. If you want a lift in, wave. If not, do a handspring over the fence.'

The hospital liked women from the bush to come in early to have their babies, and seeing this was my first, they wanted me in at least a week before it was due. I didn't want to spend a week on my own in Katherine, but Rod was flat out mustering and wouldn't be able to drive me the two and a half hours into town any closer to my due date. I waved at the plane.

Rod made it in to Katherine just in time for the birth. He stayed with me throughout the labour, and held his son moments after he was born, clearly delighted and overwhelmed at the arrival of this little person he'd helped create. Rod's parents arrived at Fitzroy the day we brought Callum home, so I had an easy transition into motherhood with my mother-in-law there to keep everyone fed and the house clean while I got used to my new role. Not that it was too exacting. Callum was a dream first baby and slept through the night from the start.

At the tender age of three weeks he spent his first night in the swag under a mosquito net. Rod was mustering away from the homestead, and had cattle in a bush yard which needed to be watched during the night, so we packed up some supplies and the swags, and took Callum out with us. All the bravado I had felt before he was born – about not needing to live in a house when I had a baby – had evaporated. I watched him anxiously all afternoon in case a mosquito or an ant found its way through the netting, and that night hardly slept for fear that something might happen to him, out here in this suddenly dangerous, unpredictable, menacing wilderness. I began to understand Rod's unhappiness with our comparative homelessness a few months earlier, and I was glad he had pushed to find us a decent place in which to live. Happily, though, this state of nervousness didn't last.

We were beginning to meet people in the area, and became very good friends with the local stock inspector, Bluey Lewis. Bluey was a great bloke. A big, red-haired, red-bearded man with a taste for loud music and fast driving, Bluey's arrival would be announced by a spray of gravel and 'The Ozark Mountain Daredevils' blaring out the window of his Toyota ute. He travelled constantly, looking after the stations between Katherine and the West Australian border. He called in often, staying for a meal or a night's sleep before heading off to the next station, and the next day's work.

One night we were down at the Victoria River Wayside Inn, and another local, Johnno, was having a few beers. It was the first time our neighbours had seen Callum, so he was being made a fuss of, and at one point Johnno, to whom I'd only been introduced a little while before, came over to me, weaving unsteadily on his feet. He was almost in tears – when Johnno got drunk, he got emotional – and gave me $10 and said, 'Here, Missus, take this for the baby and buy him some lollies.' Callum was two weeks old at the time. I took the note, and thanked Johnno gravely.

A few weeks later, Rod came back from Timber Creek with a new worker in tow: Johnno. He looked the classic Queensland ringer, from his Akubra-clad head to his cuban heeled boots, and RM Williams everywhere else. He moved into the house and became one of the family. He worked as Rod's offsider, could cook a little, and loved Callum to bits. He was a hard worker. Not the sharpest tool in the shed, but his heart was in the right place.

Every once in a while Johnno had to let loose. He would head off to the pub at Timber Creek, get rotten for a few days, and then phone to be picked up, having spent all his money on a supersized hangover. He could do really stupid things when he was drunk. Like the time he went off to the Victoria River pub with Bluey Lewis. Now Johnno was interested in the current girl behind the bar who, of course, was totally uninterested in Johnno. This salient fact totally passed Johnno by. He was busy making wedding plans as he emptied stubby after stubby at the bar with Bluey.

A road train driver was having a lot more success with her, and eventually took umbrage at Johnno's demands to 'leave my woman alone', and invited him to step outside where he decked him. They both went back inside, and Bluey sat Johnno down at the bar and told him to stop being an idiot, or words to that effect. Johnno excused himself and went outside. After a time he came back in, whispered to Blue that they had to go, right now. Once outside Blue said, 'What's the rush?'

Johnno replied, 'I fixed that bastard. I let the tyres down on his truck. That'll show him to mess with me.'

Blue looked aghast at the road train. Sure enough, all ten tyres on the prime mover were flat. He dragged Johnno over to the Toyota and threw him in, spinning the wheels in his haste to quit the scene. He may have been shocked by Johnno's actions but he had no wish to see his mate bludgeoned with a tyre lever when the truckie came out of the pub. They roared away down the road.

It was too much for Blue. 'Johnno, you're fucked in the head.'

'Hard words, Blue, hard words.'

So Bluey pulled up the Toyota, went round to the passenger side, pulled Johnno out onto the road and flogged him. Threw him back in the car and took off. A few more miles down the road, same thing. 'Hard words, Blue, hard words.' It took them about two hours to drive the 24 kilometres back to the station, and about a week for Johnno's black eyes to subside.

One day Rod and Johnno were out catching on the south side of the highway. Johnno hadn't done a great deal of catching, but he was a trier. This day they were onto a pair of scrub bulls on a good open plain, and separated to catch them. Rod ran his down, tired it out, threw the catcher into neutral, jumped out and grabbed the bull by the tail. By the time he looked up from strapping its legs, he could see that Johnno was onto his bull, near a big thicket of some prickly bush. As he jumped out to grab the bull's tail, he missed his step and the catcher ran over his foot. Yelping with pain, Johnno hopped around for a second or two while the Toyota, which he'd left in first gear instead of neutral, made a big slow circuit and disappeared behind the prickle bush.

Johnno made a dash for the prickle bush himself. The bull stopped running and, looking around the open plain, decided the best place to hide was the prickle bush. As Rod watched from a distance, unable to let go of his bull, he saw Johnno disappear into one side of the thicket, while the bull trotted into the other side. There was a lot of crashing around, and then the bull reappeared, followed closely by Johnno, who had managed to grab the bull's tail. He hopped madly behind it, barely managing to stay upright. Just as Rod was wondering how long Johnno would be able to keep hopping, the Toyota appeared around the side of the thicket, heading straight for Johnno and the bull. The bull charged the Toyota, and the three met in the middle of the plain with a crash. While the bull was busy hooking into the front of the stalled Toyota, Johnno scrambled into it.

Callum and I flew down to Melbourne in December 1979 for my parents' 25th wedding anniversary, and to attend my brother Robert's wedding. Callum was ten weeks old, and the first grandchild, so we were met at the airport by practically the whole family. When we returned, Leonie came back with us to Fitzroy and her then boyfriend – and later husband – Craig Hemsworth followed a fortnight later. It was a lovely relaxed time. Rod got along famously with both of them, and they enjoyed the station life and the work. It was a taste of the Territory that they wouldn't forget, and the first of several sojourns they made over the years that followed.

It was a big wet season that year. The grass grew thick and lush which augured well for the coming dry season's feed in the paddocks. It also gave me a green lawn around the homestead, something I'd been trying to encourage for months without any success. By February the grass inside the houseyard was so long, and becoming such a good hiding place for snakes, that Rod decided to pick up a lawnmower in Katherine. We had noticed a few big grasshoppers the day before, but nothing prepared Leonie and me for the plague of locusts that descended on us not long after Rod and Craig had left for town. I had never seen anything like it. Giant grasshoppers, up to six inches long, covered the ground and rose in noisy rattling clouds wherever we walked. The sound of them around the house all day almost drowned out the racket from the generator. By the time Rod and Craig returned that evening with the lawnmower, there wasn't a single blade of grass remaining around the house.

The university year was starting again, and Leonie and Craig had to return to Melbourne so we drove them into town the following week to catch their plane. The Victoria River was up a bit, but we managed to drive across with about two feet of water flowing over the bridge, hoping it might drop again before we came back. Heading for home two days later, we pulled up on the east side of a raging torrent, the bridge now many feet below the surface of the river. It was late in the day, so we decided to camp the night and see what it looked like in the morning. Some other people were camped a few hundred metres back from the river, high up on a ridge overlooking the river, and we joined them. We had our swags with us as usual, but apart from some pannikins, tea, sugar and a billycan, not much else. Rod had his knives and rifle inside his swag in the car. A couple of the people had been there since the night before and were short of food, so the next day Rod went out and shot a young mickey, which he butchered and shared around to the dozen or so strandees. Some of them looked askance at the bloody mound of meat on a bed of green leaves and muttered a definite no thanks, but most people happily barbequed their share on the coals with us. I had to hide a grin when I heard one person say to another, 'Hey, we're just like that fellow who got rescued from the river the other year!'

We waited by the river for another night, but the water was still raging so we drove back to Katherine and flew out to Timber Creek, where we managed to get a lift out to the station. It was another week before the flooding subsided and the bridge was passable again.

In spite of the big wet, the mustering season was well underway by the beginning of March, with meatworks prices opening at around sixty-six cents a pound for cows, which was considered good money. However it wasn't to last. Prices were dropping by April, and our overdraft was blowing out. As well as the usual bills which had to be paid long before any money came in, we had a lot of medical expenses. For at least a month Rod's health had not been good. His neck and back hurt, he had lots of headaches, and then developed nausea, stomach pain and aching joints. Several visits to doctors in Katherine failed to find anything wrong. Then one day in early April he blacked out during a helicopter muster, so I drove him into town and put him on a plane home. After five weeks of visits to specialists in Brisbane it turned out that he'd had hepatitis, but was nearly recovered, and that his spine was out of alignment, possibly due to the collarbone which had healed badly after the accident in Kununurra in 1978. It was the longest time we'd been apart, and I missed him very much. Old Mick, Nida and Johnno were still at Fitzroy, so Callum and I weren't alone, and Bluey Lewis called in regularly to see how we were going. There was plenty for Johnno and Old Mick to do checking and repairing fences, and Nida and I worked in the vegetable garden when I wasn't busy with Callum. I was also painting the house. I'd decided that the superficial improvement to our surroundings was worth the cost of a few tins of paint, even if the house was falling down in places.

The film *To Fight the Wild* was finally ready to go to air. Because it was a West Australian project, having been created by Richard Oxenburgh Productions with funding from TVW Enterprises in Perth, the Australian Film Commission and some private investors, it premiered on Perth television on 10 May 1980, screening around the rest of the country a few months later. Rod had only been home from Brisbane for about a week when he was due to leave again. TVW had provided two tickets to Perth, but Rod wanted me to stay and keep an eye on things at the station. I must have looked as miserable as I felt at the prospect of another separation, because as he was about to leave for the airport, he said, 'Quick – pack a bag and come with me. Johnno can look after things here for a few days.'

Rod, Callum and I stayed with Richard and Rachel, and I finally saw the film at a screening in the TV studios a week before its public debut. It was an odd experience, watching ninety minutes of my husband on a large screen with him sitting beside me fidgeting from time to time. I thought it was very good. It certainly captured the remoteness of the Fitzmaurice and the loneliness of his time there, and Rod's performance was first-rate. It was a media screening, so there was a flurry of questions from reporters afterwards, and later some excellent reviews.

Rod had to do several TV appearances, none of which he would let me watch being taped – he was far too embarrassed. His only consolation was that no one he knew, apart from Richard and Rachel, would see the programs. Sadly the opportunity to spend the whole two weeks in Perth with Rod was cut short when word came through from Fitzroy that Johnno had gone on a bender, so Callum and I had to return to the station after only four days. Bluey Lewis collected us from the airport and drove us back to Fitzroy, where things were a bit chaotic. Johnno had hit the bottle the day after we'd left, every vehicle had broken down, and no fencing had been done. However the situation wasn't too desperate. On the second day of Johnno's bender, a travelling mechanic turned up, a taciturn German who had worked for us the previous year. He immediately assessed the situation, moved back into his old quarters, and set to work. By the time I arrived home, he had at least one vehicle operating, so I was able to send Old Mick and a couple of young offsiders out to continue the fencing work. Johnno sobered up a day or two later, swearing off alcohol forever, or at least till the next time.

Rod stayed on in Perth for a couple of weeks. Rachel Percy's book was launched, so there were more rounds of interviews and appearances. The book, also called *To Fight the Wild*, was extremely well received and sold strongly from day one. In spite of his reluctance, Rod was a natural at publicity, just like he was with acting. I was fascinated how one minute he could be out in a stock camp, wrestling with broken machinery and recalcitrant scrub bulls, and the next minute standing in front of a camera – or several – answering questions and looking for all the world like he did it every day. He was supposed to be inarticulate, awkward and perhaps even ockerish, but he was none of these things, and the media loved him.

However, he wasn't expected to be so polished and urbane by his

My parents, Martin and Therese van Os, with me at Burwood, NSW, in 1956.

My first day at school, June 1960. Mum was expecting my sister Leonie, and the nuns took pity on her and let me start school at four and a half.

Rod at home in Murgon, Queensland, aged about eighteen.

Me, Julie Carr and Christine Steer, Port Keats, Northern Territory, 1977. We shared a house together for two years.

Me with my adopted parents, Mary and Joseph Tchembing, at Port Keats. When I went to Europe in 1977, Mary told me I was not allowed to cut my hair.

The Palumpa Station stock camp, 1976. Luke McCall is third from the right, Rupert Wodidj on his right.

Rod and me at the Fitzmaurice River in 1978 during the filming of *To Fight the Wild*. Rod jumped out of the helicopter to catch this little pig – I think it ended up in the Bradshaw pig-pen waiting for Christmas.

PHOTO: J VAN OS COLLECTION

Rachel Percy and Richard Oxenburgh discussing the script at the Fitzmaurice River, 1978. Rod built some bush tables out of tree trunks and corrugated iron, with flour drums for seats. We'd forgotten to bring chairs – we must have forgotten the tables, too . . .

PHOTO: J VAN OS COLLECTION

The camp cook at the Fitzmaurice, 1978, with bread hot from the 'dourie oven. Rod's bull catcher is in the background.

Rod about to take off after a bull, Bradshaw Station, 1978. The leather belt across his chest is for strapping the bull's legs together.

Bogged at Wombungi, Bradshaw Station, 1978. Even the horses sank into the mud and had to be helped out.

Rod and I were married in my parents' back garden at Ringwood, Victoria, in December 1978.

Rod, Callum and me in the yards at Fitzroy Station, 1980, getting ready for a day's branding. Rod was sharpening a knife to castrate the bull calves.

Rod pulling down a bull, Fitzroy Station, 1980.

Geoffrey Reemeijer keeping a bull on the slide as it is loaded into the old red International. Rod is visible on the right hand side, pulling it up with the bull catcher. Willeroo, 1981.

Callum, early in the morning, beside the stock truck, Willeroo Station, 1981.

School lessons were a little ad hoc until we set the school room up properly. Here, Callum is answering a question on the School of the Air radio while I supervise. Melaleuca Station, 1986.

peers at home. The film didn't screen in the rest of the country until the following year, so he managed to keep a low profile in the Territory for a bit longer. He was offhand and dismissive if anyone brought the subject up, but alone with me, he was excited and hopeful about the outcome: 'This movie could really make us some money – there's a lot of talk about other projects, talk shows and that kind of thing. They probably pay pretty well, I reckon. It'll all pick up speed when the film's released in the rest of the country. This could get pretty big, Jo!'

Rachel Percy had been working on a movie script, and had Rod and Mark Lee (who had played Archie in the movie *Gallipoli*) in mind to play brothers in it. Rod started to fantasise a little about a future in acting: 'It's got to be a lot less work for a lot more money, compared to bull catching,' he'd say, when I was massaging his sore muscles at night. He often suffered from neck and back pain but rarely let it stop him. I was in favour of anything that took less of a toll on his health, but privately I was a little nervous about finding ourselves living in the world of making movies full-time. However Rachel contracted Ross River fever and couldn't finish the project, and by the time she was well enough again, the opportunity was gone.

Our lifestyle might have been hard sometimes, and not the most comfortable, but I loved it. I enjoyed the closeness with the land, working with cattle and horses, and being so far from town, immersed in the bush. I liked the people that we worked with, and the interesting characters we met. Rod felt the same way, and if he was going to change his lifestyle to become a full-time actor, it would only happen if there was a big financial benefit.

I had good reason for not being too eager to see Rod get involved in the movie industry full-time. When we first started living together, Rod had been adamant that he wasn't going to be faithful to anyone. He spoke long and convincingly about how people didn't own each other, and that sex outside of a relationship didn't do it any harm, how conventional marriages forced people into monogamy and made them stale. He loved me, he said, I was the person he chose to be with, but sex was an adventure he couldn't give up. Besides, he added, it was hardly going to happen very often, given that we were mostly together and out bush. He would never do anything to embarrass me, and would never sleep with anyone in the same town or with anyone we knew. I was too young and inexperienced and, making the common mistake women make about men, thought: 'Ah, but I can change you – I'll make sure you never want anyone else but me . . .'

It's embarrassing to recall that conversation now, and to admit that I could go into a relationship accepting such terms. I can only say that I do remember thinking that he didn't really mean it, that it was just an option he needed to know he had, but one he would not exercise. I was awfully naive.

My naivety carried me through for a while. It wasn't until I was expecting Callum that I had to face the reality of the terms I'd accepted. A letter arrived not long after Rod had spent a few days up in Darwin. He had left it lying on the table after he'd read it and gone to bed. I'd noticed it as I was clearing up, and looked at it to see if it was anything I needed to keep for our accounts.

*Dear Rod,*

*It was great meeting you yesterday. I enjoyed our talks. I just wanted to say that the reason I refused to come back to your room, was because I don't do that kind of thing. And I am not a tease. I just liked talking to you.*

*Hope the film goes well, and good luck catching those wild bulls.*

It was signed with a woman's name. I sat down, feeling the bottom of my stomach dropping away at 100 miles an hour. I reread it, thinking I must be wrong, that it probably didn't mean what it seemed to. I went into the bedroom and confronted Rod with it. He denied it meant that he'd asked the girl to sleep with him, insisting that he had just wanted to continue the conversation after the bar had closed, and that she had simply misunderstood him. 'That's what you get for reading other people's mail,' he said, not looking at me, and rolled over to go to sleep.

I went back out into the living room and sat there for a while. Was marriage supposed to be this difficult? I knew it was about making sacrifices, but it seemed as if I was the one making most of them. I decided it was still early days, and things would get better as Rod let go of his need to feel like a free agent, and admitted to himself that he actually preferred being with me. Anyway, according to that letter nothing had happened. I told myself I was probably just over-reacting.

Our remoteness meant there wasn't a lot of opportunity for Rod to have 'adventures', but the number of occasions he was away, and the length of those separations, meant I began to live in a shadow of uncertainty. Later I knew that he had had some brief affairs on some of these trips away, because he told me about them. Somehow he managed to make it seem like something that happened in another universe, not something that had anything to do with 'us', and I guess I allowed myself to be convinced by him. But it was a belief that didn't hold up when he wasn't standing in front of me, reassuring me. Once he was gone, all my doubts and fears would coming rushing back in.

As well, Rod was an awful flirt. He couldn't resist making a bee-line for the most attractive woman at a party or a dinner. That familiar laser-like gaze would be focused on someone else for so long, and the suggestive banter so excluding, that I'd feel like tapping him on the shoulder and saying, *hey, remember me?* Then afterwards he would joke about how the woman opposite at dinner was running her toes up and down his leg, or how when I was out of the room, another had tried to line him up for a rendezvous. What made me feel nervous was not that these things happened, but that Rod thought they were quite accept-able. He didn't think these approaches from women were laughable, he thought they were exciting and spirited. It left me feeling like a little brown mouse in comparison. I mostly listened without making much comment. I believed that I'd negated any right to complain because I'd agreed to the terms he had laid down at the outset, so the last thing I wanted to do was behave like the jealous wife. I instinctively knew that if I tried to bind him to me too tightly, I would lose him for certain. So I held my tongue, and tried to pretend that it didn't bother me at all.

Rod certainly didn't make me think he didn't want me. At times he could be as loving and affectionate as I could wish, but the work load we were under was so heavy that it tended to take precedence over everything else. It's easy to shove personal doubts to the back of your mind when you're flat out.

Rod went to Perth for the film's pre-release publicity sometime after the letter incident, and when he came back, he surprised me with a beautiful ring. When we married, we had used the ring I'd worn in Kununurra, which was just a simple friendship ring. Now Rod presented me with an 18 ct gold ring with three small diamonds set into the heavy band.

'I couldn't afford anything when we got married, but I wanted you to have something special,' he said, putting it onto my finger, and kissing me. I was overwhelmed that he had even thought of it, and convinced all over again that he loved me, and that I was doing the right thing.

Fitzroy's owner was coming out to Australia for a visit, so the Darwin bookkeepers sent down a carpenter, plumber and electrician to make the house safely habitable – as opposed to barely habitable, which was okay for Australian workers apparently – and then I painted it inside and out. We didn't know what to expect of him, and were a bit taken aback when he turned up with a plane load of people. He began by introducing Rod to the visitors as the best this and the best that in the Northern Territory, although he knew nothing at all about him.

At that time Fitzroy would have been lucky to have brought $250 000. Rod was asked how much the property was worth by one of the guests, and he said, 'Oh, with a bit of improvement you'd probably get close to $350 000 for it,' thinking he was saying the right thing, as that was an overestimate of its value. The woman looked shocked, and Rod discovered that the guests were actually investors who believed the property was worth millions of dollars. There were wonderful plans drawn up for tourist ventures, and fruit orchards, and a sugar cane horticultural project for ethanol, but none of it ever eventuated.

Rod was happy. He was working with cattle and horses, as well as doing the odd bit of bull catching. The homestead yards were constantly busy with stock, and we were turning off animals to the meatworks, and testing cows and calves into the brand new tuberculosis (TB) free paddock. Australia had declared its intention to achieve TB free status in its cattle herds, and so a program arrived in the Territory which was to forever change the face of the pastoral industry. Instead of the old way of harvesting half-wild cattle, stations now had to comply with a lot of new rules. While animals chosen for the meatworks were sent off as before, the remainder had to be tested for TB before being returned to the paddocks if they had not reacted to the needle. If they showed a positive reaction, which meant they either had TB or had come into contact with the disease, they were destroyed. Unimaginable miles of fencing was needed to bring the open range country under control. Over the next twenty years most of the pastoral land in the top end of the Territory would be fenced and the cattle managed much more closely. BTEC – the Bovine Tuberculosis Eradication Campaign – was to become a major problem for Rod by 1986, but in 1980 he and Bluey Lewis, our local stock inspector, set up one of the first TB free paddocks in the Top End under BTEC, and began testing stock into it.

I loved it when the yards were full of cattle. You could hear the lowing and bellowing from the house, particularly at night. The smell was earthy and rich. Callum and I would go up and help out at the yards, especially when the men were branding. We were often short handed, so I'd strap Callum's car seat into the bull catcher, and with a rope tied to the bull bar, drag up the bigger calves to the yard fence so that the men could cut, earmark and brand them. The pace was frantic at times like this, and I loved the busyness and the sense of purpose. At the end of the day you fell into bed exhausted but satisfied.

Occasionally we'd take a day off. I would pack some food and drinks, and the three of us would drive out to a pretty waterhole to be on our own for a while. Rod often had something to show me that he'd noticed while he was mustering through the country, such as a perfect bower bird's bower, lined with snail shells and white pebbles, or a particularly beautiful aspect of the river and the ranges. One time he came across a big old bottle tree with a carving of a sailing ship on it, not far from the river itself. It looked to be very, very old. We always intended to go back and photograph it, but we never managed it. These were special times, when we were able to be together, enjoying the peace and the quiet around us, exploring a new piece of country and talking about something other than work.

By July 1980 we were getting into financial difficulties. We hadn't been paid since the previous October. Finally Rod sent an ultimatum to the owner, telling him that if he didn't pay us within the month, we would send a load off to the meatworks, and pay ourselves. The owner called back and told Rod to go ahead, and that he would sort it out with the accountants.

When you don't do a lot of paperwork, you underestimate the

importance of those pieces of paper. We should have insisted on a letter from the owner, or the accountants, but being young and inexperienced, and being so far in debt, we just took him at his word and went ahead. We sent them the meatworks receipts, so they knew what we had done and could adjust their records accordingly. That started a problem that was going to dog us for the next five years.

If there is any job I never want to do again, it's pet food shooting. Rod's brother Malcolm came up to help, and we started shooting pet food over the wet season to supplement our income, getting contracts on some of the surrounding stations and an agreement from the Fitzroy bookkeepers to shoot horses and donkeys on the station. Because Callum was still so small I didn't go out shooting with Rod very often, but the times I did were memorable.

We would leave the homestead well before sunrise so that we were already finding animals by the time the sun began to climb over the horizon. The idea was to shoot the animals early in the morning, so that the meat would be back in the chiller at the homestead before the heat of the day began to turn it rotten. The vehicle we used was the old long wheel base Toyota, the one we had taken into the Fitzmaurice. Rod had built a wooden box with a lid on the back of it, and patched up the front seat so that the passenger had something to sit on. We'd take a couple of bottles of water, knives, steel and stone, and Rod's rifles, a Parker Haile .270 and a Remington 22.250.

We shot wild horses and donkeys, but shooting horses made everyone feel so bad that we took donkeys as much as we could. The shot animals would be bled, skinned and the meat cut off and thrown into the wooden box. Carrying large chunks of hot bloody meat on our shoulders, in our arms, meant that we'd be soaked in warm sticky blood, with no chance of washing our hands or face until we returned home. The flies were incredible, and the smell worse. Donkey meat has a very strong odour, and the smell doesn't leave your skin or hair for weeks, no matter how much you wash.

Back at the homestead, the meat was unloaded piece by piece from the box, onto the floor of the chiller, and left to cool down for a few hours. We then trimmed the meat of excess fat and offal, weighed it into 60 pound cartons, and stacked them in the blast freezer to freeze solid overnight. It was dirty, stinking work, and we were always covered in infected cuts and scratches, no matter how careful we were. I was also pregnant again, and the morning sickness was hardly helped by the smell of donkey meat. But the dogs loved it. They were always fat!

Once the cartons were deep frozen, they would be stored in a semi-trailer freezer van, and whenever we had enough cartons for a load, a semi-trailer would arrive to take them away. We had a buyer in the greyhound racing market who was always looking for good lean meat. Donkey meat was perfect. We continued to do this for several months, and almost traded our way out of debt before the mustering season began again.

'I guess you don't know any of these people, Rod?'

'Michael, I don't even know who you are!'

Rod's first words on national television brought the house down. Michael Parkinson had invited Rod to appear as a guest on 'Parkinson' in July 1981, and the unknown bull catcher from the wilds of the Northern Territory was a big hit. Because the show's producers weren't sure how Rod would handle being interviewed, they stacked the program with three other guests, so that if Rod didn't have much to say, there'd be plenty of others to fill the gap. They needn't have. Rod was witty, funny and entertaining, and had Michael Parkinson in stitches as much as the audience.

Rod, Callum and I were flown to Sydney first class for the recording of the Parkinson interview, met by a chauffeur-driven limousine and put up at the Sebel Townhouse. I don't think the hotel foyer had ever had a swag in it before. Rod never travelled anywhere without it. A hotel maid saw it in our room the next day and assumed he'd been sleeping in it, so the story about Rod preferring his swag over a soft hotel bed was born.

It was a very flash place – especially in contrast to the stock camp that Rod had left a couple of days before. Callum wasn't impressed. There were no frogs in the toilet like there were at home, and he kept looking for them. Always one to seize an opportunity, Rod had the limo driver make a detour during a trip to the studio, to a Toyota spare parts supplier where he bought some large and heavy bits and pieces, including an entire differential, and took them home as baggage on our first class tickets.

Rachel Percy's book, *To Fight The Wild*, was doing well, already in its second printing, and *Reader's Digest* published it in an abridged version in one of its issues. It went on to be published in over a dozen other languages, and for the next few years we kept receiving copies of foreign language *Reader's Digest* as it was printed in different countries. Many people wrote to Rod after reading the story. We would frequently get letters addressed to 'Rod Ansell, near to the town of Katarina', or 'Rod Ansell, Northern Territory Australia'. The post office always managed to find him.

Fitzroy Station still owed us money by mid 1981. Rod offered the owner a deal where we would operate the property for ten years, completely at our own cost, but we would keep all the profits. At the end of ten years, we would pass the management back to him, along with a vastly improved, well-run property. He said he'd consider it, so in the meantime Rod took up a bull catching contract over on Drysdale River Station in the north of Western Australia. Malcolm's wife and baby son had joined him at Fitzroy a few months before, and went with him and Rod over to the west. Geoffrey Reemeijer, a friend of Rachel and Richard's daughter Mindy Oxenburgh, from Perth, came up to Drysdale to work with Rod as well. Johnno had shot through some time before, having exhausted his ability to stay in one place for too long. Callum and I remained on our own again at Fitzroy.

We weren't completely alone. Rod had employed a Turkish Albanian – or an Albanian Turk, we were never sure which – named Ned, who was to help keep the fences up, and whatever else needed doing around the place. Ned was Muslim, which was something not often encountered in outback Australia in the early 1980s. He was friendly and helpful, prone to getting very excited on occasion, was devoted to Callum, and had specific views about the animals around us. He tolerated the dogs, but hated them touching him. He was disgusted when the other men went pigging, and always washed the vehicles thoroughly when they came back to remove the taint of pig from them before he would ride in them himself. He had a problem with killing things. People, he assured us, were no problem if you had to do it. He had been in the army so he knew about these things, he said. But animals were something else.

One day when I was about six months pregnant, I found that the dogs had mauled a feral cat, and the pitiful creature was stuck up a tree. I asked Ned if he would put it out of its misery, but Ned was adamant: 'No!' he exclaimed. 'You can't kill a cat! Is very bad luck! More better you shoot dog than cat! No matter you build seven churches, is still no excuse!'

I picked up the gun and said I'd start building tomorrow, but the cat had to be shot. Sometimes I had to get the killers, too, when we needed meat. There were still three Aboriginal families living in the camp and, because Rod was always improving his breed of dogs, we had about fourteen dogs to feed as well. Ned would help once I'd shot the cow, but he had no idea how to bone it out, and my knowledge then wasn't a lot better, so we had plenty of stews while Rod was away. Bluey Lewis used to call in as often as he could, check that Callum and I were okay, and fill the freezer with meat for us – recognisable cuts of beef instead of my hatchet jobs.

It was around this time that I rediscovered an old friend. One day Callum had managed to eat half a packet of Combantrim tablets, an orange-flavoured worming medication. Panic-stricken I phoned up Katherine Hospital, and spoke to the doctor on call, who calmed my fears, saying: 'Don't worry, it won't do him any harm. He'll be really well wormed, though!'

I thought the voice sounded familiar, and asked the doctor his name again. It was Dr John Humphreys, whom I had become friends with while I was at Port Keats. One of my jobs was to help out at the health clinic occasionally when the AirMed doctor was seeing patients, and write down his dictated notes on the patient's card. John had given me my vaccinations before I went overseas in 1977, but I hadn't seen him since. He was now in charge of Katherine Hospital and living there with his wife Lenore and their two children. I was looking forward to introducing Rod to my old friend. I was sure they would like each other.

There was a big bay ex-racehorse called Jolly Scrabble that had ended up at Fitzroy as a stock horse. He was very hard mouthed, and very fast, so basically he only knew 'stop', and 'go as fast as possible in a straight line'. One day when they were mustering, Rod had put a young Aboriginal boy on Jolly Scrabble to bring up the rear. Somehow the horse and rider ended up in a flat gallop towards the river, where the banks were very steep. As they reached the edge, the young bloke sensibly ditched, and landed on the grass before the horse disappeared over the side. They went searching for the horse, and Rod found him in the river, unable to climb out – the banks were too steep. He couldn't leave him there to drown, or be attacked by crocodiles, so he called for the axe that was in the back of the Toyota, intending to knock the poor old horse on the head with the blunt side. It's very easy to kill a horse with a blow to the head, if it's in the right place, where the skull is quite thin. Just as Rod swung the axe, his foot slipped in the mud, and the blow struck the horse down its nose. Jolly Scrabble reared backwards in fright, and swam off downstream.

Rod came home very depressed that the horse would now suffer a miserable fate. The next morning he went out early, back to the river to see if the horse was still there. He returned a couple of hours later, and I heard him calling from the back door. I went out, and there was Rod, his shirt wrapped around Jolly Scrabble's neck: 'I found him further downstream, halfway up the bank leaning against the trees so he wouldn't slip downhill. Poor old bloke's exhausted. I don't know how he got out!'

We stabled him for a couple of weeks, looked after the cut on his nose, and fed him up. He got very used to the attention, and after we turned him back out into the paddock with the other horses, I discovered that as well as having nine lives, he had a talent for opening gates. One day I was working in the kitchen, when I heard a noise behind me and turned in fright to see a great dark shape hulking in the doorway. Jolly Scrabble had opened the gate to his paddock, opened the house yard gate, opened the screen door, and walked in through the back room to the kitchen, where he stood with his great big head poking through the door, taking a great interest in the view. There is something totally incongruous about the sight of a horse in a kitchen, especially one as big as he was. It was a trick he repeated regularly.

Meanwhile Rod was bull catching in the Kimberley. There was just himself, Malcolm and Geoff in the camp, which was run on an absolute minimum, even by Rod's standards. Much later Geoff described the camp to me:

> Even Rod reckoned this was a pretty rough camp. There was no water to speak of. Every morning he, Malcolm and I would toss to see who had to go and collect the water from the billabong, and I always lost. You had to wade out a few metres before you could scoop any up, and it was absolutely freezing first thing. Because there was so little water, there was never enough for a bogey at the end of the day, and you'd just get into your swag at night filthy. We'd wake up next morning, and there was this joke about how we would go to bed dirty, and wake up clean the next day. Dry showers, we called it.

Geoffrey was about twenty when he first came to work for us. He liked the idea of a job in the outback with this unusual bloke he'd heard his girlfriend's family talk about so much, and he'd met Rod on one of the publicity tours for the movie and the book. Geoff was a solidly built young man of medium height with a thick shock of brown hair, and a laconic way of expressing himself. It took a while to realise that he had a very dry sense of humour, and that he wasn't actually irritated by the situations he found himself in.

One time Rod and Malcolm headed into the station homestead to meet the mail plane, and didn't return for three days. Geoff was left looking after a yard full of bulls, with nothing to live on except some stale bread and a bottle of Worcestershire sauce. It was the kind of story Rod would tell about himself, and I could well imagine him thinking this was a good experience for some green young kid from the city.

My parents came up to visit while Rod was at Drysdale, so my dad flew across and spent a week in the camp with them. It was a novel experience for Dad, living in such a rough little camp, but he never mentioned that. He only told me about a close call they'd had one day. He, Rod and Geoff were tearing through the bush after a scrub bull when Geoff suddenly yelled: 'Wire!'

They all ducked as best they could, but the only thing that saved them was the wire catching and snapping apart on the windscreen clips on the bonnet. Rod drove straight back to the camp and welded up a wire catcher immediately, which was basically a length of steel sloping from the bull-bar up to the roll bar behind the passengers' heads. It had a couple of small pieces of steel welded along its length which would catch and break the wire before it hit anyone.

After three months away, Rod and Malcolm returned from Drysdale with Geoffrey, and we left Fitzroy a few weeks later. The station still had not paid us what we were owed, and when the deadline Rod had given the management passed, we moved out. We worked at Willeroo Station for the next six months or so, catching bulls on contract and making some money for a change.

On 11 December 1981, Shaun William Ansell was born. This time we were only an hour's drive from Katherine, so I remained out at the station until I went into labour. Rod stayed with me for the birth again, and we spent hours reciting Callum's favourite Dr Suess stories to each other to help take my mind off the contractions. Shaun was reluctant to show his face, and I spent hours walking up and down the corridors, trying to hurry him along, while Rod slept in my bed. John Humphreys came back on duty in time to deliver Shaun himself. He and Rod practically met each other in the labour ward, and became very good mates.

At two weeks of age Shaun developed a high fever. After spending all night sponging and showering him, I headed for the hospital in Katherine. His temperature was 41 degrees, and as soon as I arrived the nurses went to work trying to bring it down. For the next three days I lived at the hospital watching as test after test was run on this tiny little boy, culminating in a lumbar puncture after all else had shown negative. This last test proved negative as well, but within twenty-four hours, Shaun's temperature dropped and remained normal, and we were able to go home, not knowing what had made him so sick.

A week or two later, Rod returned from an overnight stay in town and called me into the bedroom, shutting the door firmly. 'Now look,' he said, grinning sheepishly. 'I've had something done, but if you're not happy about it, it can be reversed. But I think it's for the best.'

He had had a vasectomy. Without discussing it with me. This was such a huge decision for a couple to make, and yet he had taken it on alone. I couldn't believe it. I was stunned and angry, and when I raised all sorts of reasons why he should have talked to me about it, and why I wouldn't have wanted him to have one, he floored me with: 'Look,

I did it because, what if I got some girl pregnant? It would be terrible for all of us. It's better this way.'

My mouth opened and closed a few times. I looked at my two babies asleep on the floor, and for the first time I wondered just what kind of a marriage I had. It sounds ridiculous, doesn't it? How could a husband say that to a wife, and still have a wife afterwards? It's hard to explain your relationship clearly to anyone else, or to explain the attraction between you and your love. Rod was vital and exciting, and had a way of dragging the people around him along in his wake. He could get a team of tired, dispirited men up and willing to work all night repairing a damaged vehicle, even when it was the last thing he felt like doing himself. He was able to convince me time and again that the way I was looking at a situation wasn't right.

It is easy to look back now and say, 'How could I have been so weak, so readily fooled?' but I think I just loved him so much I was able to ignore the negative sides to him. I wanted to believe the Rod I loved was the real Rod, the person worth making excuses for, and worth compromising my life for. And realistically, I was a long way from home, I had no money, and I had two small children. Things had to get a whole lot worse before I felt I couldn't stay.

The other thing that worked in his favour was the isolation we lived in. I didn't have much contact with other women, and so I hadn't formed any close friendships during the time Rod and I had been together. He was my friend and confidant, and took the place that a woman friend would have filled. We talked a lot, or at least he talked and I listened a lot. I used to reflect on how lucky I was to have a husband who could talk to me, unlike the 'typical' Australian male who only discussed football or what was for dinner.

Sometimes when we talked, he would comment about how women who discussed their husbands with outsiders were disloyal, and what a destructive thing it was to a relationship. Also, he was slowly edging me away from close contact with my family and other friends. He never actually tried to forbid me from phoning or writing to them, but whenever I did, the disapproval was palpable, and I'd feel guilty, thinking that I should have been doing something else. Bit by bit, I wrote less, phoned less, and one day realised I hadn't been home for nearly six years. But that was in the future.

# 11

# Bush Musters and Oily Rags

The 1981–82 wet season at Willeroo was a quiet time. The creek came up and cut us off from the highway for a while, and the only job Rod had to take care of was keeping the grass mowed around the station buildings, most of which were deserted. So much spare time was an unaccustomed luxury, and he began to write a novel, in an old hard-covered station journal he had picked up somewhere. It was a story about a young man who comes to the Territory, and about what happens to him – like many first novels, it was obviously autobiographical, and featured characters based on people we had both met in the past few years. He could write well, and when he took the unfinished, handwritten manuscript with him to England a few years later, the editor of a major publishing house read it, and told him to hurry up and finish it.

Rod had a recklessness about him that was tempered by common sense, but this wasn't always so obvious. He flew down to Perth for some book publicity in early 1982, and came home with a new piece of bull catching equipment. It was called a 'Weedhopper'. Rod had seen it flying in Perth and decided it was the just the thing he needed for spotting bulls. It was an ultralight plane, just a few lengths of aluminium pipe, a few metres of yellow and green material, and a little engine. And a wooden propeller. Geoffrey, who had been to Perth for Christmas, arrived back with Rod at Willeroo. He was as bemused as I was appalled by the new toy. The two of them set about putting it together.

'You did have flying lessons in Perth, didn't you?' I said nervously, as Geoff handed Rod another nut and bolt.

'Nah, it was too wet and windy the week I was there. But the bloke told me what to do.'

In typical Rod style, he made a few modifications of his own as he proceeded, such as replacing the tiny, light fuel tank with a larger, much heavier one fashioned out of an empty fire extinguisher barrel. They finished it, and realised they still had a box of nuts and bolts and bits that hadn't been used up. Rod tossed them into a corner of the shed: 'Ah, probably just a few spares they chucked in for good measure,' he said, not convincing me at all. I couldn't see how an aeroplane, even a homemade one, could be put together like a bull catcher, 'a bit missing here and there, but she'll be right' sort of thing.

I was very worried about Rod taking this thing up in the air at all. It might have been possible to put it together from a manual, but I doubted if you could learn to fly from one as well. He assured me that he was only going to run it up and down the airstrip for a while to get the feel of it, and would wait to get a pilot friend out to show him what to do another time.

I could hear the buzz of the Weedhopper's engine as it trundled up and down the airstrip near the house where I was preparing lunch. Suddenly the buzz changed to a loud drone, and I realised that I could hear it above me. I ran outside, and there was the Weedhopper high in the air. I watched with my hands over my mouth and my heart racing as it slowly circled above the homestead, and tried to see if Rod looked like he was signalling for help. There was nothing I could do except wait and watch as the little plane buzzed around like a giant yellow and green dragonfly. After about twenty minutes the Weedhopper turned again and, lining up the airstrip, came down, the engine drone rising and falling as Rod worked out how to land the thing. He came down with a bump, bounced a couple of times, and taxied over to where Geoff and I had run out to the fence.

'What a buzz!' He was exhilarated, and climbed out of the seat with a huge grin on his face.

'I thought you said you were going to wait!' I was glad he was safely down but I had been terrified the whole time he was in the air, and now I was mad.

'Well, I meant to, but when I was taxiing up the strip the last time, I hit a big hard cow pat, and bounced up into the air. I had no choice but to pull back on the stick and keep going or it might have crashed. So once I was up, I thought I may as well test it out. It's going to be great for spotting bulls!' Landing was a bit tricky, he added, but he knew enough about the theory of flying that he headed into the wind, and kept the nose up as he came down, and managed not to kill himself.

The Weedhopper was moderately useful and found its share of bulls, but it was very slow, and it was too sensitive to the vagaries of unpredictable air currents. After one scary flight where he almost lost control in a down draught, and had been attacked by a pair of wedge-tailed eagles, Rod decided that chasing bulls on the ground was a whole lot safer. The Weedhopper stayed parked beside the old yellow Blitz.

The bull catching eventually dried up, and Rod and Geoff went over to Scott Creek, a station a few miles down the road, owned by the same company as Willeroo, and worked cutting and baling sorghum hay for a while. While there they met up with Tony Izod, who had been pet food shooting for us at Fitzroy the year before. Tony had a contract picking up hay bales with Duane Fishlock and his brother Aaron. Tony showed us a big impressive scar on his leg.

'Remember this?'

I certainly did. When Tony had been pet food shooting on Fitzroy early in 1981, his offsider had accidentally driven his broad-bladed skinning knife deep into Tony's calf as he made his opening cut on a brumby. Refusing to waste the animals they'd already shot, Tony insisted they finish boning out everything before going to get help. By the time he came to the homestead, the wound was already several hours old, and giving him a lot of pain.

'Whoa, mate,' said Rod when he saw the damage. 'I could stitch it for you, but I haven't got any anaesthetic.'

It was a problem. The wound needed to be stitched soon, or it would require surgery. By the time Tony got into town to the hospital, Rod believed it might be too old to be a simple job. Tony didn't want to lose any more time.

'Just stitch it up for us,' he said. 'Then I'll go in and see a doctor.'

We had no anaesthetic, but we had some whisky that a visitor had left behind. We poured as much as we could into Tony, and Rod set about cleaning and repairing the wound. I left the room. I could see that Tony was trying very hard not to make a fuss in front of a woman, so I thought it might be better if he didn't have to try and be too brave. I came back about fifteen minutes later, and the tears rolling down his face were mingling with the sweat from his forehead. When Tony finally saw a doctor in Darwin a couple of days later, the doctor commented that it was such a good job of stitching he'd leave it alone.

Rod had an ability with medical practice that always amazed me. He was always stitching up the dogs when they'd been gored by pigs, injecting them with antibiotics or lancing infected wounds, or splinting up their broken legs. His knowledge of how the human body worked was exhaustive, and he could nearly always diagnose what was wrong with someone. But he must have read a few too many textbooks at some stage, because he was forever diagnosing himself with exotic diseases. At the same time, though, he could be completely dismissive of a worker's injuries – or his own – if they weren't exactly life threatening, and insist on working regardless. That was how it was done in the bush, as far as Rod was concerned.

We had a good relationship with Luke Wise, the hands-on American owner of Willeroo and Scott Creek Stations. Luke had pulled himself up by his bootstraps as a young man in the States, going from gas pump attendant to oil company owner in a remarkably short time. He lived at the main homestead at Scott Creek, about half an hour closer to Katherine, but often came out to visit us at Willeroo, sometimes staying the night and invariably rising at 4 am no matter what time we'd gone to bed the night before. He got along well with Rod, and admired the way he ran his bull catching outfit. One afternoon he turned up with a couple of bottles of wine, and announced that he had just sold the two stations for around $5 million, and had subsequently lent most of it to the bank at an excellent interest rate.

'Well, that's great, congratulations,' said Rod, shaking Luke's hand. We couldn't even imagine that kind of money, and the thought of being in a position to lend money *to* the bank just made us both laugh.

Luke smiled, and then said, 'You don't have to worry though. I made them put a clause into the contract that said you were to remain employed as the bull catching contractors for the next twelve months.'

This was great news. We had assumed that, with a change of ownership, our contract would cease, and we'd have to move on. As it turned out, though, the manager put on by the new owners had his own ideas about how to run a cattle station, and after a few months we decided we'd had enough, and found another contract.

In July 1982 we moved to Mainoru Station, a cattle property some 250 km northeast of Katherine on the Arnhem Land border, at the end of a long and rough road. Mainoru was managed by Kevin Anlezark, a generous and friendly bear of a man who made us feel like welcome visitors rather than just the contracted bull catchers. Kevin lived there with his wife and three children, a married couple who were the cook and head stockman, a couple of old pensioned-off ringers, and a group of Aboriginal families who had traditional ties with the Mainoru country, and whose men also worked as stockmen on the property.

My sister Leonie and her husband Craig Hemsworth left Melbourne to work with us for the rest of the season, bringing their little son Luke, who was just a year younger than Callum. They had enjoyed their last visit to the Territory – when they stayed with us at Fiztroy Station – so much that when we offered them a job catching bulls with us near Arnhem Land, they didn't need long to make up their minds. Leonie took to living in a bull catching camp as if she had done it all her life. We were both very happy about being able to live with each other again, after being so far apart for the last few years.

It was wonderful to be out in the bush again, with space and air and no housework. We set up camp on a little flat surrounded by pandanus and paperbark trees, beside a cold little spring. It supplied us with good drinking water, and we kept butter and cheese cool in it as well, until Kevin Anlezark realised we didn't actually have any refrigeration, and insisted we borrow a gas fridge from the station. We dug a cooking pit, and erected a bush table and a tent for storing the food. A 20-litre kerosene drum cut in half lengthways made a washing-up sink when wedged into a square hole cut out of the table. Rod found a large slab of slate at a nearby creek, and Leonie and I turned it into a shower base, erecting hessian walls around it under a tree, and hanging a canvas shower bag above it. It was well appreciated on cold dry season nights, when hot water heated on the fire went into it.

Leonie and I cut saplings and made a frame to string up a tarpaulin over their swag and ground sheet, and were about to start on mine, when Kevin Anlezark turned up with a tent. I knew Rod's thoughts on tents, but Kevin had been so generous towards us that I just accepted his offer gratefully. It was big and airy, and for once we'd have a little more privacy than usual. Kevin looked at our fireplace, and suggested we come up to the station to eat with them at night. When I declined, with the excuse that Leonie was looking forward to lessons in camp cooking, he just laughed and said he'd send his men down with a load of firewood instead. Loads of firewood turned up regularly while we were at Mainoru, and we were often invited to eat in the kitchen with the rest of the family and staff, and for film nights in the schoolroom.

Most of our days started before dawn, the fire rekindled from the previous night's coals and the billy boiled for the first cup of tea for the day. Breakfast was usually just cereal with powdered milk, toast and tea, and then the blokes would head out in the truck and the catcher to find some bulls. What money we had earned at Willeroo went into paying back the money we owed to the bank from our time at Fitzroy, and so we started at Mainoru with very little. Everything was patched up and cobbled together. The old red International truck was a nightmare. It had a dodgy alternator, so once it was push-started in the morning, it had to be kept running all day, unless it was stopped in a place where it could be push-started again. Poor Geoff, who had come with us from Willeroo, had the truck driver's job, and spent many hours sweating in the cabin keeping the engine running and waiting for Rod and Craig to get back.

Geoff and Craig spent a few hungry days, having anticipated that they'd be heading back to the camp for lunch, but Rod was happy to go without food all day when he was working. He was never in the habit of taking food with him when he went out in the morning. If he returned to camp before dark with time to eat or have a cup of tea, that was a bonus in his eyes, but Craig and Geoff thought otherwise. Eventually he accepted that other mere mortals needed to eat in order to function, and the blokes would make up sandwiches to take with them in the morning.

Craig was a former national motorbike racing champion, on A grade super bikes, and Rod had bought a trail bike for him to use hazing bulls, that is, riding along the outside of them, helping the bull catcher keep the bull running in the right direction. The catching was difficult, in thickly timbered country with a lot of rocky outcrops. The vehicles were often damaged, but we were getting good numbers and making some money. What had changed, apart from the country, was the quarry. Buffalo outnumbered cattle in this area and Rod had to learn a different style of catching in a hurry. Craig enjoyed the work, and he, Geoff and Rod got along well together. They looked an incongruous lot. Craig had a beard, very long hair that was usually braided out of his way in a plait, and a well-muscled physique. Geoff called him 'a muscle-bound hippie', a contradiction in terms according to Geoff, and to further confuse the picture, he raced motorbikes and built and flew model balsawood gliders, and studied books on quantum physics. Evenings were very pleasant times, and after dinner we would sit around the fire talking for hours, especially when we had visitors staying, which seemed to be most of the time.

Rod was good at what he did, and really didn't need to work hard at convincing anyone else, but a large part of him couldn't resist being the showman when the occasion presented itself. He had an excellent understanding of how visitors, city people especially, felt when they found themselves in his territory, and he capitalised on it mercilessly. Geoff recalled years later how he would have to bounce around on the spare tyre in the back of the catcher when a visitor was out with them for the day, instead of being in the passenger seat ready to strap the bulls Rod knocked over: 'We'd be charging along, and spot a bull, and I'd think, here we go – Rod'll throw this one, instead of just getting on with it and catching it. And so he'd chase the bull for a while, pump it out, and leap out and grab its tail and throw it. It was impressive, sure, but it was so unnecessary . . .'

Rod would never explain why he did something, and it added to the sense of mystery and exoticism for someone who was new to the scene. One day he was driving my friend Rina in the bull catcher when he stopped suddenly. 'There was this big wedged-tailed eagle on the side of the track, gorging itself on a dead wallaby,' Rina told me later. 'It was so full it couldn't even fly away. Rod slammed on the brakes, leapt out of the catcher, whipped off his shirt and flung it over the bird's head, pinning its wings beside its body. Then he brought it back to the car trussed up like a dinner, and sat it in the back behind the seats. He never said a word about it. I just hunched in my seat beside him, absolutely puzzled as to why he grabbed this dangerous looking bird, but too intimidated to ask why he had done it. You just felt you couldn't question anything he did! It was as if asking why just under-lined your own ignorance, and somehow cast doubt on what he was doing . . .'

What he did with the bird, Geoff remembered only too well. Rod carried the eagle into camp, where Geoff was asleep on his swag, taking advantage of a lull in the work to catch up on some rest. He was awakened by a strange heavy pressure on his chest, and opened his eyes to see a fierce looking wedged-tailed eagle with a huge sharp beak scowling into his face, while Rod was in convulsions a few feet away. The eagle wandered around the camp for a day or two, until it had digested enough of the wallaby to be able to take off again.

It was very rough country around Mainoru, and we had very threadbare gear. On one memorable occasion they had to change sixteen tyres on the two catchers, and eight on the truck, all on the same day. We couldn't afford to buy decent tyres for the vehicles, and instead had a huge pile of second hand ones scrounged from the tyre dumps at the roadtrain depot and the tyre shops. Tubes were patched until they were more patch than rubber, and the tyres not much better. You never ran your hand over them – the wire poking out would take your skin off. Repairs to the equipment required imagination and improvisation, and Rod was an absolute master at that.

The red International truck had no bonnet, no doors, no lights, and only the barest of essentials to make it run as far as its engine was concerned. One day Geoff was driving it through a rough creek crossing, lurching from side to side, and the engine actually fell over. Astonishingly, it kept going. The two side engine mounts had broken, and the torque of the engine just twisted it over to one side, where it continued to thump away until they had nursed it home. Once there, Rod cut up a couple of old tyres to make new rubber mounts, and repaired it again. Sometimes the gearbox would get stuck in low range, and the only way to get it to shift into high (it was an electric shift) was to get a piece of fencing wire, and short it out from the battery – very, very carefully.

Rod preferred using Holden carburettors on the Toyotas. As soon as he brought a new catcher home, the Toyota carby would be ripped out, and a Holden version installed instead, because they were cheaper and easier to fix when they broke down. The only problem was that they had a higher profile than the original, so a hole would have to be cut through the bonnet with the oxy to allow the bonnet to close over the carby. This was usually not an issue, but one day at Mainoru a buffalo managed to clip the carby with its horn and knock it off. Geoff had to drive the catcher home with the bonnet up, peering around the side of it, while a young cousin of mine who was visiting sat wedged in the engine space, holding the carburettor on by brute force until they got home.

Sometimes the petrol tank on a catcher would get a hole in it. These were difficult to fix, and meant the catcher was off the road for at least a day. To save time, Rod would tie a 4-gallon drum in behind the driver's seat, and snake a length of reinforced plastic tubing from the drum to the carburettor. No one ever smoked in the catchers!

Bull catching took up most of our attention, but we had frequent visitors. John Humphreys and his wife Lenore had become great friends of ours by now, and we saw a lot of them. With their children Katrina and Thomas they came out to camp with us regularly, and when we went into Katherine, we would stay with them. It was the first time that I had seen Rod in a close friendship. He and John seemed to understand each other and to entertain each other effort-lessly. Their careers were completely opposite – an Australian bull catcher and an English doctor – but then Rod had an instinctive appreciation of medicine and medical practices, and John loved the bush and was fascinated by the insanity of hurtling through it after dangerous animals the way Rod did. They each recognised the other's expertise in his own area and respected that, and were no kind of threat to each other, I suppose. And they had an understanding about themselves, and the way they saw the world, that they couldn't share with Lenore and me. I think Rod found a great deal of peace and satis-faction in his friendship with John.

My oldest friend Anne Butler joined us for about two months, and her sister Felicity came up for a week in that time as well. Another old friend from Melbourne, Rina Traa, and her husband Jim Madden called through at the same time, and I had the strangest experience of being with three friends I'd known since I was eleven years old, yet feeling like I was a stranger. I started to realise then that I had changed a lot from the 20-year-old who had left Melbourne seven years earlier.

It was a great life for the children. Callum turned three while we were there, Leonie's son Luke was nearly two, and Shaun under a year old. Callum and Luke were fascinated by the big toys their fathers played with every day, and climbed into the bull catcher or the truck every chance they got. One morning we were gathered around one vehicle, all talking and concentrating on some mechanical mystery. No one noticed that Luke was sitting up in the other bull catcher until we heard it start up. It was in gear, and immediately took off, headed at a smart pace straight for the creek. Geoffrey made a record dash across the flat and reached the Toyota just as the wheels crested the bank of the creek, stalling it in the absolute nick of time. We weren't sure whether Luke was crying because he'd had a fright, or because he was cross with Geoff for stopping his car. In any case we made sure the key wasn't left in it again.

The son of a cousin of mine from Perth came to stay with us for a couple of months. He had been getting into a bit of trouble at home and his mother asked if we could give him a job for a while. Rod was always happy to help out young people, especially young city kids who needed to be reminded where the priorities in life lay – well, the priorities according to Rod, anyway. Michael almost didn't get to go home again. He was helping out at the yards one day, and had been reminded many times not to lean on the portable yards. Buffalo have long horns, and they know exactly how to use them.

'Oi, young feller, get off that panel! A buffalo's going to put a hole in you a brown dog could jump through.' Rod was getting sick of telling him, but some people have to learn the hard way.

Next minute there was a crash of horn on metal, and young Michael ended up on the ground. Everyone rushed to him, sure he was badly injured, but he stood up again, looking a little shocked. His jeans leg was split from hip to ankle, and there was a little red mark behind his knee from where the buffalo's horn had clipped him. I don't think he leant on the yards again.

As the 1982 season wore on, the weather warmed up. By October we had caught most of the bulls around Mainoru, and Rod was asked by the Bulman Aboriginal community to come and talk to them about catching buffalo. Bulman was about 100 kilometres by road to the north, in Arnhem Land, and had thousands of buffalo, as well as a remnant herd of Brahman cattle left over from an attempt to develop a cattle station some years earlier. Rod, Craig and Geoff moved up there to run a few yards and see how it went, but Leonie and I stayed behind with the kids. It wasn't worth moving our whole camp up there for such a short time, so we visited for a couple of days once a week.

An old mate of Rod's from Kununurra was in Katherine around that time, and sent a message out to Rod asking for some help. Frank was practically a pensioner, an old ex-ringer, ex-fencer, ex-bore mechanic, ex-you name it. He had a face like old boot leather from too much sun, and only one good eye, which was permanently bloodshot from too much grog. Old Frank had been on a serious binge in town for a while, and badly needed to dry out, and to be taken away from the fleshpots of Katherine. Rod said he could come out and cook for them at the Bulman camp, as long as he didn't bring any grog with him. Frank was in the DTs for a week, and kept the blokes awake at night with his nightmares and moanings until he came out of it. He couldn't go cold turkey, of course, and had smuggled a carton of beer in his swag. Every morning he'd open a beer for breakfast, the hot foam spraying everywhere as he tried to drink as much as he could before the can emptied itself in a froth. True to his word, though, he was okay after a few days, and managed to provide meals for the blokes, and helped out with the work until we left.

Back at Mainoru, the paperbark trees around the little spring burst into blossom, which attracted hundreds of flying foxes. The trees dropped their blossoms into the water, and the flying foxes defecated into it, and the whole lot started to ferment. After a couple of days the smell was so overpowering that Leonie and I took up Kevin Anlezark's offer and moved with the little ones into the empty staff quarters at the station homestead.

We ran our first ever buffalo helicopter muster in late October 1982, a major learning exercise for Rod, who had only ever heli-mustered cattle before. The set-up was basically the same as for cattle. A yard site is chosen, based on the most likely direction the animals would want to run. The yard itself is made out of portable panels, each about nine feet long and six feet high (2.7 metres by 1.8 metres), made of steel pipe welded together, and they lock into each other a bit like a Lego set. It means you can truck an entire yard around and set it up where the stock are, instead of pushing them a long way to the permanent station yards. Wire is run out from the yard entrance to form a funnel, called the 'wings', and hessian bagging hung off it so that it looks like a solid wall to a galloping cow. The choppers push mobs of animals together until they are moving towards the yards. Once a good number are inside the wings, the catchers come up behind and keep the pressure on the animals with lots of noise and movement until they are safely inside the yard, and the gate is shut.

The pilot we used at Bulman was Alan Edwards, a top mustering pilot based in Katherine at the time, who would continue to muster for us over the next couple of years. Alan was a brilliant flyer who understood cattle and buffalo, and was a major asset. We already knew from heli-mustering on other stations that a lot depended on the man in the air. You could set up the portable yards in the right place and have every other detail exactly right, and still not get any animals in the yard if the pilot didn't understand the way stock worked. And even when the yards, the pilot and everything other thing was right, sometimes it still might not work out.

One of our early yards at Fitzroy Station was a big disaster. Rod had picked the yard site, told the men where to run the hessian wings out, but had to go back to the station while the work was carried out. He didn't have a chance to check the yards again before the helicopter arrived at first light, but because the men had done it with him before, he assumed it would be all right. Several hundred head of cattle were running smoothly into the yards after hours of helicopter work, when the back panels of the yard parted company with each other and the cattle began streaming through. The pilot, John Armstrong, knew what he was doing, and just pushed the rest of the animals through the gap in the yards, and then followed them and steadied them down together a few miles further on, so that they wouldn't be scattering off in all directions out in the scrub. That way there was a good chance of getting them into the yards the next day. The problem with the yards was soon apparent. The men had only used the latches on the panels to hold the yard together, instead of tying them together with wire as well. The latches worked okay until a bull hooked the fence and lifted a panel out of its 'boot' and created an opening. John Armstrong came back the next day and the yard, with triple wire ties this time, was successful.

The helicopter muster at Bulman went well, and it looked like a contract at Bulman for the next season would be a good career move. It was now too hot to consider any more stockwork, so we packed up the camp and left Mainoru in December to go to Queensland for the Wet.

One of the most influential elements in the north of Australia is the climate. Basically we talk about two seasons, the Wet and the Dry. No frills, just the basics. The Aboriginal people of Arnhem Land recognise at least seven distinct seasons, but the Wet and the Dry is all the Europeans required, apparently. The dry season generally starts around the end of April, and is characterised by the southeasterly winds which dominate for the next few months, bringing dry cool air from the south of the continent across the deserts. It doesn't rain anymore, and the air is clear and the sky a brilliant deep blue for a few weeks until bushfires blot the sky with smoke for the rest of the dry season. Daytime temperatures in the Top End, where most of this story is set, average a comfortable 25°C to 32°C, with low humidity, but at night the mercury can drop to single figures, depending how far inland you are. Around Alice Springs in the centre of the continent the night-time temperature often plummets below zero in the winter, but in the country where we were living, a night of eight or ten degrees was considered beyond the pale. In fact for most people who have lived in the Territory for very long, any temperature below 20°C is thought to be doing it very hard indeed, and the extra blankets come out.

By the end of August, the weather starts to warm again, and the humidity rises. Man and beast become irritable and ornery as work gets harder and more uncomfortable. By October it can be around 40°C every day, often not dropping below 30°C at night. The humidity frequently reaches 90 per cent, and while clouds build up in great piles and promise relief, it won't really start raining until December or later. Once the monsoons move down from Asia, the rains set in, and cattle work in the Top End comes to a halt. The country is too wet, and it's simply too hot to work horses or cattle then.

It's a dramatic time. The Top End of the Northern Territory has more lightning strikes than any other part of the world, and there are some awesome electrical displays from October to December. Called hurricanes or typhoons in the northern hemisphere, cyclones are a feature of the tropics during the wet season. Graded from category 1 for the weakest to 5 for the most destructive, these monstrous storms are created out of big lows that develop over the sea, and build up speed and strength as they move west. Occasionally they cross land where there is a settlement and cause havoc, but often they blow harmlessly out to sea, or cross the coast at an uninhabited place, and peter out over the land. But they bring the rain which everything depends on, and life along the north coast is a lottery as to who has to pay the cost each time. On Christmas Eve 1974 it was Darwin itself that paid, when it was completely destroyed by Cyclone Tracy, a category 4 cyclone.

There's a great old saying: 'a good book for the Wet'. It referred to the time when stations were sealed off from the outside world, sometimes for months, because roads and bridges were cut by flood-waters, and the rest of the country was too boggy to move around in. It was the time when people would mend saddle gear, read that good book, or just go quietly mad. We dealt with it as our 'down time', when we repaired all the equipment, stripping down all the vehicles and giving them the attention there wasn't time for during the dry season. If we didn't have a place to live for the wet season, we would go south and visit our families in Queensland or Victoria. It was a pleasant bracketing of work and rest. We worked seven days a week during the dry season, but would stop for a couple of months in the Wet.

# 12

# From Amsterdam to Arnhem Land

I'm sure if it wasn't for Rod's great friendship with John Humphreys, I would never have been able to convince him to go to England. John and Lenore had moved back to the UK, and Rod missed the long evenings he'd spent with John at his home in Katherine, or by the fire out at our camps. We found ourselves back in Queensland at the end of a successful year, with nothing to do until catching resumed the following dry season. A throwaway remark by me about visiting the Humphreys in the UK was taken up by Rod, much to my surprise, and we arrived on their doorstep in the depths of a London winter in January 1983.

I was overjoyed to be back in England again, and I hustled Rod around trying to get him interested in the history and the country-side, attempting to share with him the feelings that England inspired in me.

'Too tame, too controlled,' Rod said. He wasn't impressed by much that he saw, and found the towns ugly and cramped. The cathedrals which I thought were magnificent he saw as overblown edifices of religions he despised. The ancient green and gentle farmlands were just tortured vestiges of what they once were, even if 'once' was more than a thousand years ago.

'But this is where you came from, it's where your ancestors started out. Doesn't that count for something? Don't you think it's fascinating to look at the evidence of the stages civilisation has gone through? Like the neolithic earthworks, the villages, these incredible structures –

even if they *are* churches – that people built in the eleventh century, without the technology we've got now?'

He shook his head. 'It's all about changing the natural environment, not living within it. All these different cultures just imposed their will on the wilderness that was here. Animals don't do that. Neither should humans.'

'Well,' I said, shaking my head. 'It's just as well there are enough places like this in the world for people to live in, to leave the bush alone for you. I guess that has to be in their favour . . .'

But Rod was very happy to see John again. We stayed with him and Lenore for a week or two, John and I doing our best to find something Rod actually liked in England. He was impressed by Stonehenge, by the sheer engineering feat of manoeuvring those massive stone blocks into place. It snowed, much to Callum's delight. Rod had never seen snow either, decided it meant it was far colder than the thermometer professed, and could not be persuaded to remove his coat and scarf even when he was indoors.

My family in Holland thought the sun shone out of him: 'Such a beautiful boy!' my female cousins exclaimed.

Rod didn't need to speak Dutch. He just smiled that flashing white smile, and acted like a special guest from another planet. Which he was.

Rod was bemused by the totally opposite lifestyle to the one he knew. Dutch homes are very much about the indoors – with a long cold winter, the Dutch have made an art form out of indoor living. Every square inch of a house is carefully considered and decorated in some way.

'Even the tables have rugs on them!' Rod whispered to me when we first arrived, puzzled by the beautiful deep crimson Turkish carpets covering most of the tables. It's a Dutch thing.

My uncles Oom Piet and Oom Loet came to the rescue before Rod was totally overwhelmed by civilisation, and took him out to see farms and cattle, while I stayed behind to catch up with my aunt, Tante Mia, and hear about my family.

He came back with a bundle of wide belts, complete with stainless steel buckles. 'Look,' he said, showing me the belts. 'Perfect bull straps!' He explained that the vet to whom my uncles had introduced him at one of the farms used them to strap down pigs when performing a procedure on them. They were made of tough woven synthetic fibre, and would last a lot longer than our leather straps.

I just laughed. Of all the souvenirs someone might bring home to remind them of their first overseas holiday, Rod brought home bull straps.

Rod had never travelled before, but it didn't faze him. Amsterdam certainly didn't. We left the boys with Oom Loet and Tante Mia in Veghel one day, caught the train up to the capital, and cruised around the city being proper tourists. We visited the art galleries, and explored the canals and bridges, and the pretty streets with their overhanging houses. I think by now he had got over his extreme reaction to being in such big cities, and could appreciate some of their attributes. At least he gave it a try. He was fascinated by Holland's liberal attitude to things such as drugs, especially when we were offered them in 'Dam Square by a dealer who may have been selling newspapers for all the concern he showed.

Another attraction for Rod was the red light district, and its laneways of windows with scantily clad girls waiting for customers. The seedier side of life fascinated him. There was something about a lifestyle that was borderline, edgy, definitely unorthodox that fired his imagination. Just like bull catching, I guess. There was always the chance of coming unstuck if you weren't careful, every turn bringing a new risk, without any safety nets. He was unrealistic about it, though. He invested the world of prostitution and other illegal activities with some kind of basic nobility. I think he would have believed in a code of honour amongst criminals. He believed that if someone had to live by their wits and not the security of a nine to five job, they were more real, more honest. I just assumed this was an unsophisticated, country-boy attitude to life in the big bad city, but I think that was only part of the explanation.

He went back to Amsterdam on his own, taking the camera and declaring that he wanted to spend a day photographing the city. When we returned to England a few days after that, he related an adventure story of a drug deal that was full of risk and danger, and how he, the backwoods Aussie bloke, outwitted them and came out on top. He met a man in a cafe who offered to sell him some cocaine. He was led up and down alleyways for ten or fifteen minutes so that he'd be confused and wouldn't remember how to get back to the place where the drug deal was to be made. He handed over his money to the man who told him to wait in a cafe and who then promptly disappeared. Rod waited half an hour before deciding he'd been duped. He managed to find his way back to the first cafe where he'd met the man, and found him sitting there laughing with his mates. Rod wrapped the strap of the camera around his hand, so that he could use it as a weapon if he needed to, and walked up to the table. The dealer moved to get up and run, but his companion said something to him in Dutch, as did the barman, and the dealer grudgingly handed over the drugs while the others laughed.

I was horrified. We had passed through customs going back into England, and he had the little packet of powder secreted in his boot. I was also horrified because this wasn't just dope: 'You're joking, aren't you? I can't believe you did that! It's completely stupid! *Cocaine!* What if you'd been caught going through customs? You'd be sitting in a jail cell right now . . .' I was practically incoherent.

He held up his hand, his eyes crinkling with amusement like I was having a little hissy fit over some very minor issue: 'It's okay, Jo, stop worrying. I didn't get caught, did I? And I'm not getting into hard drugs or anything. Look, we're here, on the other side of the world . . . I just wanted to try it, that's all. Look, you can't even get this stuff in Darwin, and besides, it's not like dope, you can get hooked on this stuff. It's okay, I'm not about to get addicted to it on one go.'

I wasn't comforted. 'Well, I'm not staying here while you mess around with that sort of crap. I'm taking the boys out for a walk.' I bundled Shaun into his pram and Callum into his jacket. He just looked at me with a bemused smile, and waved us out the door.

Drugs were certainly a part of Rod's life, if not a very important part then. In the beginning, when I first knew Rod, it wasn't a big deal. Everyone smoked marijuana. I was constantly being surprised by the numbers of otherwise conservative bush people under thirty who smoked it. I had come across it often back in Melbourne, but I didn't smoke cigarettes, so didn't feel inclined to smoke anything else. Drugs didn't interest me at all, not even out of curiosity, and no one ever pushed me to try them. I didn't have an opinion about marijuana, apart from thinking it probably did less damage than alcohol.

The first time I ever saw Rod smoke a joint was at Kununurra before we began filming on the Fitzmaurice. We had met a young couple who were travelling the country in a Kombi van, and invited them to stay at Bundaberg Downs. After dinner they pulled out some marijuana and asked if we'd like a smoke. They seemed like decent people, and I was with the man I trusted more than anything else in my life, so I felt okay about trying it for the first time. All it made me do was cough my heart out, and feel a bit sick. The others sat there peacefully smoking and apparently enjoying some effect I certainly wasn't getting.

'You okay?' Rod put his arm around my shoulders as I wiped my streaming eyes. 'It's probably the tobacco that's making you cough.'

He then rolled a joint with only marijuana in it, and watched as I tried it, encouraging me with smiles and caresses. He could be so gentle and loving, and his ability to focus on you to the exclusion of everyone else was magnified immensely when he smoked dope. Wow, if the side effects of smoking this stuff was getting extra attention from Rod, it couldn't be too bad. Except it still made me cough.

Everywhere we went, smoking the occasional joint was an accepted part of life, like drinking beer and smoking cigarettes, but it wasn't a big part of our social lives. In the late seventies no one seemed to take it very seriously. Rod drank very little alcohol and didn't smoke cigarettes, which was unusual in a place renowned for having the highest per head consumption of alcohol in Australia, and where breathing was considered an activity which enabled the smoking of tobacco. Rod's occasional joint hardly seemed like something to worry about. It was a few more years before I realised it had become something to worry about.

Arnhem Land was probably about as far away from Amsterdam as you could get, any way you looked at it. It is an enormous piece of land, some 97 000 square kilometres, in the far north-east of the Northern Territory. It was created as an Aboriginal reserve in 1931, and today remains a place that is distinctly Indigenous. Non-Indigenous people must apply for permits to cross its boundaries, and have good reasons for going there. It was a place my father had read about as a boy in Holland, and a place I had only the sketchiest knowledge of. In April 1983 we drove across its borders with the biggest catching plant we had put together so far. We had taken out a bank loan, and bought another 4WD truck, a small bulldozer, and a brand new short wheel base Toyota. For the first time Rod was not going to be spending all his spare time resurrecting an ancient battered bull catcher, night after night. The new vehicle was stripped of its cabin, doors and windscreen, and a heavy bull bar and side bars were attached.

We also employed three men. Duane Fishlock and his mate Mervyn Pringle were both Mataranka boys who'd grown up around the kind of work we were doing. Dave Simpson was the mechanic. Dave had done two tours of duty in Vietnam during the war. Rod hired him because he reckoned anyone who was mad enough to choose to go back to a war like Vietnam would be quite mad enough to mess around with buffaloes.

The first day we arrived out at Bulman, Dave was wandering around inspecting the campsite and came across a pile of buffalo manure. He looked at it in disbelief, and said: 'What is *that*?'

When he was informed it was buffalo droppings, he pulled a face and muttered: 'I ain't messin' with anything that does a shit *that* big.'

The camp we set up on the creek, about 10 kilometres out of Bulman on the road to Maningrida, was pretty idyllic, as camps go. With so many people in one spot, I insisted we dig a pit toilet rather than adopting the usual practice of heading bush with a shovel. Rod went one step further, and built a wonderful shower complete with a hot water donkey made out of a 44-gallon drum downstream on the creek bank.

It makes a huge difference to morale if the camp is reasonably comfortable. There is a lot of macho bravado in the bush about how much tougher one bloke can do it than the next. I often heard men boast about how they'd been in camps where lunch was a tin of pineapple, hot from the glove box, or where there was no water for washing and everyone stank from wearing the same sweaty clothes for a week. Or camps where the blokes were covered in boils because the food consisted of nothing more than salt beef and damper, day in and day out. The idea seemed to be that if you could live like that you were a lot tougher than the other bloke. Rod may have been content to live like that himself, and indeed expect other men to do the same, but I wasn't about to.

The men used the bulldozer to drag down an old demountable from the abandoned galena mine site a few kilometres past Bulman where Rod, Craig and Geoffrey had camped the last few weeks of the previous year, and set it up near the creek. I cleaned it and painted the inside white, and we built shelves and benches in it. This was to be the kitchen. I still cooked on an open fire, but here I had good off-ground storage for food and cooking gear, and a table to prepare things on. I also had a helper. Duane and Mervyn had brought their partners along, and Mervyn's girlfriend, another Joanne, worked with me preparing meals and doing the washing, which made life a bit easier. We washed clothes in the creek by hand, soaking greasy jeans in a plastic rubbish bin with detergent overnight before scrubbing them on the rocks with a big scrubbing brush.

We always fed people well, and I often heard visiting truckies or stock inspectors comment what a good camp we had, and how good the tucker was for so far out in the bush. No one ever quit in all the years we employed people. I can't remember anyone ever throwing in the towel and leaving in a huff.

A good part of the reason Rod had happy employees was that he never asked them to do anything he wasn't prepared to do himself. He was a brilliant driver, and he took more risks and caught more bulls than anyone else. He worked long hard hours, and I think they could see the effort he was putting in, and were prepared to do the same. He had a great sense of humour, loved telling stories, and treated his men like mates. And where as often as not in the Territory a man would get ripped off by an unscrupulous employer, Rod paid his workers well. He had a very strong sense of fairness, and would always err on the side of overpaying someone if there was any doubt, no matter how much equipment they may have damaged in the meantime. He was very much an inclusive employer. The people who worked with us ate with us and lived with us. He seemed to have a personal relationship with each of them which went beyond that of an employer and employee, and he rarely gave an order that sounded like one.

There was none of the tension that so many catching camps had, because Rod didn't try to be the biggest, baddest bull catcher of them all. In a lot of situations, the boss had to be tougher than the men he employed. If he gave an order he had to be able to back it up with his fists if necessary. I don't think Rod ever found himself in that position. He didn't act like a boss, but no one was in any doubt about who was running the show. One of our bull catchers once commented that ours was the most relaxed camp he ever worked in, and put it down to the fact that there was very little alcohol. It certainly wasn't banned, but because Rod didn't drink, no one else drank heavily. Occasionally we'd have a party or just have a few drinks, and some of the men would have a big night on the grog, but no one ever got into a fight.

One day a huge heavy parcel turned up in the mail bag. Rod's mum Eve had sent us a wonderful present, a meat mincer. When the blokes realised this, the pressure was on to make sausages. I managed to get hold of some sausage skins from the butcher in Katherine, and the next time we got a killer, they called a halt to work for the afternoon and all got into it. It was an old fashioned hand-cranked mincer, and you clamped it to a bench in order to use it. The table top, an old door, was too thick for the mincer to be clamped to, so two blokes held onto it by hand, and the other two took turns cranking the handle. It was a hard way to get a feed, but they stuck at it, and made miles of buffalo sausages, of every imaginable flavour. It was a great change to the buffalo meat we normally ate, but they decided it was too much hard work doing it by hand.

'It's got a flywheel and a belt,' mused Dave the mechanic. 'We could hook it up to an electric motor, easy.'

All eyes were turned to an old wringer-washing machine standing to one side of the camp. I had been given it some time before, but it needed electricity to run. The only power supply was the arc-welder, which was nearly always in use repairing the catching plant, so the washer stayed unused. But I still had hopes it would eventually come to my aid.

'That old washing machine'd have exactly the right electric motor, y'know,' said Mervyn, with a sly glance at me. 'Jo won't miss it, she never uses it!'

Before I could put up an argument, the motor was out of the washing machine, a frame welded up, and the mincer and the motor hooked up. Amazingly, the arc-welder could now be spared from its duties up in the workshop every so often, but it was all too late for my washing machine. The sausages were pretty good though.

We always had a lot of visitors. Even way out here, I was often cooking for half a dozen extras at no notice. We had an old kerosene fridge, and kept a supply of frozen beef in at the teachers' house in Bulman. The teachers, Tom Plunkett and Sue Farley, were old friends of mine from Port Keats, and I was delighted to have some people I regarded as practically family so close by.

Some of the Aboriginal men from Bulman worked with us. The Murray brothers, Kevin Forbes, Paddy Ryan, Lachlan Lawrence, and Spencer and Duncan Martin when they could wag school, would turn up every morning just after sunrise ready to go catching for the day in their own vehicle. As well as catching buffaloes, they showed Rod and his men the way around the country, and made sure they didn't go into areas they weren't supposed to.

Part of the contract Rod had negotiated with the community included the construction of yards and paddocks at the Mt Catt outstation to create a buffalo domestication project. Mt Catt was about thirty-five kilometres south of Bulman. The traditional owners were keen for the catching to go ahead, but didn't want to lose all their buffalo. They wanted to set up a small managed herd to provide employment and income to give their young men a future there. This was to be the start of a fascinating journey for our family.

Richard Ledgar, pastoral advisor with the Northern Land Council, an Aboriginal organisation responsible for implementing the Aboriginal Land Rights Act in the Northern Territory, came out to help with the planning and the negotiations. It was all taking a lot longer than they thought it should. Every time they reached a certain point in the plans, things stalled and they couldn't work out why. Finally everything came to a head when old George J—, one of the traditional owners, set up a camp right in the middle of the spot where the yards were supposed to be built, and brought the whole project to a halt.

It turned out that the plans for the yard and paddock laneways compromised the head of the spring which fed Mt Catt creek, which was a very sacred place. The men couldn't talk about it or show it to Rod and Richard because it was secret men's business, so they were in a Catch 22 situation. The solution was for Rod to be included in ceremonies where he was taught certain stories, and given secret knowledge. He was given a skin name, and thereafter attended many ceremonies that came through that part of the country, and had a role to play at them. Because he had a skin name, it followed that the boys and I did as well. Rod's skin name was Gojok, and mine was Kamijn. Because of my skin, Callum and Shaun were automatically Bulayn. In this part of Arnhem Land, each skin group can marry into one of two other skin groups, and the children's skin names come from the mother.

There is a strange jealousy that exists among white people where Aboriginal culture is concerned. I saw it at Port Keats, and once we became more closely involved with the Mt Catt people, I saw it time and again. Most people who become involved with Aboriginal society value the experience, but sometimes people believe that they were singled out for special treatment because of their own personality or talents. It generally follows that if you are in regular contact with Aboriginal people, especially out in a community, you will be given a skin name. Aboriginal society is extremely complex and governed by strict rules regarding relationships. It makes it a lot simpler if the Aboriginal person dealing with you knows where you fit in, and therefore how to behave towards you. I imagine that when we all first began mixing with each other a couple of hundred years ago, Aboriginals assumed that we used a skin system too; just the way that so many white people expect Indigenous people to operate by the same social rules that European society values. In any case, we often met people who scoffed at Rod's inclusion, saying 'Oh they give everyone a name, and I've been to lots of "corroborees".'

Rod was certainly given far more than that. He was very respectful of the honour, and treated it very seriously. All he would tell me about his experiences was that he was told very long, important stories, shown objects, and taken to secret places. He would never reveal any more than that, and I didn't press him. For the next few years, we attended many ceremonies, some that all of us could go to, and some that were for the men only.

I have a wonderful memory of one in particular. This ceremony travelled a long way through Arnhem Land, and had not been to Mt Catt for many years. Planning for it went on for months, and a lot of supplies were brought in. We camped at a big open area, where families set up their cooking fires and swags, and built shades out of saplings and bushes. At night, the site was a twinkling maze of dozens of small fires – there were over three hundred people there. The women cooked and cooked, laying out food on fan palm leaves, and occasionally sending it up to the men's camp, which was about a kilometre away. Every so often we could hear them singing, and the women would all stop what they were doing, and then answer with an ululation, like the singing of Arabic women. It was eerie and beautiful, and I felt very privileged to be there.

Most of the ceremonies were like that. They lasted for days, sometimes weeks, and people would come and go from their jobs at Bulman or further afield, and fulfil whatever roles or obligations they had. The rules were strictly enforced, and no alcohol was allowed anywhere near the ceremony ground. In the men's camp itself, no European clothing or accessories like hats or sunglasses were permitted, apart from shorts. Most men wore a loin cloth, or naga. A place was designated for toilet use, well away from the camping area, and no one left rubbish anywhere.

Another time, at an initiation ceremony, I was taken aside by one of the senior men and told that I would be allowed to watch the women's part of the ceremonies, but that I could never tell anyone what went on there. He said: 'Nothing bad would happen to you, but black feller might get killed.'

What I can talk about is that the initiation ceremony lasted about three days, and was an emotional and powerful event that symbolised and celebrated the journey from childhood to manhood for boys. I asked one of the women I knew well if there was anything like that for the women, but she said no. I thought that was a bit sad, but then I wondered if perhaps the women's rituals were so secret they didn't tell anyone about them, ever. Then again, all women have a maturing process that is far more obvious to them, and perhaps we don't need to have symbols like the men do, to tell us we are growing up.

So Rod was now allowed to know why there was a blockage about the site of the project, and he was able to redesign it to suit the traditional owners. Richard Ledgar and Eric Roberts, who was also heavily involved in the process, wrote a paper on the traditional Aboriginal decision-making structure used in reaching agreement on the Mt Catt project. This structure was the traditional triad of *junggayi* (policeman), *dalyin* (mediator) and *mingirringgi* (owner). Each area of land has three people with specific responsibilities for it, and they have to consult with each other about any impacts on it. Broadly, and this probably differs slightly depending on who you talk to, the *mingir-ringgi* is the actual owner of the land, by way of inheritance from his or her father, and from their father's father. The *junggayi* is responsible for seeing that ceremonies are properly conducted, special cultural sites protected, and ensuring management practices such as burning at the right time, are carried out. The *dalyin* has the job of mediating between the *mingirringgi* and the *junggayi* if there are disputes about any cultural matters. This means each individual fulfills all three responsibilities passed down through their parents. You are *mingir-ringgi* for one area (from your father), *junggayi* for another (from your mother), and *dalyin* for a third place (from your mother's mother). So, with order and propriety restored, and the old men satisfied, planning was able to continue on the yards and fencing.

Callum and Shaun thrived. Callum was at that lovely three-year-old age of asking questions about everything, such as, 'How do you make chooks?' and, 'Why don't the clouds fall down?' One morning we were having our breakfast after the men had gone off for the day, and a couple of crows flew into the trees nearby, calling and croaking.

'What do crows say?' asked Callum, squinting up at the black birds overhead.

I gave him what I thought was a marvellous reply, about how they said things like, 'Hey, there's a big fat dead buffalo! Wow! What a fat smelly one! C'mon, let's go get it!' and so on, waffling on in great detail for a couple of minutes.

Callum just looked at me as if I was a lunatic, and said: 'No they don't. They say "a-a-a-a-a-rr-gh".'

He was devoted to his little brother, and the two went everywhere together. I could see them sitting together with a book one morning, and I was stunned to hear Callum reading to Shaun. I knew that book inside out, and I could tell that he was reading every word. My God, I thought, he's learnt to read! I quietly strolled over and stood behind them, and sure enough, Callum was reading the right words on the right page. I realised after a minute that he had actually memorised the words that accompanied each picture, and that he had heard this story – their favourite – read so many times that he knew it off by heart.

We netted off a yard around the demountable for them, to keep them out of the creek, and made them a sandpit in the shade. They had each other, and the dogs, and played quite happily most of the time. One day I was watching them play in the creek and made the mistake of taking a book with me. I love reading, and get totally absorbed when I do, which is why I shouldn't have taken the book with me that day. It was peaceful and cool in the shade, and the water was shallow over a stony bottom. Perfect for kids to play in. I was lost to the world in my book, and was roused suddenly by a shout from further down the creek. Duane's girlfriend was hurrying along the bank calling to me, her little one on her hip.

'Shaun's in the water – quick!'

I looked up to see that the two boys had moved further down the creek. Shaun was against the bank and a little away from Callum, caught in a faster flow of water which kept knocking him over. As I ran stumbling down the creek I could see he was surfacing and trying to stand, but kept being swept off his little legs. I reached him as he went under again, and snatched him up. He coughed a couple of times, and whimpered a little, so I knew he wasn't in any danger. Callum followed me out of the creek, and I carried Shaun up to the camp where I wrapped him in a towel and sat holding him. We sat there like that, without making a sound, for ages, Shaun just huddling in against me and staring out of huge frightened eyes. I don't think I read another book till we left that creek.

For ages I had been trying unsuccessfully to get Rod to use some kind of safety glasses for catching. He drove at terrifying speeds through the bush, getting whipped in the face by branches, choked by dust and so on. However, he maintained that it was more dangerous to use glasses, because there was always something in your peripheral vision, such as the frames of the glasses. And besides, he'd say, they'd get scratched all the time. The only time he would wear glasses was when he went up in the chopper to spot for stock, and then he'd borrow mine, invariably losing them out the door of the aircraft when he put his head out to look at something.

One night driving back from a yard Rod caught an insect in his eye. By midnight the pain was unbearable. I drove him the three hours into the hospital in Katherine where they put in anaesthetic drops, and then the next day sent him to Darwin to have it checked by an eye specialist. For a while it looked like he would need a corneal transplant, but the infection settled down, and his vision was unimpaired. I found some plastic goggles even Rod couldn't complain about, and insisted that everyone wear them.

The country around Bulman was very rough, and Dave the mechanic earned his wages repairing the constant damage to the vehicles. The land that wasn't heavily timbered was hilly and littered with rocks like they'd been dumped from a tip truck, and tall spear grass hid the breakaway gullies.

Twice in Arnhem Land Rod was knocked unconscious while driving, but somehow always managed to avoid crashing the Toyota. His sister Christine was in the car with him one day when a stick flew up and hit him on the temple. She drove him back to the camp.

'Something hit him in the head!' she said, very worried. 'There's a cut on his temple, and he's really groggy!'

Rod was pale and dazed, and we helped him out of the car and on to the bed inside. I shone a torch into his eyes to check for concussion, and his pupils weren't responding very well. There was a hole in his temple, not big, but I couldn't tell if it was deep or not, or if there was anything lodged in it. I got on the radio and called the AirMed doctor, and managed to have him flown out to Katherine Hospital that afternoon.

Christine told me how they were chasing after a buffalo, when suddenly there was a bit of a bump: 'Rod just suddenly slumped sideways on top of me, but you know, as he went, he pulled on the hand brake, and put the gearshift into neutral. Then he was unconscious for a little while. I didn't know where we were, or which direction home was, but when he woke up again, he drove the catcher out onto the track, and told me which way to go. Then he passed out again.'

Callum, Shaun and I followed him in by road, and I managed to keep him in town for a few days before he insisted on going back. He had bits of wood in the wound, and needed antibiotics to prevent infection so close to the brain. But, as usual, he went straight back to work in spite of my argument, and suffered headaches for ages. It almost killed him. One day soon after he came back, he was on top of the truck, tying a buffalo to the overhead rails, when he blacked out and fell into the truck. He came to a moment later, and scrambled up the side of the stock crate before the buffalo could react. The only reason it didn't try and horn him was because the rope had fallen across its eyes and nose, distracting it momentarily, and giving Rod a few vital seconds to get out. The men brought him home, and made him stay there.

Accidents were always close company with bull catching. You just can't drive a vehicle at top speeds through the bush and come out unscathed every time. I worried about the dangers, but I also believed Rod when he assured me how competent he was, especially at making split second decisions. 'When I start hesitating before driving between two trees, I'll give it away,' he used to say. He seemed to go into a particular kind of focused state when he was catching. His eyes lit up with a fierce intensity, and he seemed to be able to second-guess the buffalo's every move. When I asked him how he could tell there wasn't a big hole under the grass, or some other obstacle, he just said you had to be able to read the country.

'I don't think about it, or analyse it while I'm driving,' he said. 'It all happens automatically. Some part of my brain registers, say, paperbark trees or pandanus, and I know there's probably boggy ground around, but at the same time another part of my brain is measuring the gap between two trees to see if the catcher will fit, and watching which way the buffalo is running, and where he's most likely to try and head. I don't just follow the buffalo, I push him, too. I make him go where I want him to.'

We still hosted a constant stream of city visitors, and all were keen to experience the insanity of catching a tonne of sharp-horned beast. Rod would take them out, not doing a very good job of pretending that it was a bit of an inconvenience, and scare the daylights out of them. They always came back completely enthralled with the activity, and with Rod. There are not many opportunities in our society where people can experience such thrilling speed and danger legitimately. It probably explains the present obsession with extreme sports.

Rod had a way of making people believe that what he was doing was the most important, relevant, real job in the world. Everything else was just wanky posturing. He spoke about the land, about the

bush, and I could see people envying his knowledge, and his com-
munion with a nature that most of us are distant from. What made
him more fascinating was that he could also talk about anything else
with the same credibility.

Michael Parkinson was in touch again, wanting to do an interview
with Rod in the bush, a big departure from his usual format. Then
they organised for Rod to fly to Sydney instead, wanting him to
appear with a special guest they had lined up. It turned out to be Koo
Stark, famous for being Prince Andrew's girlfriend at the time. The
studio people thought it would be good to contrast two people from
opposite ends of the spectrum. However two days before Rod was due
to fly out, they cancelled his appearance, as apparently Ms Stark
refused to appear on the program with anyone else. The blokes in the
camp were very sad. Rod and I weren't so sad – well, Rod was probably
more disappointed than me – because we felt that Parkinson had
exhausted all the interesting stuff out of the Fitzmaurice story, and we
didn't really know what else he'd find to talk about. We thought that
was probably the end of the media interest by now, but we were
wrong.

We had a great year in 1983, and made some good money, most
of which went into term deposits at the bank. Rod's biggest dream
was to own his own station. We had considered a few places, from
St Vidgeon's in the east of the Territory to stations in the remote
Kimberley, but never had enough money to get started. Sometimes we
talked about the kind of house we'd want to build, and doodled with
designs and layouts, but it always seemed a long way off. Generally,
though, life was so busy and frantic that there wasn't a lot of time to
ponder the future.

We had, however, bought a small piece of land the year before.
Duane Fishlock had the option to buy a 20-acre block for $12 000 in
Mataranka, but had no money. Rod was sympathetic and wanted to
help him get his land, it being something Rod valued so much himself.
Instead of lending Duane the money, we came to an arrangement
in which we bought the block, subdivided it, and gave Duane half,
keeping the other 10 acres ourselves. We figured that 10 acres for
$12 000 was still a good deal, and it helped out Duane as well. He
immediately put an old house on it, put up some fencing and moved

in. Some years later, he sold it for a very good price, and kick-started himself on to eventually being able to buy a cattle station just north of Mataranka. Rod was always very satisfied that he'd been able to give a young bloke a hand like that.

The Bulman people wanted us to stay on, and invited us to move our camp into the community at the end of that year. Rod had formed a solid friendship with some of the Bulman men who had worked with us all year, and they were keen to be involved in the mustering next season. Rod would be bringing back only one European offsider, Mervyn Pringle, the following year and it was agreed that the rest of the team would be made up by the Bulman fellows.

When we arrived in the beginning of 1983, Bulman had about thirty-five inhabitants including children. There was a small, two-teacher primary school, housed in the old 'silver bullets', large mobile schoolrooms found all over the Territory that were meant to be temporary but ended up staying put for a long time. Its students came from Bulman, and from the Weemol community just a few kilometres away. The people lived in a collection of houses of varying styles and condition, from the high-set former manager's house to shabby, one-room tin sheds. There was no store or shop of any kind, but there was some arrangement with one of the Aboriginal organisations that pensioners' cheques were cashed for them in Katherine and food sent out once a week. It seemed like a difficult way to live, and it was obvious that sometimes there wasn't enough food to go around. A large power plant generated electricity for the community and was maintained by the NT government. Most buildings weren't properly wired up, and there was a spaghetti of extension cords snaking all over the place. The old manager's house had a cool room beneath it, which was used by the community to hold beef for a few days whenever they killed a beast.

The demountable was dragged up behind the little bulldozer, and left in position beside the school for next season's camp. Most of our other gear was sent on ahead into Mataranka for storage over the Wet. We had a full load of buffalo in the yard ready for the meatworks, but for some reason Rod went into Katherine, promising to come back out that night, so we could load the buffalo onto the road train the next morning. Everyone else had left.

He called me in the afternoon on the community's radio-telephone: 'Do you think you can load the buffalo with the Bulman fellers? I'm going to stay in town with Ruth and Rolly. You can get a lift back in with the truck driver tomorrow.' He made a half-hearted excuse about his neck being sore.

'But you took the swag in with you! *And* everything else!'

'You'll be right. You won't need the swag – it's not *cold*!'

Callum, Shaun and I spent the night on the verandah of the teachers' house. Tom and Sue had already left to go south for the holidays, and the school was bleak and deserted. We didn't have a swag, or any cooking gear, just some food I had kept for the last night and the trip in. It poured with rain, and we huddled in a chair under an old coat that had been left outside by mistake. The wind blew the rain in on us, and it was freezing. I stacked up a couple of cane chairs behind us to make a bit of a windbreak, and convinced the boys this was a really funny way to sleep. Then some camp dogs tried to share the verandah, and started growling and barking at us until I pelted them with the rocks that Tom and Sue kept on the verandah for just that purpose.

Eventually the boys fell asleep under the coat, and I held them, feeling utterly alone and miserable. Here I was, with my two little children, we didn't have a home anywhere, not even a camp now, and we were huddled like refugees under someone else's old coat, and we were cold and wet. I started to feel quite desolate, when a voice in my head said, yeah, and we have money in the bank and about $20 000 of buffalo sitting in the yard waiting to go to the meatworks. You'll be dry tomorrow. I convinced myself it wasn't much to put up with in the scheme of things, and hugged my boys a bit closer.

# 13

# The Best Christmas
# Present Ever

In 1984 Rod came back to Bulman a few weeks ahead of us, and built an annexe onto the demountable out of upright barked logs, and laid a concrete floor with pieces of local slate set into it. He built some cupboards, a wall of flattened stringy-bark, and a double bed in the annexe, and a bed for the boys up in the demountable. He also built himself a rough desk to write at – the novel begun at Willeroo was still in progress. A roof of leafy branches laid over chicken wire and tied down and covered with a plastic tarpaulin to keep out the rain finished it off. Seeing we were going to be living 'in town', Rod said we couldn't very well be camping like we usually did. It was wonderful! After the past two years of sleeping on the ground in swags and living under tarpaulins out in the open, it was so good to have a bit of privacy.

We also had electricity. Our neighbour Tex Camfoo invited us to run an extension cord over to his house, so we were able to have a washing machine and a deep freezer. Bliss! We added on a cold water shower screened with corrugated iron, and a kitchen sink for washing up. I dug a trench from the shower to the contour drain nearby, and laid a piece of poly water pipe to take away the waste water, and planted bananas at the outlet. I was very happy. I guess after not having had a house of my own for so long, I was very easy to please.

I was easy to please, but I was also easy to fool. I guess I just loved my husband so much I was prepared to put up with an awful lot, and chose not to believe things I didn't want to know about. A few days after the boys and I came back to Bulman, my friend Sue, the schoolteacher, came to see me. Sue looked at me with a pitying expression, and shrugged in a helpless kind of way: 'Look, I don't know what to make of this, but Connie [not her real name] is saying that something was going on with Rod while you were away. She's quite upset, and I don't know what to do about it.'

Connie was a lovely young woman, not long married, who lived nearby. My stomach plummeted, and as usual my first reaction was to defend Rod: 'I'm sure it's nothing – everyone was helping Rod build this house, and maybe she just developed a crush on him or something then . . .?'

Sue gave me that look again and shrugged awkwardly. I told her to tell Connie to come and see me to talk about it. She came in, clearly agitated, and I made a cup of tea. What else do you do when another woman is sitting in your house telling you she is in love with your husband? We had a conversation of sorts, but I wasn't sure in the end if Rod had seduced her or not, and finally I asked her what she wanted to do about it.

'I don't know,' she said. 'I've never been in love with a white man before.'

My hands were shaking a bit. I summoned all the strength I could muster, and just said to her gently, 'Connie, he is married. You are a married woman, too. You have to forget about him, and just think about your husband. I don't know what Rod has done, or what's happened, but nothing else is ever going to happen. Okay?'

She looked a bit distraught, but she nodded, and left soon after. I sat in my little house feeling shellshocked. A roller coaster of emotions ran through me – anger, grief, shame, and a kind of hopeless resignation. Why did it have to be like this? We loved each other, we had a great sex life, we could talk to each other. Why did he have to chase other women? I recalled the conversation we'd had when we first began to live together, when he told me that he would never be faithful to one woman. Maybe it was time to accept defeat, and admit that I couldn't live like this.

Callum and Shaun ran in, laughing and talking about the bulls they were 'catching', and gave me quick fierce hugs and demanded food. The brief thoughts I had of leaving their father withered. How could I wreck these two little boys' lives?

I don't think Rod meant to hurt me – I'm sure he didn't. It was just the way he was. His affairs with other women, as far as he was concerned, were not a reflection of how he felt about me. To him everything was a challenge – could he catch that enormous bull, could he muster that rough country, could he seduce every woman he set his sights on? I came across a quote he'd written down some years later, which went a long way towards explaining his view of life. It said: 'Only two sights give a man real pleasure: land he owns, and a woman he doesn't.' He didn't yet have the first, but the world was full of the second.

When Rod came home I confronted him about Connie's visit, and he denied anything had happened between them, claiming it was just a young woman having a crush on an older man. I warned him that might well have been the case, but if he messed around here, where we lived, I wouldn't be around to watch.

We were mustering and bull catching again in earnest, with Mervyn Pringle and the Bulman men. Rod's fame from the Fitzmaurice story followed him even here. One day a couple of stock inspectors arrived to check a yard, and as they were being taken to the yard site, one of them said to Mervyn in a slow drawl: 'This is that feller who got lorst in the bush, ay? Sleeps in holler logs, ay?'

Mervyn just grinned at him and shrugged. A few minutes later they pulled up at the yards and were walking over to where Rod was unloading buffaloes. There were several long narrow rolls of hessian on the ground, and Mervyn nudged them with his foot, and said to the stockie following along behind: 'See these? Holler log swags . . .'

Callum started with Katherine School of the Air, and we began the first of many years of correspondence schoolwork. A couple of days a week he went over to Tom and Sue, and joined in with the preschoolers at the Bulman school, which he really enjoyed. He and Shaun often disappeared for hours at a time to play with other little kids in the community, coming home well fed by someone's mother or aunty. I realised just how well fed when we were visiting some friends in Darwin one day. They were very serious conservationists – vegetarians to boot – and they had been talking about various animals in the Bulman area, notably some species on the endangered list. Callum and Shaun were listening eagerly. Talking about animals was one of their favourite activities.

'Do you ever see any of them?' said our friends, asking about some particular little furry mammal.

'Yeah!' answered Callum and Shaun, very enthusiastically. 'They taste great!'

Our neighbour's wife, Nellie Camfoo, often used to take them fishing, and digging for sand frogs to use for bait. They went hunting for bush tucker with their friends' families, and spent many hours unconsciously learning about the environment around them. Callum and Shaun soaked up knowledge like sponges, and developed an affinity with the bush, and with our Aboriginal hosts, that has remained a strong part of both their characters.

If Rod came back early from mustering, he would often take them down to the yards in the bull catcher, their eyes shining with excitement. There he would explain everything that was going on, and talk about what was happening to the buffalo, and translate their bellows for Callum. Fishing was another passion they shared, and we spent many afternoons by the river, the boys watching everything their father did, learning early how to catch fish and bait their own hooks. Rod always explained slowly and carefully when he was showing them something, and was unstinting in his praise when they got it right. He took them out into the bush with him often, teaching them to recognise the tracks of different animals, and how to catch ant lions in their little sand traps with a piece of grass.

Their biggest treat was being allowed to go down to the yards to watch the buffalo being drafted and loaded onto the road train. They would line up along the fence rails with all the other kids and yell at them as the animals were pushed up the race. Most of their games consisted of playing at mustering, and creating bogs for their toy trucks. I guess they saw so many vehicles being pulled out of bogs, that's what they thought grown-ups did. We had a television and video player at Bulman, courtesy of Katherine School of the Air, so that Callum could watch videotaped school activities, and programs like 'Playschool' (there was no TV reception outside Katherine). Friends then began to keep us supplied with tapes of wildlife documentaries and other TV programs, and Callum and Shaun incorporated lots of this information into their games. So as well as bull catching and finding echidnas under logs, they now hunted dinosaurs, and built trucks out of cardboard boxes and milk tins, and talked about albatrosses and elephants.

Rod and I had noticed the year before that the community frequently had food shortages. He talked about it with the men who were working with us, and they came up with the idea of pooling some of their wages, and buying provisions from Katherine. Every fortnight they would give me an order, which I radioed into the general store in town, and the food would come out freight-free with our next road train. The men used a locked shed to store it in, and looked after the distribution themselves. The old pensioners didn't go hungry any more.

The Bulman community had been asking me for a while to start a shop. It was such a long way from town, and so few people had cars, that getting hold of simple items like washing powder or nappies out at Bulman was a formidable task. On my occasional trips to town, I would frequently take a list of requests and an envelope of money to bring things back for people. Barr Enterprises, a camping and army disposals store in Katherine, used to do a hawker's run every couple of months, and bring a wide variety of goods out to the communities for people to buy, but if your cheque hadn't arrived the day they were there, you missed out. When we got to know the owners of Barr's, Ruth and Rolly Shoesmith and Bill and Anne Midgely, they asked if I'd think about taking over the Bulman sector of their run, and open a shop out there instead.

I was a little hesitant about the idea, as I had never had any experience in sales or business, but when I mentioned it to some of the Bulman women they were very excited, and I was virtually steamrollered into taking it on. Rolly taught me the rudiments of the bookkeeping I needed, and I discovered it was actually a lot of fun. The shopkeeping, that is, not the bookkeeping. Life was busier, but I enjoyed the extra contact I had with everyone in the community. Katherine was a three hour drive away, and the women in particular didn't get into town much. Being able to buy hardware and clothing at Bulman made a big difference.

I ordered a garden shed from Katherine, and some shelving and trestle tables. The stock was basic, but pretty much covered everything from axes to underwear. The Bulman community thought it was great, and on the days the shop was open, I didn't get out of there until the sun went down and it was too dark to see.

I also became a stand-in nurse. Bulman eventually had its own full-time health worker, but there was no one when we first moved there, and I would often be asked for help. It was the same at Fitzroy Station, where I looked after the families of the Aboriginal men who worked for us, making calls to the sisters at Timber Creek for advice when necessary. Most cattle stations operated the same way, and used to be kept well stocked with medical supplies by the Health Department for this reason, but Bulman wasn't a cattle station as such. The nursing sisters from Bamyili (later called Barunga) came to the rescue when I'd exhausted our personal medical kit, and kept us well supplied so that I could continue to treat people as before.

In today's litigious public liability climate, I doubt there'd be any support for an untrained person to perform such a role. Liability was the last thing that I thought of. A lot of the time it was simple first aid, changing a dressing, or having a look at someone who was sick. If it was more than I knew what to do with, I would call up the AirMed doctor and describe the symptoms, or the injury, and then do as I was instructed. I had to deal with miscarriages, road accidents, boils, burns and scabies, and the usual run of colds and flu. I didn't mind doing it at all, and I was chuffed one day when the doctor on the other end of the radio thought I was a nurse.

'Okay then, sister, just give him an injection of antibiotics to start with, then commence oral A-Bs.'

'I can't give him an injection,' I said, 'I'm not a nurse.'

'Oh! Well, you sure sound like one,' he replied, and thanked me for providing the back-up in the community when there was no medical staff.

I became involved with the medical profession more closely than I had bargained for. Ever since Callum was born I had suffered from recurrent chest infections, eventually to be told I had asthma. That year was particularly bad. I was either just going down with or recovering from another chest infection all the time. Finally I ended up in hospital with pneumonia and a collapsed lung. It seemed that the biggest cause of my problems was an allergy to the cobwebs and dust in the bough shed roof of our home.

While I was in hospital recovering, Rod decided it was a good time to tell me about his latest affair. We had met a woman who lived on a property just outside Katherine, and she and Rod had begun sleeping together. I was upset. I liked the woman and had thought of her as a friend. When I didn't seem to be accommodating enough, he turned on me and hissed, 'Well, don't think you're the only one suffering! We're feeling awful about this too – we hardly got any sleep last night! Everyone's worrying about how *Joanne* will take it. What about how bad *we* feel?!'

I just looked at him in disbelief and walked back to my bed, dragging the drip stand with me. I climbed in and stared at the ceiling. How had we got to this point? Maybe it was my fault for not being brave enough to say '*stop it*', for thinking that if I could live with Rod's terms everything would be alright. It certainly didn't feel alright.

When I came out of hospital and we were back at Bulman, Rod asked me if I'd mind if he and the woman continued to see each other. Well, I thought, there's an improvement. This is the first time I've ever had a choice about being cheated on. This time I didn't care about being subjected to a lecture on faithfulness equating to ownership.

'Yes,' I said. 'I do mind. I don't want you to.' To my surprise, he accepted my answer, and didn't continue the affair.

Rod was becoming quite moody and irritable. At the time I put it down to the constant neck and back pain he lived with, but in hindsight things were changing. He was smoking marijuana more regularly, mainly because it helped him deal with the pain, but again this increase was something that only became obvious with hindsight. Life was a constant adrenaline rush of helicopters, musters, drafting yards, road trains and stock inspectors. Everything seemed to happen on the run, and I felt anxious most of the time, like there were one too many balls in the juggling act. There wasn't a lot of opportunity to sit back and evaluate things like relationships.

In November 1984, Rod's lifelong dream came true. The year before Point Stuart Station, up on the Mary River flood plains some 200 kilometres east of Darwin, had been purchased by the Northern Territory government, divided into four blocks to be used primarily for buffalo grazing and these put up for tender. Rod heard about it and immediately lodged an application. When the successful tenders were announced, only blocks A, C and D had been allocated, and none of them to us. Block B hadn't been allocated to anyone. We weren't too surprised, as there would have been people with a lot more money than us tendering for them, we supposed. Rod went into the Department of Lands to see if there were any more pieces of land coming up, and to make enquiries about what was happening to block B. He spoke to someone who floored him with:

'Look, you didn't hear this from me, but your tender was actually approved in the first place, and then the approval was withdrawn. If I were you I'd take this a bit further.'

Taking it further resulted in Rod having several confrontations with senior public servants. It was clear that something odd was going on, and that we had blundered into the middle of it. Rod told me about it in detail, finishing with: 'There I was, toe to toe with this bloke across his desk, both of us really fired up. Then he says, "You want block B? You can have it. Don't ask any more questions. Now piss off!"'

Just when he thought it was all a lost cause, he was told he had block B. Sixty thousand acres (25,450 hectares) of magnificent flood plain country. It was an absolute dream come true. The contract required the fulfilment of certain covenants, such as boundary fencing, internal paddocks, water supply, yards, livestock and a residence within five years. Once the covenants were completed, then by paying the purchase price of $115 000, the land would be ours. The covenants and purchase prices were different for each of the blocks. It was an unusual arrangement, but one that gave people already working in the industry a chance to get in on the ground floor. It was a big challenge, developing a property from virgin unfenced bush to a fully operational station in just five years, something that every other property in the Territory had taken a generation to achieve, but it was the chance of a lifetime.

With the money that we had saved in the previous three years, Rod immediately bought $70 000 worth of fencing materials to start fulfilling the fencing covenants – the boundary fencing was the immediate priority. We went to see our bank manager in Katherine about a loan.

He looked at our proposal, and frowned. 'Oh, we would have given you a loan, but you've taken out the money you had on term deposit,' said the manager. 'You no longer have any security.'

Rod and I looked at each other, looked at the title deed to 60 000 acres of prime land on the bank manager's desk, and looked at him.

'Fine,' said Rod, picking the document up from the desk. 'We'll go and see your competition across the road.'

We crossed the road, asked to see the manager, and walked out later with a loan big enough to get us well started on the development of the property.

Rod had flown over the block a week before with Paul Josif, but I still hadn't seen it. As Executive Officer of the Northern Land Council southern regions, Paul had been overseeing Richard Ledgar's work at Mt Catt, and we had all become good friends. He was as excited about the new property as we were, and was a great source of support and encouragement for the next few years, as was Richard.

The weekend after we had acquired the bank loan, Ruth and Rolly Shoesmith and Bill and Anne Midgely, our friends from Katherine, drove up with us to the block. We followed a rough little track that left the Shady Camp road halfway along, and wound its way between ironwood, stringy-bark, pink flowered turkey bush and tall milkwoods to arrive at a breathtaking vista of flood plain stretching out to the western horizon. We were standing on the top of a long gentle slope that marked the boundary between the drier, timbered high country and the green carpet of the flood plains. Below us was a line of paper bark trees and bright green grass, crowded with water birds and buffalo. I glanced at Rod, who had a look of sheer bliss on his face, and a grin he couldn't hide.

There was an enormous banyan tree beside us, the grass and weeds beneath it flattened by buffalo and wallabies seeking shade from the midday sun.

'This is where we'll build the house,' said Rod. 'Right beside this tree. Imagine waking up to this every morning . . .'

We lit a fire and boiled a billy right there, our first meal setting the tone for all the ones that followed – shared with friends. Later we walked around exploring, and found a crystal clear stream running the length of a remnant rainforest patch just a couple of hundred metres to the north of our planned homestead site. Water would not be a problem. It was pure and sweet, and flowed from a spring at the top of the rainforest. The forest itself looked like a scene from one of Tolkien's books. Lichen covered trunks with massive buttressed roots towered up to a dark canopy overhead. The forest floor was sandy and littered with a thick carpet of fallen leaves, and the creek threaded its way through this like a river in miniature, with tiny waterfalls and bridges of mossy roots. It was full of darting fish, and the occasional long-necked tortoise, and it was shallow and clear over white sand, perfect for kids to play in.

The forest was also beautifully cool, like walking into a dim, air-conditioned room from the bright glare outside. It was quite small, only about three kilometres in length, and perhaps 200 metres at its widest point. The little creek flowed out into a paperbark swamp, where it disappeared into the plains. This was the hottest, driest time of the year – we were seeing the country at its worst, and it was still beautiful.

Callum, Shaun and I returned to Bulman, while Rod stayed at the block, erecting a rough camp and making many forays into Darwin to deal with covenants and fence line positions at the Lands Department. The covenants were very tight and, amongst the list of developments required in the first five years, demanded that someone be in residence all the time. He employed a team of contractors, one of whom was Bob Thomas, the wonderful old camp cook from Bradshaw Station. Bob had his mate Baker, another old cook and fencer, and a young bloke to help them, and they worked over the wet season and into the new year erecting the boundary fencing and completing the first part of our covenants. I was happy Bob was there, because I knew that at least Rod would eat well, and the camp would be kept clean and well organised. At the top of the rise overlooking the flood plains, beside the giant old banyan, they set up a huge tarpaulin stretched over an A-frame of cut saplings, positioned some camp stretchers and mosquito nets under it, and cleared a space out in front for the cooking fire and the camp ovens. This was the first residence on what was to become Melaleuca Station.

I think it was at least a year before we began calling it Melaleuca. It was either referred to as Point Stuart, or The Block. 'Point Stuart' was confusing, because that was the name of the whole area, and 'The

Block' didn't identify it to anyone but ourselves. Eventually I decided to make a stand, and named it 'Melaleuca' for the many species of paperbark that grew there, and slowly the name slipped into everyone's vocabulary.

Rod came back down to Bulman to catch a last load of buffalo before the 1984 season ended. The animals were gathered in between storms and many boggings, and were sent away on a road train only hours ahead of seven inches of rain. I'd left getting our Christmas presents and food till after the buffalo were gone, so we missed out when the rain came and the river flooded. We had lentils and canned vegetables for Christmas dinner, and for presents the boys had to settle for whatever was left over in the shop. But that was okay, because we had the best present we could imagine – getting our own land.

The day after Christmas we started repairing the catching gear. Working on the vehicles was tough because there was little shade, and everything was roasting – a thermometer reached 54°C laid on the road beside us in the sun. The only respite was when it was actually raining, and then the searing heat would be swapped for steamy dampness. Storms are wonderful when you are watching them from inside a well-roofed house. They're something else again when you can't find a place out of reach of the spray. We unrolled tarpaulins to cover the gaps in the sapling walls, but it was still pretty wet. However, we could cook inside on a little gas burner, and thanks to Tex and Nelly we had electricity for lights and a fan at night. Life seemed pretty good, and when the rain sealed us inside our camp, I felt safely cocooned with my family.

However, isolation has its terrors, and that was brought home to me thoroughly one wet night. We had been watching a video, and when it finished, the two boys were asleep on the bullock hide rug on the floor. The only light came from the TV screen, and I left it like that as I stepped up into the demountable to get their bed ready for them. Suddenly Rod charged in, a child hanging by an arm from each of his hands.

'Quick, grab me the air rifle! There's a death adder on the floor!'

He had been stepping over the boys to go to bed himself when, in the half-light from the TV, he saw a snake curled up against Shaun's back. He took the rifle, held the barrel an inch from the snake's unmoving head and shot it, while he held its twisting body down with the broom. Then he took it outside and beat it to smithereens with the broom, destroying the broom as well.

Nellie Camfoo heard the disturbance and came over to see what was happening. 'That's a really cheeky snake, that one,' she said, looking extremely serious when we told her where Rod found it. 'He'd kill that little boy dead, if he bit him.'

After the fuss was over, I went outside and was sick. I realised that I wouldn't have seen the snake, and that I would have rolled Shaun over onto his back to lift him up, right on top of the snake. It was about 46 centimetres long, a healthy, mature death adder which had come down from the rocky hillside looking for a warm spot out of the rain. Death adders are one of the most dangerous snakes in the world. Shaun was only three years old. If he had been bitten, he would never have survived. It was night time, the airstrip was under water, and the Mainoru River was in flood, blocking the only road to town.

1985 ushered in a confusing year of travel and work – too much of both. Rod headed for Melaleuca as soon as possible to continue the boundary fencing work and begin the next development phase.

The year before, the Katherine manager of the Department of Aboriginal Affairs (DAA) had asked if we would set up a resource centre at Bulman, and so in 1985 Rod and I were employed as manager and secretary of the Gulin Gulin Resource Centre, which was to be responsible for the administration of government grants, in particular a housing grant to build five houses, and to be an official point of contact for the Bulman community. I was also to set up and operate a full-time shop and office, so I closed up my little garden shed and arranged the building of a large shed to house the new community-owned store and the resource centre office.

Earlier in the year Rod had helped some of the local Bulman men organise their own bull catching operation. Kenneth Murray's older brother, whose name I can't write because he has since died, was the mainstay, and had been since we first met him in 1983. He was a natural leader, a truly good man, and was looked up to by the entire community. He was a big man, with a big heart and a great sense of humour. He and Rod were very close, and spent a lot of time together.

They worked out a plan to set the Bulman men up managing their own bull catching contract. The profits would stay in the community, and the men would be employed. We staked them some money to get started, and Rod came down from Melaleuca at the beginning of the season to help them set up their first muster and get vehicles ready. They repaid us our money out of their first load of buffalo, and ran a very successful operation for the rest of the season, almost entirely on their own. I looked after the paperwork for them, and ordered the helicopters and the road trains. Rod came down occasionally when they had any major breakdowns, but basically they were doing it on their own.

In addition to running the resource centre office and keeping the books for the bull catchers, I was supervising Callum's first year of schoolwork for a few hours a day, training some girls to work in the shop, keeping the books, and managing the shop itself. I also had to write lots of reports, organise the building of the houses, pay wages, and attend meetings with the Gulin Gulin board of directors. And somewhere in this I tried to keep an eye on Shaun, who luckily for me was a self contained little fellow who was usually happy to follow me around and amuse himself on the sidelines on the days Callum attended the school. At nights I would try and catch up on our own bookkeeping, and usually fell into bed at about nine o'clock, utterly exhausted.

I missed Rod very much, but it did me a lot of good to have to rely on my own skills without him there. After a couple of months of doing all the work, and only getting the secretary's lower wage (Rod was only paid when he was actually at Bulman), I went to see the head of DAA in Katherine.

'I think I should be getting the manager's salary, because I'm doing the job of manager as well as secretary,' I said to the director. 'You can pay Rod the secretary's wage instead when he's at Bulman. I think that's fair.'

He looked at me sideways, and said: 'But you're female. The men at Bulman won't have a female manager. Besides, there are no other female resource centre managers.'

'I've already talked to the committee about it, and they don't have a problem with it.'

I stuck to my guns, and eventually he relented, but he was still sure that there would be difficulties out at Bulman. A month later we were at a resource centre conference at Daly River, and I had the pleasure of catching his eye when I turned up late to be greeted by all the Bulman committee men with, 'Hey, here's our boss!'

Fate had decided that we weren't going to do any of this the easy way. Rod had been out fencing at Melaleuca in early March 1985 when he arrived back at his camp to find that fourteen summonses had been left on the table. All were related to the old allegations from Fitzroy, back in 1981. Now, instead of being a civil matter, they had become criminal charges. The police had investigated these matters in 1981 and no charges had ever been laid. It bothered us that almost as soon as we moved onto our block on the Mary River floodplains, these charges suddenly reappeared. Rod felt that they were somehow related to his confrontation over the allocation of the lease. Whether improperly inspired or not, the revival of these charges had a dramatic effect on our lives from that moment on.

The charges were mostly related to pet food shooting, with Fitzroy's owner claiming that we had not been permitted to shoot pet food; that all the meat was bull meat and not horse or donkey; and that all the pet meat we had shot came from Fitzroy Station. The others were alleged cattle theft, about the cattle we had informed the owner we were sending off in order to be paid some of the money the station owed us. None of the charges were true, but they set us on a long and arduous course to prove it.

When you live in town, and the time of a scheduled meeting is changed, it's an inconvenience. When you have to travel 200 kilometres to get into town for that appointment, and have to line up someone to look after the place while you're gone, it's a major disruption. Scheduled court appointments were frequently changed at the last minute, meaning Rod had wasted the best part of two days, costing us time and money.

The case was to be heard in the Darwin Magistrates Court in September, putting Rod under intense pressure for the next few months. If he was found guilty he could go to gaol.

Throughout this time I was sick with chest infections so often that finally I was tested for tuberculosis. I was given a Mantoux test, an injection on the inside of the forearm. A red lump appears a day or so later, and its size gives an indication of a positive or a negative result. There was too much to do at Bulman for me to stay in town to get the test results checked by the doctor, so I said I'd ring him the next day. Dr Paul was our regular AirMed doctor, and appreciated the importance of privacy in the bush. Having a consultation over the radio is a bit like holding a private conversation over loudspeakers at a football match.

'Just phone through the measurement of the red area, and the lump, if there is any,' he said when I saw him in Katherine. 'We don't have to discuss it over VJY. You don't want everyone who knows you thinking you've got TB, do you!'

Dr Paul wasn't there when I called the next day, so I spoke to someone else: 'I have to give you a Mantoux reaction measurement to pass on to Dr Paul,' I told the doctor, trying to be circumspect. 'It's about five centimetres across, and there's a large red lump in the middle. Over.'

'Oh, that's a positive reaction! You definitely have TB. You'll have to come straight back into town for treatment. How soon can you get here?'

I was dumbfounded. I was also angry. This doctor had just told the whole VJY network I had tuberculosis. So much for confidentiality.

'Thanks a lot for that public announcement,' I snapped. 'I've just got home from Katherine, and I'm not about to turn around and go back in. When will Dr Paul be back? I want to talk to him!'

I spoke to Dr Paul later that day on the radio-telephone up at the old manager's house. He calmed me down and said the reaction didn't necessarily mean I had TB, but that I had probably been exposed to someone with the disease. However, I did have to go back in for testing, and the boys would also have to be screened. It turned out that I didn't have TB, but I continued to get sick.

# 14

# Melaleuca

Throughout 1985 Rod came and went between Bulman and Melaleuca every couple of months, and in between the boys and I would make the long trek north. It was a 1600-kilometre round trip, a lot of it over bad roads, but we had agreed we had to make this effort so that our relationship would stand up to the time apart. We were in regular contact through VJY, and occasionally through the radio-telephone, and we wrote to each other as well.

Sometimes, if we were going to be meeting up again soon, he would take Callum back to the station with him. Shaun, being only three years old, would watch them go, feeling very sad to be left behind because he was too small. One day Rod was about to leave, this time by himself, and Shaun was sitting watching him load up the bull catcher, looking sadder and sadder.

Rod glanced up at me with a raised eyebrow, I nodded, and Rod said to Shaun: 'Hey, mate, do you think you could come and give me a hand at the block for a few days?'

I can still see his little face, trying very hard not to smile too wide, so that he looked grown up and important enough to go to work with Dad. A week later, Callum and I followed them up. Shaun was a proper man now, he told me, and he would look after me when Rod was away, because he knew how to do all kinds of things. He showed me how they washed in the creek using sand, and delivered all this information in a very deep, gruff voice.

Every so often we would arrange to drop the kids for the night with friends in Darwin, and book into a suite in one of the classier hotels, just so we could spend some time on our own. One time when we were meeting in Darwin, Rod said he had a surprise for me that evening but wouldn't tell me what it was. We went shopping for some clothes for me to wear, and he was very loving and attentive all afternoon. With such a build-up I was expecting a candlelit dinner in a beautiful restaurant, followed by something incredibly romantic. We drove off in the car, waving goodbye to the boys, who were staying with Rod's sister Christine and her husband, and pulled up in the car park of a sports stadium.

'Here we are!' said Rod, smiling broadly, looking very pleased with himself. It was a boxing match. A boxer from down south was in Darwin for some kind of title fight – I can't even remember his name – and this was my big night out! I just tried to look suitably grateful and impressed, and spent the evening trying not to feel too out of place in my glad rags.

The worst part about leaving my little house at Bulman for any length of time was that the local wildlife tended to move in. One time the boys and I returned after several weeks' absence to find that a mob of camp dogs had been living in our place. It was disgusting. There was rubbish, old bones, and dog crap from one end of it to the other, and it smelled beyond belief.

Callum's teacher was coming out on a patrol the next day, so I set to work madly tossing out the wrecked stuff, and cleaning and scrubbing what I could. The next morning I was standing in the annexe, looking around and trying to identify a terrible stench. I had searched everywhere for its origin, cleaned under everything, even raked underneath the demountable in case some animal had been half eaten under it, but found nothing. Just as I heard the teacher's plane overhead, I glanced up and saw what looked like the frayed end of a rope. Or the frayed end of a cat. That was definitely where the smell was coming from.

I ran outside, grabbed the first bloke I saw, and said: 'Quick! The schoolteacher's here, and there's a dead cat on my roof! Can you get it off for me while I go and meet the plane?'

He promptly delegated the job to a couple of young boys standing nearby, and I took off. I dallied as long as I could at the airstrip, chatting to the pilot, and waiting for the plane to taxi down its length and take off again, before driving the teacher slowly back to our camp. We arrived just in time to see the remains of the cat being scraped into a plastic bag, which only intensified the stench. I made a weak joke about the hazards of life in the bush and hurriedly sprayed the area with some floral car deodorant in an attempt to cover up the awful smell. Dead cat is one thing. Dead cat with floral car deodorant is something else again. We gathered up the books and went down to the river for the rest of the day.

By August there was 70 kilometres of fencing erected at Melaleuca, and Rod was able to start catching some buffalo. He had met Greg Keogh, a keen young bull catcher from Humpty Doo, and offered him some work. Greg and his wife Josie drove out to Melaleuca to have a look at the prospects. As they stood beside the big banyan tree looking out over the flood plain at the buffalo feeding out across the flats, Rod said to Greg: 'What do you reckon? I'll pay you twenty-five dollars a head for everything we catch, you supply your own catcher and look after it. I'll provide the truck and the rest of the gear.'

Greg had just come back into town from an eight-month stint at Urapunga. Catching jobs were getting harder to find, and all the places he'd worked were a long way out in the scrub. The most he'd ever been paid was $10 a head. He frowned for a bit, considering the offer, and said: 'I'll just go and talk to Josie about it.' He walked over to where Josie was sitting in the shade, and his face cracked into a huge grin.

'Can you believe this? Beautiful country, all the buffalo you could want, an hour's drive from home, and twenty-five fuckin' dollars a head! Shit!'

Greg walked back over to Rod after carefully rearranging his face, and said, 'Yeah, mate, we'll give her a go.'

They started almost straight away, catching fifteen buffalo the first day. We didn't have any bionic arms then (a mechanical arm operated by a winch, to hold buffalo against the side of a bull catcher – invented by Kal Carrick), and all the bulls were rolled with the catchers and pinned under the bull bar while an offsider jumped out and strapped the bull's legs. Josie, who was pregnant, drove the pick-up truck. The first muster was a boundary muster with Swim Creek Station, and involved swimming buffalo across the Mary River, pushed by the helicopters. The fishermen's nets were in the way, and the buffalo had to be pushed upstream away from them before they could come across. Angliss in Darwin was the only meatworks operating at the time, as Mudginberri was closed down with an industrial dispute. Jay Pendarvis, Mudjinberri's owner, had run afoul of the unions by employing his meatworkers on negotiated contracts, and they picketed his meatworks for two years until Jay finally won a court case which attracted national attention in a landmark decision.

Greg was very impressed with the old fellows who were doing the fencing, old Bob and Baker. Bob refused to take any payment from Rod before he had inspected their work in person. It was all timber work, all the holes bored out with an auger, every rail adzed into shape and fitted into the posts, all the post holes dug by hand and the posts rammed in place with crowbars. So they drove around the entire line, checking every strainer assembly, post, rail, twitch and join until Bob's sense of honour was satisfied and Rod handed over a cheque.

'I thought, what a grand old bloke, a real, old style sense of honour in the bush,' Greg told me later. 'Then the next night they grabbed my bull catcher and went to the Bark Hut and brought back a pallet of beer on the back of it.'

The three fencers took themselves off into the bush behind the main camp, and began drinking their way through an entire pallet of hot beer. On a visit to the camp, Greg thought he'd do the old fellows a favour, and cooled a dozen beers down in his esky for them. When he presented the cold cans to them, old Bob placed his next to the fire to warm them up. 'Cold beer hurts me teeth,' he said.

After ten days Rod went to see them, and told them the break was over and they had to start work again soon. He would give them two more days, but they had to come back to work then. No problem, they said and waved him off. The blokes were still very drunk, and looked a bit hostile as Rod and Greg drove up a couple of days later. The youngest member of the crew, a solid young fellow about twenty-five or thirty, was looking very much the worse for wear. The two old blokes had given him a flogging, and were eyeing off Rod and Greg as if it would be no trouble to give them a touch-up as well.

'I'll give you two days to sober up, and if you're not back at work by then, I'll take an axe to this lot,' Rod said, indicating the remains of the pallet, which still had several dozen cartons of beer left on it. He and Greg drove off, with Greg wondering just how well he and Rod would do if the blokes turned nasty.

Two days later, still no workers, so Rod and Greg returned to Bob and Baker's camp.

'You're not back at work yet,' said Rod.

'We're not movin' till we've finished the beer,' muttered Bob in a threatening voice, staring Rod in the eye.

Rod just nodded, picked up the axe and smashed up the entire remaining beer supply. 'It's finished now,' he said. 'See you tomorrow.'

They turned up the next morning, and the fencing continued.

In September 1985 Rod's case was heard in the Magistrates Court. The boys and I travelled up to Darwin, and waited in the hotel for the outcome. We were completely unprepared for the verdict. Our lawyer Patrick Loftus had been confident it would be thrown out by the magistrate, but was puzzled why the Crown seemed to be spending so much money on what looked like a civil matter. They were flying witnesses in from all over Australia, and from the US, and almost all of them turned out to be witnesses in favour of our side of the argument. The Crown's case looked like it was crumbling, and Patrick was sure that most of the charges would be thrown out, with only one or two sent up to trial. He was flabbergasted when all fourteen charges were sent up to the Supreme Court. He turned to Rod and asked him who he'd upset. Outside the court a helicopter pilot we knew, who had been called as a witness for the other side, said to Rod: 'I don't know what all this is about, but I hear it's political. I wish you luck.'

A couple of months after the Magistrates court appearance, Rod had to go to court again. Some time earlier, we had been advised by a solicitor to start up another company in a measure to try and protect Melaleuca if Rod was found guilty at the end of the Fitzroy case. In the meantime our focus changed, the new company never traded, and we forgot about it. Then we received a summons to go to court for not putting the necessary paperwork in to the Taxation Office. I had only just returned to Bulman again after two trips up to Melaleuca in quick succession, and was trying to catch up on work when Rod called from a public phone.

'How did the court case go?' I asked him. He had gone into town the day before to deal with it, and when we'd talked about it together a few days earlier, it seemed like it would be a nuisance, but no more than that.

'Yeah, it was okay. Judge just gave me a lecture about keeping better records or something. Do you think you can come up for a few days?'

I had barely unpacked the car from the last trip. 'Rod, I've only just got back! I've been away so long, and there's so much to do here. I can't come now. Maybe in a couple of weeks?'

I was tired, and feeling overwhelmed by the mountain of work waiting for me in the office. The prospect of another 1600-kilometre round trip just then was the last thing I needed. Rod sounded all right, said he was all right, but it was difficult to tell just what he was feeling. Telephones are not always the best form of communication. The next time we got together, he was unhappy with me, and attacked me for not coming when he'd asked.

'I needed you!' he stormed. 'All I wanted was for you to come up, and you couldn't be bothered! It was terrible in court . . . it was just like the last time all over again . . .'

He was really upset. Apparently the judge had railed at him for being careless and lax over the forgotten company records, and tore strips off him in front of the court. Coming so soon after the Fitzroy matter, and especially in the light of that being sent up to the Supreme Court, the judge's words cut deeply, and Rod fell in a bit of a hole afterwards. I felt awful. I hadn't realised how badly he'd been feeling about it, or I probably would have gone back again. It didn't matter. He just accused me of being cold and callous, not caring about him. It was to become a source of bitterness for him, and he brought it up many times when he was moody and depressed. Our relationship was gradually changing.

Callum, Shaun and I were back at Melaleuca in early December 1985. My sister and brother-in-law, Leonie and Craig Hemsworth, were coming to take over the Resource Centre from me in January, so we took a break to spend Christmas with Rod.

I was looking forward to us being a family again, but Rod was very stressed and bad tempered. The previous year had been difficult, and

I accepted that his frequent bouts of bad temper were due to many factors, but I had expected things to improve when we were all together again. He acted as if I'd been holidaying at Bulman all year, not bearing as much of a load as he had. He insisted we go out fencing every day whether it rained or not. It was the middle of the wet season, and the temperature was close to 40°C by 10 am. Everyone else had left by then, and everything felt bleak and sad. Rod wouldn't let up on the work for anything, and we were loading up the Toyota on Christmas morning to go out fencing for the day, when Paul Josif and his girlfriend turned up unexpectedly, bearing eskies full of food and cold drinks. Rod was persuaded then to take a day off, considering it was actually Christmas Day. It was good to see a smile back on his face, but it was disheartening to think I couldn't put it there.

The boys and I returned to Bulman when the Hemsworths arrived in the new year. Leonie and Craig had two sons now, five year old Luke, and Christopher who was three years old, and were looking forward to living in the Territory again. The six of us crammed into the caravan which had replaced our old demountable and annexe the previous year, and I set about introducing them to the Bulman people and explaining the Resource Centre operations. Three weeks later, we headed off down the corrugated road to Katherine for the last time. I had said my goodbyes to everyone, and I think I cried most of the way to town. The whole idea of Melaleuca, and of my family being able to be together again, was exciting and wonderful, but I was still sad to be leaving behind a community that had taken us in and made us feel like we belonged there.

After years of moving from one property to another, having a place of our own was wonderful. It wasn't much to brag about, just a large tarpaulin stretched over an A-frame of saplings, with camp stretchers under mosquito nets to sleep on – the same camp that had served the fencers the year before. It was awkward when it rained: no matter where you are under a tarp, you always seem to get wet. The rain hammers down close above your head, and if it's not dripping down your back, it's blowing in at the sides. There can be something very dismal about sitting under a piece of canvas way out in the bush, with the rain coming down so hard it's like being inside a drum at a military parade. You suddenly seem to have walls – very wet, white ones you can't see through. You scurry around lifting everything – such as kids – up off the ground to keep them dry, while a torrent of muddy water swirls around your feet. We dug ditches around the camp in an effort to direct the run-off away from us, but when the rain is truly monsoonal, you just have to pick up your feet and wait for it to stop.

Cooking outdoors in the wet season is a real challenge. The campfire had a solid windbreak, and another sheet of corrugated iron across the top to keep out some of the rain, but it was only a gesture if it really came down hard. Sometimes it was just too wet to do anything, and we had to be content with bread and canned food, and a drink of water instead of a billy of tea. Eating dinner before the mosquitoes carried you off was another challenge, and if you weren't back home in time to cook before the sun went down, both the cooking and the eating were done in a mad slapping frenzy. We bought a fourteen metre demountable in February, something that was mosquito proof, and this was to be our temporary house until we could build the proper homestead.

We used the demountable as a bedroom for the four of us, a schoolroom during the day, and a bug-proof dining room for everyone to eat in at night. Everyone else slept in tents scattered around it, with a flash tent for visiting dignitaries such as grandparents.

Callum and Shaun were happy. They didn't find anything unusual or difficult. I suppose they had lived in so many different kinds of accommodation in their short lives that they accepted wherever they found themselves, so long as Mum or Dad was around too.

On 14 February 1986, I wrote to my parents that we had started work on the house. Because we couldn't afford to build the house in one go we were compromising, and building it in stages. The first stage was to put a roof over the demountable and a verandah in front of it, which would form the front half of the house later on. Water wasn't yet connected to the homestead site, and every couple of days we had to load a 44-gallon drum in the back of the ute, drive it down to the creek about 500 metres away, and fill it with a bucket. This was for cooking and drinking. Bath time meant a visit to the creek with soap and a towel, stepping lively to try and dodge the clouds of mosquitoes. If we were going to be pouring concrete, we needed a better water supply, so we ran poly pipe about two kilometres to the spring, and set up a pump. The budget didn't stretch to a holding tank at the house site, so we only had water while the pump was on.

We cut and barked ironwood posts out of the bush, and concreted them into deep holes around the demountable, and with the help of Rod's then brother-in-law Peter, erected a roof over the lot. The roof extended outwards about four metres to provide for a verandah. The next job was to lay the concrete slab underneath.

Peter knew a few concretors who loved pig shooting, so a satisfactory barter was arranged where the concretors brought out their gear and some extra labourers, we invited a few more friends, and all of us spent a couple of weekends setting up formwork, digging the foundations, and mixing and pouring a large concrete slab by hand, using little concrete mixers and wheelbarrows. Just before the slab was poured, Greg Keogh came out and set up the plumbing for the bathroom which was to be built at one end of the verandah. When he wasn't catching bulls, Greg was a qualified plumber, but he much preferred chasing buffalo to digging trenches and laying pipes. His payment was a buffalo calf. I thought the barter system was wonderful. In later years when we were in financial trouble with the Government and the bank, I used to fantasise about paying our debts with a cheque written on the flanks of a big bull buffalo . . .

Rod and I continued with the fencing. I would spend the morning with the boys supervising their school work while Rod worked on his own, and then we would join him out on the fence line for the rest of the day. Duane Fishlock and his wife-to-be, Jane Michell, came to stay for a couple of months. Jane was the eldest daughter of Val and Graham Michell, great friends of ours from Maud Creek Station near Katherine. Duane worked with Rod and me on the fencing, and Jane helped Callum and Shaun with their lessons, and studied a correspondence course herself. They camped on the back of their truck, under the big banyan tree. Duane continued to come up and do some bull catching with Rod at the end of each season for the next few years, and did a lot of fencing on Melaleuca the following year as well.

Greg Keogh came back out at the end of the wet season ready for another go. He brought some mates with him, Chris Penhall and Richard Lovegrove, two other young blokes from Humpty Doo whose idea of bliss was being allowed to hurtle across the flood plains after buffalo. Being paid was practically just a bonus. Rod worked out a contract with them where they had responsibility for setting up the yards and hiring the helicopter, and supplied their own catchers, loading ramp, and hessian for the wings, in return for 40 per cent of the meatworks price of the buffalo. We would supply the portable yards and the truck, and retain the remaining 60 per cent of the proceeds.

The men began work in April 1986, and the first muster was called Terry's Yard, to mark the arrival of Greg and Josie's firstborn son whose birth date had dictated the timing of the muster. A few weeks later Josie came out to Melaleuca with the newest little bull catcher, and they set their camp up on Number One Billabong, about five kilometres away from the homestead site. Richard went on to another job after a few months, but Chris and Greg mustered for the rest of the season.

April also brought us some very welcome visitors – our dear friends John and Lenore Humphreys were back in Australia for a few months. John had agreed to do a locum for a doctor in Katherine, who in turn was looking after John's house and practice in Oxford. They came out to Melaleuca with their three children for a short stay before heading down to Katherine. John's eyes lit up when he saw the flood plains for the first time. He knew how much this land meant to Rod, and the two of them spent a lot of time driving around the property, just looking.

The plumbing might have been in the concrete slab and ready to go, but it was a long wait before I had a functioning bathroom. In the meantime I bought a second hand bathtub in Darwin, stood it up on blocks at the bathroom end of the verandah, and attached some poly pipe to the outlet to carry away the waste water. Some old tarps strung between the posts granted a little privacy, and when the pump was running, I could have a real bath!

Callum and Shaun thought this was the best fun ever – their own private creek – and filled it with plastic crocodiles and tortoises, and occasionally the real thing. A visitor had been taken to admire the bathtub by the boys one afternoon, and was about to pat the lifelike tortoise bobbing near the surface, when Shaun said: 'It might bite you if you touch it!'

She snatched her hand back in fright. She'd thought the tortoise was a toy, and gave the plastic crocodile on the ledge a wide berth.

But we still needed a toilet. I thought it would hurry things up if I just dug the hole for the septic tank myself. The new toilet was set into the slab, and all the plumbing was in place. It just needed a septic tank to connect to. And a transpiration trench of course . . . I needed a hole six foot by six foot, by about six foot deep, so I marked out the site one morning and started digging. About a foot down I hit coffee rock, and had to get the crowbar. After that I got smart, and whenever I knew someone was coming out from town, I would make sure I was down in that hole, crowbarring away. The visitors would watch with interest for a minute or two, and then of course offer to take over from me for a while. I especially liked it when the visitors were government employees – your taxes at work!

My parents were coming to stay, and the toilet wouldn't be completed. There were just too many buffalo to be caught to worry about domestic matters like bodily functions and indoor plumbing. However, I couldn't picture my mum staggering around in the bush with a shovel and a roll of toilet paper, so I did what every good daughter does in this situation. I built a nice little pit toilet away from the house, just on the edge of the bush. I dug a good deep hole, found half a 44-gallon drum to prop over it, cut a hole in it with the oxy-acetylene, and fixed a toilet seat on the top. A few star pickets and some metres of hessian pinched from the buffalo yards, and I had a neat little loo. A twist of wire and a stick made a fine toilet roll holder. The only thing I hadn't considered was that I had erected the structure right on a wallaby path.

This weakness in the plan became apparent when the dogs scared up a wallaby one day while Mum was visiting the toilet. The wallaby was doing ninety when it hit the hessian wall across its accustomed escape route. Shrieks from Mum and hysterical laughter from her grandsons brought Dad and me running outside. I'm not sure who got the biggest shock, Mum, or the wallaby when he got tangled up around Mum's feet. Fortunately for her grandsons, once Mum realised it wasn't actually a buffalo attacking her, she could see the funny side of it. However, she made them tie up the dogs the next time she went to the loo.

Finally, I did get a proper toilet. There was no way I was going to spend another wet season digging holes for myself and two little boys amid the mosquitoes in the rain. When I watched the back hoe ripping into the hole I had spent so much effort on, and tearing out the transpiration trench in about twenty minutes, I almost didn't mind the wasted blisters. At least it was happening!

When it was finally hooked up, I dragged a bemused Rod over to the smallest room. 'This is a transforming moment in your life, Rod,' I said. 'Listen to this . . .' and I pressed the button of the toilet. 'That is the roar of civilisation. From now on, shovels are for digging *post* holes.'

I was still cooking our meals on an open fire off the end of the verandah, dodging wet season storms and a billion mosquitoes. The rain eventually stopped as the dry season arrived, but the mosquitoes, which bred enthusiastically in the warm, slow waters on the flood plains, were even worse. You could wave your hands around and hit them in the air as thick as raindrops. It was possible to eat outside on the verandah during the day, but in the evening we were driven indoors. Chris Penhall earned my undying gratitude one day when he roared into camp with a gas stove strapped onto the back of his ute. He had been demolishing a house in Humpty Doo, and it had an old but working stove to be removed and dumped, so he loaded it up and brought it out to me, along with an old Hills hoist clothesline, so I could pull down the miles of rope I had strung up between trees. A tiny part of Melaleuca became forever and unashamedly suburban the day the Hills hoist went in.

Chris, like Greg and Josie, became as close as family to us. He was always laughing at something, always saw the lighter side of a situation, even when everyone else was down in the dumps. He and Greg had known each other since primary school, and were forever entertaining us with stories about growing up in Darwin. They were both classic Darwin boys – rough around the edges but warm hearted and generous, extremely hard working, able to see the funny side of any situation, and armed with more war stories by the time they were twenty than most men acquired in their whole lives.

They were complete opposites. Greg was over six feet tall, clean shaven with crewcut hair with a strong, powerful physique. He had a direct, no-nonsense manner which, coupled with a loud voice, could seem aggressive if you didn't know him well. But he was quick to see the funny side of anything, and had a laugh that started in his boots. In fact Greg's laugh was the first thing about him that Rod described to me when he told me he'd hired him. Chris was short, solid and had long blond hair, a thick full beard, and twinkling eyes that disappeared behind round, rosy cheeks when he laughed, which was often. He reckoned he had turned down more requests to play Santa Claus at Christmas parties than he'd had hot dinners. Both men were fantastic with Callum and Shaun, and spent a lot of time talking to them when they were around. As well as bull catching and mustering buffalo, they helped with fencing, building the house, collecting rocks for the walls, concreting, eradicating mimosa – they were part of every stage of the development of the station.

Greg's wife Josie was a huge asset too. Originally from Tasmania, she had moved to Darwin in her teens. She and Greg had met at high school here and had been together ever since. She coped with the demands of a new baby and looking after the camp for Greg and Chris as though she had been born to it, and had a lovely relaxed attitude to everything. Nothing ever seemed to upset her, and she was always happy to pitch in and help with whatever needed to be done, whether it was preparing a meal, or loading a road train in the middle of the night.

Rod shared a sense of the ridiculous with Greg and Chris, and it didn't go astray on the rest of us either. We all became addicted to board games for a few months, playing games like *Trivial Pursuit* and *Risk* till late at night. One morning we were planning to run a yard up at Deep Lake. To catch the buffalo here we had to get in position several hours before the buffalo wandered out of the trees and down to the edge of the water to feed on the green grass. So to while away the time, we took a board game with us. The stock inspector turned up a little early to check the buffalo, arriving before we had even run the yard. He was dumbfounded to find four burly bull catchers (and a couple of less burly ones) crouched in the grass under a shady tree, intently rolling dice and moving pieces around a board, playing *Risk*.

My brother Rob visited later that year, and was so taken by the excitement of catching buffalo that he stayed for two months. He went home at the end of the season, bought himself an old short wheel base Toyota, and arrived back the following year ready to start. Within an hour of him arriving, Rod, Greg and Chris had him outside, and had stripped the vehicle down to the bull catching basics – cabin off, doors off, bull bar strengthened up and old tyres cobb 'n' 'coed on to it. I don't think Rob had even had time to take his bags out of it!

Rod still had contractual obligations at Mt Catt, and periodically would go down to organise the next stage of the fencing for the buffalo domestication project. During these times, if Greg and Chris weren't mustering, we would work on building the walls around the verandah.

We had opted to build rock walls rather than buy concrete blocks for the outside of the house, and there was an abundance of good material on the ridges not far from the homestead site. The walls were to be 600 mm high, and 225 mm thick, and would run around the edge of the concrete slab between the ironwood posts. Flywire between the top of the rock walls and the roof would close in the verandah and make it insect proof. To secure the house against rain and cyclones, Rod designed heavy steel shutters to hang from the top beams between the posts. These would stay open on steel supports and the height could be adjusted to let in light and breezes.

I hired form work from town to make the job of building a rock wall simpler. Once the form work was set in place, we laid a bed of concrete down inside, and then began placing rocks carefully in between the two sides, making sure the best and flattest rock faces were against the forms. Then the gaps were filled in with concrete and small rocks. Once the concrete had set firmly enough, the form work was pulled off, and we'd scrape back some of the mortar to expose the faces of the rocks, and scrub them with brushes and sponges to clean them up before the concrete set completely. It looked fantastic. Whenever we had a spare few hours, we would go out rock collecting, one person driving the tractor, while the rest of us walked ahead picking up suitable rocks and tossing them into the lowered tractor bucket.

The bathroom was the first objective. We ended up with a very grand looking bathtub, set in rock with a step up into it, also built of rock. It was level with the top of the rock wall, and had a magnificent view out across the flood plains, but with only fly wire on the windows, it wasn't exactly private, so baths were usually taken at night with the lights out. It was finally finished one day in early October

1986 when my brother Rob and Chris, who was a plumber like Greg, hooked up all the plumbing, and tiled the bathroom as a surprise for my birthday when I had gone to town for the day.

In that first year we'd become aware of a serious weed problem on the station. *Mimosa pigra* is a virulent noxious pest that infiltrates flood plains and watercourses, turning good country into an impenetrable, thorny desert useful only to feral pigs for hiding in. Each plant can produce up to 90 000 seeds a year. It grows very quickly into a tall, woody, heavily thorned shrub and it has no natural predators apart from buffalo grazing on young plants. It had been introduced to the Top End in the late 1800s as a novelty plant, interesting for its ability to close up its leaves when touched. By the 1940s it was recorded as far south as Adelaide River, but wasn't recognised as a weed problem for a few more years. It thrived on the black soil flood plains, being able to tolerate saline conditions and seasonal flooding.

There were some infestations on Melaleuca, and Rod had been spot-treating them with a soil sterilant called Velpar in early 1985. In April of that year Cyclone Gretel dumped 58 centimetres of rain on Melaleuca in two days. The sudden flush of water spread the mimosa seed far and wide, turning what seemed at first like a reasonably manageable infestation into an explosion we couldn't imagine. Here was another expensive problem. We were horrified at the idea of aerial spraying the flood plains with herbicide, and contacted the Environment Centre to come out and give us their opinion, thinking there must be some other way to get rid of this invasive weed. Lyn Allen, the coordinator, was as stunned as we were by the extent of the growth. We drove around taking photos and feeling completely overwhelmed. Even Lyn said we had no choice but to spray.

There was one plant that indirectly benefited from the mimosa spraying. Rod had left a couple of young blokes working at the station one time when he had to go to Bulman for a week. He'd given them instructions on how to use the Velpar, and left them to work their way around the edges of the flood plain, treating individual outbreaks as they went. He came back a week later and the 20-litre drum was empty, but Rod couldn't see any evidence of where they had used the herbicide. A couple of weeks later, the magnificent old banyan tree beside the camp began dropping its leaves, and within a week was completely bare. Rod immediately thought that the boys had just emptied the drum of herbicide under the banyan so that it would look like they'd been busy, when instead they'd just had a holiday for a week.

He raced into Darwin the same day and bought several litres of seaweed fertiliser, mixing up 44-gallon drums of solution and tipping it out around the old tree in an effort to save its life. We must have poured about 500 gallons of seaweed solution onto that tree over the next couple of years, until one day someone who knew more about banyans than we did pointed out that they actually lost their leaves once, sometimes twice a year, and that the old tree was not dying as Rod had believed. The bloke at the hardware store must have wondered just what were we growing out there to require so much fertiliser.

Mimosa, fencing, building, money worries, catching buffalo, all this kept us completely occupied, but the looming court case was still hovering like a vulture throughout. No matter what we did, or how busy we were, it was always there in the background, like a monster under the bed. By August 1986 it had cost us over $5000 in legal fees, and didn't look like slowing down any time soon.

Now that we knew we would be fighting in the Supreme Court, we needed a barrister to represent Rod. Kevin Murray QC, from Sydney, agreed to take on the case. Murray's fees were normally $2000 per day, plus airfares and expenses, but the case had caught his interest, and he agreed to do it for fifty head of buffalo, no matter how long it took. He said it would make an interesting story for his memoirs. Patrick Loftus, who had previously been our solicitor, was now a barrister, and was to act as Murray's junior.

We booked rooms in town in mid August 1986, and moved in for a few days, leaving Callum and Shaun with Greg and Josie. Murray arrived in a dramatic swirl, barking out orders left, right and centre and leaving Rod and me feeling like complete babes in the wood. He was scathing about the charges and the case the Crown had, and declared it would be wrapped up in twenty-four hours. Hearing this my heart sank. No one could be this much of a prima donna and be any good, I thought.

That night Rod and I talked about what would happen if he went to gaol. He was tormented by the thought of being locked up: 'You know I couldn't stay there, Jo. I can't be locked up in a cell. I wouldn't hurt anyone, but I'd have to get away. I'd have to break out and go and live in the bush somewhere . . .'

We made vague plans about putting a cache of survival gear in a place where Rod could find it if he needed to, but that was as far as it went. I don't think my imagination could stretch to seeing Rod in gaol, and we had too many other, more immediate worries.

The first day in the Supreme Court was 19 August 1986. Rod, Patrick, Kevin Murray and Bruce McCormack, who was now our solicitor since Patrick had gone to the Bar, headed off for the court-house while I stayed behind in the hotel room, pacing the floor and wondering what was going to happen to us. They were back by lunchtime, Murray, Bruce and Patrick beaming from ear to ear, Rod looking completely shellshocked. The judge had dismissed eleven of the fourteen charges straight away. After a hurried conference early the next morning, the prosecution decided it was not going to present any evidence, and so the judge instructed the jury to find Rod not guilty on the three remaining charges. So all the witnesses, including those who had been flown in from all over the country and the US again, went home without having to say a word.

For eighteen months we had been living with the possibility that Rod might actually go to gaol. It was a salient lesson in keeping written records, and not making verbal agreements. But at what a price. Financially it was bad enough. It had cost us over $15 000 in legal fees, but that didn't take into account the lost time, and especially not the mental trauma and stress. We could have sued the government to claim back some of what we had been forced to spend, but it just wasn't worth trying.

Rod was severely affected by the court case. His greatest fear in life was of being locked up, unable to be in the bush. He had hardly slept a full night in over six months, had lost weight from a frame that had none to spare, and worry lines had etched themselves permanently into place around his eyes and mouth.

After the court case was over and the dust settled, I packed Rod off to Timor for a holiday. Kupang had recently reopened to tourists for the first time since the Indonesian invasion of East Timor in 1976, and I thought that it might be good therapy for him to have to cope with a foreign language and culture for a few days, and perhaps help him put things into some kind of perspective. He had been getting quite paranoid in the last few months, seeing plots and secret agendas in every letter or communication we had with anyone in government. He badly needed a break. It was also the cheapest holiday I could send him on, but we couldn't afford for both of us to go.

Somehow in spite of all the distraction of the court case, we had managed to muster over 1500 buffalo, poison a lot of mimosa and clear most of the fence lines for our future paddocks. We had also made a good start on our homestead, and had a reasonably mosquito-free place to live in. While Rod was in Timor, the rest of us built the stone walls around the verandah on the concrete slab.

The buffalo blocks, like all pastoral leases in the NT, had to comply with the Bovine Tuberculosis Eradication Campaign (BTEC). The campaign had been around for a while, and Rod had been one of the first managers to begin a tuberculosis testing program in the early eighties at Fitzroy Station. In the more closely settled parts of Australia, where farms were smaller and easier to control, implementing a TB testing program was not difficult. Cattle were in smaller paddocks, and generally quieter and easier to handle in comparison to the vast reaches of outback cattle stations with their free ranging semi-wild herds. BTEC meant that the pastoral industry had to change from a largely harvest-based practice, where cattle might only be mustered twice in their lives – the first when they were branded and earmarked, and again when they were sent to the meatworks – to a more intensively managed system, which required a lot more fencing and regular handling of cattle for testing.

The problem that Rod saw with BTEC was when it was applied to buffalo. As part of our lease agreement for Melaleuca, we had to stock the station with a certain number of TB-free buffalo. The station had about 3000 feral buffalo on it when we first arrived, and we either had to catch all of them, test them for TB, and put the clean animals into paddocks and destroy the reactors, or start over from scratch, which meant removing all the feral stock, and replacing them with TB-free buffalo from elsewhere.

The test for TB was originally designed for domestic cattle. However when it was used to test wild buffalo, many animals gave a false reaction. This was said to be because they were stressed from being caught, or pregnant, or perhaps not in good condition. Mustering wild buffalo meant that you ended up with a yard full of angry or just plain terrified animals which had been chased by helicopters and bull catchers, and penned up in a steel yard for the first time in their lives. A high stress situation. The same day or the next, they had to be TB tested, which involved making them run up a narrow race where they were given an injection beneath the butt of their tails. A day or so later they were run into the race again, and their tails felt to see if a lump had developed which indicated a positive reaction – a lump meant a buffalo had TB antibodies in its system.

If they reacted positively, they were slaughtered and post mortemed by the Government vets, and often found to be free of TB. The other, bigger issue from Rod's point of view was that the test on wild buffalo also drew false negatives, meaning that a buffalo actually infected with TB could produce a negative result, and then be put out into the paddock with the clean-tested animals. This meant that the chances of producing a clean herd were highly compromised.

Rod investigated this as deeply as possible, reading everything he could find, including the Federal Government's own conflicting reports and recommendations. In particular he argued that Australia was just being used as convenience by the Americans. Under the GATT (General Agreement on Tariffs and Trade), the US had agreed to take a certain amount of our beef. At the time of the agreement they couldn't supply their own requirements for lean beef, but now they had an oversupply at home. US farmers were complaining loudly because Australian beef was competing with their own product. The only way for the US to get out of their commitment to buying our beef was to insist that we have TB-free status from wherever export beef was sourced.

Rod argued that this was blatant hypocrisy because the US didn't have TB free status itself. TB was almost impossible to catch from cattle because of the limits of contact with the general population, and because even slightly heating infected meat destroyed the TB organism. But if the Australian government wanted to insist on cattle being tested, he believed that buffalo should be left out of the deal. We didn't export buffalo, dead or alive, to the US. It would be cheaper, Rod maintained, to rid the Top End of the Territory of cattle, and allow the infant buffalo industry to find its feet without the demands of BTEC. He became very active within the Buffalo Industry Council, and argued the issue with every Government employee he met – which didn't increase his popularity with any of them.

We therefore decided that we would completely destock our property of its feral buffalo herd rather than capture them and try and test them clean as our neighbours were doing. The wild buffalo in southeast Arnhem Land around Bulman and Mt Catt had been monitored for several years through the meatworks and were declared free of TB. Rod had a contract with Mt Catt that instead of taking payment for the continuing work on the buffalo domestication project, he would take a share of the young breeding females that were being caught. That way, Rod figured we would comply with our stocking covenants a lot sooner, and have a chance of remaining TB-free for a lot longer. Besides, we needed the income the feral buffalo would bring from the meatworks so that we could continue to develop the property. We were allowed to send untested stock to the meatworks, because if a buffalo was found to be infected with TB when it was slaughtered, the carcass was immediately dumped.

It took a while before Melaleuca was officially named. For the first year or so everyone had referred to the station as 'Block B', or 'Point Stuart', or just 'the block'. I decided that we had to choose a name, and came up with 'Melaleuca'. It had a nice ring to it, and was the name of the dominant species of tree on the flood plains. I wrote to the various departments and told them the new name, and gradually they started to use it in their correspondence. But there was one particularly unpleasant public servant in the Primary Industries department, who had decided his role in life was to make our life as difficult as possible. Months after I had notified him of our station's proper name, he still addressed our letters as though we were just temporary tenants – 'To The Leaseholder, Block B'. This chap had a large scale map of the Point Stuart area on his office wall, and one day when Rod and I were in there for a meeting with him, I noticed that all the other properties in the Point Stuart region had their names on the map, except for us. We were still 'Block B'. I picked up his pen, and said, 'It's about time you updated your map, you know . . .' and marked MELALEUCA in bold letters across his wall.

# 15

# 'Crocodile Dundee'

Legal battles, BTEC and running the station weren't the only items on the agenda. We were having a break from work one morning during 1986 when we received a call over VJY from an assistant in Clive James' office, wanting to line Rod up for an interview.

'Why does he want to interview me?' Rod asked the assistant. 'The Fitzmaurice stuff's a bit out of date, isn't it?'

'He wants to talk to you about the new movie, "*Crocodile Dundee*". Have you seen it yet?'

'No, mate, never heard of it. We don't get to the movies much out here. What's it got to do with me?'

We received several more calls over the next few days from various friends who had seen the film, and wanted to know why Rod had kept it all such a secret. 'But it's *you*,' they said. 'We just assumed you must have been collaborating on it. You mean you're not even making any money out of it?'

We went to see the movie for ourselves, and thoroughly enjoyed it. We probably laughed in places no one else did because so much was familiar. The shaving with a knife scene in the movie made us smile – Rod shaved for *To Fight the Wild* because continuity was too hard to maintain if he grew a beard like he had on the river, so he stayed half shaven most of the time. Hence the attempts to shave with his skinning knife in the film.

The scene where 'Mick Dundee' pretends to tell the time from the sun was hugely funny to us, because it happened just like that during filming on the Fitzmaurice. The crew came back to camp one afternoon laughing about how Rod had fooled the producer, Richard Oxenburgh. Rod, Richard and sound recordist Roly McManus were talking about telling the time by the sun. Richard thought it was just another bush myth, that it was all guesswork. He said to Rod, looking up at the sky, 'So what's the time right now then?'

Rod and Roly were standing behind Richard. Rod grabbed Roly's wrist, checked the time, and squinted up at the sun. 'Ah, I'd reckon it's pretty close to ten past ten.'

Richard checked his watch, astonished, while Roly had silent convulsions in the background.

The media began making the connections for themselves, comparing stories and sequences from the Parkinson interview with the movie. In an interview with Paul Hogan and John Cornell for the *Sydney Morning Herald* on 23 April 1986, reporter Paul Byrnes wrote: 'According to his (Hogan's) long time writing collaborator, Ken Shadie, the idea for the character of Mick "Crocodile" Dundee came when Hogan saw Michael Parkinson interviewing a Territory man who had been savaged by a crocodile, but the guy didn't even know who Parkinson was.'

Rod had brought the house down in the 1981 *Parkinson* interview when he told Michael Parkinson 'I don't know any of these people, Michael. I don't even know who you are . . .'

Highly respected Melbourne journalist Keith Dunstan interviewed John Cornell just prior to the movie's release, and wrote: 'Parkinson, according to Cornell, brought him down to Sydney, and he was so tough, he wouldn't even sleep in his bed at the Sebel Town House. He had to sleep on the floor.' Rod's swag on the floor of our room at the Sebel Town House caused a stir with the housemaids, and Parkinson referred to this in the interview. I think the Toyota diff wrapped up in a piece of canvas beside it caused a bit of consternation as well.

In June 1986, *New Idea* magazine featured a story about *Crocodile Dundee* scriptwriter Ken Shadie: 'The idea of Crocodile Dundee was sparked by an interview on one of Michael Parkinson's specials. Parkinson interviewed a man who had never been outside the

Northern Territory. [According to Ken Shadie] 'Paul thought this was the "ideal character for Hoges . . ."'

The media wasted no time making comparisons, and overnight the phrase Rod came to hate – *the real Crocodile Dundee* – began appearing in newspaper and magazine articles. As far as I was aware, he was rarely mentioned in the media again without that tag appearing alongside his name.

Early in January 1987, we received a call over VJY from a reporter with the *Sunday Territorian*, congratulating Rod on being chosen as the inaugural Territorian of the Year. The paper had run a story about Rod and the movie the previous November, after sending Colleen Mackie and Clive Hyde out to interview Rod and take photos.

'Buffalo station owner and author, Mr Rod Ansell, has been named *Territorian of the Year*. He was nominated for the inaugural *Sunday Territorian* award for being "the real-life Territorian who inspired *Crocodile Dundee*, a film which put the NT and Australia in world focus . . ." the nomination read.'

(*Sunday Territorian*, 11 January 1987)

'You'll get a plaque with your name on it,' said the reporter. Rod and I looked at each other, and up at the virtually nonexistent walls of our abode.

'I'll have to build a wall to hang it on then,' answered Rod with a grin. But we never did see the plaque.

We were going to run out of feral buffalo to sell before too long, and we needed an income to tide us over while we built up our clean TB-free herd from southeast Arnhem Land. Tourism was the ideal vehicle. We had contacts in the tourism industry in the US who were keen to promote our property as a tourist destination to the high-end market.

Rod had met Dominick Macan the year before when Dominick was travelling around Australia doing some research for his tourism business. He visited the station, and he and Rod discussed the idea of using Melaleuca as a homestay destination, and Dominick was certain it would do well. Using the connection with *Crocodile Dundee* would get our product noticed amongst all the others out there. Rod said, 'They did okay using a bit of me, maybe I can use a bit of them . . .'

Rod contacted Paul Hogan asking if he could use the phrase 'the man who inspired the movie' or something similar, in promotional material in the United States. He made it very clear that he was not interested in seeking any financial reward or compensation from Hogan. He said he'd be happy to sign any kind of document to guarantee that.

At the end of March Rod received a letter back from Hogan's business partner, John Cornell, warning him off, and threatening legal action if Rod either claimed to be the real 'Crocodile Dundee', or used the words to promote his tourism venture. Looking back, I think Rod had a sense of terrible unfairness. He was severely shaken when he received the letter. He couldn't see the harm in him benefitting a little from Hogan's success, when as far as Rod was concerned, he had been a part of the inspiration for the Dundee character.

Coming only a few months after the court case, Rod found it a lot harder to bounce back from this. All the subsequent media attention was salt in the wound. The centrepiece of every story was that Rod was 'the real Crocodile Dundee', but he couldn't even use *that* to improve the chances of a tourist business. So he ran with the publicity. Over the next two years Melaleuca hosted a bewildering array of journalists, film crews and photographers from Australia, the US and the UK, who made their way out to the station to talk to Rod, film and photograph him, and have the daylights scared out of them in the bull catcher.

The late 1980s should have been the happiest time of our lives. We had achieved the goal we had been dreaming about for years, and Rod for most of his life – having our own land. We had the opportunity to pursue the life we wanted, and to work at it together. We had two gorgeous, healthy little boys. We were young and healthy ourselves – Rod was thirty-two, I was thirty-one, and apart from his constant neck and back pain, he was still very fit. But he was increasingly moody and unhappy. When people were around and there was work to be done, he was fine, and full of energy and direction. He laughed and told stories at dinner in the evenings, was animated and lively, and during the day he worked like there were never enough hours to go round. But over the wet season of 1986–87, when the catching had given way to the heat, the humidity and the torrential rains, and the other workers had all left, he was prone to deep depressions, and the moodiness which had been relatively rare until now became a feature of our life together. What should have been the happiest time of our lives so far descended into the worst, most despairing time of mine.

Rod was becoming more and more critical of me, of what I did or didn't do, and nothing seemed to please him. We had some terrible fights, late at night when the boys were asleep, which would end in him haranguing me about all my faults, and blaming me for everything that was going wrong. There was something inside him that was eating him away. It was as though he thought there was more to life than what he had, something more important or more satisfying, and he wouldn't be happy until he found it. He was the kind of person who had to look deeper into everything, had to answer the unanswerable questions in life, and wouldn't be content until he had done so.

I think where other people are content to conduct their own private search for the meaning of their lives, Rod had to induct me into his search as well. I had to feel as tormented as he did by the absence of whatever it was that was missing from his life, or I wasn't being honest or real enough for him. He would keep me up till the early hours of the morning, lecturing me about my faults and shortcomings. I was lazy, stupid, useless, unimaginative, weak – if it wasn't for me, we wouldn't have so much difficulty.

Rod excelled at convincing argument, and I was very poor at it. I hated arguments and confrontation, and he could tie me up in verbal knots in a very short time.

I began to live in a constant state of anxiety, never sure how to answer a question for fear it would spark another mood which would build up to another numbing tirade in the middle of the night. He kept this up until eventually I was shorn of every vestige of self protection I had, except for my brilliance at 'keeping up appearances', making sure no one ever suspected there was anything wrong between us. It's how brainwashing works, repeating something to a person when they're exhausted and uncertain, and eventually they agree with their tormentor just to get some peace. I became a kind of shell, all shiny and effective on the outside, but a big empty space inside. I didn't know who I was or what I believed anymore.

It wasn't like this constantly. There were enough good days in between the bad ones that I could convince myself the bad days were just passing storms. Sometimes, if we had visitors who could stay at home with the boys, Rod and I would take off on our own in the bull catcher for a few hours, and he'd show me something new he'd discovered, like the perfect white-flowered Calytrix bush in amongst all the pink ones, up near Deep Lake. Another time we crept quietly up to Duck Lake and watched in awe as thousands upon thousands of native ducks floated in massed ranks on the shallow water, and we laughed in amazement as they rose into the air in a deafening storm, showering us with feathers, when they became aware of us.

At times like this I felt we hadn't lost what had brought us together in the first place, and that we would survive this rough patch. I'd tell myself that he was just worried about the many things we had little control over – the sheer scale of the challenge we'd taken on with Melaleuca in the first place, for example. He struggled with pain every day, and he knew that the success of this venture depended on him being able to keep up a high level of work and effort. The spectre of becoming unable to work physically left him in absolute dread. I could find endless reasons for why he would be feeling depressed. So when he was in a good mood, and things were how they used to be, I convinced myself that *this* was what my life was about.

Christmas 1986 was not a happy time, and by the end of January Rod and I were barely talking. In early February 1987, my mother called me over VJY with sad news. Anne Butler, my friend since we were nine-year-olds in the playground at Our Lady's, had been killed in a horse riding accident. Rod didn't want me to go to the funeral, but he knew he couldn't stop me. I left for Melbourne carrying two kinds of grief – it was clearer than ever that our marriage was in meltdown.

In 1987 I hired a governess for the first time. I was finding it difficult to keep up with the boys' schoolwork and my own jobs. Mary was a young English woman travelling around Australia, and answered an ad I'd put up at the backpacker hostels in Darwin. She was very sensible and down to earth, but possessed of a great enthusiasm and imagination when it came to teaching school to two young blokes who would have preferred to be outside doing anything else at all. After putting up with Mum, whose lessons were constantly interrupted by telephone calls, station and business matters and visitors, a dedicated governess all to themselves must have seemed like torture! Mary had them putting on plays, making costumes, cooking cakes and generally enjoying most of their time in the schoolroom. And I could go back to just being Mum, instead of being the boss all the time.

Our contract with the people at Mt Catt took us down there in early April, building a set of buffalo yards and fencing several paddocks. Mary went with us to Katherine, where she caught a bus to the next stop on her holiday, and I picked up Lucy Burrows, a relative of John Humphreys in England. When I first met Lucy I thought she wouldn't last very long. She was a sweet young thing with a peaches and cream complexion and a very upper class accent. She didn't look like she would cope with the bush very well, especially not a rough little camp like we had at Mt Catt. We had set up on a creek, with good fresh water and a handy supply of yabbies. We weren't going to be there for very long, so it was just the basics – a tent to house the food and other supplies, and swags under tarpaulins. I didn't worry too much that Lucy might pull the pin, because I was going to be picking up a permanent governess in two weeks.

While backpackers were happy to work for their keep and a bit of pocket money, they didn't stay long and a succession of different ones every few months would not be good for Callum and Shaun. Anne's sister Felicity quit her teaching job when Anne died, and in April I wrote to her offering a very poorly paid job, but with great bonuses like living in the outback, watching helicopter musters and never knowing what was going to happen next, all in a really beautiful environment on the borders of Kakadu National Park. I must have caught her at a weak moment because she agreed immediately, and arrived in time to relieve Lucy, who vastly preferred coming out to the yards all day with Rod and me to cut and weld steel rails. I had seriously underestimated Lucy's thoroughly British country upbringing. She surprised us all by thriving in the rough conditions, absolutely loved bull catching, and stayed until October.

Felicity must have found her new classroom a bit strange after the rural Victorian schools she'd been teaching in. Our schoolroom consisted of a patch of shade which had to be followed around as the sun moved across the sky. The school radio was hooked up to my car battery for on-air lessons, and the desks were rickety old card tables, with flour drums for seats. After school Callum and Shaun would play in the creek, floating around in the old tin bath we'd used at Bulman, and catching ant lions in the soft white sand of the creek banks.

Yard building is hot, hard work. We were building steel yards, impervious to white ants and weather, and while we didn't have to go out and chop down trees, knock the bark off logs, and dig enormous holes by hand like the yard builders of old, it was still a tough enough job.

Every morning I donned long pants, a long-sleeved, heavy cotton ex-army shirt, and found my gloves. Hat essential. Racing to beat Rod's impatient 'Hurry up', I'd throw some lunch together, and lug a big container of water to the Toyota. The yard site was a couple of kilometres away, with a scattering of small trees around that offered scant shade.

Several tonnes of steel pipe had been delivered there a few weeks before, and were now baking relentlessly in the sun. Each 7-metre length of pipe had to be dragged over to the cut-off machine, measured, cut, and its ends bashed flat with a sledgehammer so it could later be welded in place on a post. Everything was hot. The steel was hot just from being in the sun all day. There was a continual shower of sparks from the cut-off machine and the white hot flashing from the welder, specks of molten slag leaving tiny charred dots all over any exposed skin. The noise was deafening. In the background the welder's engine hammered away, rising and falling in response to the load on it. The cut-off machine screeched and screamed its way through the steel pipes, and the sledgehammer pounded both our ears and our hands. After a while you stopped noticing, and it was only when the welder was finally shut down at the end of the day that quiet came rushing back in like a tidal wave.

Occasionally we would go into Bulman and spend some time with Leonie and Craig. Rod had been doing a little bit of catching with the Murray and Forbes brothers who lived at Bulman, and our catcher was a bit the worse for wear this particular time. The brakes were almost nonexistent, but they were never terribly good anyway, so it didn't seem like too much of a problem when Felicity, Lucy, the boys and I headed in one evening to Leonie and Craig's for dinner. I just used the gears and the engine to slow down, instead of the brakes. The moon was already up, and cast deep shadows across the track, but we could follow it well enough. Suddenly I realised I'd missed the turn I should have taken, and a wide, deep washaway loomed directly in front of us. The brake pedal went straight to the floor, no resistance whatsoever. I did the only thing I could think of – if thinking was what I did – and jammed the gear stick into reverse. There was a terrible screeching and grinding from the gearbox, and the vehicle slid to a stop, just as the wheels began to drop over the edge of the hole across the road. No one said a word. Then Lucy breathed, 'My God . . . we would have been killed in that . . .'

When we finally reached Bulman and saw Rod, who was already there, the others gave him a hard time about the brakes on his catcher. Instead of looking sheepish, he just stared at me and said, 'You should look where you're going.' I flushed hotly, and hoped that no one else had heard him.

The yards were completed in about two months. They looked great, and we were proud of the job we'd done on them. The community was very happy too, and one bloke said to Rod, prophetically, 'That yard'll be here when you die, old man.'

Sammy Bulabul and his wife Christine were at Mt Catt then, along with old George J—. They were some of the senior traditional owners for the area, and the people we dealt with the most. Although I had met them before, we became very close friends during this time, and they came up to stay with us at Melaleuca several times in the following years. George was a shrewd, clever old man with a wicked sense of humour. He was short, stocky and gnarled, and had played the character Goggle-Eye in the classic Australian film *We of the Never-Never* some years before.

He'd look at you for a while, and then say something like: 'I don't like white fella, but you all right.' And he meant it. He didn't like white people generally, but he was good at dealing with them. He knew exactly who he was, and he was on his own land. White people were just an intrusion into his life, generally, and out at Mt Catt, on his own country, he had no doubt about who had the upper hand. Europeans might come to his camp with rules and regulations, and policies and submissions and a host of paperwork and problems, but to him it was just like playing with children. He told them what he wanted them to hear, and got on with his own business.

Christine embraced us as her own family, treating Callum and Shaun like her grandkids. She taught me the skin names and the marriage laws between them, and she and I spent a lot of time on her front verandah drinking tea and talking about our families. Christine was plump and comfortable looking, with a lovely face and a rich laugh. She looked after her grandchildren with a languid playfulness that belied the watchfulness she maintained over them. Her husband Sammy Bulabul was a fine man. Powerfully built, with a smooth, handsome face, Sammy was the kind of person you wanted in your corner. He was quiet and gentle, but he exuded an aura of authority, fairness and strength that identified him as a leader, wherever he was. Sammy and George worked with Rod on the details of the buffalo domestication project, organising groups of young men to provide labour where it was needed, and kept up a level of enthusiasm and excitement about the progress of the project that was infectious.

At the end of May 1987 we packed up the camp and headed back to Melaleuca. Felicity and I arrived at the station before the others. She was a very quiet person, not given to voicing her opinion unless her life depended on it, and I wasn't sure if she was happy working with us or not. But I knew Felicity would cope with our not-quite-normal lifestyle when we had to stop a few miles down the Point Stuart Road.

'Bloody hell,' I said. 'The engine's overheating . . .'

Being well trained by Rod, I drove with one eye on every possible gauge in any vehicle I was in. We got out, and I lifted up the seats – the Hi-Ace engine was underneath them. The radiator was dry. We waited till it had cooled a little, and poured the last of our water into it, but it wasn't going to be enough.

'What about the window-washer tank?' suggested Felicity hopefully. The washer tank of course was bone dry.

'I don't think the window-washer even works,' I said. 'We'll just have to sit here till someone comes along.'

Felicity was quiet for a moment, and then said: 'There's ice in the esky. We could melt it in the hubcaps and pour it into the radiator.'

I was to discover that Felicity was a natural at coming up with unusual solutions to problems, and she wasn't the least bit fazed by breakdowns, discomfort or inconvenience. The perfect bull catching camp employee!

We pulled into the homestead just before dark, and I put my hand up on top of the post near the doorway to retrieve the key to the demountable. I felt a series of smooth bumps where the key was supposed to be. I leapt away from the post with enormous strides. I dragged a chair over, and climbed up to have a better look. The bumps were several orange and white striped coils of snake. I was pretty sure it was a brown tree snake, which were venomous but not dangerous, being rear fanged, but I wasn't about to take it for granted. I poked at it with a broom handle a few times, and eventually it started to move away, finishing up draped beautifully over the roof beams for the next few hours as we unpacked the car. Snakes were never much of a problem at Melaleuca. Once in a while one would venture up onto the verandah, hunting geckoes and frogs, but apart from a large king brown who lived in the tool shed, and whom we were very cautious about but could never catch, snakes kept their distance.

Goannas, however, were not so shy. There were lots of them around the homestead, and several used to come up to the verandah looking for food. We had been given about twenty muscovy-cross ducks by some friends in town. They were mostly black with some greenish tinges and sported a lot of fleshy red wattling on their heads. Some had more red wattles than the others, and were much uglier looking, so I concluded they must be the drakes. When one of the ducks nested right beside the back door, I was pleased that we were finally getting some population expansion, although not so thrilled about the location. After six or seven weeks went by with no sign of little yellow bits of fluff, I decided I didn't know very much about ducks, and that perhaps we didn't have a drake after all. Just some very ugly ducks. The ducks had all been laying in the same nest, which by now contained about thirty very stale eggs. No one was game to move them in case one broke. An enormous old goanna discovered them, and every morning he would stomp across the flat to the back door, completely ignoring the humans nearby, and scoff a few eggs. Eventually he cleaned the lot out, and we didn't have to worry about exploding duck eggs anymore. Goannas must have extremely strong constitutions, because we didn't notice any exploding goannas either.

Soon after that, someone offered me a real drake to look after our poor frustrated ducks. I realised then that our ducks weren't nearly ugly enough to have been drakes. This bloke was twice the size and had far more red wattles on his head than the girls. When I brought the new head of the barnyard home, I opened his crate on the back of the ute to put him in the yard with the ducks. I didn't even lay a hand on him. He stuck his head up, spotted a duck, leapt out of the box and over the fence, straight onto one of the poor ducks. He didn't even hit the ground. He introduced himself to the rest of the flock in a similar manner, and before we knew it we were knee deep in ducklings.

Mustering began straight away, and with a full complement of catchers. Greg and Chris were back, and we had another young fellow named Brett – or Blunder, as Greg christened him. It was good to get back into our 'real' work, as I thought of it. A typical mustering day began well before daylight, with a hurried breakfast on the verandah – that is, for those who could eat. There was always a tangible nervousness in the air before the helicopters arrived. Were the yards in exactly the right place? Would the wings hold? Would everyone get through the day uninjured? And most of all, would we get a mob into the yards? A billy of tea was as much as most of the blokes could manage before the mounting tension was brought to a climax by the clatter of the helicopter arriving in the pre-dawn gloom.

We frequently used two helicopters for a muster, because two could cover more country in less time, and control the movement of the buffalo a lot better. Simon Taylor and Clinton Brisk did most of our mustering in Robinson R22s, tiny machines in comparison to the Vietnam war veteran Bell 47s we'd used before. After a quick consultation with Rod about the area to be mustered, they would settle back for a coffee while the catchers went on ahead to get in position. Generally the buffalo were feeding out on the flood plains early in the morning, moving up into the shelter of the tree cover as the day warmed. The yards were set up the day before in the direction the buffalo would be most likely to run, close to a well-used pad. Lucy and I erected a lot of these ourselves, after Rod had chosen the site, and given instructions on how he wanted them constructed. The wings stretched for a kilometre or more from the yards out onto the flood plain, forming a huge funnel with several kilometres between their ends. They were nothing more than a few pickets, a strand or two of wire, and miles of hessian bagging, enough to trick a galloping buffalo into thinking that because he couldn't see through it, he couldn't run through it.

At the prearranged time, the choppers were in the air, the whap-whap-whap of the rotor blades coming and going as they swept far and wide pushing little mobs of buffalo in the direction of the funnel mouth. Herd animals like cattle and buffalo find safety in numbers, so once a mob is running, other individual animals will usually join them. Gradually a sizeable number were heading in the right direction, and once they entered the funnel, the bull catchers roared in behind them, pushing them on as the sides of the funnel narrowed down to the yards. The yard itself was built in a figure of eight, with another gate at the waist, making two separate yards so that the first mobs of buffalo could be shut in the far yard, and more animals run into the receiving yard on the next pass.

Rod had spent a lot of time developing a gate that was self locking. One of the most dangerous times at a muster was getting the gates closed on the yard. The catchers would follow the buffalo into the yards and park at the gateway to keep them penned while someone climbed over the vehicle to reach the gate, and try to slam it shut while the catchers revved their engines to frighten the buffalo away. It was awkward, and after too many near misses, and one not so near miss when Greg had his shoulder dislocated by a buffalo hitting the gate as it was being closed, Rod invented a self closer that could be operated by someone safely outside the yard with a rope. It consisted of a latch that rode up a sloping angle of steel plate and dropped down into a gap to lock the gate when the gate was pulled into the gate post with a rope. Simple but effective, and strong enough to withstand a tonne of buffalo hitting it at full speed.

This was the best time, just after a completed muster. The choppers would land in front of the yards, one by one the vehicles would pull in and shut off their engines, and everyone would gather near the buffalo, grinning with relief and satisfaction. Water canteens were pulled out, smokes rolled, and all the near misses and disasters of the day recounted. Watering troughs would be set up for the buffalo, a pump started up to spray them with water to cool them down, and then usually they were left alone overnight to settle before being trucked out to the meatworks the next day.

In between musters we caught small loads individually as well. We also caught at night, something everyone said couldn't be done. Rod graded a dead straight line on the flood plain across the Mary at Shady Camp, and the catchers would use this and the stars to get their bearings. On that side of the river there were no trees, and the catchers had many square miles of good running to chase buffalo. We went through countless spotlights, smashing at least one every night, and bought them by the carton from Kmart in Darwin. We ran animals into yards sometimes, marking where the yard was by its position in relation to the Southern Cross, which hovered above the horizon that time of the morning. A kerosene lamp marked one side of the wings, and one person was stationed at the yards to open the gate and let animals through as they were pushed up the wings. It's amazing just how much you can see in open country by starlight. It was cool work, and the buffalo stayed fresh and relatively unstressed. As soon as it was light, the truck went out to pick up the night's haul. We caught several hundred bulls that way.

Christmas 1986, Greg had broken his leg badly in a fall from a roof. After bull catching all year, courting death and serious injury every other day, he returned to his 'normal' job as a plumber, and was badly injured the first day on the job. Rod and I went in to see him the night before he was to have an operation that could have resulted in the loss of his lower leg. Greg was in a lot of pain, but most of all he was worried about the future. He had a young family to support, and that was going to be a hard road if he ended up with only one leg.

'Don't worry about next year's contract, mate,' Rod said to him. 'She'll be waiting for you when you get over this. The job's right.'

And it was, as it turned out. Greg didn't lose his foot, but he spent months in rehab learning how to walk again, and came back desperate to find out if he could still drive a bull catcher. Driving was fine. A couple of modifications to his catcher, and a place to stow his crutches, and he was away. Spencer Martin from Bulman was working for us then, and he spent the first few months riding with Greg and strapping his bulls. When Spencer had to return to Arnhem Land, I stepped into the passenger seat, and strapped for Greg for most of the season.

There were some near misses. One day Rod and Greg were out running some bulls with a young backpacker couple along for the ride. Rod took the girl, an Israeli soldier, in his catcher, while her partner, a young German, was keen to give Greg a hand. Greg explained to him exactly what he had to do, and the man assured him he was fine. When the crunch came, the young German froze, and wouldn't get out of the vehicle to rope the bull. Greg told me the story later:

> The German bloke just froze – couldn't bring himself to get out of the catcher once we had a buffalo. All he had to do was get the rope on its horns and tie it off on the bull bar, but he wouldn't get out. I was fucked if I was gonna lose a good bull, so I hopped out to do it myself. With all the rocking and stuffing about, the bull got loose and galloped off a bit, and as I turned to get back to the catcher my bad leg collapsed under me and I was in a heap on the ground, this bull and me just lookin' at each other. There was nothing I could do. He put his head down and started to charge, and I just shut me eyes, waiting for it. Next thing I knew, Rod came out of nowhere, scooped me up in this flying tackle and rolled with me under the bull bar just as the buffalo went past hooking for me. I still dunno how he did it – he saved my life. I was sure I was dead.

It was quite a feat. Rod never weighed more than 55 kilograms at the best of times, and Greg was a good six inches taller and weighed about a hundred.

Another time we were running a trap at Shady Camp. The men had been working nonstop for nearly three days, catching and loading out small numbers of buffalo to the Point Stuart meatworks, and were completely exhausted. Finally in the middle of the night, Rod, Greg and Chris had a puncture on the way back to the yards, along the Shady Camp road. They pulled off the flat tyre and were gathered around it trying to make repairs when somehow they all fell asleep.

PHOTO: J VAN OS COLLECTION

Rod and me at Mount Isa in early 1979, on our way back to the Territory after we married.

PHOTO: J VAN OS COLLECTION

Shaun used to grab the skin on either side of my neck and pull me towards him with an evil grin, and then give me a big kiss. Bulman, 1984.

PHOTO: J VAN OS COLLECTION

Rod and Geoffrey in the catcher with Shaun and Callum, Willeroo Station, 1982.

Nellie Camfoo teaching Shaun and Callum how to find sand frogs for bait, Bulman, 1984.

Inside the camp Rod built for us at Bulman. Blue tarps could be rolled down to keep out the rain in the wet season. It was actually quite waterproof.

Josie Coleman and Felicity Butler taking a break from loading buffalo at
Melaleuca, 1988.

Number One Billabong, Melaleuca Station. This was a beautiful lake, perhaps 10 or 15
acres in size, which we sometimes paddled a boat on, but never swam in.

This was the first camp at Melaleuca Station from late 1984 till early 1986. The 'kitchen' is just in front to the right. You didn't get a cup of tea if it rained hard.

The things you put up with to have a real bath! It was rough, but it worked.

Melaleuca homestead, 1989, built of local stone, ironwood posts, and corrugated iron. Rod's mum planted the grass on one of their visits. Every day she planted a few rows in the cool of morning and evening, and a few months later we had a good lawn to keep the dust down.

Photo: Josie Coleman

Rod and me after a helicopter muster, Melaleuca, 1989. I had cut my hair short for the first time in about fifteen years.

Photo: J van Os collection

Greg Keogh and Rod with a good buffalo bull, held in the bionic arm on Rod's catcher.

PHOTO: J VAN OS COLLECTION

Four boys in a tub – from left: Luke Hemsworth, Shaun, Callum and Chris Hemsworth pretending butter wouldn't melt in their mouths. Melaleuca, 1986.

PHOTO: J VAN OS COLLECTION

Callum and Shaun with lunch. They took their fishing very seriously.

Wet season storm about to hit Shady Camp, 1991. This was my bedroom, a mosquito-proof tent wrapped up in tarpaulins to keep out the rain.

Making a table in the 'shop' at Shady Camp. We built the same style rock walls here as at Melaleuca.

The first day of the Shady Camp Boat Hire business. Greg Keogh takes some of the kids for a run on the Mary River, August 1989.

Howard Springs, December 1993. From left: Callum, Shaun, Lex and Tom playing cards, while Ali does her best to distract Tom.

Lex and me in Darwin, 2005.

Callum, me, Ali and Shaun in June 2005, Darwin.

Greg woke up a few hours later with a torch being shone in his face, and someone crying out, 'This one's alive!'

Some men arriving before dawn to fish at Shady Camp had turned a corner to see a vehicle on the side of the road and three bodies lying scattered about a loose wheel as if they'd all been thrown out in a terrible accident. The blokes went home and had a good sleep.

One day towards the end of the season Rod told me I was to organise the next muster myself. I was to choose the site of the yard, build it, and position the wings. I didn't sleep much the night before, but I was determined to prove I was more capable than he thought. There were still a few mobs of buffalo up at Deep Lake, and a number of pads led off the water up into the trees. I chose a yard site a hundred or so metres back into the trees, and returned the next day with Lucy Burrows, another backpacker and seventy panels of portable yard on the truck. Each panel took two people to lift it. We carried them one by one into position, and built the yard in the usual figure eight design. The next day we ran out the wings, hanging the hessian on the wire with pieces of tie-wire. That night we were ready. Rod came out and inspected the work, and couldn't find any fault with it.

The chopper turned up early next morning, and the men ran the yard. I didn't drive with them – I'd tried my hand at catching before, and decided my kids needed a mother more than the station needed another catcher. However, I was crouching behind the wings at the yard when the first buffalo ran in, and couldn't hide my jubilation when the final draft topped ninety head. Not a huge number, but respectable nonetheless. Everyone else congratulated me, but Rod was almost dismissive. Why was I so excited about something he did every day? I was flattened, but not for long. I knew I'd done well, and I also knew I'd surprised Rod.

Later that evening, he came up to me and said, with an almost grim look on his face and a hand on my shoulder, 'You did okay, you know. That was a good yard.'

It meant more to me to hear him say it than he could ever have imagined.

It was a busy household. We all ate together, shared the one bathroom, and spent most of our evenings with each other, talking or playing games if the men weren't out repairing vehicles half the night. The generator was only used at night so that we had lights to cook and eat by, and was shut down when we went to bed. We had water to the house, but only in the bathroom, not the kitchen, and then only when the pump was going, as we had not put in a holding tank yet. There were twelve of us most of the time, and that number was often swelled by the regular visitors who came through.

We had enormous numbers of guests during those years. Some were backpackers who had called by in the hope of some work, and ended up going bull catching for a few days. Some were there on business, but most were friends, family, or distant relatives of acquaintances. It seemed that the opportunity to visit a real Australian buffalo station was just too good to pass up, so we played host to a wide cross-section of people. The place Rod was most in his element, after the bush and bull catching, was at the table over a billy of tea, captivating guests with his stories and his own philosophy of life. He had an ability to hold his listeners with that laser-like gaze, his face alight with such intensity that he seemed to sweep them up and carry them along with him. He thrived on the contact and the conversations, and the exchange of ideas, even if that was largely one-way.

One guest, a British university professor who knew a friend of ours and was keen to experience the 'outback' during his stay in Australia, said to me as he was leaving: 'Remarkable chap, your husband. You know, he had me quite convinced with his arguments last night. It was only after I went to bed and thought about it that I realised I disagreed with him!'

Of course, not everyone thought Rod's arguments were so compelling and irresistible. He didn't have much luck convincing the various government officials we had to deal with!

Rod had met the Australian country singer John Williamson on a trip to Sydney that year, and when John came to Darwin for a concert some months later, he came out to Melaleuca for a couple of days during his tour with his wife Mary Kay and his back-up people. When he first arrived, he looked a little uncertain about just what he'd let himself in for. The rest of us weren't sure how to treat this bloke either – we didn't know anything about him except that he sang some pretty good songs. Rod solved that initial awkwardness by putting the visitors in the bull catchers, and headed out to catch a few buffalo. By the time they returned, they were all completely relaxed. There's nothing like having the living daylights frightened out of you a few times to get a proper perspective on things.

Felicity's parents were staying as well, as were four young British backpackers who'd arrived in a Kombi van the day before. As usual there were multitudes to feed, but Felicity, Josie and I got stuck into our usual loaves and fishes act, and had enough to feed everyone several times over by the time dinner was due.

'Well,' said John after the meal, 'you've given us a pretty amazing day. I guess I have to do something in return,' and he picked up his guitar, much to everyone's delight. No one had mentioned the idea of him singing for us. It seemed too rude to presume he'd just toss off a few numbers on request. He started singing, and didn't stop for well over an hour. It was brilliant, our own private concert on the verandah at Melaleuca, while John's bottle of scotch was passed around. Not bad – he provided the entertainment *and* the alcohol.

# 16

# Midwinter's Day

In March 1987, Rod's movie *To Fight the Wild* screened again in Australia, billed as 'The Real Crocodile Dundee' in the southern TV guides. We hosted visits from several film industry people who had movie or TV projects in mind, and many more journalists. *People* magazine in the US sent Margot Dougherty to interview Rod for a lengthy article which was published the following June, Rod sharing the cover with Paul Hogan. As well, Rod was invited to appear as a guest on the *Mike Walsh Show* and Channel 9's *Today*, both national TV programs.

In December the BBC contacted us, wanting to set up a visit. Before they arrived, Barry Wigmore from the *London Daily Mirror* was on the doorstep, and spent several soggy days with Rod, driving around where it was still possible in the Wet, and questioning all of us about how we lived out here. His article featured over two days in late January in the UK, and was syndicated into some Australian Sunday newspapers as well. The BBC crew arrived in April 1988, and filmed a segment of a program they were producing about characters who may have been the inspiration for *Crocodile Dundee*. Later someone sent me a clipping from the December issue of *The Independent* TV guide in England that previewed the documentary featuring in the *Wideworld* series on BBC2, and said: 'Behind the caricature, is there a real Crocodile Dundee? This is the question that a young Australian photographer, Kos Evans, set out to answer. She found buffalo catcher Rod Ansell (*above*) who fits the bill quite neatly.'

Rod didn't chase the attention. His first reaction to yet another request for a story was invariably a grimace and resignation. In addition to establishing a buffalo property, we also wanted to operate Melaleuca as a tourist destination. The media attention became useful. The interviewer may have come out to talk to this man labelled by the press as the 'real Crocodile Dundee', but that premise quickly gave way to fascination with the lifestyle we led. Before long, the focus of most interviews was very much on Rod, buffalo catching and the bush, and not on any movie character. However, I think the constant attention was skewing his sense of himself. He had to perform for each of these occasions. He was conscious of having to sell himself, while at the same time trying to still appear nonchalant about it all. And in the background, every time, were the men, the mates he worked with. It must have been a hard balancing act, performing for the cameras in front of the toughest audience imaginable – other bull catchers – and yet trying to give the media what they wanted.

The cracks were showing though. Rod was smoking dope every day when he had it, and not just a joint at night to relax. One before breakfast, if there were no visitors around, several through the day, as well as another at night. The other catchers noticed how much he smoked, and commented on it. It made them uncomfortable. Some of them smoked a joint occasionally too, but they shared one between themselves, and smoked cigarettes the rest of the time.

There were a dozen people for dinner most nights, and always someone living with us. We were never on our own, with just the four of us, let alone the two of us. Juggling a disintegrating marriage, the daily demands of the station, and the social pressures of living with a lot of people, many of whom were total strangers, meant we both had to keep pretending that everything was fine. It also ensured that we never had the opportunity to really talk to each other properly. I think it also prevented me from stepping back at some point, and asking myself – *what is happening to me?*

This lack of proper communication, combined with Rod's regular lectures about my faults and shortcomings, kept me in a tight corner. If you isolate a person, make them feel uneasy and unsafe, and keep telling them the same thing over and over, eventually they believe it, no matter how irrational that might be. It was obviously irrational – I was believing all this stuff, yet I was still keeping everything running. I couldn't have been the weak, stupid creature Rod had me convinced I was. But from my perspective, he was right, and I was hopeless.

I never confided in anyone about what was happening, never criticised Rod to anyone else. I was too well schooled after so many years with Rod that our marriage was our own business, that no one else had a right to an opinion or to give advice about it, and I could not even imagine how I'd broach the subject with anyone I knew. I just kept thinking, it's okay, I can get through this . . . Exactly what I was getting through *to*, I had no idea.

By February 1988, Rod wanted a divorce. He believed that he'd be better off if he could put a legal distance between us. We'd still own the station together, and life would go on as normal for the boys, but we would no longer be married. The general plan was that we would continue to share the house, because Rod would be away in Arnhem Land a lot of the time anyway, and that when we could afford it, we'd build another house for me. We'd talked about developing a camping ground down at Shady Camp, the popular fishing reserve on the Mary River, and that would be my business, and where I'd eventually live. Whatever, it was going to take a while to put it into effect.

Maybe if it had all been bad, I would have rebelled, but he would veer from being vicious and cruel one day to affectionate and gentle for the next few. It was just enough to keep me thinking it might get better, just enough to keep me holding on. I was unable to think clearly on my own behalf. I had considered leaving a couple of times. I spent at least one day in a complete fog, vaguely sorting out things I should keep, completing all the outstanding paperwork in the office, with the idea of leaving the next day, just driving away. But there was no way I could leave my sons. And equally no way I could take them away from their father. If he had been cruel to them, if they had been affected by what was happening between their parents, I would have snatched them up and run. But Rod was a good father, and they adored him. They never saw us argue, and they never saw the way Rod spoke to me in private. Divorce was not something I had seriously considered, but I listened to him with what felt like relief.

In the meantime, Rod convinced me that we shouldn't tell anyone at all about the divorce yet: 'Let's just wait until the formalities are done, and we can tell everyone after that. It's not like there's going to be major changes. And it's no one else's business anyway.'

As well as that, Rod's mother had been ill with heart problems, and we didn't want to give her anything else to worry about. We filed the application at the end of March 1988, claiming that we'd been separated for the requisite twelve months already. In more ways than one I guess we had. It was just two weeks before our first tourists were arriving. If I didn't know anything about stress by then, I was about to start a crash course.

Rod had taken a phone call from Dominick Macan in the US in February and told me: 'Dom's got some people who want to come out in a few weeks' time. They're in the travel business, so he reckons it would be a good thing to give them a taste of what the place can offer. They'll be here about the sixth of April.'

I looked around me and felt a wave of panic slowly rising. There was a half-finished house that wasn't yet mosquito-proof, no kitchen to speak of, and running water only when the pump was going, just to name a few problems. We were a long way short of appearing like a desirable international tourist destination. We made a list of what had to be done, and rang Peter Berry in Katherine.

Somewhere in the middle of everything last year, we had decided to do a bit more on the house. Peter Berry and his mate Gert had built some wonderful stone and timber houses at Mt Catt, so we asked them to come up to Melaleuca and finish off ours for us as we were too busy to do it ourselves. Rod and Greg had already cut enormous ironwood posts which Peter and Gert stood in position and erected the roof overhead, joining it to the original structure we had put up in 1986. It was six metres high in the centre, and sloped away either side to about two and a half metres. Peter and Gert left, and would come back when we were ready to do the carpentry inside.

We had lined up the same concreting friends again, dragged the demountable out from under the roof with the bulldozer, and poured an enormous concrete slab under the shade of the new roof. For the remainder of the year we were once again building rock walls every chance we got, right around the outside of the slab as well as walls for the interior rooms, all 600 mm high. Greg, Rod and I worked for most of the 1987 to '88 wet season to finish them off, and now they were ready for Peter and his men to return. The plan was to erect timber framing on top of the stone walls, and clad it with cypress pine planks which we ordered from Queensland.

Peter managed to squeeze some time for us into his schedule. The cypress pine arrived in the nick of time and was stacked up in fragrant bundles on the new slab. Peter arrived a couple of weeks before the US clients were due, and he and his men worked like Trojans putting up the framing for all the rooms. They started on the cypress panelling, but only had time to complete the main bedroom and make the doors before they had to go back to another job in Katherine. In the meantime Greg and Chris and a couple of other helpers did as much as they could, and were nailing the last of the flywire in place just as Rod drove through the gate with the American visitors on board.

It had been a gruelling few weeks, making sure I'd thought of everything we'd need, trying to second-guess what the clients would expect, worrying about the state of the house, and how much it was all costing. The tension between Rod and me wasn't helping any either. I was about to go outside to greet the arrivals, when Chris and Greg came in to wash up.

'Whoa, mate! You better have a look in the mirror, Jo – what have you done to yourself?'

My chest and neck were covered in bright red blotches. I looked like I'd come off second best in a beetroot throwing contest. All I could put it down to was nerves. My stomach had been in a knot for days, and if I looked I could see my hands shaking slightly. I rushed into the bedroom and changed into a shirt that hid the blotches a bit better, and hoped the guests wouldn't think I had some exotic disease.

Bob and Cari Koch were our first guests, and we didn't even have a name for our business yet. Cari was a travel agent in Los Angeles, and she and Bob decided their honeymoon would be a great opportunity to check out this new destination. Dominick had explained to them before they left the States that our house was still under construction, but I don't think they really appreciated just how unready we were. Our bedroom was the only room completely finished, and we installed the Kochs in there. Rod, Callum, Shaun and I unrolled our swags in what was to be the boys' bedroom, behind the kitchen. We hung blankets up on the unfinished wall frames for privacy, but it must have seemed very Third World stuff to Bob, who poked his head through the blankets at one point, and said: 'Are you guys sure you're okay in there?' He looked a little nonplussed. He and Cari must have been wondering just what they'd got themselves into.

Greg stayed on to help, but Murphy's law was in full flight that week. I don't think there was a vehicle on the place that didn't break down. Even the four wheeled motorbike had a flat tyre. There were no buffalo to be seen anywhere, and the bull catcher got bogged a dozen times. Rod came jogging back to the homestead one day having left Bob and Cari out in the bush, because one of the back wheels parted company with the Toyota. Another morning he came trotting in, covered in mud, to get another vehicle to pull the bogged catcher out again.

'Shall I put lunch on now?' I called as he left to start up the tractor.

'Yeah, should be back in about twenty minutes. Bloody catcher's stuck in the crossing at the bottom of the rainforest.'

That creek crossing was always wet but generally had a hard base, and Rod must have thought he could rush it and give his passengers a bit of excitement as the black water sprayed out either side of the Toyota. I started preparing lunch.

An hour and a half later, three very hot and dirty people straggled up to the verandah, on foot. Cari looked distinctly unimpressed. As I gently shooed the Kochs into the bathroom with soap and towels, I looked inquiringly at Rod.

'Bogged the bloody tractor. I'll have to take the grader out there and pull them both out.'

'It's not going very well, is it?' I said ruefully. 'They seem a bit unhappy today.'

'Nah, they love it,' said Rod with his usual confidence. 'They've never had a holiday like this before! It's all fascinating stuff to people from the city.'

I doubted that getting bogged or breaking down every other day was quite the experience anyone would be looking for, but Rod was very sure of himself. He took them fishing, looking for wildlife, chasing a buffalo when the country let him, crocodile spotting on the river, birdwatching and anything else that came into his head. At night he entertained them with stories and Territory history, and his own bush philosophy.

The visitors, once they'd grown accustomed to the idea that this wasn't a 'normal' holiday, seemed to thrive on the unexpected, the disasters, and even the bogs. Rod kept them interested and entertained with his knowledge of the bush, I kept them well fed, and Callum and Shaun took them for 'Harry Butler' wanders in the rainforest, something the boys were very good at. On the last day Rod organised a helicopter flight over the station for them, and the Kochs finally saw that we did indeed have a few herds of buffalo. But the thing they enjoyed the most was staying with us, as part of the family. They shared our home, our meals and our daily lives, and I guess experienced an 'outback' way of life for real, instead of glimpsing it in a short visit, or driving by in a bus. This was to become the template when I started running homestays in earnest a couple of years later, though I think the travel agent in Cari decided that, while she and Bob had had a wonderful time, perhaps the average US tourist wasn't ready for such a 'real' experience. We didn't get any more of them!

Rod and I went to court in May 1988, and my strongest memory is of the judge having a chuckle about the fact that our application said we intended to continue to reside at the same address after the divorce. It was all over with fairly quickly. The other memory is that while I took an affirmation, having renounced my Catholic faith a long time ago and not actually considering myself officially a Christian, Rod, the religious sceptic and challenger, swore on the Bible.

It was odd leaving the courtroom. Rod opened the door for me, and we walked out together, conscious of the curious looks from the other people in the courtroom. Our old friend from Kununurra, Gavin Perry, met us at the hotel we were staying at. He was the only person other than Felicity and my friend Sabrina who knew we were divorcing.

'This is really weird, you know. The three of us are sitting here chatting pleasantly, drinking tea. Aren't you two supposed to be at each other's throats?' Gavin shook his head and laughed, but he looked a bit bewildered just the same.

It *was* weird. But what was even stranger was that Rod still didn't want to tell anyone.

'Other people – our families – will only try and get involved, and want to help,' he said. 'If we wait a while, when we tell them and they say "but what about the boys?", we can say, "look, we've already been divorced for this long, and they're fine." They can't interfere then.'

I didn't tell my sister Leonie, not wanting to put her in the position of having to keep such a secret from our parents. That was hard, because she and I were very close, and I valued her counsel. I had talked to Gavin and to Felicity about it, and to Sabrina by letter, not trusting my own judgement enough to carry me through. I wasn't so sure it was a good idea, but as usual I went along with Rod – if one thing was certain, it was that Rod never did things the usual way.

The decree nisi came through on 21 June 1988, midwinter's day, which I thought was eminently suitable. The time when life was at its lowest ebb, either dying, or waiting to be rebirthed in the spring.

# 17

# End of an Era

One of the less popular features of the Northern Territory is the bushfire smoke that stains the sky for months. It always seemed a complete conundrum to me – you burned the country so that it didn't burn. Early in the dry season, as soon as the grass had dried out but there was still plenty of moisture in the soil, we'd begin burning off at Melaleuca. The idea was to prevent serious hot fires later in the Dry, when they would be much fiercer and kill young trees and shrubs, and possibly get out of control and burn pastures and fences. We reduced the fuel load of the vegetation by lighting fires along the edges of the paddocks and the roads early in the year. This way we achieved a 'cool burn', where the fire licked through the bush while it was still relatively green, leaving most of it untouched but thinning it out so that if it did burn later, there would be less damage to the environment.

All of us would go along on these expeditions. The tractor usually went ahead a week or two before, slashing a broad swathe beside the fence line so that we had a clear place to start from. Lengths of old poly pipe were set alight, and they burned slowly, dripping blobs of flaming plastic onto the long grass at the edge of the mown area. The rest of the crew followed along behind with old mail bags, beating the flames out on the short grass side, and allowing them to move out into the bush, where they eventually reached a green patch and went out. It was hard, dirty work, but a big group of us working together like that always made it feel like more of a social gathering than a grinding job.

It was in 1988 that Butje, a young Timorese man Rod had met in Kupang eighteen months before, arrived to live with us. Rod had taken a liking to him, and was impressed with his efficiency and hard work. He really wanted to help him, and give him the opportunity to come to Australia if that was possible. We sponsored Butje to come to Australia to work for us. Rod had an idea that Butje could help out with managing the books and so on, but when I collected him in Darwin, I realised that Butje's English wasn't up to handling much correspondence.

Well, I thought, he's spent lots of time working in a hotel, and Rod says he can cook, so there's a good job for him. It would be a change for me not to have to cook all the time. I soon discovered that Butje had a repertoire of two – a soup made from jackfruit which no one could eat, and stir-fried meat. The meat dish was basically large chunks of meat, stir-fried. That was it. Sometimes some vegetables were added, but basically it was just rice and meat. The second time he cooked it, I thought I'd make a salad to serve with it, and left it in a bowl on the bench while I set the table for lunch. By the time I returned to the kitchen, the salad had disappeared.

'What happened to the salad, Butje?'

'I cook it with the meat.' He smiled and nodded, showing that he'd remembered my comment about a few vegies with the meat being a good thing.

'Oh! Well, that'll be different!'

Stir-fried salad was actually not too bad, but the general consensus was that the troops preferred their lettuce cold and crunchy.

Butje may have been completely out of place on a Northern Territory buffalo station, but he tried harder than most people I ever saw. He was in a strange country confronted with scary looking bull catchers, buffalo that weren't the least bit like the quiet ones at home, and an isolation that he would never have experienced amongst the losmens of Kupang. As if that wasn't enough, he went to southeast Arnhem Land the following year to live in one of Rod's rough camps at Mt Catt while they chased buffalo for a few months. Butje took over the cooking, such as it was, and kept the camp much cleaner than it would have been otherwise, but he never really got used to the fierceness of the wild buffalo. In Timor, buffalo are very domesticated. Little children can control them with a stick and a rope. These Australian buffalo were terrifying for Butje. And to add to his fears, old George J— had scared the daylights out of him by telling him, with a huge grin, that he was going to eat him one night. I think Butje was quite relieved to be leaving the Territory in one piece when he went home to Kupang at the end of his twelve month stay.

In July 1988 producers and directors Bill Paolantonio and Chris Pechin from *Incredible Sunday*, an American program, came out to Melaleuca to do a four-day shoot with Rod, using an Australian film crew. They also brought a female presenter, Brianne, whose job it was to follow Rod around in the bush for a few days and be the 'New Yorker' to his 'Crocodile Dundee'. They started out the first day with a very tight schedule of shots they wanted to get. We looked at the list over breakfast, looked at each other and shrugged. They'd discover soon enough that they weren't in LA anymore.

The first upset in the timetable occurred straight after breakfast, when the camera gear was being loaded into the catchers. The resident goanna, he of the egg-eating inclinations, strolled across in front of the Americans, who nearly had heart failures in their rush to get the camera crew onto it.

'Bring him back again!' demanded the director. 'We need to get a second shot of that!'

Chris Penhall walked past on his way to his catcher, shaking his head and rolling a smoke. 'Ah, bad luck, mate. I don't think he signed his contract, ay?'

It took all day for them to realise that their schedule was subject to a host of uncontrollable variables. A buffalo might not be found at 1 pm. The pigs might not cooperate at three. And the unexpected mob of wallabies that allowed themselves to be filmed for a full half-hour hadn't been slotted into the timetable in the first place. The only thing we could almost guarantee was the weather. Once they accepted this, and discussed with Rod what they wanted to film each day, he was able to organise things so that they'd get the footage they wanted.

They were fascinated by pig hunting. Rod and some of the other men had begun hunting pigs with spears a few months before, and this was irresistible to the Americans. They had seen the size of the huge black boars on the flood plains, and couldn't believe anyone would be so crazy as to go after them with a spear instead of a big gun.

The blokes had fashioned the spears out of grader blades cut and ground to a sharp edge, and welded them onto lengths of steel pipe, or wired them onto bamboo poles. Then, with the dogs kitted up in their stout leather vests and wide collars, they'd drive out onto the flood plain and venture on foot into the mimosa thickets after the pigs. The dogs would flush out a mob of squealing black porkers, latch onto the biggest boar, and keep it occupied while the men ran in and killed it with the blades.

I never went along on these hunts. 'Too much testosterone for me,' I'd say, only half joking. I found the idea of killing for sport, even if it meant the elimination of a few more feral pigs, unappealing and faintly unsettling. I wasn't squeamish about killing animals when necessary, or butchering them for food. But while I didn't share Rod's penchant for pitting himself against the wilds, I did understand it. He needed to feel that rawness of experience, that uncertainty of putting yourself in danger, and testing yourself against the natural world. I think he felt unreal and out of place in the world the rest of us inhabited.

These elements about him were what appealed to the film makers. They wanted to capture this Daniel Boone character who was running out of wild places to lose himself in. People like Rod represent all the things we faintly remember, when a dog howling at the moon at night raises the hair on our arms and necks; when an unidentified sound in the dark makes us think first of a wild animal, and not a burglar.

They spent four days heading out every morning to film Rod in various scenarios – bull catching, butchering a buffalo, killing pigs, finding bush tucker for his co-star Brianne to gag on – and they slowly relaxed. One of the benefits of having so many different people to stay, and especially overseas visitors, was the exchange of experiences and ideas. Evenings were full of conversation and comparisons of lifestyles and philosophies. Once people stopped being the Hollywood Producer, or the New York Director, or the BBC Journalist, they discovered they had a lot in common with the rest of us.

They signed our visitors' book when they left, and Chris Pechin wrote this:

Rod and Joanne,

This is the way I'll remember Australia – the life of the bull catchers. The catching of the bulls, the killing of the pigs, getting stuck in the bog – and pulling each other out.

That's what happened most . . . Hollywood people rushing into the bush to make a movie, trying to rush to make the schedule, and getting caught in the bog, and being rescued by the Australians who worked with us and made us laugh like hell . . .

In September 1988 Rod flew to Los Angeles to film the second part of the *Incredible Sunday* program, where Brianne got to exact some revenge for the mud and the bush tucker, but somehow I don't think Rod having to eat a corn dog from an LA street vendor was in the same league as her witchetty grub.

He landed back home just two days ahead of the next film crew's arrival. This time it was *A Current Affair* and Neil Kearney and his crew stayed for three days filming buffalo-catching sequences, and talking to Rod about his life. We had some other visitors at that time, and with Felicity's help I was cooking for eighteen people at each meal. I blessed Chris Penhall every time I turned on the gas stove.

In amongst all the film crews and other distractions, we were mustering and bull catching at full speed. Often we would load the buffalo out at night, when it was cool. Sometimes I'd take a swag out for Callum and Shaun to sleep on while the rest of us helped push the buffalo up the race and into the truck – Josie, Felicity, and anyone else who happened to be around would come along. One vehicle would shine its headlights onto the race to provide a little bit of light, and another would work in the back yard, pushing up animals and forcing them to run towards the loading ramp. We would stand ready with lengths of timber to slot though the bars of the loading ramp to stop the buffalo from backing down the ramp again. The dogs helped too, biting at the buffaloes' hocks when they stopped and jammed themselves in the race. Off to one side, away from the yards, a billy would be brewing on the fire, hot tea keeping everyone's spirits up in the small hours.

When we were bull catching rather than mustering, instead of booking a road train to take the buffalo to the meatworks in one load, we would use our own truck which had a stock crate on the back and could carry about twelve to fifteen head. I often drove it and unloaded it by myself at the abattoir at Point Stuart, about 20 kilometres away, while the men went out and caught more buffalo.

*To Fight the Wild* was being screened in the UK and the United States that Christmas, and Rod was flown to London and Los Angeles to do a round of interviews with TV, radio and newspapers. The BBC were talking to him about doing a short series, which Rod was very hopeful about, but after several months of consideration, the money wasn't forthcoming, and the project didn't go ahead.

Rod was constantly being encouraged by various people in the film industry who wanted to work with him on some kind of film or television project. In 1987 and 1988 Melaleuca played host to at least five producers and/or directors who were keen to involve him in something. Scripts were flourished, ideas tossed around, treatments produced. I could see Rod getting hopeful about being able to make that tantalising change of direction, the one that had seemed to beckon nearly ten years earlier. I wished for his sake that it would happen, but all the enthusiasm and all the ideas eventually came to nothing.

Rod saw television as the means to get across his passionate beliefs about nature, and about living. He believed that people needed to reforge their connection with the natural world or mankind had no hope. In December 1988 he appeared on the *Wogan* program in London, and spoke about wanting to teach people about the bush, how to respect it, how to survive in the kind of country he loved. He struck a definite chord with a lot of people and he received dozens and dozens of letters over the next few months from people wanting to come out to Australia and do exactly that.

But 1989 was the year in which we had to meet the development covenants on Melaleuca. We had completed the boundary fencing, built a homestead, and fenced off several paddocks. The main one now was the stocking covenant, and we had to have 200 TB-free breeder buffalo on the property by the end of the year in order to comply with it. The pressure to get the buffalo and meet the covenants swung attention away from tourists and television, and Rod would spend much of 1989 shuttling between Melaleuca and Mt Catt.

Almost all the buffalo on Melaleuca had been caught and sent to the meatworks by the end of 1988, and all the calves shot as part of the demands of acquiring our 'Provisionally Clear' status. Greg had the deadening job of shooting hundreds of them when they came into the yards with their mothers, and taking their ears for the $40 per head compensation payment. The carcasses were left out in the scrub for the dingoes, goannas and hawks to feast on. A few months after the last yard was run and the last beast removed, the government stock inspector came in by helicopter and flew over the station to shoot any remaining animals. He found fewer than twenty, so we had managed a very thorough and efficient destocking in the four years we had been operating at Melaleuca.

Chris and Greg didn't return to Melaleuca to work in 1989. The writing was on the wall for them as it was for so many other young blokes in the bush. BTEC was quickly reducing the numbers of feral buffalo, with tens of thousands being shot from helicopters all across the Top End. Very soon there would be no more wild buffalo, no more buffalo catching. And for Greg this was compounded by his leg injury, which meant he couldn't jump up and down off trucks and around stock like he'd been used to doing. He began a full-time course at university, but when the mid year holidays came, he and Josie went down to Mt Catt and spent a month working with Rod catching buffalo there. Chris went back to plumbing, but at the end of the season old George J— and Sammy Bulabul convinced him to come to Mt Catt to work for the community as the mechanic. They were getting the buffalo domestication project going, and needed someone to look after the vehicles.

Michael Parkinson called Rod back to Sydney for another interview in mid 1989. It was a very different Rod in the chair this time. The beaming, cheeky young bull catcher who'd made everyone laugh so much back in 1981 had been replaced by someone much more guarded and wry. He looked strained and uncomfortable on the screen. I felt very sad when I watched the program.

Felicity decided she'd finally had enough of teaching, two years after she'd first given it up. She found me another governess while she was down south for the Wet, and instead came back to help me run the station, while Rod was away at Mt Catt.

Felicity and I continued the fencing and yard building. We dug holes and concreted in corner assemblies, ran fencing wire, hammered in pickets, strained up the wire, and tied on droppers. Then we'd sit down and work out the intricacies of the solar panels which powered the electric fences. We electrocuted ourselves so many times I think our hair was permanently standing on end. It's not a dangerous shock, but it hits you like a solid punch to the body. It wasn't so bad in the dry season, when the humidity was low, but in the wet season we were always jumping and swearing at the bloody fence.

Callum and Shaun had lots of fun with the electric fences. One time I came across them, with their cousins Luke and Christopher Hemsworth, standing in a line near the fence, all holding hands. Mystified by this unusual display of sibling affection, I watched for a while. They called out to another child who was staying with us, Sabrina's son Bill, 'Bill! Bill! Quick – grab Shaun's hand!' Bill obediently trotted up and took Shaun's hand, and Callum immediately grabbed the positive wire on the fence. Bill jumped, and danced around shaking his hand while the others fell about laughing hysterically. It was obviously worth getting a shock if you could trick someone else into it too.

Felicity and I had quite a learning curve, working our way through the different problems we encountered every day. One time we were driving home after spending the day working at a creek crossing on the east side of the station. We were in the Hi Ace, when suddenly it sputtered and died. I checked all the obvious things, like fuel, oil, temperature, and then found the fuel filter was completely blocked with sludge.

We had no spare fuel filters with us, so I decided the only thing we could do was to bypass the filter just to get home. The problem was how to reconnect the two cut ends of the plastic fuel line. Felicity came up with another of her imaginative solutions, and we fitted the empty barrel of a biro into the line, and twisted some soft tie-wire around each end. We got home in time for dinner, feeling very proud of ourselves.

We serviced the diesel generator ourselves, changing its oil and filters, replacing some simple parts whose names I can no longer remember, and bleeding the air out of the fuel lines when it ran out of diesel. It wasn't a big generator, so it was started with a crank handle. One day I cranked it up but for some reason the handle didn't spin off the way it should have when the engine coughed into life, and it stayed on the shaft, spinning around in a deadly blur. I stood outside the shed for a few minutes, wondering how the hell I was going to get the damn thing off without getting killed. Felicity came over and we tossed a few brooms at it, hoping they might dislodge the crank handle. We ducked away from the door as they were slammed into the metal roof with a terrible clatter. In the end I cut off the fuel supply to make the engine shut down. And had to bleed the damn generator again.

For most of 1989, at least while Rod was away, Melaleuca was a woman's domain. Apart from Callum and Shaun, there was Felicity, Gilda Müller the governess and me. Simon Clark, a young Scottish backpacker on his second stint at Melaleuca, was a cheerful and willing worker for a couple of months before going to Mt Catt to help Rod with the buffalo, but otherwise it was only women. We would spend longer on a job than the men might have, but we always got it done without anyone having a dummy spit. Consensus was the marker. Sometimes we really had no idea how to do something when we started a job. For example, I had been told to put in the creek crossings in the fence lines. Where the fence lines crossed the creeks, there was a need for something that would stand up to the floodwaters in the Wet, and yet still create a barrier to buffalo in the Dry season. Rod had decided that the best way to do this would be to run heavy wire cables across the creeks themselves, and attach lengths of rubber conveyer belting to this, so that the belting would hang down to the creek bed in the dry, but would be lifted up by the floodwaters in the Wet without breaking the fence.

I knew what I wanted to end up with, but there were a lot of things to consider, such as the force of the water flow, the direction of the force, where most of the strain would be concentrated, what angle the strainer posts should be at, and so on. And none of us had studied physics at school. We sat and looked at the crossing for a while, discussing the different aspects. That particular day we had with us a young bloke who had been working with Rod down at Mt Catt. He'd been sent up to help at Melaleuca for a while, but he was only about seventeen, and had no practical skills at anything. However, he was irritated by the length of time we were taking to work it all out. He huffed and puffed, and behaved as if we should all be deferring to him simply because he was the only male there.

'Gawd, just get on with it!' he erupted finally.

'This one's been apprenticed to Rod for too long, I think,' I muttered to Felicity.

We ignored him, and eventually came to a decision about what we should do, and started work. Putting in the strainer assemblies was the hardest part of the job, because they had to have deep and enormous bell-shaped holes filled with steel reinforcing and metres of concrete to hold them in the sandy banks. It took most of the day, and we tried very hard not to make a comment when our token male collapsed under a shady tree with blisters and a sore back long before the rest of us. The steel cable was strained across a week later after the concrete had set hard, and when the rubber matting went up a few months later, it all worked perfectly. We dropped the young bloke in Darwin on the next trip, and left him to find his way back to Rod.

I used to say, when people asked how we were managing with no men around to do the heavy work, that we didn't need any men. What we needed was a wife: 'It would be great to have someone there who would do all the little things, like fuel up the generator, and do the oil changes on the tractor, and service the car, you know, that sort of thing. Oh, and cook dinner sometimes too . . . . A *wife* is what we need, not a bloke!'

The household was certainly peaceful and calm, and full of laughter. I don't think Callum and Shaun suffered too much from the absence of continuous male role models. I knew I must have been doing something right when Callum's teacher, out on a school patrol, told me about the last school camp Callum had been on: 'We were playing "Farmer in the Dell",' she said, 'and I picked a girl to start off the game, to be the Farmer. One of the boys objected loudly that she couldn't be the farmer because she was a *girl*. Do you know, Callum piped up: well my mum's a *bull catcher*, and *she's* a girl! I was so proud of him!' I was proud of him too.

Girl bull catcher or not, the fencing to be done was more than Felicity and I could manage on our own, and so a succession of backpackers began to come through, working for their keep. Some stayed a few days, some stayed a few months, but they all thoroughly enjoyed the experience. The lifestyle on a station was so different from anything any of them had come across. It was the opportunity to actually *live* what the tourist brochures talked about and the buses drove past. They all boarded with us, as part of the family, and I imagine for young people away from home for months, this wasn't such a bad thing either. They came from all around the world, from all walks of life. Some were students on summer holidays from Europe and America, some were older travellers, taking a break from work and routine. Dinnertimes were like meetings of the United Nations. One night we realised we had seven different nationalities seated around the table – English, German, Canadian, Israeli, Swedish and Japanese, as well as us Australians. It was wonderful for Callum and Shaun. They were learning at an early age about the different people in the world, and the countries they were from. That not everyone lived like we did, or spoke the same language.

The backpackers did whatever we did, whether it was buffalo catching (in the early days), or getting up in the middle of the night to light fires, and they loved it. Without exception they worked willingly, and were pleasant and friendly – well, I guess one wasn't quite such a success. Gunther – or Goitre, as Felicity called him – only stayed three days. We had arranged his journey out to the station, and when he turned up, he decided it was much too hot, and that the work was much too hard. He also had a huge appetite, in spite of not working, and had us watching in glazed fascination as he had second and third helpings before anyone else had finished their first. After the third day of Gunther lying in the shade complaining about the heat while the women slogged away, Felicity drove him to Shady Camp with his bags and suggested he find a lift back to town from one of the tour operators.

Another we dubbed the Credit Card Kid. 'Randy' told us he was an air traffic controller in San Diego. We thought he looked a little young to have so much responsibility, but who were we to judge? He stayed a couple of weeks, and charmed everyone with his friendliness, his hard work, and in particular his willingness to cook. Shortly after he left, we heard he was arrested in Darwin for fraud. Apparently he'd had a racket going where he'd steal a fellow traveller's credit cards, go out for the evening with other backpackers and pay for everything on the stolen card, while the others would quite innocently pay him their share in cash. By the time the poor backpacker realised his cards were missing, 'Randy' would have moved on to another hostel. He was finally caught trying to use a stolen card in a chemist shop. We never did find out if he was really an air traffic controller.

Towards the end of 1989 I had an Israeli soldier, a Japanese truck driver, and a Swedish university student helping me to build the stock yards and tackle the creek crossings. BiBi, Hiroshi and Peter were very hard workers. Peter the Swede spoke excellent English, but BiBi the Israeli, and Hiroshi, the truck driver from Tokyo, struggled a bit more. Hiroshi had practically no English at all, but BiBi had lived for a time in Japan, and spoke enough Japanese to translate for him, so we managed to communicate very well, if through a kind of relay system. BiBi, Hiroshi and Peter hung the rubber matting on the creek crossings – no small task, as each piece of matting weighed at least 100 kilograms, and had to be manhandled across steep banks.

Rod had marked out the stock yards on his last trip up to the station, and so I drilled the holes with the post hole digger on the tractor, and we concreted in the posts for the forcing yard. We were running steel cable through these posts instead of welding on steel rails, so I blew out the holes with the oxy-acetylene, and the blokes threaded the cable through. Doing it that way meant that I could get on with it, otherwise we would have had to wait for Rod to come back and do all the welding. My welding was okay at a pinch, but the yards needed to be able to withstand big buffaloes smashing into them without the rails snapping off the posts.

In August 1989, I convinced the bank to lend us some money, and I bought five dinghies and outboard motors, and started hiring them to fishermen at Shady Camp. We'd had absolutely no income all year, and with Rod down at Mt Catt getting together the new buffalo to restock Melaleuca, we wouldn't have any for a while to come. I made up some advertising cards and dropped them into all the hotels and backpacker lodges in Darwin, and placed regular ads in the *NT News*, and a couple of popular fishing magazines. Before too long, we were getting a regular trade, and covering some of our day-to-day expenses.

Earlier in the year, the boys' governess had rolled the Hi Ace on the gravel road. Fortunately Gilda wasn't hurt at all, but the poor old Hi Ace was a write-off. I had been musing about starting some sort of tourist venture on the station, so when the Hi Ace was towed home, Chris Penhall, who had come out for the weekend, picked up the oxy gear and cut off all the squashed and damaged panels, right down to the floor. He turned it into a beaut people carrier for the station, welding roll bars over it, and putting in extra seats we found at the wreckers' yards in Darwin. Shade cloth wired onto the tops of the roll bars made a shady roof, and we were in business. Mostly, though, we used it to tow boats down to Shady Camp. It carried twelve people easily, and looked completely ridiculous – particularly when Felicity and Gilda painted it in pink and grey zebra stripes.

My father was coming up to stay for a few weeks in the middle of 1989, and I insisted that we tell our parents about our divorce. Dad had stayed with us the previous August, and I couldn't face another period of pretending that everything was okay between Rod and me. Rod was away at Mt Catt so much that we didn't meet to talk about it until the week before Dad was due to arrive. We wrote letters to both sets of parents, explaining the situation, and Mum and Dad received theirs the day before Dad left for Darwin. Not exactly good timing.

I was in town to pick up Dad, and phoned Mum from the hotel. She was not happy. So we yelled at each other for a few minutes, nearly hung up on each other a few times, but managed to calm down and talk about it rationally. She was angry that we hadn't told them for so long, and then only the day before Dad was due to leave. It had come as a massive shock. Then she surprised me by saying that she was relieved to see me out of the marriage: 'I could never bear seeing the way he treated you,' she said. 'That time we stayed up there, you and he would both be out working all day, and when you got home he'd sit down and say "Cuppa tea, Jo," and you'd rush around and chop the bloody firewood and get the dinner ready and everything else. And I couldn't say anything – you would have just defended him. That's why I haven't come up again – I would've had to bite my tongue off.'

I was stunned to hear this from Mum, but it wasn't to be the last time I heard it. As more people learned of our divorce, several women confided the same sentiments to me. They all said that although they liked Rod for himself, they thought he wasn't a very nice husband. I'd always believed that we presented a devoted, united front in spite of what was happening behind the scenes, but to my shocked surprise, lots of people saw me as very much the downtrodden wife, running around in the background keeping Rod happy. It gave me a lot to think about.

As well as the quiet, steady support I had from Felicity, I also had some other good women friends through this time. If I didn't confide in them about what was happening, it was only because of Rod's influence, not because of any lack of trust in them on my part. One of them was Jane Miles, who I first met through the Katherine School of the Air in 1984 at the annual school conference. One of the teachers, Leonie Rosevear, introduced us: 'Jo, I have someone I want you to meet. I've been wanting to introduce you two for a long time – I think you'll get along really well!'

Jane lived in Kakadu National Park, with her husband Greg, a senior park ranger, and their two children, Carlia and Bunitj. They had been in Kakadu since 1976, three years before it actually became a national park, living at remote places like Cannon Hill and the East Alligator River. Jane was a very talented artist, and painted the wilderness outside her back door. She also edited and produced a little magazine called *Bush Buzz*, which went out every couple of months to isolated families in the Territory. Jane soon involved me in it, and with her constant encouragement and infectious enthusiasm I began writing regular articles, and eventually illustrating them, something that was to become a major part of my life in the future.

I had met Sally McLeay and Harry Craven around 1988, and they became great friends of both Rod and me. They loved coming out to the station, and we often stayed with them when we went into Darwin. Sally's house was a sanctuary of normality for me – I stopped in to see her every chance I got, for a cup of tea and a chat about something other than buffalo, BTEC and the bush. She was at home with a small daughter at that stage, but still vitally interested in the arts, books, and life in general. I treasured her intellect and her outlook, and she was to become a real lifeline for me in the next few years.

Another woman had become a very important part of my life until her death from cancer in 2003. Barbara James had first come to Darwin in 1967, from rural Nebraska in the United States, and had lived here ever since. Gavin Perry introduced us in late 1986 – he had not long moved to Darwin from Kununurra, and lived in a little flat under her house. Barbara was a trained journalist, and was now a respected historian and writer, in the middle of her first major book, 'No Man's Land', about the history of women in the Northern Territory. She lived on East Point Road in a house famous for its verandah, which was a magnet for all kinds of interesting and diverse people. A 'verandah session at Barb's' was characterised by lively debate, lots of laughter, and plenty of red wine. If Darwin had an intelligentsia, its meeting place was Barbara James' verandah. She encouraged me to write, and to draw my first cartoon strip, which eventually ran for some years in several newspapers, locally and inter-state. She was my mentor, and had been pushing me to write this book for years.

My long friendship with Sabrina kept me afloat too. We had first met in 1967, when we were eleven-year-old students in first year at Aquinas Girls' College in Ringwood. Although we hardly ever got to see each other, being at opposite ends of the continent, we wrote long letters regularly. Mine were full of daily details, but nothing about my relationship with Rod, until it had really broken down. She had made her own observations about the relationship on the occasions she'd stayed with us over the years, and the times we'd visited her, but had kept them to herself until I'd admitted things weren't so good. Wise and practical, she helped me to sort through what was happening to me at my own pace, never pushing, and never judgemental.

An era ended in 1989, when the telephone was connected to Mela-leuca. For the past seven years, from the time we went out to Mainoru, I had regularly fronted up to the Codan two-way radio, answering the call of 'VJY Darwin calling Eight Sierra Oscar Juliet mobile, over,' with 'Eight Sierra Oscar Juliet standing by, over.' One by one the call signs around the Territory were disappearing as technology put us in direct contact with the rest of the world. It was sad to witness the end of a long tradition, even though it gave way to something a lot more efficient and private. But the Out Post Radio system had its own efficiencies. There were many times when someone standing by to make their own call would chip in with an answer or a suggestion after you'd completed yours. For example, one day at Bulman I was calling the meatworks to find out if our buffalo had arrived. The meatworks hadn't seen them, and when I finished the call, commenting to the VJY operator that I wondered how you could lose a whole road train of buffalo, a voice clicked in: 'Just saw your truck at Emerald Springs an hour ago – he had tyre trouble but he's on his way again now,' followed by another voice: '. . . and it's real easy to lose a road train of buffalo, mate!'

VJY broadcast the news, and relayed the running of the Melbourne Cup every November, and helped a lot of people feel a little less isolated and forgotten by the rest of the country. It was a living network, an absolutely vital support in the bush that saved lives and preserved sanity, operated by a team of women with often wicked senses of humour. At Bulman I had ordered some seed worms by mail for my compost heap – the hard red soil in the community was absolutely devoid of earthworms. When I knew they were on their way, I phoned up the mail plane company to ask them to make sure our mail bag wasn't left out in the sun, so that the worms wouldn't cook. For weeks afterwards, I would be asked when I called in: 'Roger, Eight Sierra Oscar Juliet – and how are your worms now, Jo? Have you tried some Combantrim, dear?'

A real telephone was great for privacy and for fast and efficient communication, but it was lacking in a few other attributes.

The clock was ticking for Melaleuca – our lease was up for review at the end of 1989. We had completed most of the covenants except for the stocking requirement, and we were certain we could manage this by the end of the year. The yards were well underway, and we had already bought a flash new cattle crush to build into it. Things would continue to be tight financially, but we had hopes for the tourism venture to provide some income once it got going properly. The boat hire business was up and running and looked successful. And we had destocked the property, and were almost ready to take on the first shipment of TB-free buffalo to begin restocking.

We had been working for months with a professional financial consultant on our plans and projections for the station and provided this information along with our tourism ideas to the Lands department ahead of time. In September Rod and I went to see the bank about extending our loan, so that we could build the yards, and get the stock from Mt Catt. The initial response from the bank was positive, but when we called back to see when the new finance would be approved, we were in for a rude shock. The loans manager told us that the bank could not lend us any money now, because they had been informed that our lease was not being renewed. We were completely stunned. Our lease still had four months to run, and it looked like someone had already decided that we weren't going to be staying, even without the requisite inspection by the Lands department. This just smacked of the worst kind of interference imaginable, not least because it was so incredibly blatant. We immediately began writing letters complaining about it, and finally after waiting for four miserable months, we were told we could have another five-year lease. Then to top it off, we received a letter congratulating us on being the first clean property in the area with a tested-negative herd. Coming at the end of five years of criticism because we had opted to destock rather than test clean, because we had no faith in the test, this was a pretty sour victory.

# 18

# Concrete and Cocktails

New Years Day 1990 was no different from any other day. The backpackers and I spent it slashing and poisoning mimosa out on the flood plain, but the next day I took Callum and Shaun to see a movie in Darwin. The other two backpackers were leaving, but BiBi, the Israeli, had agreed to stay on for another month, much to my relief. He was a cheerful fellow and a very hard worker, and with his help I'd get a lot more done than I would on my own.

The new governess started in mid January. Lesley [not her real name] was a university student, taking some time off from studies in her third year, and not sure if she wanted to keep following that course. She was an energetic, happy young woman, got along well with Callum and Shaun, and the teaching got off to a great start.

Rod slept in the boys' bedroom, on the rare occasions he was actually at the station. He was smoking a lot more marijuana, but as it made him calm and helped him deal with things better, it seemed like the lesser of two evils. He came and went a lot, spending time in town on BTEC matters, writing letters and submissions to various organisations and government departments. Because of the *Crocodile Dundee* attention, Rod's criticisms of the BTEC program were regularly aired in the paper, or in media like the *Bulletin*, and current affair programs. He was also often down at Mt Catt, getting things ready for the coming season there. The plan for the year was that he would go to Mt Catt and catch the rest of the young TB-free buffalo for Melaleuca to fulfil the stocking covenants on our block, and continue the work on the Mt Catt infrastructure, while I would finish off the fencing, and maintain the rest of the place in the meantime. The boys were very used to his absences, and accepted his comings and goings in their lives as normal. I accepted it with a great deal of relief.

The wet season brought a lot of storms, and BiBi and I were kept busy checking fence lines and cutting fallen trees and branches off them with the chainsaw. There was the usual maintenance, such as stripping down engines, repairing fences, checking on the new buffalo which had arrived a few months earlier from Mt Catt, slashing the fence lines not yet underwater, and pulling out mimosa as it emerged with the rains in new places. Mimosa was a constant, grinding battle. We sprayed again in February – another thirty drums of Starane adding to our debt with Elders in Katherine, but it had to be done now, not when we could better afford it. In an effort to keep the re-growth at bay, we would harvest *Hymenacne* grass out on the flood plain, and replant it in areas where the mimosa had been killed. This was to give the mimosa seedlings heavy competition when they emerged, as the *Hymenacne* grew thick and dense once it got going, plus it was a native grass suited to the area, not another imported potential weed.

Felicity arrived back at the station in late February, and I was never so pleased to see anyone. I had missed her calm steadiness, and the feeling she gave me of having someone in my corner. I'd been finding it increasingly difficult to go out and work on my own. Just having someone else to work with, and talk over ideas and plans, made a huge difference to my outlook. I was also getting sick again, one chest infection after another, and the doctors ordered more TB testing. Callum and Shaun wanted to know whether I'd be destocked if I tested positive.

The boat hires were improving as the fishing picked up at Shady Camp, and my plans for the campground development down there started to take shape. When I wasn't working outside, I would write up submissions and do some financial projections, ready to be handed over to the consultant in town who was going to tidy them up for me and run the figures through his computer.

Charlie Garske, a tourist operator running backpacker adventure tours into Kakadu National Park, started bringing his tours through

Shady Camp in January, hiring my boats three times a week, and paying rental on a permanent campsite. As well as being a top barramundi fishing destination, Shady Camp was famous for having the largest concentration of big saltwater crocodiles, and the backpackers loved it. The crocs were a powerful attraction, because Shady Camp also had the densest concentration of mosquitoes in the country, and this still didn't deter the tourists. The mosquitoes were at their most voracious at dawn and dusk, and of course these were the times we were usually down at the river launching and retrieving boats.

A few months later Ivan Paton, who owned a backpacker hostel in Darwin, started running his tours through Shady Camp as well, and set up a similar arrangement to Charlie's, hiring boats, and camping on our land. I had to buy another boat and motor to cope with the increased hires, and started to feel like I was actually getting somewhere.

Lesley wasn't enjoying teaching, but she was keen to stay on at the station. Rod was back at the time, and we had been working on the yards. I took over in the classroom again, and Lesley went off to work with Rod at the yards instead. In May, Rod began a relationship with her.

We had been divorced now for nearly two years, but I hadn't made that psychological leap into single life yet. That was one of the downsides of having pretended to be happily married for so long after the legalities were finalised. I was completely unprepared to see Rod turning his affection to someone else. Logically I could sort it all out, but whenever I saw Rod with Lesley, I was absolutely gutted. In hindsight it seems absurd to think that I could have carried on living in the same house as my ex-husband, while he was plunging into a romantic affair with another woman right in front of me. But I did, and I managed, and eventually they left and went to Mt Catt, and I stopped coping for a little while, and fell apart at my friend Sally's for a day or two.

The fact that I liked Lesley helped me deal with this dramatic change in my life, and the part of me that could stand back and be rational decided that it was a good thing. At least Rod would have someone with him at Mt Catt. The other thing I reflected on was that Lesley was vehemently anti-drugs. I hoped she might be able to slow down his marijuana use. Someone new, who hadn't been part of the last few years, might be able to make him see himself differently, and perhaps find a place where he didn't feel the need to smoke so much. Lesley seemed like a much stronger person than me, someone who wouldn't lose herself in Rod's personality, like I had.

It also seems absurd to think that I could still have cared what Rod did. But the truth is that I did care. I think it was a combination of the lack of reference points, due to the isolation I'd been in for so long, and the pretending for so long that everything was all right. It took a while before I could step away and feel I was my own person again. It happened quite unexpectedly, a few months after Rod had left.

I was up earlier than usual one morning, outside in the garden by myself, watching some wallabies feeding on the wet grass and listening to the racket of the birds as the sun came up. I wasn't thinking about anything in particular, just breathing in the peace, and being aware of a gentle balmy breeze, that perfect temperature you almost can't describe, where the air lies against your skin and makes you feel it, but no more than that. I realised that I felt good, that I really felt content and happy for the first time in a long time. I suddenly became aware that there was a part of me that Rod had never got to, never affected. It was as if there was a little box inside me that had stayed safely locked up until now. I felt a spreading warmth, a slow rush of tingling energy and a welling of peacefulness, as if the box had opened up and let something wonderful out. It was like I had come out of a tunnel into the light. Suddenly life seemed full of possibility and hope, and I knew it would be all right.

It was the fishing season for the Mary River, and as well as getting the boats ready for the backpacker tours, we were busy with guides and their clients coming to stay at the station and fish Shady Camp. The rest of May was a blur of cooking and making beds for visitors, cleaning boats, and burning the fence lines.

Mary Hodgson, a lovely, sprightly 70-year-old, arrived at Melaleuca in June to teach Callum and Shaun for a few weeks, under the Volunteers for Isolated Students Education (VISE) service. In return for free board and lodging, these volunteer ex-teachers go out to the bush and give mothers a break from the classroom. Mary stayed with us for six weeks, and the boys just loved her. I loved her too, because I was able to stop being the big bad bully all the time to Callum and Shaun. That's the trouble with teaching your own children. Mum's always the one giving orders and making them do things they don't want to. They can't exactly come home after school and complain about the teacher to you.

We'd made a start on the campground early in the year while Rod was still at the station, and had built half of the shop, erecting a roof over a concrete slab. Now, whenever we had a spare few hours, Felicity and I, and whoever else we could press-gang into helping, filled form-work with rocks and mortar. The walls looked good, and there was definitely something therapeutic in the absorption it took to construct them, choosing rocks of the right shape and size to fill the space, and a few hours later pulling off the formwork and cleaning away the excess mortar to expose the stone. My brother Peter was visiting for the first time, and spent the whole month he was with us carrying rocks, washing boats and putting out fires. It may explain why he's never been back! He wrote a poem in our visitor's book, part of which said:

> . . . There's feral pigs, and awesome crocs,
> Sick of boats, come pick up rocks.
> Flocks of jabiru, so graceful in flight,
> Tired of the bush? Help set it alight! . . .

Now that the country was drying out again we started burning fire-breaks along the fence lines. We would start off by mowing the grass either side of the fence with the tractor slasher to reduce the fuel load as much as possible. We could have graded the fence lines and not needed to burn, but then we'd have erosion problems, so we did it this way. It took weeks and weeks to cover all the property's fences, often requiring cooperation from the neighbours to do the boundary fence lines. Because it would get so hot and windy during the day, making it difficult to control the burn, we did a lot at night, getting up at two in the morning when the air was damp and still, lighting fires to burn away from the fence and into the paddock where they would die out in the green grass. It was quite lovely walking along in the cold June air in the middle of the night, watching bright little jewels flaring down the length of the line.

It wasn't all just work. Callum and Shaun had gone to Mt Catt to spend the school holidays with their dad, which left Felicity and me out at the station on our own for a while. We were invited to a cocktail party in Darwin. We thought if we could finish work by five o'clock that afternoon, we'd have enough time to get ourselves showered and dressed up before commencing the two hour drive into town. We were up at five thirty in the morning to get boats ready for an early hire, and started working on the rock walls at the shop as soon as it was light enough. The rock work went slowly, with only a break to collect and clean the boats for the next day's tours, and we couldn't finish till 6 pm.

We raced back to the house, starting up the water pump at the spring as we passed. The water took forever to make its way down to the house, so we gave up on the idea of a bath and left just as we were, hot and dirty and covered in cement dust. Speeding down the Arnhem Highway past Tom's Gully mine, I ploughed into a wallaby at 110 kph, which pushed the radiator cowling up into the fan. For once we had no tools with us, not even a torch. A caravan convoy of farmers from Wagga stopped and helped us make enough repairs to get going again, and insisted on following us into town to make sure we didn't have any more trouble. We gave them the station phone number, promising a fishing trip in return for their help.

We dragged ourselves in to Sally's at nine thirty, showered and changed into our glad rags, and got to the party by 10 pm. When we finally sat down, cocktails in hand, catching our breath, Felicity and I looked at each other and burst out laughing. The extremes of our day were too ridiculous. From mixing concrete and cleaning boats to sipping cocktails in our best dresses, with a 200-kilometre drive in between. Not to mention a dead wallaby. The Wagga farmers took us up on the fishing offer, too, and turned up a few days later.

In mid July Callum and Shaun came home from Mt Catt in George Westmacott's little plane, with vague news about a muster that had gone wrong the day before. Rod had been having a bad trot at Mt Catt, and there were still no buffalo to be seen. The bank was pressuring us regularly about the repayments that weren't happening, and making ominous noises about not extending our credit. At least the boat hire and the homestay business kept us fed.

A week later Lesley phoned from Katherine to say that Rod was in trouble. The muster that the boys had mentioned had taken place on the boundary with Mainoru Station, and Rod had erected the yards 100 metres over the unfenced boundary, on the Mainoru side. Mainoru's owner, John Harrower, had turned up, and when he found animals mustered into the yard and no one there, he let the tyres down on the grader and the other vehicles. Rod arrived back at the yards and was wildly angry, threatening Harrower with a star picket. The stock squad was called in, and now Rod had a court case to answer.

A couple of days later Rod called. After a few terse sentences about the problems with Mainoru and the stock squad, he said: 'Elders want their money now, and the only way we can avoid going bankrupt is to sell the block.'

The stock squad had frozen Mt Catt's account with Elders and effectively stopped the catching operation there. In turn Elders demanded we pay our account. We owed them about $40 000, mainly for herbicide to spray mimosa. I guess they could see the writing on the wall – if we couldn't catch buffalo at Mt Catt, we wouldn't be able to pay their account either. *Sell the block . . .* I couldn't believe it. Those were the last words I ever thought I'd hear Rod say. He was still talking: '. . . it's the only way we can salvage something out of all this. We haven't got any choice. I'm coming up in a couple of days to put it on the market.'

I couldn't believe he could give up so easily. We had a very large mortgage with the bank, but Melaleuca was still worth a lot more than what we owed. I decided he was probably just overreacting because of the trouble he was in with the stock squad. I hoped so.

I went out with the backpackers and finished concreting in the posts for a new section of fencing, and wondered if I was just wasting my time. As I worked, I thought about the ramifications of what Rod had said. If we had to sell Melaleuca, then all our dreams of being able to have an amicable divorce, with Rod working the station and me running my own business at Shady Camp, and Callum and Shaun able to shuttle between the two, would remain just dreams.

Greg and Josie had spent a few weeks with Rod during the year, and had come back very disturbed about the way he was behaving, and about the whole place in general. At the time Greg didn't voice his worries to me, but I could see that he was unhappy with Rod. Much later he told me that he and Josie had serious doubts about Rod's mental state, and how much dope he was smoking: 'I worked with that man a long time, and I knew how he operated. But at Mt Catt that year he was making some very bad decisions, things I knew just wouldn't work. Completely irrational decisions. But you couldn't talk to him. After a while Josie and I decided we'd had enough, and there was nothing we could do about him, so we left. It was really sad, like everything was just over. We'd had such good times with Rod, but he wasn't the same person anymore . . .'

As much as the quantity Rod was smoking, the other thing that really bothered Greg was that Rod was trying to hide it from him: 'He'd disappear for a while, and come back and light up a joint, but you could see that he'd already had some. It was like he was trying to cover up just how much he was smoking.'

Greg and Josie were disturbed by the whole atmosphere at Mt Catt. The previous times they'd been there, they felt welcome and enjoyed the interaction with the Mt Catt people. This time there was a palpable feeling of unease and unhappiness, and an undercurrent of something ominous they didn't understand but knew was connected to traditional 'business'. It's not for me to comment on Aboriginal traditional practices. I don't know enough about it, and it would be arrogant and foolish if I even tried. But some bad things were happening, some laws were broken, some people got very sick, and some died. Greg and Josie felt like they were in the middle of a completely foreign country, a long way from any friendly consulate, and didn't speak the language. And Rod's condition only made it all worse.

A few weeks earlier, I had started a relationship which did a lot to restore my self esteem and happiness. Sally and Harry had introduced me to a friend of theirs, and before long I was feeling a lot less lonely. The first time Pete was coming out to spend a weekend at the station, I wasn't sure how to handle the prospect of Mum having a 'boyfriend', with Callum and Shaun. They got along well with Pete, and he liked them, so in the end I just tackled it head on and said: 'I really like Pete. When he comes to visit, I'd really like him to sleep in my room. What do you think about it? Is that okay with you guys?'

Shaun looked very serious and nodded, while Callum said, with great maturity for his ten years: 'That's okay, Mum. It's good. Dad's got Lesley, so you should have somebody too.'

It was a wonderful relationship for me at that time. Pete was an Air-Med doctor who knew nothing about the bush, or anything very practical, so I was in the unfamiliar position of being the teacher, of being the one who knew how to do things. He was full of admiration for the things I could do, another unfamiliar experience for me. It was great for my battered ego.

Ironically, the very first time Pete came to stay was also the weekend Rod and Lesley came back to the station. I was so tense at the prospect of Rod being here at the same time as Pete, that I think I would have snapped in half in a good breeze. We were concreting in more steel posts and digging new holes, so I had something to concentrate on for most of the day. That evening, Pete arrived first, and when he saw how nervous I was, he handed me a glass of wine and took over preparing the dinner. Then, shortly after that, Rod's sister Christine and husband Peter turned up unexpectedly. Felicity and I just looked at each other and started to giggle hysterically. There were going to be fifteen people for dinner, tonight of all nights: Felicity, Callum, Shaun, Wendy the governess, Christine and Peter, four backpackers, Wayne Miles, who was bringing Rod and Lesley out, and Pete and me. If my new relationship was going to get a road test in tact and diplomacy, this was a good start.

'Oh well,' I muttered to her, 'at least if there's murder there'll be lots of witnesses!'

Wayne and his passengers arrived about 8 pm. I was startled by their appearance. Rod looked like he hadn't had a bath in weeks. His hands and bare feet were grimed with ingrained dirt, and his clothes were the same. Lesley didn't look a whole lot better and she seemed tired and strained. Perhaps they had to rush up here from Mt Catt and didn't have time to get cleaned up, I thought. I'd done the same thing many times myself.

Rod had a grim, sour look about him, but he was polite when he was introduced to Pete, and shook his hand. In a quiet moment, I offered them towels and the bathroom, but Rod just snorted, and said loudly, almost as an announcement: 'Some of us have got to work.

Nothin' wrong with honest dirt.' I noticed the backpackers, who'd been digging holes and mixing concrete with Felicity and me for the last few days, look at each other and raise their eyebrows.

They ate their food sitting cross-legged on the floor of the verandah, as if to underline the difference between 'honest' workers, and the bourgeois types who bathed and sat at tables. Christine and Peter obligingly sat with with them, so the tension was lessened somewhat, and the rest of the evening passed in a civilised manner.

Pete, the backpackers and I put in a few more posts on the flood plain in the morning while Rod took Callum and Shaun fishing, and in the afternoon Rod and I spent a couple of hours together to discuss our options for the station. I was relieved to find that he'd reconsidered his idea about just giving up and selling. He would try and get the rest of the buffalo we needed to fulfil the stocking covenant demanded by the Lands Department, and we'd see what happened after that. There was still the chance we could be successful in our latest application for a Buffalo Development Grant. If necessary perhaps we could find a partner to buy half the station and bring some capital in, which would satisfy the bank. But the next hurdle was the Mainoru business.

'This is all your fault. It wouldn't have happened if you'd got those maps for us,' Rod accused me in a quiet voice.

I was floored. Now his disaster at Mainoru was my fault. I stared at him for a few moments, memories of similar occasions flashing through my mind, times when I took on the burden of guilt for failed musters or broken-down trucks. Not anymore.

'No,' I replied, a lot more firmly and steadily than I felt. 'I'm not wearing that. Not at all, not in any way. You had every opportunity to get those maps ever since you went to Mt Catt, and you didn't ask me till the last minute, when it was too late.'

Rod looked at me as if I'd spoken Swahili, but didn't argue any further.

That night they went back to town, and the release of tension broke over the rest of us like a collapsed building. Callum and Shaun were in an awful state, restless and upset. The tenseness of the past two days was affecting them far more than I realised. I lay on the bed with them talking quietly to calm them down, and eventually they fell asleep, exhausted. I lay beside them and wondered again if I was doing the right thing, if it would be better for all of us if I just took them away where they'd have a more 'normal' life. The only trouble was, I wasn't sure what normal was any more.

# 19

# The Cosmic
# Hit List

In August 1990 we had a full house again. Rod's parents, Eve and George Ansell, were visiting from Queensland, so he came up from Mt Catt to spend a few days with them at Melaleuca. As well as the Ansells there were two backpackers staying with us, six fishing clients booked in for a couple of days, and Felicity's parents. Sixteen all told. I was getting so tired of dealing with so many people all the time. However, it was good to see George and Eve again. Despite the divorce, I still had a warm relationship with them, one I wanted to keep that way. We had become very close over the last ten years and I didn't see why Rod and I divorcing should change that relationship. They went off with Rod and the boys to stay at Mt Catt for a few days, and Callum and Shaun came home by bus a week and a half later.

That same month we were informed that we would not be getting a Buffalo Development Grant. In the wake of so much criticism over BTEC and the damage it had done to the buffalo industry, the government had offered buffalo producers financial assistance in the form of a grant of $100 000. Almost every producer in the industry was given one of these grants, including the Sultan of Brunei who owned neighbouring Opium Creek Station at the time. However, we were told that there was no money left, and that we had missed out. Then the bank started bouncing our cheques. It felt like our options were drying up rapidly.

Felicity and I spent several weeks welding pieces of steel picket onto the posts we'd been putting in over the last few months, to carry the plastic insulators which held the positive wires on the electric fences. My welding was improving considerably, to the point where I was scavenging leftover pieces from our steel dump, and making up fence assemblies with them. I tacked two long straight lengths together side by side, and used them as a guide in which to lay the smaller pieces I was joining. My proudest moment came when Otto Sutter, the government weed control officer and a former welder, praised my efforts as 'not bad!'

Fires were starting to become a problem by September. We had fought several small ones on Melaleuca, and I'd also sent our portable water pump over to the neighbours to use for a fire on their place. It was shaping up to be a very bad bushfire year, but so far we were okay. Then the buffalo started dying. Just one or two at first. I was completely puzzled. They didn't look sick, and there was no sign of any trauma on them, but every few days we'd find another one on the ground, weak and unable to get up, and I would have to shoot it.

When I was able to reach Rod at Mt Catt and tell him about it, he said it was the water, and that I had to get the troughs installed at once. I didn't have any money to do it with, so Rod said he'd organise for $800 to be available at some friends' place at Humpty Doo.

I arranged with Chris Penhall to collect the money and buy the materials I needed. But when Chris arrived at the Humpty Doo house, there was only $350 waiting for him. He was told that Rod owed them the money for his dope, so Chris used his own money to pay for the things I'd ordered in town. Luckily I had some unbanked boat money at the station, and I gave it to Chris with a cheque for the rest, and hoped it wouldn't bounce. Rod's dope habit was starting to look like a much more serious problem than I'd imagined. Nothing like this had happened before. I wondered briefly if I should try and front him about it, but I knew what the response would be. There was enough friction between us already.

Wayne Miles was a Darwin-born and bred photo-journalist, who had become a close friend of Rod's in the past two or three years. He had spent a lot of time photographing the landscape and activities at the station, and shared a passion for the bush with Rod. He also shared Rod's views about BTEC and the buffalo industry, and viewed every obstacle to Melaleuca's progress as a personal injury. Wayne went out to see Rod at Mt Catt about this time, and he called me when he got back to Darwin. He was angry and disillusioned about what he'd found. Rod had told me that he had buffalo in hand and would be sending them up in a week, but Wayne said he didn't have any, and that most of the workers had left as well. 'I don't know what he thinks he's doing out there!' exploded Wayne. 'He's spending heaps of time in Katherine, he's not catching buffalo, and he's just smoking shit all the time. Everyone else has left.'

Wayne knew as well as I did that if we didn't get the buffalo to Melaleuca, our chances of holding on to the station were pretty thin. I didn't know what to do. There was no point in me trying to talk to Rod. I knew he'd only get angry and blame me for whatever was slowing him down, so I just kept on with my jobs and hoped that somehow Rod was going to pull success out of a hat, like he had done so often before.

Felicity and I were really proud of the job we did on the troughs. Neither of us had ever put one in before, but it looked pretty simple. 'How hard can something that has no moving parts and three bits of concrete be?' I said, surveying the pile of stuff Chris had unloaded at the yards for us.

It ended up taking us the entire day – two days counting the curing of the slab it had to sit on. The hardest part was getting the trough perfectly level, requiring the tractor bucket to suspend the half-tonne concrete basin while I wedged stones underneath to hold it all in position for the concrete to set. In the end, when it overflowed, water ran over every side of the trough evenly. We were so pleased with ourselves we went home and opened a bottle of champagne.

Rod turned up suddenly, flying in to Opium Creek airstrip, and requiring a cheque to pay for the chartered flight, which I also hoped wouldn't bounce. He looked a mess. No swag or clothes with him, just himself, filthy dirty but this time with bark off him everywhere. At Mt Catt a couple of nights earlier, he said, he had tried to stop some drunks who had come in from Ngukurr from stealing petrol and terrorising some women and little children. He had been badly beaten. He was covered in grazes and welts, and could barely walk.

I took him home and ran him a bath with plenty of antiseptic, treated the grazes and cuts, and put him to bed in the spare room, starting him on some antibiotics from the medical kit to deal with the infections. A couple of days later he was feeling well enough to start picking on me, but this time it wasn't bothering me. He criticised me for not getting the troughs in soon enough, saying that I should have been able to see the buffalo needed better water. All the old stuff, that I was slack and lazy and stupid. But this time he didn't affect me. I just stopped listening, and felt sorry for him. He looked so unhappy. I felt more like his mother or sister than his former wife. I told myself that the things he was saying didn't matter. They weren't true, just his opinion. It didn't have to affect me at all.

In October 1990, Rod decided to run as an independent candidate for the seat of Arnhem. I lent him my car, against all my better judgement, to go out to Arnhem Land and collect nine signatures for his nomination. He said it would be the only way he might be able to make a difference to the BTEC issue, and what he could see it doing to the buffalo industry. Privately I thought it was a complete waste of time, but I knew that if I didn't lend him my car, I would forever be the only reason he lost the election.

The buffalo wouldn't come up to the troughs to drink, so we had to go out into the paddock in whatever vehicles were going, the old Hi Ace, the four-wheeled motorbike, on foot, and push them up to the spring so they could drink there. Rod's sister Christine and brother-in-law Peter came out as often as they could to help, and at one point made the decision that Peter would stay and continue to help with the buffalo while Rod was away getting his signatures. Peter also helped me to continue work on the shop, and with the help of another friend, Owen, a tour guide, we put up the other half of the building started earlier in the year. Christine loved her brother, practically idolised him, but in spite of Rod's and my differences, she and Peter never took sides, and gave me a tremendous amount of support. Whether it was building, watering buffalo, or just coming out for a weekend and insisting we take the day off to go fishing with them, they both encouraged and helped me immeasurably.

In spite of our efforts to get the buffalo onto good water they were still dying, one every few days. Rod was still away getting his nomination signatures, and I couldn't track him down anywhere, so I rang one of our neighbours to come and have a look at them. Geoff Newton came up from Opium Creek, and we went out to the paddock.

'The ridge country round here has really poor soils. The feed looks good but there's not much in it,' said Geoff. 'You better get some mineral supplement blocks for them to lick. The water's okay.' Geoff said he had the same problem at his place from time to time. So I ordered some blocks and put them out in the paddocks. The buffalo also had lice, he said, and recommended we inject them with some anti-parasitic vaccine.

The yards weren't ready to take any stock through them, so the next day our neighbour Alan Fisher lent me 30 panels of portable yard, and two blokes to help put them up. The vaccinations and vaccine guns arrived, and we yarded the buffalo, and then found the needles were the wrong size, so I had to let the buffalo out, and order the right needles. We'd have to do them the following week.

The election a couple of days later saw all our faint hopes of a Labour win pulverised along with the Labor party's, which only gained two seats. Rod had pinned his hopes on a change of government meaning a change of policy might be likely, but in hindsight it probably wouldn't have made any difference. The public servants didn't change, and BTEC was a federal policy anyway.

Rod and Lesley arrived back, and my car was a wreck. He'd obviously gone far and wide in an effort to drum up votes, taking two and a half weeks instead of the three days he'd promised. The brakes were gone, lights broken, and it was filthy inside. They picked me up from Sally's place the day after the election, and we drove home in total silence.

We ran in the buffalo the next morning and injected them all, and then I left to drive to the Bark Hut to pick up Wendy the governess. The brakes failed completely as I approached an intersection, and the car slammed into a small tree. I wasn't hurt, just stunned and bruised from the seatbelt, but the car didn't look too good. However it was still driveable, and I was able to get it back to the station. Luckily it was an old car with a strong chassis. There wasn't any other damage except to the body work and lights. That afternoon we had an appointment in town with the Ombudsman about our latest rejected application, so Rod drove back to town with all of us – Lesley, the boys and me. We'd been told by someone who worked in the DPIF that our application for a grant was rejected for 'political reasons'. We saw the Ombudsman, and then a lawyer, who both told us the same thing, that basically the Ombudsman could force the department to review our application but it would just be knocked back again. There was no point pursuing that one any further. We were just not going to get a Buffalo Development Grant.

Rod never missed an opportunity to have a go at the government, whether it was about TB testing, helicopter shootouts, or even environmental issues, such as the government's encouragement of pastoralists to plant Gamba grass on their properties. We had numerous arguments about it with departmental officials who visited. We weren't the only people who could see it had the potential to become a dangerous noxious weed, but we were treated like rabid greenies because we were concerned about what it might do – and what in 2005, it is now doing – to the country outside of the Gamba grass paddocks. The Territory government of the time, the Country Liberal Party, was notorious for its inability to cope with public criticism. Rod's outspoken opposition to BTEC, and to other government initiatives, had marked him for retaliation.

The rejection of our last application, coming so soon after his failed election bid, did nothing to improve Rod's frame of mind. I asked him to fix the brakes on my car as I couldn't afford to take it to a mechanic, but he said he didn't have time. Charlie Garske had just given me a cheque for boat hires, so I cashed it at the bank, rang Chris Penhall, and we went and bought the parts we needed to fix the brakes. I had never seen Chris so angry. He lay under the car looking at the damage, and said: 'The sooner you get away from that bastard the better. He may as well have put a bloody gun to your head and pulled the trigger as let you drive this car!'

I listened to him, knowing what he was saying was right, but feeling really sad. Chris had been such a big part of our family, along with Greg and Josie, for so long. For him to talk like that just underlined just how much Rod had changed.

While Chris was working on the car I went to see our pastoral inspector, Ted Easton, in the Lands Department. Ted had always been scrupulously straight and fair with us, and we needed to know if they would allow us to sell Melaleuca before we were foreclosed on. It seemed that Lands wouldn't have a problem, but that the bank had the final say, as they were the first mortgagee. As Ted said, they didn't want to see us walk off the property broke. Sometimes it was difficult to believe that. While we were in town, I drafted more letters to Lands and the Department of Primary Industry and Fisheries (DPIF) while Rod saw Brian Ede, the leader of the Opposition. Rod thought that while the new Cabinet was being formed after the election, there may have been an opportunity to approach the head of the DPIF in the absence of a Minister, to put our case about being refused assistance. But the same Minister was still in the saddle as it turned out, so it was a waste of time.

Rod wanted to move back to the station, and demanded that he be allowed to live in the house, especially as it looked as if we were going to lose the station before long. I could see the fairness of this. I'd been living in it for the last two years while he had largely been camping down at Mt Catt. All I wanted was a rainproof camp down at Shady Camp, I said, and I'd move out. Rod seemed to think this was an unfair demand. He wrote me a vitriolic letter listing all my faults and threatening me with custody proceedings if I didn't do exactly what he wanted. He said that I could move to Shady Camp, with no power or water, no refrigeration, and that I would have nothing more to do with Melaleuca once he got back. It was so full of hate and bitterness that I was stunned for a while. I didn't know what to make of it, but I knew that no court would give him custody of my children, and that was all I cared about. I would be more than happy to have nothing to do with the station, and there was no way I was going to share a house with him and Lesley. I had nearly finished the shop, at least enough to make a temporary home, and that sounded like a much better place to be. I tore up the letter and pretended it never happened.

Just when you think life's not worth living, something else happens to make you wonder if you're not on some cosmic hit list. November was an incredibly busy time. There were numerous trips to town for meetings with the bank, DPIF, the Northern Territory Tourist Bureau and the Lands Department. The buffalo were still dying in the paddock despite the supplement blocks, the worming, the vaccinations and the watering. Everything was breaking down. I had three flat tyres on the tractor in one week, and four on the Hi Ace, which was using engine oil at an alarming rate. A short trip to town ended up taking longer than planned, and I found myself racing around in circles one Saturday morning buying supplies for the coming week. Six fishermen were booked in that night for a week's stay, and an AAT King's bus was arriving at 3 pm to camp on one of the billabongs. I was already running late when I met Charlie Garske, who told me there was a bushfire at Melaleuca which might need checking soon.

I dropped Shaun and Callum at Greg and Josie's, and rushed off. The car kept breaking down all the way, and when I got to the Shady Camp road turn-off, I could smell the smoke. By the time I reached the homestead, the AAT bus right behind me, there was thick smoke everywhere, and a fire only about 400 metres from the house, with a strong wind pushing it closer. The flood plain below the house was alight as well. I wasn't worried about the safety of the house – the ground around it was well cleared, but our sheds were close to trees, and we couldn't afford to lose the feed in the paddocks which were waiting for the new buffalo to arrive. I rang Alan Fisher, Donny Stewart, Geoff Newton and the Wildman ranger station, and within the hour there were twenty-five people at the station, with grader, tractor and fire units, clearing firebreaks and back-burning to protect the paddocks. While I was waiting for everyone to arrive, the phone rang.

'G'day, what's happening?' asked a familiar voice. It was Greg. 'Josie said you looked a little strung out when you left here. Everythin' okay?'

I babbled into the phone about the fire, and the fishermen, and the bus, and Greg said: 'Just hold the fort, we'll come out and give you a hand.'

They arrived just an hour later, when I was trying to work out where to start back-burning, and I was so relieved to see them I nearly wept. Greg knew the station geography much better then me, and would know where we should be putting our main efforts. He took over the direction of the firefighting, and I started to calm down.

In the meantime, Donny's wife Grace took over in the kitchen, expertly cooking up huge amounts of food for everyone while I was at the fire. The fishermen and their guide Les Woodbridge had arrived, and after making sure there was nothing they could do to help, sat outside drinking their beer and watching the entertainment.

We worked till late into the night, saving the paddocks but unable to stop the fire out on the flood plain. It would have to burn itself out.

And then to cap it all off, the next morning the first thing I did was put a stake through the radiator of the Hi Ace when I went out to check the fire. Donny and Grace picked me up walking back along the road, feeling very sick of everything. Donny offered me seven hundred bales of hay, which he said were just going to get wet if they weren't used. Later Greg told me that the night before, Donny had asked him if he thought I'd be embarrassed if he offered them to me.

I felt like an absolute charity case, always having to get friends and neighbours to help me sort out problems on the station. Things Rod should have been doing, or paid station hands, at least. I was doing the best I could, but there was so much I didn't know. I was so angry with Rod, and so dispirited at the mess we were in with the bank, that I almost refused the hay, but I knew I'd only get into more trouble without it, so I thanked Donny wholeheartedly, and swallowed my pride. Everything may have been going wrong, but I was buoyed up by the knowledge that I had some bloody wonderful friends and neighbours.

Rod and Lesley turned up at the homestead two days later, breezing in with an ABC film crew to do an interview about BTEC, and left as quickly as they'd come. It was all getting a bit surreal, I thought. Then our local stock and station agent, David Loveridge, phoned the following day to tell me Rod had been to see him about putting Melaleuca on the market. I got the strong impression that he wanted to make sure I knew about it. We made plans to meet and talk about marketing.

We were kept awake by falling trees for the rest of the week. All through the night, trees that had burnt during the day would suddenly fall, crashing down with a sound like cannons going off in the distance. With the sound of exploding trees, and the smoke that wreathed the house for days and days, it was as if we were in a 1917 battlefield.

You get to know certain sounds out bush. Bird calls, animals noises, the different sound of every vehicle on the property. You monitor them without even being aware of it. Just two days after the fire, I was woken early by a sound from the generator. In a split second I knew the generator was about to stop, but also that it shouldn't be stopping, because I'd filled the diesel tank only the day before. I was out of bed and halfway across the yard before I realised I'd even left the house. 'A blur in a sarong,' as Les Woodbridge put it later. He was on his way to the shed for the same reason but I beat him to it, and managed to shut the machine down before it stopped itself. I soon saw the problem. All the engine oil was lying on the floor of the shed. The sump plug had vibrated itself loose and fallen out. It was a near disaster, because if the engine had run out of oil and seized up, I would not have been able to afford to get it fixed. Then I would have had to stop taking fishing guests, and a good part of our income would have been lost. Not to mention having no electricity at all.

At the end of November, the government put a caveat on the property. We had to spray the mimosa again, but we had no money, and no credit. I had the income from the boat hire and the homestays, but it wasn't going to buy much herbicide. I went in to see Graeme Schultz in the Weeds Section about our options. We needed thirty drums of Starane again, at a cost of $18 000 which we had to pay before we could claim back the subsidy. But even if they only charged us the subsidised amount, we still couldn't afford it. If we didn't spray, the government would put a notice on us under the Noxious Weeds Act. I asked Graeme if the department would carry out the spraying program, and if we could pay our share on the sale of the property. This was agreed to, and a caveat was placed on our title.

The very next day Elders rang in a panic because we owed them $54 000 – as well as the weed spray from the beginning of the year, Rod had been purchasing gear for Mt Catt after its account was frozen, and now we had a substantial debt. The only thing they could do to secure the debt was to take out a stock mortgage over the property, which they promptly did. I was feeling like Melaleuca was being chipped away from us piece by piece. That afternoon the engine of the Hi Ace blew up, and I had to buy a second hand engine. I needed the Hi Ace to be able to tow the boats to and from the water, so there was no choice about repairing it. I found one in town, and Greg came out and put it in the car for me.

I was trying to get an excision of the campground. I wanted my life to be as separate from Rod's as joint custody would allow, and the best way I could see was to live close enough that the boys could see their father whenever they liked, but to have nothing to connect me to the station in any other way. If I could excise the land on which I was building the campground, I could own it outright, and not have to deal with Rod any more than I absolutely had to. I took my proposals into town again, and contacted sympathetic people in the various departments to write letters of support for my plans. Everyone seemed to think it was a great idea, a sensible solution in the light of the inevitable sale of the station. But the government said no, they would not agree to an excision before all the covenants were completed. I decided to wait a while and apply again.

Greg and Josie came out in early December for a few days to help me pour the concrete slabs for the shop down at the campground. I had hired a couple of backpackers, so we fired up the cement mixer and got stuck into it. Halfway though the first mix the tyre on the wheelbarrow exploded spectacularly, stopping everything. Greg took a wheel off the mixer to fix the wheelbarrow, and then had to weld up a support for that machine. In the meantime the concrete mix was going off, and we were trying every trick we knew to keep it soft, like mixing washing up liquid into it. It actually works . . . Everyone was helping, even the little kids, and by the end of the day I had a floor to put a few more rock walls on.

Rod came back from Mt Catt, but without any buffalo. By now it didn't seem to matter. Unless a miracle happened, we would have no choice but to sell the station. Everything seemed bleak and hopeless, even my relationship with the AirMed doctor had finished – very amicably, but nonetheless. I had one extremely bright spot on my horizon. I was going home for a holiday, for the first time in six years. My parents had sent me the airfare, and Callum, Shaun and I were leaving straight after Christmas. I packed up all my things, left the boys to spend Christmas with Rod at the station, and went into Darwin.

Sometime around then I watched the movie *Parenthood*. There is a scene in which the dotty old granny talks to herself. She tells a story about going to the fair when she was a girl, about how wonderful the roller coaster ride was. How she'd never been so scared, thrilled, terrified and exhilarated all at the same time. She said that some folks preferred the merry-go-round, but they just went round and round. She preferred the roller coaster. I thought to myself, that's me. My life might be a hell of a roller coaster, crazy and stressed out, and all ups and downs, but it's a lot more exciting than a suburban merry-go-round.

# 20

# Shady Camp

'Well, here's to déjà vu!'

Felicity and I clinked our wineglasses, and dived for cover. It was our first night at Shady Camp, 26 January 1991. Arriving at midday, we spent the afternoon getting boats ready for the next hire, and barely had enough time to throw up our mosquito nets before the hordes of hungry, stinging insects swarmed us at dusk. Dinner was bread, cheese and a glass of wine, taken inside our nets to be eaten by torchlight. This was basically where I'd started thirteen years earlier, sleeping in a swag on the ground, no house to live in, and with none of the things most people consider essential. And certainly not with the cheese and wine.

'Do you think we're nuts?' I asked Felicity.

'Probably!' She shrugged. 'Here we are, two grown-up women huddling under mosquito nets at Shady Camp in the middle of the wet season. No power, no water, no toilet, no walls. It seems pretty crazy. It's not what most people would do, I guess.'

'You know, there was a point, just when we reached the Shady Camp turn-off, when I could've turned around and gone back to Melbourne. I just didn't want to drive down this road one more time . . .'

'I know, I felt like that too. But what choice have you got?'

I didn't have a choice, really, unless I was prepared to walk away from my boys and Melaleuca, or take them away from their father.

'Hey, listen,' she said, 'there's a storm bird!' A channel-billed cuckoo began its raucous shouting call, somewhat like a kookaburra with a sore throat, and as the cadence died away I thought how glad

I was to have Felicity with me again. She was blessed with the ability to focus on the small wonders around us, which shrank problems back into their proper size. Whatever else was going on, there were so many amazing things under our noses, things we'd never appreciate if we were inside comfortable houses watching television at night instead.

The next day we set about making ourselves a home. We went up to the homestead where I'd stored my things while I was away, and brought back the refrigerator – Rod could keep the freezer – as well as the table I'd made a couple of years before, four folding chairs, a small gas camping stove and, of course, the champagne glasses. Most of Callum and Shaun's belongings came too. Shaun was in town staying with Greg and Josie, but Callum came back with us to help set up the camp.

Water was our main concern. Chris Penhall had come up with the brilliant idea of cutting a piece of 8-inch PVC pipe down the length of one side, and forcing it over the edge of the corrugated iron roof. This would be the guttering to collect rainwater for the tank. Rod welded up a sturdy tank stand for us, and we concreted it in, installing a 5000-litre tank on it the next day, purchased with money I'd saved from the boat hire business. I connected it to the PVC pipe guttering, and we had a water supply.

Monty Dwyer, an English backpacker who'd worked with us before Christmas concreting the shop floor, arrived back at Shady Camp and pitched in immediately. He thought we were crazy too, but he liked our little camp, and was more than happy to be part of it. I was very glad to have him back. Not only was Monty a hard worker, he was cheerful and energetic, and he was a much better mechanic than Felicity or me. The mosquitoes appreciated him even more than we did, though, and he was a mess of itching infected lumps after a few days. No matter how much insect repellent or how many layers of clothing he wore, they still managed to get to him.

Our bedroom tents were great. First we built A-frames out of long straight saplings, and stretched large tarpaulins across them, with the ridge pole wrapped up to prevent it rubbing holes in the tarp. Then we laid a bed of sand underneath, and erected mesh tents in the shelter of the A-frames. They made very dry, snug abodes, reasonably shaded during the day, and delightfully cool and airy at night.

The kitchen was another 3m × 3m mesh tent, erected under the roof of the shop, with tarpaulins stretched between the roof and the rock walls to keep out the driving rain. Now we could eat after dark and not have to race into our beds to escape the mosquitoes as soon as the sun went down. But so far meals were very basic – whatever didn't require cooking – as I hadn't thought of bringing gas with me for the little camping stove. One night Callum and I decided we were sick of cold meals, so we dragged a piece of corrugated iron into the building, raised it up off the concrete floor on bricks, and lit a fire on it so we could cook a proper meal out of the rain. It worked just fine, but I made sure I filled the gas bottle next time I went to town.

The kitchen sink was outside the building. We built a frame to hold an old double kitchen sink we had, and ran a pipe to carry away the waste water to a nearby clump of pandanus. Dishes dried in the sun – when it wasn't raining.

The toilet was a 'long drop', basically just a hole in the ground well away from the camp, with a screen erected around it for privacy. We used ashes from the fire and earth from the hole to keep it covered up after each use, and when it filled, we dug another hole and shifted the screen.

We had the loveliest bathroom. We brought an old enamelled bathtub down from the homestead, formerly used by the ducks, set it up on blocks inside yet another mesh tent, and ran some piping to carry away the waste water into the same pandanus clump. Some old slate tiles made a floor to step out onto beside the tub, and a bamboo screen donated by Sally and Harry made it a bit more private. A few lush green potplants completed the effect. When it was cold – in the dry season – we left black plastic water drums out in the sun to heat up through the day, providing us with hot water for bathing that night. During the wet, if no one was around, Felicity and I simply stood under the overflow from the rainwater tank, and showered to our heart's content.

We even had a telephone. When the phone was installed at Melaleuca the year before, I had a tower erected at Shady Camp as well, looking ahead to when I'd start the campground there. The Telstra man who came out to make the final connection was very amused, and said: 'I've put phones in some odd places, but this is the first time I've put one in a tent!'

We made a point of setting the table for dinner every night, and cooking proper meals. Just because we were camping, we weren't about to live rough. Most of the time we cooked on the gas stove, but occasionally I'd light a fire outside and bake something in the camp oven. But with Darwin being so close, and traffic coming in and out so regularly, most of the time I ordered bread from town, and didn't bother making my own.

We didn't have any electricity, but we didn't need it. The new telephone was solar powered. The fridge was an old kerosene refrigerator we had converted to gas, and it worked well. Lights were provided by a couple of kerosene lamps, or more often just candles. When we needed brighter lights, I would hook up a fluorescent strip light to a 12 volt battery which also powered the school radio. If I needed to use any electrical tools, such as drills or saws, I'd borrow the tractor and the welder from the station – the welder produced a 240 volt supply while it was operating.

The front half of the building became the public area, where we serviced the boat motors, stored tools and equipment and dealt with clients. We sold some fishing tackle as well, such as lures, hooks and handlines. The back half, screened from view by tarpaulins, was where we lived. I hoped it wouldn't take too long before I could close it all in properly with doors and windows and flyscreens. Not to mention a few solid walls to keep the rain out.

Often people would call in to book a boat, and look around at the tents and the kitchen, and say, half jokingly, 'But you don't actually *live* here, do you?' They were always amazed when we assured them we did. Eventually I got to the point where I'd say, 'Oh no, this is just where we operate the business from during the day . . .' As far as I was concerned, it was a lot more comfortable than any of the stock camps I'd been in.

Our days settled into a routine of towing boats, cleaning and refuelling them. We did all the maintenance ourselves, and were able to repair most things with a bit of instruction by phone from the boat suppliers in Darwin. I was back in the schoolroom, teaching Callum and Shaun in the kitchen tent. Eventually I acquired another tent to use as a classroom, but for now we just cleared away the breakfast dishes and got out the books. We tried to get as much done as we could early in the day, before it became too hot. They loved being on the river. We would often take a boat out when it was quiet and fish for barra, or just count the crocodiles we could see. The boys had grown up with a healthy awareness of crocodiles, and never went into the river. Later Shaun, ever the entrepreneur, started a little business for himself retrieving lost lures from the crossing at low tide, and selling them back to the fishermen.

I didn't see a lot of Rod. When I did it was usually stressful, although he was very helpful when we were setting up Shady Camp. I think the reality of him living in a proper house with electricity and fans and so on, while his children and ex-wife were living in tents in the middle of the rainy season, may have made him feel a little guilty. But it didn't last long. It almost seemed like the happier we were down there, and the better we operated, the more difficult he became.

The station finances didn't make it any easier. I approached the bank in February for an overdraft on my personal account – which was in credit with the proceeds from the boat hire business – to buy two more rainwater tanks for the campground. I barely got started on the purpose of my visit when the two bank officials across the desk interrupted me abruptly and told me they were calling in the loan on Melaleuca. One handed me a letter of demand, and said they were going to sell the property if we didn't repay our loan immediately.

We contacted lawyer Geoff James, who immediately went to work to find us some breathing space. He did a great job, and over the next few months negotiated a position where the bank agreed to lend us enough money to finish the yards, survey the campground for excision, maintain the station, and mount a professional advertising campaign for the auction of Melaleuca in July. We couldn't avoid selling up, unless we found an investor before the auction, but at least it wasn't going to be a fire sale.

Rod and I met with the bank a few days later, and it was clear that they were in no mood to negotiate. We sat down and talked for a long time about what we should do. The best solution that Rod could see was to find a buyer for half the station, to bring in the money to clear the debt.

'But we owe the bank almost four hundred thousand dollars now!' I said. 'There won't be much left for development after the bank is repaid.'

'Melaleuca's worth over three million dollars,' retorted Rod. 'There'll be plenty left over to pay you out, and finish the covenants.'

I wondered why the bank was forcing a sale on such a valuable property, if we only owed a portion of its value.

'How can you be sure it's worth that much?'

'Don't be stupid! Look at it – it's the last available flood plain, it's close to Kakadu, it's got unlimited tourist potential, it's got stock yards and fencing and a nucleus TB-free herd. It's right next to the best fishing in the Top End. Of course it's worth that much – it's probably worth a lot more.' He went on outlining the various ways a deal could be set up, where I might retain a percentage of the ownership and rights to the campground instead of being paid out, and I began to feel a familiar sense of being overwhelmed.

I took a deep breath. I had some things to say that he wasn't going to want to hear, but I pressed on: 'I just want to make something very clear. I'm entitled to half of our assets, by law. I won't force a sale of the property – assuming we've got any choice – just to get my share, but at the same time I'm not going to be ripped off. I'll look at any offers you get but I don't want to be in a position where you're managing my finances, as you would be if I retain partial ownership of Melaleuca. I don't want to be connected to you apart from the kids – and I'm sure the feeling is mutual. I have to be able to live and support the boys, and even if I manage to keep the campground out of all this, I still need to be able to develop it so that it can operate properly. I'm not going to go out with nothing just so you can stay here. That's not fair. I have worked as hard as you for the last twelve years to get here, and I deserve a fair share.'

To my absolute surprise, we managed to stay calm and reasonable, and Rod more or less agreed with me.

Rod wanted to attract an investor to buy 49 per cent of the property for one and a half million dollars. It was obvious that this was unlikely, but I didn't know what else we could do at the time. We talked about different scenarios to divide up the property, and in every one, I ended up with very little. Rod seemed to think it was eminently fair that I should get the campground, which was undeveloped and would need huge injections of finance to build, plus $30 000 cash, and yet be liable for half of Melaleuca's debts, while he would retain

51 per cent of the property, and the investor would pay the rest of the Melaleuca debts. I was no economist, but even I could see the inequity of that. Every time I refused to agree to the terms, he would go off in high dudgeon.

One day the boys came back from a stay with their father, very quiet and upset. When I asked them what was wrong, they said that Rod had told them I was forcing him to sell Melaleuca, and that because of me, they wouldn't be able to live there anymore. I was horrified. The one thing we had agreed on, and managed to stick to, was that we would never criticise each other to the boys. Our break-up was our problem, not theirs.

I steadied them down and explained, as well as you can to an eleven- and nine-year-old, about how I had worked very, very hard with Rod to keep Melaleuca all these years, and that it wasn't fair that I should go away with nothing just so Rod could stay there. I explained that it was the bank that was forcing the sale, and that we were trying to find the best way through the problem so that we both ended up with something. I said it was very likely that we would lose the station. Losing it would be very hard, but I also said that you didn't have to own something to love it.

I realised then, more than at any other time, I think, just how much Rod had changed. The Rod that I used to know would never have hurt his sons like that. The pattern of the last few years became very clear, and I could see a man who was simply falling apart. I had always relied on the fact that whatever his behaviour, he had a firm grasp of the reins of his life. He always came up with a solution to our many troubles – the practical business ones, that is. He always had a plan, or could find a way through to get to the point he was aiming at. I sat for a long time wondering just what was happening to him. Was it the divorce, was it the dope, was it just a combination of all the pressures of the past few years, and was he cracking under the strain?

Money was very short. Boat hires were down as the backpackers hadn't returned to the Top End in any numbers yet, and the fishing wasn't happening either. After a meeting in town one day I asked Rod to help with some of the bills I had to pay, like the boys' school fees and clothes. He and Lesley were on the dole, and had over $500 a fortnight to live on, but Rod maintained it was barely keeping them alive.

'That's bullshit!' I yelled at him. 'I kept *five* of us alive on $400 a fortnight a couple of years ago, when we had to go on the dole one wet season, don't you remember? *And* I managed to keep some of the bills paid! These are your kids!'

Rod just shrugged, and said he couldn't help. Increasingly now he seemed to be someone else altogether. The man who once would have given anybody a helping hand now wouldn't even help out where his own sons were concerned. I felt like I was talking to a stranger most of the time. I wanted to say that if he didn't spend so much money on his dope he'd manage, but I wasn't brave enough.

I had many nights where I couldn't sleep, and lay in my tent in the small hours worrying about all the things that could, or were, going wrong. I'd be gripped by the most awful feelings of dread, and have nightmares, when I finally did sleep, that I was stranded in the middle of the Shady Camp crossing at night, clutching Callum and Shaun, while the river rose around us, and the crocodiles closed in, and there was no one to help.

By mid April it all caught up with me. People were commenting that I looked tired, but I didn't pay a lot of attention. I'd been rushing around town for a couple of days seeing lawyers and the banks, and called in to collect my things from my friend Barbara James' house, where I'd been staying. I'd been talking to her at a hundred miles an hour, and obviously seemed a bit ratty. She looked at me closely and said, 'You're not really going home now, are you? You look completely exhausted.'

That was all the encouragement I needed. I decided to go home in the morning, had one gin and tonic, promptly collapsed on the table, and had to be put to bed, where I slept for twelve hours. A week later I was back at Barbara's again, and had a bad night where I couldn't sleep. I was anxious and shaky, full of the most dreadful feelings of hopelessness and misery. At 3 am, a sobbing mess on the bed, I was afraid I was going crazy, so I went downstairs, woke Gavin, who lived in the flat under Barbara's house, and asked him to drive me to the hospital.

The doctor was wonderful, listened to my woes, told me I wasn't going crazy, just suffering from a lot of stress, and gave me a prescription for some sleeping tablets. She also gave me a couple of pills for that night. I went back to Barb's house and slept till 10 am. After that I threw the prescription in the bin. I was too afraid of ending up like Rod, needing some chemical fix to help me get through the day.

It was around that time that I started to get to know Lex Silvester. I had seen him at fishing and tourism industry functions, but I'd never really spoken to him, although I'd always noticed the tall, good looking man with the grey hair and the surprisingly young face. One evening I was at a farewell dinner for my good friends Sally and Harry who were leaving the Territory, and Lex passed my table, and stopped to say hello. We had a brief chat, and I thought, well, he's very nice, but my life is far too complicated to get involved with anyone else. I thought no more about it. Then a couple of days later, Barbara suggested I talk to Lex about an issue I had with boat hiring liabilities. He was an old friend of hers, and he'd recently returned to practise law after a few years in the tourism industry. It seemed like a reasonable suggestion.

Meeting Lex was a turning point in my life. He had not long finished building a top flight resort out at Cobourg Peninsula called Seven Spirit Bay, a lot more remote than Shady Camp, and was very interested in what I was trying to do. He had grown up on a sheep and cattle property in Victoria, which the family had to sell when his father became ill, and he identified strongly with our problems at Melaleuca. His marriage had ended a few years earlier, and he had two children, Sophie who was sixteen, and Tom, ten. Lex came out to visit at Shady Camp a few times, and in spite of my determination to keep my life uncomplicated, we began seeing each other, fell very much in love and, before we knew it, were juggling lots of long drives between Darwin and Shady Camp to see each other, four children and two very different careers.

I spent Mother's Day guiding an Austrian couple down the river to photograph crocodiles, and found plenty, most bigger than the dinghy we were in, and several well over four metres long. The best shot of the day came right at the end, as we were quietly motoring back to the barrage. Just twenty metres in front of the boat, a massive head broke the surface of the water with an equally enormous barramundi in its jaws, and as I frantically jammed the motor in reverse to stop us running into it, proceeded to chomp up the fish without the least concern for us. We watched in stunned silence until the crocodile submerged again. I suddenly felt a lot less confident about the river than I had all day.

The next morning we were up at 6 am to deliver boats to the river, but then I had to get back into bed so that Callum and Shaun could bring me the breakfast they'd planned for Mother's Day. I sat up eating pancakes Shaun had cooked, while the boys sat on the bed watching me, telling me about their fishing trip the day before. They went off to do the dishes – the other part of my Mother's Day present – and I sipped my tea, watching some wallabies grazing nearby and listening to the sounds of doves and kookaburras floating through the cool morning air. It was one of those perfect moments, when the light is soft, and the humidity feels like silk on your skin, and you can't think of anywhere else you'd rather be.

The next few months were a whirl of talking to banks, to Rod, to lawyers, to government officials, to real estate agents. Our lawyer Geoff James had managed to get a stay of execution, in which the banks agreed to give us time to find an investor or a buyer before the property was auctioned on 22 July. They also agreed to an advertising budget. David Loveridge organised a brochure and Rod revised his three million plus sale price to a more reasonable one closer to two million dollars. The occasional investor came out of the woodwork, but none of them was serious. They all thought the price was way too high, and I guess they could see a chance to get the place cheap at auction anyway.

In the meantime, a friend in the Lands Department called me and said, 'Look, this is none of my business, and it shouldn't be any of the department's business either, but I have to ask you: are you and Rod divorced?'

I told him that we were, that we'd been divorced since 1988.

'Then put in another application for the campground excision, and make it very clear that this is *you* applying for yourself, and that Rod has nothing to do with it. Make it very clear that Rod is not going to be part of the new title.'

The old feelings of resentment about how the government always reacted to Rod automatically resurfaced, and I found myself about to say to the friend to tell the Lands Department to go jump, but I managed to bite my tongue. It seemed that as long as the department thought that Rod was involved with the campground excision, it was never going to be approved. I reapplied.

Lex guided me through putting together a comprehensive plan for the development of the camping ground. I had to present a Preliminary Environmental Report to the Conservation Commission about what I intended to do there, as well as a host of other proposals and documents.

The water which we had collected in the rainwater tank over the Wet lasted us for several months. We carted river water from the upstream side of the Shady Camp crossing to wash the boats and ourselves, and kept the tank water just for drinking and cooking. I realised it had probably passed its use-by-date one day when someone commented on the funny taste. By the next day it was seriously bad, so I got Callum to climb up and have a look in the inspection hole with a torch.

'Uh-oh,' I heard him say. 'Shaun! Come and have a look at this!'

Felicity and I glanced at each other apprehensively. Neither of us really wanted to know what else we had been filling our water bottles with for the last few days – or weeks.

The remains of a large snake were curled in the bottom of the tank, and the water was rotten. An evil-looking froth was beginning to collect on the surface. Feeling a bit sick, we drained it and scrubbed it out with a broom, leaving it to stand till the following wet season's rains could flush it out properly. A couple of years earlier, we had drilled several bores in the vicinity of the camp ground, but they were all too salty to drink. I planned to supply the camp with water by pumping from the river about a kilometre above the crossing, but I couldn't afford to do it yet. In the meantime we carted our drinking water from upstream too.

A month or so after this, Alan and Sheree Fisher, our neighbours at Swim Creek Station to the north of Melaleuca, dropped by for a cup of tea. When Alan noticed our water situation, he offered to lend us a water tanker. I was completely stunned when he arrived the next day, driving his semi-trailer and towing an enormous, 30 000-gallon tanker full of water from their bore at Swim Creek. We didn't have a water problem any longer!

The day I'd dreaded came, and we filed in to the Travelodge Hotel in Darwin on 22 July 1991 for the auction of our hopes and dreams of the past twelve years. Lex came with me. The auctioneer David Love-ridge opened the bidding in a room full of people holding auction cards, but not a single bid was made, and Melaleuca was passed in. It was a reprieve of sorts, but it meant I was still in limbo, not able to move ahead with my plans for the campground, and still shackled with the worry of the huge debts hanging over our heads.

After the failure of the auction, Lex spent weeks putting together a document outlining the attributes of the station, putting a pro-fessional gloss on the potential of Melaleuca for buffalo grazing and ecotourism, which we sent to everyone we thought might be interested in buying or investing in the property. He put a huge amount of effort into it – he didn't want to see me end up with no home *plus* a huge pile of debts to pay off. In any event he thought it was unlikely that either Rod or I would end up with anything after the creditors were paid off. Rod surprised me by ringing Lex about the document, and cooperating with him on it. By this stage, though, Rod was feeling under siege, as he'd had to appear in court over the Mainoru charges from the previous year.

In August 1991, the government granted me the excision of the campground from our title to Melaleuca Station. My third application had been approved by Cabinet, but title to the land would not be given until survey work was completed, and all the money owed to the government by our company repaid, that is, the costs of the last couple of mimosa sprayings – about $40 000 – and the purchase price of the station, some $115 000 plus the annual rental since the new lease had been granted. I decided to hold off on the champagne for a bit longer. But I was still hopeful it would all work out, and I had the surveyors come out and survey the fence lines.

Lex and I were very happy together. He came out most weekends, and when I had to go to town I would stay with him at his apartment in Fannie Bay, a suburb of Darwin. He was great with Callum and Shaun, friendly and fatherly towards them, and made me feel very secure and comfortable. He was loving and considerate, and he made me laugh. We talked all the time, and I felt I had met a true partner. I felt stronger and more hopeful than I had for a long time. Whatever Rod threw at me, or the government, or the bank, I felt I could deal with now, because I had someone in my corner to back me up completely.

# 21

# A New Life

I had been involved with Landcare quite heavily for the past few years, first as secretary for our local Lower Mary River Landcare group, and later as president. It took up a lot of time, but it was interesting, and it gave me much enjoyable contact with all my neighbours. We were conducting trials of some mimosa treatments on the infestations beside my campground, because they were so accessible there, so I occasionally had to go to town for a few days to be away from the herbicide spraying, seeing I was pregnant. In November 1991 I had to present a paper to the Threatened Species Network conference, about the conflict between conservationists and pastoralists, and I couldn't tell if it was nerves or morning sickness that was making me feel sick!

Having a baby at that time was not what most people would have chosen to do, I guess. Neither Lex nor I had any money. He was just starting back in the law after several years doing other things, and I still had the fate of Melaleuca hanging over me. We had four children who were still at school, and God knew what was around the corner. But it felt right. Everyone seemed to be very happy for us, especially the kids. Callum and Shaun began talking to my stomach immediately, Tom seemed pleased, and Sophie, who was away at boarding school, wanted to be kept abreast of every development in the pregnancy.

It was hard being out at the campground now. Rod was as difficult to deal with as ever, and always seemed to be needing a lift in to town whenever we were going in. I had no normal kind of relationship with him at all anymore – there was just stifling, silent tension whenever we had to share the same space for any length of time. I wondered if it would ever change.

Felicity left for the Christmas holidays, and Simon Clark, the young Scot who had first arrived at Melaleuca as a backpacker in 1987, came back to look after Shady Camp for a few months. We were hoping that when the campground got underway, Simon would take over managing it, and in the meantime he was looking after the boat hire and caretaking the place for me.

One afternoon in early December, a vicious squall blew through the camp, destroying the school tent, the bathroom tent, the kitchen tent and ripping most of the tarps to sheds. It also blasted a year's paperwork to the four points of the compass. We picked it all up as best we could. The next day Simon was up at the station, doing a job for Rod, and I was home by myself. I was trying to repair the kitchen tent, but I couldn't do it. Suddenly it all seemed too hard. Everything always had to be done from scratch, there was no proper place to live or to store anything, and I just felt as if everything was caving in on me. I sat in a corner amidst the wreckage of the tent and cried my eyes out. After that I felt better, and I fixed the tent.

A couple of days later, Les Woodbridge, who had become a good friend of both Lex's and mine over the past year, was camping at the Shady Camp reserve with some fishing clients. He called in to have a cup of tea and a chat, and as he walked into the shop, he looked around, looked at me and said, 'You're doin' it hard, girl.'

I was just glad I'd had my crying fit already.

1992 brought a final decree from the bank. They had allowed us another six months or so to find an investor, but now they were calling in the loan. There were still potential investors inspecting the property, and Lex met with the bank and squeezed some more time out of them.

In an unexpected positive move, the Minister for Lands wrote to me in March saying that he was removing the requirement that our company's debt to the Lands Department be repaid before I could be granted my excision, and wished me all the best with the development. The Tourist Commission was ready to help out with financial assistance once we had the title, and it seemed like it was really going to happen at last. The champagne cork was almost out. But the bank refused to allow the campground to be excised from Melaleuca while the mortgage was still there. I even offered to buy the land separately, arguing that they would get the price on top of whatever they got for the station at auction. It was just four hundred hectares out of Melaleuca's 25,450, but the bank wouldn't budge.

Early in April, Rod was in court over the Mainoru boundary matter from 1990, and was found guilty on all counts of assault and cattle stealing. Rod was so sure he'd be acquitted. Lex and I attended the court, and, along with seven or eight other people, handed up character references to the magistrate. Despite how I felt about Rod, I didn't want Callum and Shaun's father to go to prison. Instead of a likely gaol sentence, Rod was given a two-year good behaviour bond and a fine of $500 plus costs of $4000. He had wanted to bring Callum and Shaun into court, reasoning that they should see how justice worked, but in reality he expected the magistrate to be swayed by the vision of two young sons. I refused. If it had gone badly for Rod, the sight of their father being led away in handcuffs would have been much too distressing for them.

Rod hadn't reacted much when I told him about my pregnancy, but by the end of the nine months, he was behaving very badly. I hadn't had a lot of direct contact with him. Callum had been at boarding school in Darwin since the previous July, and was having a difficult time. Finally things came to a head and Rod and I agreed he would go back out to the station where he'd re-enrol with the School of the Air, and be tutored by Rod and Lesley. I wasn't happy about it, but Rod insisted, and Callum said he wanted to go back to live with his father. Fair enough. I was days off giving birth to my baby, and in no position to do much about Callum at that point. Felicity was continuing to supervise Shaun's lessons, and he could see his dad whenever he wanted, so Shaun was happy to stay where he was.

A few days later I had a bitter phone conversation with Rod. Felicity had sent me into town a couple of weeks before, banning me from any further trips out until after the baby was born, saying she didn't want to deliver it in the bush. Rod rang me at Lex's apartment in Fannie Bay, ostensibly to talk about Callum's change of schooling. He began ranting and raving, that it wasn't fair to Callum and Shaun to drag them into this 'episode' and expect them to have to deal with this child: 'Callum doesn't want anything to do with this baby. He's confused by it all, and besides, this is nothing to do with Callum and Shaun! There's no blood relation between them and this baby. You are being really selfish. It's got nothing to do with them!'

I closed my eyes and tried to stay calm. 'Oh?' I said. 'Then if there's no blood relation, who exactly was their real mother?'

He was silent for a few moments, but then just proceeded to harangue me about the boys being neglected and feeling unwanted. I tried to reconcile this with the images I had of two boys cuddling me and talking to my belly, and peppering me with questions about it. I wanted both the boys to be nearby when the baby was born, but Rod maintained Callum wanted no part of it. I let him carry on for a bit, concentrating very hard on staying calm and quiet, and then asked to speak to Callum.

'Callum, I don't know if you want to come into town for the baby's birth or not, but whatever you want is okay. I'll miss you but I won't be upset with you. Maybe it's a good idea if you stay and look after your dad for a few days, and I'll see you afterwards.'

He seemed happy to no longer be the meat in the sandwich, and I let him go. I so wanted this time to be special, and I didn't want Rod spoiling it by making me feel miserable. I knew I could sort Callum out later on, so I just let it go, and turned all my attention to the impending birth. I was determined this time I was going to get it 'right'.

My sister Leonie arrived in Darwin, and we spent three serene and blissful days together, going out for lunch, having coffee in little cafes, and buying 'baby things'. We also talked at length about what I wanted in the labour, assuming it all went smoothly and I had a choice! I had been reading lots of books about childbirth methods, and Lex had come to all the antenatal classes with me, so this time I was well prepared. When I gave birth to my first two babies, I had virtually no support apart from Rod, and no information. I knew how babies were born, theoretically, but living over 200 kilometres from the nearest hospital, I couldn't attend antenatal classes, and had no women friends to talk it over with. Both labours were long and painful, and I was flat on my back for about fourteen hours each time, finishing with an episiotomy for the first, and tearing in the second.

I didn't realise then that there were other ways of giving birth, and that I could actually make choices.

The preparation paid off, and at 3.20 am on a Sunday morning in June 1992 Alexandra Maria – Ali – was born after a peaceful, drug-free, almost painless three-hour labour with Lex and Leonie supporting me. Shaun and Tom came in a few hours later to meet Ali. They sprawled across the bed, looking at her and stroking her, each clearly pleased to have a little sister.

Callum came in a week after, and was very happy to see Ali. But he barely looked at me, nor did he give me a hug, which was very unusual. We sat out on the verandah, and started talking, and it was easy to see that he was confused and upset. When I tried to draw him out, he began shouting, 'You never listen to me! You're never there for me! All you care about is the baby!'

He jumped up to run away, but I held on to him and hugged him until he settled down. I was upset now. Callum had never used words like that before. Eventually we both calmed down and talked quietly for a while. Rod had used the week or two Callum had been with him to paint me as black as he could. Rod's difficult life, all his problems, were my fault, because I was unfair and mean. I was very disturbed at what I heard. I remembered how hysterical Rod had been a few nights before Ali was born, and wondered at his state of mind. It seemed as if he was losing the plot altogether.

I gave Callum a hug. 'It's okay, Callum. Rod's just worried about all the problems with the bank and the station, and he's saying things he shouldn't say, and that aren't true anyway. Don't worry about it – you don't have to decide who's right or wrong, or choose between us. Both your dad and I love *you*. That's the main thing.'

I had to get Callum back into town as soon as I could. I wanted to ask him about Rod's dope smoking, but thought better of it.

I had just paid all the outstanding Shady Camp bills and was feeling positive about the future prospects, when Peter, the backpacker I'd employed to help Felicity with the boats rolled the ute on the way home from town and wrote it off. I had some money put aside, so I was able to get another car, but it seemed like it was forever going to be a case of one step forward, two steps back.

Then, just three weeks after Ali was born, the bank announced they would be taking vacant possession of Melaleuca in a fortnight. Once again Lex managed to get a little more time, and Rod continued to chase up his last possible investor.

Ali and I moved back out to Shady Camp, and erected a new insect-proof tent, one with a proper floor and no gaps for nocturnal snakes to get in. During the pregnancy, I had been asleep in my tent one night when I was awoken by the sensation of something sharp grabbing my finger. As I sat up I saw a long dark tail sliding off the bed, and then a snake disappearing out the gap in the zip-up door. I inspected my hand carefully, but I could only see a red mark, like the skin had been pinched but not broken. With a little baby I was taking no chances, and the new tent was definitely snake-proof.

It was hard being back out in the camp. It was August, and the cool of the Dry was gone. The mosquitoes were as thick as ever, and there was nowhere to put a change table, or a pile of clean nappies, or even a sleeping baby, it seemed. With a very young baby in tow, there was a limit to how much I could actually do out there. After a couple of weeks I decided I'd earned my stripes washing nappies in buckets years ago, and that Felicity and Peter were doing just fine by themselves. Shaun was going well with his schoolwork under Felicity's supervision, and was happy to be near his dad, so I returned to town, making Lex's place in Fannie Bay my home, and just came out to Shady Camp on weekly overnight visits.

The correspondence school had contacted me at the end of the school term because they had received so little work from Callum. He came in to stay for the October holidays, and when Rod didn't turn up to take him back again, Lex and I decided to keep Callum with us and send him to day school in town. I phoned Rod, braced for abuse and argument, but Rod just said, 'Yeah, fine, okay.' I couldn't work him out.

Melaleuca was scheduled to go to auction again in November. Lex had managed to get several months' extension from the bank for Rod to come up with his investor, but once more nothing happened. However, just a few days before the auction, Melaleuca was sold to the Paspaley Pearling company, for the amount of money owed on it. It was almost an anticlimax. Instead of the emotional roller coaster

I'd experienced when Melaleuca went to auction in 1991, I just felt tired and relieved it was finally over. The huge burden of debt was gone, but so too was the hope of embarking on our own development project at Shady Camp. Rod was to stay on as manager for Paspaley's, which he seemed to be happy about. I wondered how long he would last following someone else's agenda, particularly on a piece of land he had regarded so completely as his own. At least he had a place to live and an income, without the financial responsibility. It seemed to be the best solution under the circumstances.

Lots of people asked me how I felt about the sale, assuming that I must be devastated to finally lose Melaleuca, after hanging on to it with our fingernails for so long. One night after the sale had been finalised, I was at Shady Camp with Felicity, sitting in the warm evening air watching the sun set across the flood plains. I said to myself, that land doesn't belong to you anymore, and waited for the response. Nothing. No sadness welling up, no lingering regret. The threat of losing Melaleuca had lasted for so long it had become a state of existence in its own right. There had been so many reprieves and extensions and last chances that it was a relief to be able to clear the board. And I felt that I'd lost it a long time before anyway. The sunset I was watching may not have been illuminating flood plains I owned, but that didn't change the sunset. I thought about all the good things we had done on the station, all the fencing, the building, the bull catching, all the people who had been part of those years – they were still my experiences and memories whether or not Melaleuca belonged to me.

I was allowed to continue my business at Shady Camp for the time being, and was invited to submit my development proposals to the new owners, which I did. In December, Lex and I decided that the little flat in Fannie Bay was bursting at the seams, and we bought a house down at Howard Springs, some 35 kilometres south of Darwin, and half an hour closer to Shady Camp. A three-bedroom house on a two-acre block, in the rural area, with lots of room for a few kids, a garden and some chooks. It wasn't much of a house, but we could see the potential for improving it when we could afford to. The following year Callum started at Taminmin High School as a Year 8 student, and Shaun went into Grade 6 at the Howard Springs Primary School just a

2-kilometre bike ride away. Tom continued to live in town with his mother, and Sophie was back in Victoria, working as an assistant for a year at her old boarding school.

It was a great compromise for all of us. Lex was still close enough to work in town. It wasn't too far for Tom to visit, and I was less than two hours from Shady Camp. Callum and Shaun may not have been out bush exactly, but at least it wasn't a small suburban block. We all felt the flush of a new beginning; even our teenage boys got into the spirit of it, helping to build a chook run, and sorting out the overgrown garden with surprising enthusiasm.

Felicity stayed on at Shady Camp, keeping the boat hire business operating. Antony Butters, a young fellow from Leicester in the UK who had worked with us the year before, arrived back again in time to replace Peter early in 1993, and stayed for another couple of months. He was a keen birdwatcher and fisherman, and for him Shady Camp, with its myriad bird life and its fishing, was like heaven on a stick.

Felicity left in July 1993. Her parents had both been ill, so she returned to Victoria to care for them, and to decide what to do next. It was time for her to move on to the next phase of her life. She had been keeping me sane for almost seven years, and we had gone through a lot together, mostly good memories. Life wouldn't be the same without her around.

I employed Mal Stockton as a full-time manager when Felicity departed, in view of the planned developments, and withdrew a bit more from running the business, apart from regular trips out to deliver fuel or equipment. Instead I started drawing a lot more, and in early 1994 started a commission for the Territory Wildlife Park, drawing a series of cartoons for their new reptile exhibit. My friend Jane Miles had brought me in on an art job she was doing for the park, after years of coaxing little cartoons out of me for *Bush Buzz*. By now I was doing a full page cartoon strip for the *Bush Buzz* cover every two or three months, and feeling that I'd like to see what lay in that direction. As Ali got older, the prospect of spending half our time in the car between Howard Springs and Shady Camp was looking less and less attractive.

The year went on, and the boys and I got used to living in town permanently. Shaun still considered the station his real home, and Howard Springs just a base, but he made friends and did well at school, and was happy. Callum seemed happier at Taminmin High too, and began to take an interest in cricket. I still had plenty of contact with the bush, as I was still the president of the Lower Mary River Landcare group, and on the board of Landcare NT.

Rod and Lesley were living at Melaleuca. He appeared to be coping with the change in his circumstances, being the manager of his former home, but I was worried about his effect on Callum and Shaun. He would phone the boys, make definite plans to collect them at the end of the school week to go out to the station, and then just not turn up. No phone call, no message. The boys would call him, and phone friends who might know where he was, but all too often they would spend a miserable weekend waiting, passing up other offers to go fishing or out somewhere in case their dad turned up to get them.

I complained about it to Rod one day, and he retorted hotly, 'Well, they don't say anything to me. They're just pleased to see me.'

'Of course they don't say anything to you. They're already worried that maybe you don't want to be bothered coming to get them, so they're not going to say anything that might make you cranky! Just phone them if you can't make it. Don't leave it for days and days.'

He snorted and left in a huff, and told the boys not to complain to me when he didn't turn up, because then I gave him a hard time.

For a while he made an effort but pretty soon he was back where he'd been, not turning up for a week to collect them, without any explanatory calls. Callum took it in his stride, but Shaun would get very upset about it, torn between being angry with his father and sad that he hadn't come to get them.

Sometimes when Rod came in on his own, he would stop and have a cup of tea, and talk about the station, and what was happening out there. These conversations were rare. I always dreaded the prospect of talking to Rod. If I knew he was coming to the house, I would be nervous and on edge, unable to concentrate on anything. An uneasy fear would creep over me, tying my stomach up in knots while the rest of me was unravelling. When I tried to pinpoint just what I was afraid of, I couldn't. I hated myself for being so pathetic, that he could still make me feel insecure in my own house, but I didn't know what to do about it. But on those occasions when calm and civil conversations did happen, it was almost like the old Rod was back, and the hope would flicker that maybe we could be friends, that it didn't have to be so fraught and difficult.

However, things were not going well for him. Lesley had been ill, and they'd had to go south for some medical treatment for her. She had quit her degree altogether. He was still fighting the government over BTEC, and was working up a compensation case with Geoff James who had represented us in our struggles to keep the station.

Rod told me the police raided Melaleuca some time in 1993, looking for drugs. They came in with a SWAT team, men wearing camouflage gear and carrying assault rifles. He was walking back from the water pump, and Lesley was alone inside the house. As he approached, he saw a figure in camouflage fatigues, carrying a rifle and creeping around the side of the house.

'It could have got very ugly if I'd been out shooting wallabies or something. I mean, what do you think when you see someone armed to the fuckin' teeth sneaking under the windows, and you know your partner is inside? If I'd had a gun I would have used it thinking I was shooting some homicidal maniac!' He was almost hysterical with rage about it. I could certainly understand the reaction to seeing armed strangers at your house, but I also wondered why the police thought it was necessary to go out there like that. You didn't do a drug bust with an armed force for a few ounces of marijuana, surely?

I didn't have any contact with Lesley, apart from the occasional phone call to try and arrange the boys' pick-ups. She could be friendly sometimes, just like the Lesley who first came to work for me, but at other times she was almost hostile. Whenever I saw her and Rod together, though, they seemed happy and were very affectionate with each other. Lesley seemed to have taken on Rod's whole attitude to life while they were at Mt Catt. Since then she dressed mainly in old army fatigues, and went barefoot like Rod, repeating his stands on issues, and seeing the same hidden agendas in anything to do with the government. So I was totally unprepared when Rod phoned one day in January 1994. Callum and Shaun had been staying with him at Melaleuca, and he was going to bring them back to me: 'Lesley's left, and I've kind of lost my marbles. Ah, I've got an appointment to see a shrink, and try and sort things out . . .'

I couldn't believe it – Rod was voluntarily seeking help for his mental state. I replied very cautiously, 'That's fine, just drop them off when you come through. I think it's a really good thing you're doing, Rod.'

He dropped the boys off that afternoon. About midnight, I was woken by the sound of a car engine and headlights shining into our bedroom. I slipped out of bed to go to the back door, and switched on the verandah light. It was Rod.

'Sorry, sorry – it's me,' he called out. 'Sorry to wake you up.' He looked awful, all shrunken and tight, like he was expecting a blow at any moment, and he was holding himself like he was injured.

'I had to get out of town quickly, and I didn't know where else to go.'

'Come inside. What's happened? Are you hurt?' I closed the door behind him, and started filling up the kettle for a cup of tea. Rod turns up, Jo puts the billy on. Old habits just don't die.

He wasn't injured, at least not physically anyway. In the bright kitchen light his face looked haggard and wretched, and his mouth was a tight pinch. His eyes were dark blue hollows, staring out around him as if he expected to be attacked at any moment.

'I got a hotel room in town, and I was talking to the doctor I'm supposed to see tomorrow, because I was feeling pretty bad. He decides I'm suicidal, and tells me to sit tight, because the police are on their way to have a chat and a cup of fuckin' *tea* with me, to make sure I'm okay. So I just got out of there. The bastard'd lock me up in a psych ward and I wouldn't get out.'

I poured a mug of tea and handed it to him. 'Were the police following you?' I asked him.

'No, I pissed off before they got there, just left the phone hangin' while he was talking to me. He was tryin' to keep me on the phone till they got there.' He clutched the tea, and stared into space.

'Well, you better stay here for now. I'll make up the bed in the spare room. We'll sort it out in the morning, okay?' I sounded a lot calmer than I felt.

He looked at me like he was about to cry, and nodded, biting his lip.

I left him in the kitchen, and went down the hall to our bedroom, and woke Lex. I explained what was happening. Lex said it was fine with him, and we'd make sure Rod got some proper professional help in the morning.

The next day I phoned our family doctor, arranged for a referral to a private psychiatrist, and drove Rod up to town for the appointment. He was in with the doctor for two hours. Great, I thought. Maybe after all this time he'll start confronting himself, and stop blaming the rest of the world for his troubles.

That afternoon the psychiatrist rang me at home. 'Rodney is very mentally ill,' he said. 'He should be in hospital, but he has no private health cover, so he would end up in the public system under the same doctor who called the police last night. I've put him on some medication but he really needs to be under supervision while he's on it. Could he stay with you, and can you monitor his medication?'

I staggered a bit at that. The prospect of having an officially mentally ill Rod in my house for a few days was the last thing I wanted. But if I didn't, he would just go back out bush, and probably get worse. I hoped the psychiatrist knew what he was doing. Maybe this was the break Rod needed to pull himself together. Reluctantly I agreed, but I said I would call my partner first to talk it over with him.

Lex was a lot more comfortable about Rod staying than I was. He thought we couldn't do much else anyway: 'You don't have a lot of choice, Jo. He's Callum and Shaun's dad. It'll be okay. Might be a good thing for him.'

I spent the next five days in an increasing cloud of apprehension. At first Rod was quiet and subdued, and we even had a couple of chats about his condition. He told me that all Lesley's friends, and the doctor she'd been seeing, had talked her into leaving him and wouldn't tell him where she was. All he had was a phone number. He was worried about her, he said, because she was depressed like him, and might harm herself. I couldn't imagine the Lesley I remembered being a potential suicide, but then I knew how much I had been changed by Rod, and I said I'd call her, just so he knew she was okay.

Later, when he had gone out, I rang the number I'd been given, half expecting a very aggressive response, if she would speak to me at all. An hour and a half later I reeled off the phone with a very different view of things.

Lesley had always appeared to me to be a very strong, confident young woman, highly intelligent and outgoing. Not the sort of person to put up with any nonsense from anyone. Yet her relationship with Rod had followed a very similar track to mine. She had lost all her brightness and confidence, had stopped seeing her friends, and reduced contact with her family. Rod convinced her that she had mental problems, and that she was the cause of the problems in their relationship. Finally when she told him she was leaving, he said that she made him feel like he wanted to kill her. He put this into a letter, and threatened to show it to all her friends, so that they could see what a terrible person she was, to have brought him to such a point. What was even crazier was that he did show it to her friends, who straight away put her on a plane south.

Once she had got away from him, she immediately began seeing a counsellor. She only realised then what kind of an impossible situation she had been in. She encouraged me to do the same: 'It doesn't matter that it's been a few years since you were with Rod, you're still affected by it. It would probably do you a lot of good to get some counselling.'

Ironically, I had made up my mind to do exactly that just the week before. I had decided I was fed up with continually feeling on the back foot whenever I had to deal with Rod, that it was way past time to be rid of feelings of anger and anxiety where he was concerned. I wanted to put it all behind me and move on, and be able to deal with him from a position of strength. Later that year I spent ten weeks seeing a counsellor, and it was the best thing I ever did.

I came off the phone with my head spinning, but also with a strange feeling of relief. It wasn't just me. If someone as strong willed as Lesley could get sucked into the same kind of maelstrom as I had, then maybe I wasn't as completely weak and stupid as I had thought.

Most of the time Rod was in our house, he was in the spare room sleeping, rarely even coming out to eat. But slowly he was turning back into the man I was used to. The misery and dejection were replaced by a familiar bitterness, and he began blaming everything and everyone but himself for what had happened: If Lesley's friends had stayed out of it, if Lesley had only listened to him more, if she hadn't talked to other people, everything would have been all right still . . .

I heard all this without making any comment, apart from saying at one point, 'But you threatened to *kill* her, Rod. Don't you think that's pretty scary? It's not surprising that her friends got her out of Darwin, is it?'

'I didn't actually *threaten* to kill her, I only said that she made me feel like I *wanted* to,' he replied emphatically.

I knew better than to try and point out that there really wasn't a lot of difference between the two. I rang his mate Wayne Miles to come out and talk to him. Wayne made up a story that he had to write a feature article about crocodiles for a magazine, and whisked Rod away out bush with him for a fortnight. I didn't hear from Rod again for weeks. I didn't know if he'd gone back to see the doctor, but I decided to keep out of it. The old familiar cockiness had replaced the subdued introspection, and I didn't feel comfortable.

After he had left, I paced up and down, hating the feeling of uncertainty he'd brought, and the fact that he'd made me feel unsafe here, in my own house. I tackled it in the only way I could think of, and I completely stripped the guest room. I took all the furniture out and put it in the bright sun on the clean grass, aired the mattress out in the hottest part of the day, scrubbed the walls and floor and the overhead fan, and washed the sheets and the curtains. Then when it was all back together, I lit candles all through the house, and mentally erased him from my home. Maybe it was a silly ritual, but I felt better.

Rod was on his own for a while at the station. The next time we saw him, he had shaved his head. It was like a kind of staged grieving, what you do when someone dies – you shave your head, cut off your hair. A symbolic disfigurement, like the Aboriginal practice of slashing yourself with sharp stones at a funeral. In spite of everything I felt a twinge of pity for him, out there by himself. I knew how much he hated being on his own, but I knew from experience it wouldn't be for long.

Sometime during 1994 he took up with a couple of different women, and one stayed for the next eighteen months or so. Callum and Shaun went out to the station when they could, but they didn't like Rod's new partner much. Rod became more and more unreliable about picking the boys up – or returning them when they were out there. Several times I had to drive out the 100 kilometres late at night to collect them from the Bark Hut, so that they could go to school the next day.

Meanwhile, our lives flowed on at our own pace. Sometimes it was possible to forget Rod and his problems for weeks. Lex left his law firm and went to the Bar, joining William Forster Chambers as a barrister. Callum was in Year 9 at Taminmin, Shaun in his final year at primary school. Ali was two years old. I had begun drawing seriously, and had various freelance jobs. We finally gave up on doing any campground development at Shady Camp when we couldn't reach an agreement with the new owners, and in April 1994, I sold Shady Camp Boat Hire to Michael Dunbar, who operated one of the backpacker tour groups that hired my boats.

It was a wrench to sell it. I felt sadder about the end of that part of my life than I did when Melaleuca was sold. I had started the business myself and, with Felicity's constant help, built it up into a reasonable little operation which kept us fed and clothed for a few years. It had given me a sense of achievement and confidence at a time when I badly needed it. And best of all, it gave me a degree of independence I had not had in a long time. However, it was the right time to move on. I also resigned as president of the Landcare Group, now that I was no longer a landholder or a business owner out there.

At the end of 1994 Rod rang to warn me that he might be arrested for not paying the fine that had been imposed on him two and a half years earlier at the Mainoru court hearing. I wondered why he didn't have any money, when he was being paid a good wage by the station owners. It probably should have occurred to me that he may have been spending it on drugs, but I assumed he was only smoking dope, and that he probably grew his own, or at least some of it. In the end he managed to arrange an advance on his wages to pay the fine and stayed out of gaol.

There had been another police raid at Melaleuca, and much talk around about drugs out there. Talk about other kinds of drugs, not just dope. I didn't know what to believe.

In September 1995 the station was again raided by the police. Rod actually phoned me about it this time, to my surprise, but his story was so full of intrigue and paranoia, I thought that he had finally lost his mind.

'I can't say much, the phones are tapped,' he muttered conspiratorially. 'There's a lot of bent cops in the force, and they're behind it. But there's a couple of good ones, and I'm slowly putting it all together . . .'

His life had been threatened, he said, it was all a plot to silence him. Silence him about *what*, he didn't say. The government was involved, and the police force. Writing this down now, it looks so ridiculous I hesitate to put it on paper. But Rod could always invest what he was saying with a certain credibility. You could never be quite sure whether it was *all* rubbish – maybe there was just a kernel of truth in there, but how to know which bit? In any case, I just put it down to his constant paranoia, brought on by smoking too much marijuana.

I didn't think it was any more than Rod overdramatising something that was most likely quite ordinary. He was probably being threatened with the sack because he wasn't performing well, or because he wasn't getting along with the managers in town, and he'd built it up into a conspiracy whirling around him. He had certainly done it before. It was the only way he could deal with failure rather than admit that he was at fault. In any case, he said that he wouldn't be able to have the boys to stay with him now, because the threats against him might put the boys in danger. I wondered how I was going to explain that to them.

Before too long he did lose his job at Melaleuca, and in late 1995 he was asked to resign. He had been allowed to catch brumbies on the station, and had slowly been building up a herd of good horses, which Callum and Shaun would spend time handling and riding on their trips out to the station. Now he had to find somewhere for the horses, as well as for himself.

The horses were running in Calytrix paddock, and Rod was permitted to leave them there until he found somewhere else for them. For about six months he and his girlfriend drifted around different people's houses at Humpty Doo and Darwin River, staying here and there, or camping out in the bush. The boys saw little of him during this time, and there was sometimes as much as seven or eight weeks between contacts. I saw him unexpectedly in town one day. He looked terrible – dirty and unshaven, in filthy clothes, his hat jammed tight down on his head. I immediately had a panic attack. My hands were shaking and sweating, my pulse rate soared. It wasn't fair that he could still have this effect on me after so long. I understood that it was a normal reaction, and that eventually it would recede, but I wished it would stop. I didn't tell Callum and Shaun I'd seen him – it would have upset them to know he had been so close to home, and not phoned or called in to see them.

Rod's latest relationship ended sometime in the first half of 1996, and we wondered what would happen to him now. The boys seemed happier to have their father to themselves again, and the occasions I saw him, he looked a bit calmer and steadier. Maybe, I thought, he can pull himself out of this. I didn't know how he was going to do it, but I believed that the ability was still there, if he made the effort. He had his horses, and he still had his dream of riding through Arnhem Land. Maybe something good could come out of it.

# 22

# The Waler Expedition

Taking packhorses through Arnhem Land was something Rod had talked about for years, from when we lived at Bulman in 1983. At first it was just an idea to travel through the land at the pace of a horse, exploring, living off the land, seeing what was there, and just living the life for a while. After Rod had been inducted into the special relationship he held with the Rembarrunga people, he began to understand the concept of Dreaming trails or song lines, the routes the ceremonies travelled from one important place to another. The concept of following the song lines by horseback, combined with a study of the flora and fauna along the way, started to form. But it was one of those things you plan to do when you've 'got time' to disappear for a few months. It obviously wasn't going to happen while we were trying to build up a buffalo station, and the idea was pushed to the back of that dusty shelf where we store those 'one day' dreams.

When the station sold and Rod was employed as manager, or perhaps after he left it, he could see the possibility of finding that time. I imagine once the financial pressure of trying to hold it all together was gone, he was able to muse about things he would like to do sometime. Somewhere along there, the 'Waler Expedition' began to take shape.

The brumbies on Melaleuca were old Waler stock. Strong, nuggetty and sure footed, they were completely adapted to the heat and the rough terrain. We used to watch them flying across the flood plains, negotiating the potholes and the buffalo wallows like they were galloping across a bowling green. The stations in the area – such as Mt Bundy – used to supply remounts for the Indian cavalry around the time of World War I, and the Waler was the horse the army wanted. There is a lot of uncertainty surrounding the origins of the Waler, but it is generally believed that they originated in New South Wales in the 1800s, using the stockhorse for strength and hardiness, and thorough-bred stallions to contribute speed and size. Perhaps the first of the overlanders, like the Duracks, brought them up here in the early days, and they spread out from there, suited to the harsh conditions on the emerging stations in the Territory. Rod knew these were the horses for the job he had in mind, and he had gathered about twenty together before he left Melaleuca, choosing young healthy mares and gelding some young stallions.

After the demise of his last relationship, Rod went back out bush, and camped at Shady Camp. Every day he would make his way out to Calytrix paddock, and follow the horses, tracking them through the pink turkey bush and the paperbark trees on foot, and working out where they usually ran. After a week or so, he was able to stay in sight of them, and gradually approach them on foot. He concentrated on one horse, a young mare called Icecream, who he'd broken in the year before, and soon had her eating out of a bucket of horse feed. He caught her then, and was able to follow up the others on horseback and muster them all into a yard.

The O'Briens on neighbouring Carmor Plains agreed that he could bring the horses to their place, and in return for doing odd jobs and helping with the occasional muster, Rod was allowed to camp at Raintree Bore on the station, looking after that water point for them as well. Callum and Shaun went out there in June 1996 for the mid year holidays, and helped him to move the horses over to Carmor.

Raintree Bore was infamous for big poisonous snakes, particularly king browns. Several men had been bitten by snakes there over the years. The first night they were camped at the bore, the boys were sleeping in a two-man tent, while Rod was a little distance away from them under a mosquito net strung up between two trees. They had thrown their camp up at the end of the day in a bit of a hurry, and hadn't checked the ground beforehand. There was a lot of deep leaf litter on the ground.

During the night Rod was woken by the sound of the leaf litter being rustled. He listened for a while, and then realised it was a snake coming towards him. A very big snake. It was moving quite fast, spooked by the changes to its environment, with the camp gear around, a fire nearby, and strange smells and objects. It was making a beeline for its hole, which happened to be on the other side of Rod's mosquito net. Rod caught sight of the snake streaking across the leaf litter towards him, and just as it hit the wall of his net he lunged backwards away from it, and the net ripped and fell on him. He lay there paralysed while the snake writhed over his chest and head and slithered off and away into the litter behind him.

Callum and Shaun woke up hearing: 'A snake bit my neck! A snake bit my neck!'

Two adolescent boys in a hurry to get out of a little tent is not good for the tent, which was completely destroyed. When they reached Rod, expecting only to be able to hold their dying father's hand as he breathed his last, Rod was fighting his way out of the remains of his mosquito net, and looking around for the snake.

'Dad! Lie down! Lie down! Show us your neck!'

'What?'

'You said a snake bit your neck.'

'No! I said *a snake hit my net*! Look, there it is . . .'

In the torchlight they could see the tail of a very large snake. Just as Callum went to grab it, as he had seen his father do many times, Rod knocked his hand aside: 'Don't touch it! Look –'

He shone the torch around and found where the snake had gone down its hole. The great thick body had disappeared into the opening, but right beside it at the entrance was the snake's head looking out, ready to attack. Rod grabbed a rifle and shot it. When they were sure it was dead, they pulled it from its hole. It was nearly 2.5 metres long, a monster king brown and one of the most venomous of all Australian snakes.

After the holidays, Callum and Shaun went back to town for school, and Rod was alone again in the bush. He put up an advertisement at Shady Camp asking for someone to help him break in horses. Cherie was a young woman who had been working as a tour guide in the area. She didn't know anything about horses, but she was a willing pupil.

We met her, and she seemed okay. The boys appeared to get along with her, and she made an effort to be friends with them. Rod and Cherie camped at Raintree Bore for the next eight months, living rough under canvas. Cherie didn't seem to mind living like this, and she clearly idolised Rod. The boys spent the occasional weekend and most of the school holidays out there, happy to see their father doing something more constructive with his life. He was doing some work for Carmor Plains, and breaking in and handling his horses, something Callum and Shaun loved being involved in.

He was also gearing up for the Waler Expedition. The boys told us about the preparation and planning, and it looked like it was really happening. There was support for the venture from bodies like the Northern Territory University, and ERISS, the Environmental Research Institute of the Supervising Scientist, and he had been promised equipment such as a GPS, a solar powered water pump, a two-way radio set, animal and bird traps, specimen collecting bags and textbooks. Rod prepared a letter for potential sponsors, which in part described the expedition's scope:

> . . . The expedition itself is quite unique in this day and age. It is a two year horse mounted environmental and anthropological study based primarily within Arnhem Land. The horses will allow the expedition to follow the 'Kunapippi' dreaming trail that transverses Arnhem Land. The expedition will undertake standard European studies of small mammals and flora, and record Aboriginal knowledge of environment and human history. In these tasks we will be guided and assisted by people of the 'Rambungha' language group.
>
> This expedition was instigated by 'Rambungha' people interested in the exchange of knowledge and maintenance of environmental and cultural values. The expedition will also undertake an Aboriginal environmental assessment survey where the expedition members will assist the 'Rambungha' people to record the information . . .

It displayed all of Rod's hallmarks – it was imaginative, different, attention grabbing and epic. A venture like the Waler Expedition would generate a huge amount of interest. It would have had its detractors, for sure, but the idea of taking a slow and measured journey by horseback, in company with the traditional custodians of the land, was inspiring, and reminiscent of the explorers of the previous century.

The expedition was to begin at Urapunga, a small Aboriginal community east of the Roper River, and about 290 kilometres southeast of Katherine. Rod intended to begin in the 1998 Dry season, and finish up in northwestern Arnhem Land in the middle of 2000. ERISS would meet up with the expedition on a regular basis to collect the data and resupply the team. ERISS was also planning to help develop methodologies for data collection, and to assist with publishing the information at the other end. There were plans for spin-off publications, like magazine articles, coffee table books and calendars.

The project had all the perfect ingredients for Rod: horses, the bush and freedom to ride through it, Aboriginal involvement, and a sense of being central to something important and relevant. It sounded positive and exciting, and it seemed that he might have found a way to pull himself out of the morass he had sunk into. But in spite of this encouraging activity I had a constant nagging feeling that it wasn't going to be that simple. He didn't look very healthy for a start. He was thinner than ever, and none too clean. His skin, which had always had a healthy tanned glow, looked greyish and dull. The keenness of his eyes had been replaced by a wariness, and they flicked around when he spoke to you, like he was constantly scanning for danger.

It wasn't just me who thought he was deteriorating. Many people mentioned that they had seen Rod in town, and were shocked by his appearance. Our old friend, Bluey Lewis, ran into Rod in Darwin one day and told me a few weeks later: 'I didn't even recognise him for a bit. I saw this long-grasser across the road, dirty, barefoot, scruffy and ragged looking, and bugger me if he doesn't wave and sing out to me. Once I heard him I realised it was Rod, but, my God, what's happened to the man? He seemed really strange too, like he was on something . . .'

It was becoming a sadly familiar story. Yet sometimes Rod would turn up at our house, clean and clear-eyed, talking sense. And he still had some good friends, people who weren't part of any drug scene, and who held responsible jobs, had families, lived normal lives. Geoff

Stewart and his wife Mary Willems saw a lot of Rod over the years, either out bush or when Rod came to town. Geoff was a doctor and worked mainly with Aboriginal communities in the Territory. Before their children were born, Mary had spent several years setting up and running horticultural training programs for Aboriginal women in remote communities. Both of them had a deep love of the bush and of the remoter parts of the Northern Territory. They first met Rod in about 1990, and were fascinated by his connection with the bush and with Aboriginal culture, and spent a lot of time with him exploring both. They also developed a close bond with Callum and Shaun, watching them grow up from eleven- and nine-years-olds to young men. I was always a lot happier on the occasions I knew the Stewarts were going to be around too when the boys were spending time with their father.

Shaun begged me to let him go on part of the Waler Expedition with his father. They were setting out early in the new school term, but I let Shaun have a week off. It would be a great experience for him, taking a mob of horses overland. There was not much opportunity left any-more to do something like that. It might also send Rod the message that we supported this positive, constructive direction he appeared to be taking.

They left Carmor Plains one morning in early August 1997, with Rod and Shaun on horseback and Cherie driving their car down the road, keeping the little mob of ten horses held against the fence that ran along beside the Point Stuart Road. They went very slowly, getting the horses used to travelling together, and becoming accustomed to the occasional vehicle roaring past in a cloud of dust. They took two days and nights to reach the Bark Hut on the Arnhem Highway, and camped on nearby Annaburroo Billabong for a day or two before moving on.

Shaun came back to town, and Dwyn Delaney went on with them. Dwyn was the owner of 'Delaney's', a country and western outfitters store in the city, and had become a mate of Rod's in the last few years. He was very supportive of the ride. He contributed equipment towards it but, more importantly, a lot of moral support. Dwyn, like Wayne Miles and Geoff Stewart, was worried about Rod's very apparent deterioration, and believed that the ride could only be a good thing.

Rod had collected permission from all the landholders along the way before they set out. They headed south, following the McKinlay River upstream, then crossed west to the Margaret, with two of them on horseback, and one driving Dwyn's Toyota and towing Rod and Cherie's vehicle behind. Dwyn was startled to find that they spent a lot of time lost. Rod hadn't brought a compass, just a map, and a vague idea about where they were headed: 'There were just dozens of billygoat trails all over the place – Rod had no idea which way to go. We went around in circles for the first three days.' It wasn't like Rod at all.

About the third day after they left Annaburroo, Dwyn took a bad fall from his horse, a gelding called Bushman. The horse had been playing up that morning, and when Dwyn went to climb back on after a lunch stop, Bushman pelted him twenty feet through the air. 'I just flew up this high arc, straight for a big stick poking up out of the lagoon we were stopped at. I hit the stick headfirst, but my hat stopped most of the damage. Then I landed flat on my back, and I was sure it was broken.'

Dwyn lay on the ground in terrible pain while Rod hurried over to him. Just then, an army vehicle drove up. Dwyn relaxed slightly, thinking that at least they would have a decent first aid kit, and some painkillers. But to his dismay he heard Rod tell the soldiers they were fine, and didn't need any help. The soldiers drove away, and Dwyn lay in the same spot till the next day, when he carefully got to his feet, helped by Rod and Cherie, and managed to get into the driver's seat of his vehicle. Propped up by pillows and blankets, he had no choice but to drive along behind the mob. The horses were still too fresh for one person to handle alone, so both Rod and Cherie had to ride. They reached Ban Ban Springs after about four days, and set up camp on the dam. The horses had settled into a good travelling habit, and were averaging about 35 kilometres a day. Dwyn left Rod and Cherie to continue on their own, and drove himself back to Darwin, where he spent the next six months in physiotherapy, repairing the damage. He had four fractured vertebrae in his lower back.

Rod and Cherie reached Katherine by October, and spelled the

horses for a few days at Graham Michell's property, Maud Creek
Station, just a few miles outside the town. Graham was a long-time
friend of Rod's and mine. We'd spent many pleasant nights and
weekends over the years staying with him and his former wife, Val
Hristova, and talking long into the night. Graham may have thought
what Rod was doing now was unusual, but then he was used to Rod's
different way of looking at things.

Geoff and Mary Stewart caught up with Rod and Cherie at Maud
Creek and travelled with them as far as Mataranka, a journey of just a
couple of days, following the old railway easement. Geoff and Mary
remember there being a lot of tension between Cherie and Rod by
then, and she left Rod once the horses were in the stock yards at
Mataranka, and went to live in Katherine for a while.

The weather was too hot for the horses to travel very far now, and
Rod made arrangements with Elsey Station to agist the horses there
over the wet season. He also had to do some work for a local station
owner who was owed money by Mt Catt for a grader Rod had
arranged for the community to purchase a few years earlier, but which
had never been paid for. So he spent several weeks breaking in horses
to pay off the debt.

Callum finished Year 12 at the end of 1997, and took a year off to
work and earn some money before starting university the following
year. He and Shaun hadn't seen their grandparents or the rest of the
Ansells for some time, so before Callum started work, Lex and I sent
them down to Murgon for a few weeks after Christmas.

When they came home again, Callum began working for Paspaleys
as a shell cleaner on one of the pearl farms on the northwest coast of
Western Australia. Shaun went to spend some time with Rod, who
had moved up to Darwin during the wet season, and was living at
a mate's place at Humpty Doo for a while. Cherie had returned by
then as well, and was also with Rod at Humpty Doo. When the 1998
school year started, Shaun continued to live with his father for a few
more weeks, coming back to us at Howard Springs when Rod returned
to Mataranka.

Callum finished up with Paspaleys in May 1998. He was due to
begin university the following year, and knew that he wouldn't be able
to spend much time with his father then, so he decided to spend the

rest of this year with him. He travelled down to Mataranka, and went out to Elsey Station where Rod was doing some work. They walked the horses to Roper Valley Station, about 100 kilometres to the east, where Sammy Bulabul was living at the time, taking part in a land claim hearing for his traditional country.

In a stroke of incredible irony, Lex was asked to represent the government in this particular case. I was very distressed. Of all the land hearings Lex could have acted in, and he didn't do many of them, that he should appear on the other side to my old friends was very difficult for me. But as Lex pointed out, the hearing was basically a formality, and there was no doubt about Sammy's legitimate claim to the land. I just hoped that Sammy would see it that way too.

In another coincidence, the day Lex turned up at Roper Valley for the hearing, Callum arrived at the station with the horses, and was astonished to see Lex's familiar Land Cruiser parked under a tree. Lex was only there for a day, but Callum stayed about a month before moving the horses over to Urapunga Station sometime in June, a journey of another 70 or 80 kilometres.

Urapunga Station was chosen as the starting point for the Waler Expedition by the old people at Mt Catt, because it was in need of some help. Rod wanted to travel the Kunapippi ceremony track, collecting information along it, and correlating factors such as fuel loads, and fauna and flora biodiversity with the track, to see if there was a connection with the route this traditional dreaming track followed, and the land itself. The custodians of the country Rod was going to be travelling through had a trade-off though: they would give their support to Rod for this venture, and provide knowledgeable old people to accompany him on various sections of the track, but Rod had to do something in return. They wanted him to stay at Urapunga for a while, to work with the young men there, and to go through some more ceremony himself.

Felicity was back in the Northern Territory again, studying science at university after working on some remote properties in New South Wales and the Territory for the past couple of years. In July 1998, she, Ali and I drove the seven hours to Urapunga Station to pick up Shaun from his two-week stay with Rod during the mid year school holidays.

We arrived at the community around mid morning, and found our way to Rod's camp.

It was a bit of a shock, walking into the place where they were staying. They had the use of quite a good little house, a sort of large bed-sit, with a kitchen and a huge bathroom complete with a four-person spa. Apparently it was the building used by the Northern Land Council staff when they visited, and the community had told Rod and Cherie to camp there. Rod was sitting on a bare mattress on the floor, a mound of blankets tangled beneath him, rolling a smoke. There was rubbish around the room, dirty plates and open tins of food on a filthy table. Rod was grubby and unwashed, and his clothes were torn and dirty as well. I couldn't understand it. I think that was the first time I truly realised just how far he had sunk, in terms of self respect and any kind of a normal life.

Outside, I chatted with Callum and Shaun for a while, trying to get some idea of what was happening. They were plainly embarrassed at me seeing Rod like that, but at the same time they were defensive of him. It was so difficult for them. They loved their father dearly, in spite of how strangely he behaved. They were always so intensely loyal to him, but they must have known that he was getting worse and worse. The man they had grown up with at Bulman and on Melaleuca hadn't behaved like this. He was someone they had idolised, the man who could do anything, the man who caught more buffalo, drove faster, worked harder, and did everything better than anyone else. He taught them about the bush, and about life, and as far as they were concerned, Dad knew everything. He was the same man who teased them and made them laugh and cuddled them and loved them. That was something Rod had never stinted in. He had always given them enormous amounts of affection, and had often told them he loved them, at every age. It was an enormous transformation for them to deal with, even if it had been a gradual one.

Shaun was having a rough trot at school that year, and by the end of it, having battled teachers, an inflexible school system, and a frightening episode with a bone tumour, he announced his intention not to go back and do Year 12 in 1999. I made a deal with him that he could have the following year off, provided that by the end of it he either went back to school or got a proper job. He wanted to spend time with his father. I could see that Shaun was terribly worried about him, although he would never say as much. As soon as the Year 11 exams were over, he went down to stay with Rod. Callum came back, and went out to work on the pearl farms again until university started the following March.

In hindsight, it was clear that Callum and Shaun were endeavouring that one or the other of them was with their father as much as possible.

# 23

# 'We Will Look After Him'

Nineteen ninety-nine, and Lex and I had a very quiet house, with just Ali at home now. Callum was living on campus at the Northern Territory University and studying engineering, and Shaun was with Rod at Urapunga. It worried me that Shaun was out there, isolated with his father and Cherie, and not doing anything very constructive. That was okay for a few weeks, but not how I wanted to see my son living his life. When I spoke to Shaun occasionally by phone, or on the even rarer occasions when he came to Darwin that year, he talked of lots of activity – building spear traps to catch cattle for the community, meetings to try and raise government and Land Council support for community projects, yard building, fencing. The Waler Expedition seemed to be on hold for a while, but Shaun was confident it was still going to happen. The horses were in a paddock nearby, and were being worked occasionally. According to Shaun Rod was using the time at Urapunga to get the remainder of the support system in place so that the expedition could begin.

It all sounded good, but it just didn't fit with the impression we got of Rod's state at that time. Whenever I saw him, which wasn't often now, he seemed evasive and edgy. He was short with words, wouldn't look me in the eye much, and held his mouth tightly. As often as not he would just wait outside in the car, or squat beside it in the grass smoking and waiting for the boys to be ready to go. Now that Callum and Shaun were all but grown up, there was no longer much for us to say to each other. Lex and I very much doubted that Rod was capable of organising anything anymore. And after the fiasco at Mt Catt, I couldn't see how any funding bodies would take his propositions very seriously.

The very last time I saw him, about May 1999, he was picking up Shaun from our house at Howard Springs after a brief visit. I had to go out, and had left Shaun at home waiting for his father to collect him to go back down to Urapunga. When I returned, I passed them on the road. They stopped, and Shaun came over to kiss me goodbye. As they drove off in Rod's little blue car, Rod and I gave each other a wave and a nod. The barest of civil recognition. I watched the car disappear in the rear-view mirror, and thought just how far we were from the young couple we had once been, so much in love and with such a future in front of us. Now we waved at each other like vague acquaintances.

At the ripe old age of seventeen, Shaun had fallen in love with a teacher at the Urapunga School. Tamara was a few years older than Shaun, but was a delightful, happy young woman who provided a complete contrast to the lifestyle he had been living with Rod. Shaun ended up spending quite a lot of his time with Tamara at her house in the Urapunga community, especially after Rod and Cherie moved their camp some 20 kilometres away from the community, out on the Wilton River near Lake Allen. She called in to meet us when she came to Darwin on a school trip, and I was relieved that Shaun had some healthy normality to balance his life a little at that time.

It was to be my father's seventieth birthday in August 1999. Lex was flat out with court cases and couldn't get away, so Ali and I went down to Melbourne on our own, planning to stay a month at least and catch up with Lex's father Alec Silvester as well. We travelled out to Bairnsdale in eastern Victoria, to spend a few days with Alec and his partner Lois. Lex's daughter Sophie was visiting at the same time, and she and I drove up to Mt Hotham on Monday 2 August, to show Ali the snow. It was a perfect day. The weather was mild, the snow was brilliant, and I was happy to be back in my favourite part of the world for the first time in twenty-four years, even if it was just for a few hours. I sat on a boulder by the side of the road overlooking

Mt Feathertop, and remembered the wonderful times I'd had up here so long ago.

That same morning back in the Territory, Shaun and Callum had dropped by the house at Howard Springs, and Callum had left a note for Lex asking him to cancel his accommodation at the university residence. Callum wrote that he wanted to take some time off and see his father, that he was driving back to Urapunga with Shaun, and that he knew Lex would be furious at him for quitting his degree. He called Lex that evening from Urapunga, and Lex told him he had to tell me himself, and gave him the phone number of Alec's house in Bairnsdale. Callum decided it was too late to call me that night, and planned to do so the next day.

Ali and I went into town on Tuesday 3 August, to get the photos of our visit to Mt Hotham processed. Ali chatted away to the shop assistant, and when I approached the counter, the woman said to me, 'You're from Darwin, are you? Did you hear about the shooting up there this morning? Apparently a policeman was killed.'

I said that I hadn't heard. I couldn't remember the last time a police officer had been killed on duty in the Territory, but I was sure it was a long time ago. A little tendril of apprehension uncurled in the pit of my stomach. I just put it down to the fact that this kind of event was so unusual for Darwin, and hoped it was no one I knew.

That night, the story from Darwin led the news reports. An unidentified gunman had shot dead a police officer at a roadblock south of Darwin, and had wounded several other people. Two men had also been shot and wounded the night before in the same area, and several houses had been fired on. The gunman had been shot dead by another police officer, but his name had not been released yet.

We watched the reports like everyone else, shocked by the violence, mystified, puzzled, but so far untouched. We were about to walk next door to have dinner with Lois's daughter, when the phone rang. Lois called me inside, saying:

'It's Lex – he sounds *very* serious.'

'I bet I know what it is – Callum quit uni yesterday, and Lex is really unhappy about it.'

Lex had called me the night before to tell me about the note from Callum, but I hadn't heard from Callum yet. I wasn't too concerned –

the phone was often out of order at Urapunga, and he probably wasn't relishing the thought of a nagging from his mum either.

I picked up the phone.

'Jo – I have very bad news . . .' For a split second, I thought that it would be about a young friend of ours who had been seriously injured in a car crash a few days before, and was completely unprepared when Lex continued: 'Rod's dead.'

'*What?*'

I heard Lex take a deep breath. 'Have you heard about the shooting up here? It was Rod, Jo . . .'

I couldn't get any sound out then. It was too big to take in, too impossible to comprehend. But then I suddenly remembered Callum and Shaun; my stomach dropped a thousand feet and my knees buckled.

'Where are my boys? Where are my boys!' I gasped into the phone. I couldn't get any more words out. Visions of my sons hiding in the bush, or being witnesses at the scene, being held by police, just flooded in, and I couldn't think straight.

'They're okay, they're okay – they weren't there. They're at Urapunga – they don't know anything about it. I've arranged a charter plane to take Geoff Stewart down there first thing in the morning, to be with them when the police tell them, and to bring them home.' Lex sounded like he was barely holding things together himself, and we both ended the conversation in tears.

Ali and Sophie were standing over me as I crouched on the floor clutching the phone: 'What is it? What's happened? *Who* is it?' Ali and Sophie were crying themselves now, and Sophie was almost shouting.

I lurched to my feet, and gathered myself together, but I still couldn't speak. No sound would come out, no matter how hard I tried. I just pointed at the television, and whispered: 'It was Rod . . .'

The others decided to go on to dinner, taking Ali with them, while I stayed behind and tried to get my head around what had happened. I phoned my sister Leonie, but neither of us could talk. We just wept together over the phone. What was there to say? The horror that some-one close to us had killed another human being – it's not something you could ever be prepared for, something so terrible, and so irrev-ocable. My mother called next, and then the phone rang again. I answered it, thinking it would be Lex with details of the flight home he was trying to arrange for us.

'Hi, Mum! How are you going?'

My heart almost stopped, and my throat closed up. I took a deep breath and then began the best acting performance of my life. 'Callum – where are you?'

'I'm at Urapunga with Shaun and Tam. I guess you're pretty mad with me for quitting uni, huh?'

The only thing in my favour was that Callum was expecting me to be unhappy with him, so my flat voice didn't sound too strange, I guess. I made an excuse about coming down with a cold and that I felt very tired, and said we'd talk about his decision to quit his studies when I got home. I promised to talk to him again soon, and hung up the phone feeling as sad and hopeless as I ever had in my life. I couldn't tell Callum and Shaun about their father, not when they were on their own, out in the bush. I felt like I was giving them a night's reprieve. There'd be enough grief to come.

We flew into Darwin at 10.30 pm the next night and Lex met us at the airport. Leonie came with us, to stay and help us through what was going to be a very tough time. Callum and Shaun were already at home, having flown up from Urapunga with Geoff Stewart that morning. It broke my heart to see them, their faces a mixture of un-utterable grief and incomprehension. It is bad enough to lose your father at any time, but to lose him in circumstances like this was beyond imagining.

We just held each other for a long time, and sat quietly together on the couch for an hour before I made them go to bed. There wasn't anything to say yet. It was all too close.

The next morning, their father's name was in the papers, identified as the gunman who had killed a young police officer. We also knew by now that he had been using amphetamines heavily before he died. The phone began ringing constantly, and Lex and Leonie took over answering every call, keeping a record of the people who rang to express their sympathy, and fending off the media.

That morning, Callum and Shaun had to go into the police station at Berrimah to give statements. I went in with Callum, and Lex went in to support Shaun. Both the boys were amazing. They handled an unimaginably difficult situation as mature young men, only a day after learning of their father's death. They were treated well by the interviewing officers. I was worried that there would be palpable resentment on the part of the police, but both boys were treated with respect, like boys who had just lost their father, not like the sons of a man who'd murdered one of their colleagues. Both Callum and Shaun expressed their sorrow for the dead policeman's family as well.

After their interviews were over Shaun and Callum, with Geoff's help, began searching for Cherie. She had disappeared, and they were afraid she might be dead too. I guess it gave them something to do, something to focus on, and they spent a couple of days combing every track and turning off the Stuart Highway in the Acacia Hills area. By Saturday we heard that she was in Brisbane, and she contacted us by phone that night, wanting to know if the boys were okay. It was a strange call, and she sounded quite detached from everything that was going on.

Rod's family left Murgon on Thursday morning to drive to Darwin. Almost his entire family came – his parents Eve and George, Eve's sister Ruby, his brother Malcolm and his wife Julie, his oldest sister Jennifer, her husband John and their children Kasey and Regan. Rod's younger sister Christine was already in Darwin.

The Ansells arrived on Saturday night and came out to see us on Sunday. In a strange twist, they realised that they had actually seen Cherie themselves at a roadhouse as they passed through a town in Queensland. They noticed her because they'd heard the truck driver she was with asking her if she was okay when she came out of the bathroom, and then they recognised her photo in the paper when they got to Darwin.

It fell to me to organise Rod's funeral. We discussed several options, but the only thing we were all certain about was that Rod would have wanted to be buried in Arnhem Land, at Mt Catt. I was the only person who knew all the people who would have to be consulted. Sammy Bulabul and his wife Christine were living in Darwin most of the time now, as Sammy was suffering from kidney failure and was on regular dialysis. I went to see them by myself to talk about the burial.

Sammy and Christine were distraught. They didn't want to believe it was true, and quizzed me about whether the newspapers had got the wrong person. They also refused to believe that Rod used drugs. It just didn't fit the person they had known for so many years. It was like talking to Rod's parents. They could not believe that their son had come to this. They knew that he had smoked marijuana, which horrified them enough anyway, but it was almost beyond their comprehension that he could have been using amphetamines. But then there was no other explanation for what happened.

'He was injecting drugs into himself, Sammy, and it made him go crazy. I didn't know he was doing this either, none of us did. He just went crazy, and shot all those people.'

Sammy was very certain that Rod should be buried at Mt Catt. He said that Rod had told him once that he wanted to be buried there when he died. I was relieved to hear it. Both the boys and I thought it was the best place too. I knew how difficult this was going to be to arrange, so I needed to know that it was really what Sammy wanted too, or it would never happen. For a start, there was a Kunapippi ceremony taking place at Mt Catt right then. It would be next to impossible to reach the right traditional owners to give their permission for the funeral to go ahead. The Northern Land Council (NLC), who had no fondness for Rod Ansell, would have to be involved, and might be awkward. The distances might be too much for Rod's parents, who weren't well people. Permission had to be sought from the authorities to bury a body outside an official cemetery. And most of all, the actual grave site had to be organised from Darwin, to happen at a very specific time because the plane bringing the coffin down had to take Sammy back to town for dialysis, and couldn't be delayed at all.

I spent several hours with Sammy and Christine waiting outside the NLC office in Darwin, while they tried to contact people at Mt Catt for permission. It seemed like it would take a miracle to make it happen from here, hundreds of kilometres away, depending on people and machinery I had no control over, getting all the necessary permits from every authority, and make it all happen on time. I organised what I could in town, and just had to trust that the Aboriginal people at Mt Catt would do their part.

A few days before the funeral we held a quiet memorial service at our home in Howard Springs. The Ansells and about forty old friends came, people from the bull catching days, Melaleuca, Arnhem Land, all over the place. It was a sad affair, and most people were too upset to speak, but Callum and Shaun were wonderful. They spoke to the assembly about their father, and when one faltered, the other would pick up where he'd left off. They spoke about remembering the good times, the good things about their father, and not how it all ended. They mentioned Glen Huitson and his family and expressed their grief for that loss too. I was so proud of them.

Rod was buried on 12 August 1999, at Mt Catt, next to his old friend Old George J— who had died some nine years before, in a ceremony that was a mix of traditional Aboriginal and Christian practices, managed and led by the Mt Catt and Bulman people themselves. The community backhoe wasn't working, something I had worried about from Darwin, but Rod's old bull catching compatriots – Kenneth Murray, Lachlan, Paddy Ryan, Kevin Forbes and others – left the Kunapippi ceremony and came and dug the grave by hand themselves.

It was a very moving occasion. There were so many conflicting emotions, so many memories. In a speech made during the proceedings, Annette Miller, on behalf of the Bulman and Mt Catt communities, turned to Eve and George Ansell, and said: 'Rod is back where he belongs, with us, and we will look after him for a thousand years.'

# 24

# Roadblock:
# August 1999

**M**uch, much later, when things had settled down, and it was a little less painful to talk about it, we pieced together what had happened.

Unknown to Callum, Shaun, Lex or me, Rod had been using amphetamines for several years. The boys had never seen any indication of this, except for one time when Callum found a syringe out at one of their camps after Rod had left Melaleuca. He had recently finished the DARE program at school, a drug education initiative sponsored by the police in Australian schools, and recognised the syringe as something used to inject drugs. He asked his father about it, but Rod told him that it belonged to a girl he was seeing, and not to worry about it. Neither of the boys ever saw any other evidence of drugs apart from marijuana.

Rod was in the habit of taking off with his partner for a few days if Callum and Shaun were staying for a while. They would go out bush and camp by themselves away from the main camp, and it was clear to us later that this was when Rod was injecting speed. By the time Rod and Cherie were living at Urapunga, drugs had become the controlling aspect of his life. Every fortnight meant a 1200-kilometre round trip to Darwin to collect dole money and buy food, and marijuana. What the boys didn't know was that Rod was also bringing back a supply of speed. Shaun recalled that his father would get back from these trips, often high as a kite, laughing and talking animatedly for hours and hours.

The flip side of this animation and energy was that afterwards he would become depressed and fixated on the conspiracy ideas that were taking over his life. There was a kind of pattern, Shaun recalled, which didn't have an explanation till much later: 'Most of the time, there wouldn't be enough work to keep busy. Then all of a sudden we'd be working really hard, fixing up fences, or building a spear trap or something, just racing like there was some huge deadline, working late into the night. We were using old hand augers to drill the holes through the posts, and old wire we stripped out of burnt fences. Then there'd be a kind of lull, where the work would stop, and no one would be doing anything for a day or so, and then the delusional stuff would get going again.'

Somewhere along the way Rod became obsessed with the Free-masons. He gradually wove an elaborate conspiracy about them as a dangerous, evil cult that ritually abused and murdered children and other people. Rod was convinced that Cherie was escaping from this cult, and that the Freemasons were after her, intending to kill her to keep her silent.

Rod tried to tell Callum and Shaun about the danger he believed they were all in. They listened with a lot of scepticism, and even though their father's insistence was contagious, it all seemed terribly far-fetched. 'Just the same,' Callum said later, 'Dad could convince you of anything. He could make you believe the sky was green, if he wanted to, and you'd look out the window just to make sure it really was still blue. And even though you didn't believe it, all the stuff he was saying played on your mind. I was often there by myself when they'd gone to town, and some nights I'd start thinking about what Dad had been going on about, and start wondering if maybe it was true, and really get spooked out there by myself . . .'

When Shaun went to Urapunga to live with Rod at the end of 1998, Rod met him in Katherine, and took him into the Shell Roadhouse where they sat all night, drinking coffee to stay awake while Rod wrote a long, long letter. It was an exposé of the Free-masons, pages and pages detailing their practices and their intention to kill Cherie, and Rod mailed it to Franca Arena, a New South Wales Member of Parliament who was well known for her stance on paedophiles. This was Shaun's introduction to the conspiracy. He, too, listened with the same scepticism as Callum had. And being just as isolated – in fact even more so when they moved their camp out to the Wilton River – Shaun occasionally wondered whether his father's obsession might not have some basis to it. However, about a month before the tragedy, Shaun and Rod had a huge confrontation about it. Shaun was refusing to take it all seriously, Rod became angry, and the two of them had a fierce shouting match. The same thing had happened to Callum not long before he left the previous November. Callum had questioned some of the things Rod was telling him, Rod had become apoplectic with rage, and they'd had a serious argument over it.

Rod was getting more and more agitated about the Freemason conspiracy, and Shaun was feeling very uneasy. It's one thing to dismiss the ravings of someone you have no respect for. It's quite another when that person is the father you've looked up to all your life. Shaun decided to talk to Callum seriously about their father at the next opportunity.

Some weeks before, bow hunters wearing night vision goggles had been seen in the bush around the camp, and near the Urapunga community. It turned out that they were just friends of the storekeeper who were doing some pig hunting with bows, but for Rod it was another sign that the enemy was closing in on them.

Shaun went away for two weeks in July 1999. It was the school holidays, and Tamara's sister had come up to stay, so Shaun and Tamara took her off for a bit of sightseeing. They returned at the end of July, and Shaun arrived back at the Wilton camp just on sunset, finding the camp in total disarray, and Rod and Cherie both very fearful. There was a very bad feeling in the air. Rod was absolutely adamant that Callum had to come back to Urapunga. He told Shaun that they were all in great danger, the Freemasons were closing in, and that everything he had been telling him was about to come to a head. He told Shaun he must go to Darwin and bring his brother back.

Tamara's sister was leaving in a few days to fly south, so Shaun and Tamara left with her on the Friday afternoon, 30 July, and drove to Katherine where they booked into a motel and went out for dinner. They drove on to Darwin the next day, picking up Callum and going out on the town for the night. It must have felt worlds away from the brooding little camp on the Wilton.

Tamara's sister flew out Sunday afternoon, and Callum and Shaun made plans to leave the next morning. They had discussed their father's extreme paranoia, and his obsession with the Freemason conspiracy. They decided it was all getting too crazy, and that they had to do something about him. They agreed they would go back to Urapunga and take Rod away from there now, either by himself or with Cherie, and bring him to Mt Catt. For them, Mt Catt was a symbol of the good times of their childhood, of the times they remembered their father at his happiest, and a place they knew he would feel safe, surrounded by the old people.

'We wanted to get him to Hitler,' Shaun said. 'We just felt that old Hitler would know what to do with him, and we were just going to stay there with him until he got better.' Hitler Wood was a famous medicine man, a healer, and Rod had spent a lot of time with the old man in the past. If anyone could have got through to Rod by then, it would have been Hitler.

Callum, Shaun and Tamara left Darwin on Monday morning, 2 August, stopping off at home in Howard Springs to leave a note telling Lex that Callum was quitting uni, and asking him to cancel Callum's room at the student residence. They arrived at Urapunga that evening to find no sign of Rod or Cherie, so they sat down at Tamara's house to wait for them to return. Callum was only nineteen, Shaun seventeen, but they were determined to convince their father to come with them to Mt Catt.

Another conversation about Rod had taken place just a few days before. Geoff Stewart and his family had been on a holiday, a three-month trip through Arnhem Land, visiting old friends in the various communities he and Mary had been involved with over the years, and in mid-July 1999 they arrived at Rod's camp on the Wilton River. They hadn't seen him since he'd reached Mataranka the previous October with the horses. They knew Rod had been using amphetamines for some time, and nothing Geoff had said to him could convince Rod to confront his addiction and the effects it was having on him. Cherie would often stay with Geoff and Mary when she was in Darwin. She would talk to them about herself and Rod, and several times made the decision to leave him. However each time, after a day or two, she would lose her resolve despite their support, and go back out to Urapunga. By late 1998 Rod's deteriorating personality and mental state, and his and Cherie's increasingly dysfunctional relationship, were things Geoff and Mary could no longer tolerate. Their offers to help were rejected by both parties, so Geoff and Mary decided to cease contact with them, and hadn't seen them for about nine months. Now, however, they were on holidays, were going to be in the area, and thought they should see how he was getting on.

A few weeks earlier, they contacted Rod at Urapunga, and made arrangements to meet at the community on a certain day. As they drove down the gravel road to Urapunga, they passed Rod and Cherie headed in the opposite direction. When they arrived at the community, an embarrassed Shaun greeted them, and told them that Rod had just left for town, and would be back in a couple of days. He took them out to the Wilton, and helped them set up camp not far from Rod's.

Rod and Cherie turned up four days later, and made a very brief appearance. Rod was very obviously high on speed. They didn't reappear for another couple of days, when the effects had begun to wear off. Over the next few days, Geoff and Mary had many conversations with both Rod and Cherie, all of which were dominated by Rod's insistent obsession with Freemasons and the enormous conspiracy to get to them. Geoff and Mary listened with total scepticism, but it was a waste of time trying to argue against any of it. They could see that Rod had deteriorated even further from the state he'd been in the previous October. In spite of this, Mary remembers Rod sitting in the dust with her little boys, playing trucks with them for hours. She thought he looked very sad.

Rod's attitude to his dogs was an indicator to Mary of just how much he had changed: 'It was the way he treated his dogs that really said things were going seriously wrong. His dogs were such a big part of his life, but at Lake Allen we noticed how badly he was treating them. He'd beat them savagely for some little thing, and they weren't being looked after, chained up all the time, barking constantly. Rod's dogs never used to bark.'

When it was time to leave, they met Rod and Cherie in Urapunga, and spent a last few hours with them, and again Rod spoke passionately to them about the people he believed were hunting him and Cherie. He tried to convince them that they too were in danger by association, that the Freemasons would target his friends and family as well. Then Rod began naming people Mary knew. By coincidence, Mary and Cherie had come from the same large country town in Victoria, but had never met each other before Cherie began living with Rod. However, they did know some of the same people, and now Rod was building an almost convincing argument backing up his theories, and using the names of people Mary remembered. Both she and Geoff began to feel very uncomfortable. They knew logically that what Rod was talking so passionately about had to be rubbish, but there was a seed of doubt creeping in, just the same.

They left the camp and headed for home, talking over what they'd heard back in Rod's camp. By the time they got to the Stuart Highway, they had shaken themselves free of the tendrils of Rod's ravings and could see them for what they were. But they were bothered by the fact that he had been able to persuade them, even for the briefest time, to entertain any idea at all that what he was talking about could have been true.

Geoff felt like Rod was spinning out of control. Rod hadn't made threats of violence against anyone, but he was clearly becoming completely delusional. When Geoff got back to Darwin, he contacted Wayne Miles and they agreed they had to do something about Rod. They made plans to go to Urapunga together in two weeks' time, on the weekend of 7 August, and convince Rod to seek some professional help. Geoff didn't know how they were going to do this, but he was planning to take medication with him to sedate Rod if necessary. It did cross his mind that, given Rod's paranoia and the weapons in the camp, this could be a dangerous thing to do.

At the Wilton camp on Saturday night, 31 July, Rod used the last of the speed, and began to become fixated about the absence of Shaun and Callum. He decided the boys should have been back by now, and was convinced that the Freemasons had kidnapped them, and were going to torture and kill them in an effort to get to himself and Cherie. At Urapunga they borrowed a car from Peter Woods, the community's manager, and drove to Darwin on Sunday evening.

They arrived at a friend's house in Humpty Doo about three in the morning, and Rod woke him up asking if they could swap cars with him, in order to put the imagined pursuers off the trail. The friend refused, as did the next one. They looked up Tamara's surname in a telephone book, and found one listing, for an address in McMillans Road. Tamara had no relatives in Darwin at all and the name was pure coincidence, but it was enough to convince Rod there was a connection to the boys' whereabouts. They spent most of Monday hiding in scrub nearby, observing the house.

Sometime during the afternoon, they went to Geoff Stewart's home at Rapid Creek. Geoff, Mary and their children were away for the day, and Rod and Cherie climbed in through a window. While in the house, Rod had trouble using the phone, and decided it had been tampered with. They rang our house in Howard Springs and recorded a garbled, rambling message, but then left the phone off the hook, resulting in a confused lot of sounds and words on our answering machine. When Lex listened to it the following day, he could make nothing out.

Rod decided that the Stewart family had been taken by the same people he believed were pursuing them. Hoping to find Callum and Shaun still alive, Rod took two first aid kits from the house, and they left.

Around sunset they turned up at the caravan where their friends Gary and Meg lived, just off the Stuart Highway near Kentish Road, Noonamah, about 50 kilometres south of Darwin. They often used to stay there when they came to town, and had known them for around six years.

Rod tried to convince the couple that they were in danger, that the Freemasons were closing in on him and Cherie, and that by association Gary and Meg were also in danger. When this didn't work, they left the residence and drove a short distance away. After about an hour, Rod returned to Gary and Meg's place on foot, armed with a 30/30 rifle, and fired four or five shots around the caravan, apparently to frighten them into believing what he had been warning them about. One shot hit the caravan itself. Cherie drove away when she heard the shooting, stopping a few miles further down the highway near the Acacia Hills store, while Rod crept away. By this time Gary and Meg were cowering on the floor of their van, wondering if Rod might have been telling the truth.

Rod moved across the Stuart Highway down Kentish Road, and within minutes began firing on the first house he came to, where Brian Williams lived with his partner and her ten-year-old daughter. Their neighbour Dave Hobden heard the gunshots and jumped into his truck to drive over and see what was going on at his mate's house.

Just as he stopped the truck outside Williams' house, a bullet exploded through the windscreen of his truck showering him with glass which pierced his right eye. Williams saw this happen, and ran out to help his mate, who had started to grope his way across the grass, blinded by blood and pain. While the two men were crawling behind some cover, Rod climbed into the truck and tried to drive off, but couldn't release the brake. At this point Williams picked up a baseball bat and rushed the truck, swinging wildly at the driver's side window, where he could see a head. Rod fired at Williams, shooting him in the hand and blasting off his right index finger. Later Williams found he had shotgun pellet wounds on his abdomen as well, and it appeared that Rod had picked up Hobden's shotgun from the seat and shot Williams with that.

While Williams and Hobden were getting to safety inside the house, Rod was yelling out a garbled mix of accusations about child killers and Freemasons, and Hell's Angels and child thieves. He kept shouting, 'Give me back my kids!' The two men had no idea what he was talking about. The shooting began again, through the walls, door and up through the floor of the elevated house. Williams hid Hobden, his partner and her daughter as best he could, and they stayed huddled like that against the bullets and the flying glass until the shots stopped, and the yelling grew fainter as Rod moved away into the bush.

The police arrived on the scene, and the two injured men were taken to hospital by ambulance – they had received calls about multiple gunshots in the area from many people by now, including from Gary and Meg several times. The Tactical Response Group (TRG) followed soon after. They established a roadblock at the intersection of the Stuart Highway and Livingstone Road, to the north of Kentish Road, and proceeded to work through the area, looking for the gunman, whose identity was unknown.

It was decided that it would be safer to set up a second roadblock from the south side of the danger area, rather than have Darwin police travel through the area to do so. At 3.30 am Sergeant Glen Huitson, officer-in-charge of Adelaide River police station, arrived with Senior Constable Jamie O'Brien and the two set up the roadblock at the junction of the Stuart Highway and Old Bynoe Road, less than a kilometre south of Kentish Road. In a few hours there was a line of trucks and road trains stretching down the highway to the south. They had been told to look out for a male, armed with a 30/30 lever action rifle, and a 12 gauge shotgun.

Around 5 am on Tuesday, the driver of one of the road trains heard a noise and felt his cabin rock. He saw someone in his rear-view mirror, so he turned up the radio in his cabin, climbed into the sleeping compartment, and called his wife on his mobile phone to tell her to call the police.

The TRG made a full search of the line of vehicles, but there was no sign of the gunman. The line of cars and trucks was building up as people attempted to get to work, and finally they were allowed to detour around the roadblocks via Old Bynoe Road, Hopewell Road, and Cox Peninsula Road, giving the danger zone a wide berth. The TRG vehicles left to conduct some house searches, and Sergeant Huitson and Constable O'Brien remained on their own at the southern roadblock.

As the morning wore on, it was getting very hot in the middle of the bitumen road, exposed to the sun as they were, and both Huitson and O'Brien removed their ballistic vests for about ten minutes to cool off, and then replaced them.

Sometime after 9 am, Anthony Hobden and Jonathon Anthonyszz, removalists who had stopped at the roadblock a couple of hours earlier on their way to work, came back. They had gone home to have some breakfast while waiting for the road to clear, and needed to get to Kentish Road to meet Anthony's brother, Dave Hobden, about the day's work. Both men were unaware of the night's events, or that Anthony Hobden's brother Dave had been injured. By this time, the two officers had taken some folding chairs out of their vehicle, and were sitting on the passenger side of the car in its shade. Constable O'Brien had taken his ballistic vest off again, and left it on the back seat of the police car. Sergeant Huitson was still wearing his vest.

The men were relaxed, expecting the roadblock would soon be dismantled. The last gunshots had been heard many hours earlier, and the sighting at the road train was nearly six hours ago, and to the south of the roadblock. It seemed likely that the gunman had detoured around them during the night, and would be well out of the area by now.

Jon Anthonyszz was leaning against the front end of the police car, on the passenger side, while Dave Hobden was squatting in front of the two police officers. The four men were chatting when a shot rang out and Anthonyszz was flung to the ground, screaming in pain. Huitson and O'Brien reacted immediately, O'Brien pulling out his pistol and crouching beside the back of the vehicle looking over the boot. Huitson reached into the car for the radio and called for assistance. O'Brien scanned the area from where the shot had come, and saw someone lying on the ground, propped up on his elbows with a rifle aimed straight at them. He was about 40 metres away from the car, on the east side of the Stuart Highway, behind the water pipe that supplies Darwin's water.

As O'Brien watched, he saw the gunman crawl forward on his elbows towards a ridge of dirt left by a grader, which gave him some cover. The rest of the area was clear, and the gunman had an open view of the four men.

Huitson picked up a shotgun from inside the police car. O'Brien fired four or five shots in rapid succession, causing the gunman to drop his head. Huitson then fired the shotgun through the vehicle, shattering the driver's side window. Both officers continued firing in the hope that they could keep the gunman pinned down and unable to return fire before the TRG arrived. They were worried about the civilian, Anthonyszz, who lay exposed to the gunman on the road.

Suddenly O'Brien heard the gunman fire again, and Sergeant Huitson spun to the ground, clutching his stomach. Then Anthonyszz began screaming, afraid he would be shot again. O'Brien yelled to Hobden to go and get his mate while he stood up and began firing at the gunman to keep him pinned down. Hobden quickly ran out and dragged Anthonyszz behind the cover of the vehicle.

O'Brien picked up the shotgun that Huitson had dropped, and

commenced firing at the gunman. During the exchange of fire, a car drove up to the roadblock from the south. Both O'Brien and Hobden yelled and waved at the car to go away, and it disappeared. At this point O'Brien tried to formulate a plan of retreat, but it was obvious that he could not move two injured people without exposing everyone to the gunman's bullets. They would have to remain where they were until help arrived.

They continued to exchange fire, O'Brien very aware that he had a limited supply of ammunition. As he reached into the vehicle to get some more, he noticed the gunman begin to move forward. He told Hobden to stay down, and he stood and fired two more shots. The gunman fired a shot back, which O'Brien heard narrowly missing his head. As he reloaded, he heard the sound of vehicles approaching fast from the north.

The TRG had been gathered at Kentish Road, preparing to conduct more searches of the bush beside the highway heading south, when they heard gunshots, and received a message that the southern roadblock was under fire. They immediately raced towards the scene, and as they neared it, the leading TRG vehicle was clipped by the following one, and rolled onto its side.

As the TRG officers scrambled out of their vehicles, calling out to O'Brien to tell them where the gunman was, O'Brien saw the gunman rise up into a kneeling position, turn slightly and aim his rifle at the new arrivals. The gunman's attention was shifted from O'Brien, and now the officer was able to take careful aim. He fired two rapid shots, and the gunman dropped to the ground. He appeared to still be moving, and in a firing position, and O'Brien fired again. This time the gunman lay still.

At forty-four years of age, Rodney William Ansell was dead, in a manner that would cause so many people grief of the worst kind. He had killed a young policeman who had a family of his own, and injured three civilians, two seriously. Ironically, 38-year-old Sergeant Glen Huitson was the kind of policeman Rod Ansell would have respected. He was known for his fair and gentle manner with Aboriginal people, and had a very close relationship with the people of Daly River, where he had previously been stationed. Highly regarded by his fellow officers and his community, Sergeant Huitson was about to

receive a Valour Award for bravery, only the fourth time the medal
had been awarded in the Territory. In February 1999 he had disarmed
a gunman who had hijacked a tourist bus in Litchfield Park, without
even drawing his own weapon.

Rod was identified by papers he had on him. A friend of Wayne
Miles in the police force knew he was a good friend of Rod's and called
him when the police had identified Rod at the scene. Wayne called
Lex, and later had to identify the body of his friend.

Back at Urapunga, Callum and Shaun were completely unaware
of what had taken place. Peter Woods had told them that Rod had
seemed very upset and worried about them when he borrowed his car
on Sunday night, but he didn't know where Rod and Cherie had
gone. They drove out to the Wilton camp on Tuesday to check that
their father hadn't come back during the night, but it was deserted.
When Rod hadn't returned by Wednesday morning, they tried to
phone around to see where he was. The telephones at the community
were out of order, so they went to the Roper Bar Store a few miles up
the road. They rang all the numbers they knew, but none of their calls
were answered until they reached a friend of Rod's in Humpty Doo,
who asked them if they had seen the morning paper, which they
hadn't.

'I can't tell you anything for sure, but some pretty bad stuff's goin'
down. That's all I can say.'

They sat by the water at the Roper River crossing for a while,
discussing possible scenarios, whether the things Rod had been
raving about for so long had actually happened, or if he'd perhaps
finally lost the plot and had some kind of a breakdown. The brief
communication from the Humpty Doo friend had such ominous
overtones. They didn't know what to do, whether they should go back
to town and look for their father, or stay and wait for him to contact
them. A meeting was about to start, one that Rod was supposed to
attend, with the local people, the land councils and the Elsey Station
manager, to discuss the proposed meatworks and the future of the
Urapunga cattle operation. Peter Woods had asked them to stand in
for their father, so they drove slowly back to the community. At least
this prearranged activity took the pressure off making a decision
straight away.

About fifteen minutes into the meeting, they saw the police vehicle from Ngukkur pull up at Rod's old camp in the community. Callum and Shaun immediately got to their feet and excused themselves. A stranger bringing bad news is easier to bear than someone who is close to you. They were braced for it, whatever it was. They walked towards the police car, recognising the officer from Ngukurr. Then they saw Geoff Stewart get out of the passenger side, and it was all they could do to continue walking towards him. His appearance could only mean one thing.

They flew back to Darwin in complete silence, unable to speak to Geoff or to each other. Lex brought them home to Howard Springs, I arrived home a few hours later, and gradually we all began to deal with the reality of the terrible events that had taken place just a day before.

# Epilogue

In the course of writing this account, I spoke to many people, old friends from the early days, friends from the more recent past, and people who had known Rod through professional contact only. Every time I contacted someone to ask if I could talk to them about Rod for this book, I was nervous about the reception I might receive, half expecting disapproval or rejection of what I was trying to do. Without exception, they were all eager to help, and glad that the real story was finally going to be written.

I spent hours and hours reliving old times with friends, reminiscing about the wonderful bull catching days, the crazy things everyone did, and listening to them talk about the impact that Rod Ansell had had on their lives. And the impact that the manner of his death had on them.

They mostly remembered him as a storyteller, as a natural born entertainer, who could keep everyone laughing and the stories flowing. They remembered him next as a consummate bushman, possessing an uncanny, intuitive connection with the bush, and an endless reservoir of knowledge about it. And they remembered the bull catching. Whether it was cattle bulls at Fitzroy Station, or buffalo in Arnhem Land or on the Mary River flood plains, they all recalled these times with great humour and satisfaction. These were the times about which they told *their* stories.

They talked about the decline they had seen taking place over the years. Some were angry that Rod had let them down by not remaining the bush icon they had held him to be. Others were just puzzled at how someone like him could have slid down into the depths of squalid drug addiction the way he did. All of them were deeply saddened at how his life ended.

At my fortieth birthday party in 1995, Greg Keogh, Chris Penhall, Geoff Reemeijer and Duane Fishlock sat down together and talked about the man they had each known so well since the early eighties. They talked about going out and kidnapping him, and taking him away somewhere to get him off drugs and straighten him out, get him back to what he was.

Even if they'd been able to carry out the plan, I doubt it would have succeeded. Rod never went back, not anywhere. The world he inhabited was long gone, and he didn't seem to be able to survive in any other. The biggest hurdle they would have had to overcome was making Rod accept that he had taken a wrong turn, got lost, stuffed up badly, and he never did that. I think they knew it too. It was just something they wished they could do. Rod had given them the best time of their lives, and they felt powerless in the face of what was happening to him.

Certainly Rod had had a lot of highly stressful situations to contend with, many of them simultaneously – court cases, severe financial stress, a failed marriage, media attention, constant back and neck pain, and the loss of his land. Added into this mix was the spectre of change. The pastoral industry was changing. Gone was the romance of the open range, tall tales, hard men and hard living that he had grown up revering. Bull catching was almost consigned to history, and he no longer owned his station. And to not put too fine a point on it, he had suffered the humiliation amongst his peers of losing his land, watching while it was auctioned publicly and offered to people who thought it wasn't worth his price.

A lot was said about the fame going to his head, and that he was terminally bitter about missing out on making a fortune from his association with *Crocodile Dundee*. Rod handled the media attention better than most, but as time went on, and he was still getting airplay either through *Crocodile Dundee* references or the BTEC fight, some people thought that he was seeking the attention, and that it had given him a swelled head. I don't think this was true at all. Rod always had a good-sized ego – it made him who he was. Media attention was something that didn't faze him, and I don't believe it changed him much at all.

However, I do believe he was a lot more affected by the *Crocodile Dundee* episode than I appreciated at the time. People have their stories. Aboriginal artists can only paint stories they have a right to, their own stories which they inherit by birth. Rod's story was his epic on the Fizmaurice River. He had lived through it and survived it, and for that reason, owned it. When the media began to refer to him as the real 'Crocodile Dundee' his own story was, as he saw it, usurped and trivialised. Contrary to myth, he did not attempt to seek a share of the proceeds. As far as I know, he never gave it a thought. 'Crocodile Dundee' was not Rod Ansell's story. When Rod contacted Hogan and asked for permission to refer to himself as the person who was an inspiration for the movie, or something similar, for the purpose of promoting overseas a very small scale tourist operation on Melaleuca Station, he was merely adopting, wryly perhaps, the media's parody of himself. Implicit in Rod contacting Hogan was his acknowledgement that 'Crocodile Dundee' as a trade name belonged to Hogan. When John Cornell's letter turned up warning him off, he was genuinely surprised and disappointed.

These were all aspects that influenced him strongly. But lots of people suffer great disappointment in their lives, suffer terrible tragedies and the loss of all their dreams, yet they don't kill people.

Rod had already demonstrated that he was looking for more in life. He was not content to settle for what most people wanted. He needed to understand the big questions, the whys rather than the hows and whens. But he confused happiness with acceptance and surrender.

He didn't want to be ordinary, and he didn't want to *feel* ordinary. He had a dangerous streak, a self destructive force that he managed to keep in balance most of the time. He had an outlet for it in the excitement and the dancing-with-death of bull catching. He craved that whole body exhilaration it brought. After a muster, or having just caught a bull, his eyes were bright and focused, and he was in a state of high alert, every muscle fibre practically vibrating. Doing a dangerous physical activity is like that. It's why people love extreme sports like base jumping, or snowboarding down mountains, or bungee jumping. It's that whole body buzz it gives, being right on the edge.

Perhaps he searched for that feeling with amphetamines. Speed puts the user in a state of alertness and euphoria, makes them animated and excited, *speeded up*. But where the downside of bull catching might be injury, the downside of amphetamines is much more complicated. Users can become irritable, hostile and aggressive. They can turn violent for no reason. Their appetite is suppressed, and they lose weight. They can feel a sense of power and superiority over other people. And they can become psychotic, experiencing delusions, hallucinations and paranoia.

I used to believe that marijuana was a simple, 'safe' drug. I don't believe that any longer. Like my peers, I used to laugh at the conservative notion that it 'led to harder drugs'. People who smoked dope became relaxed and mellowed. That had to be a lot more desirable than the aggressive, lurching drunks staggering outside the hotels.

Perhaps if your life is going well, if you are content, feeling in control of your life, and in good health, maybe sharing the occasional joint doesn't do you much harm, although recent medical opinion is that even very light use might be dangerous for some people. Maybe it's in the same category as having a glass or two of red wine. Perhaps the damage occurs when you smoke dope because your life is none of those things, and you smoke it to escape your problems.

Rod smoked to 'chill out', calm down, to stop feeling angry, sad, worried – all those things. But before long, he was smoking from sun-up to bedtime. You might be feeling good when you're stoned, but you don't make good decisions. It became a snowball effect, as one bad decision after another just gave him more to feel bad about, so he smoked even more to be able to deal with it.

Hindsight's a great thing. Lots of us thought that Rod was starting to smoke too much, but when you're dealing with the busyness of living at the time, you don't always see things for what they are. And even when those around him believed he was overdoing it, it was quite another thing to front him about it. Rod would never admit he had a problem. Not even when he was seriously addicted to amphetamines. His good friend Geoff Stewart talked to him about it several times in the last few years, trying to convince him to seek help with it, but Rod would never admit the problem was as bad as Geoff thought. As far as Rod was concerned, he was in control of what he was doing, he could stop any time he chose.

I know that many of Rod's friends have wrestled with the notion of 'if only we had . . .' As the Coroner Mr RJ Wallace put it in his report:

Both Stewart and Miles . . . and Ansell's other friends . . . were therefore faced with delicate questions as to when and how they ought best to intervene. Such questions are awkward enough when faced by friends, relatives and health professionals in a case involving a person living an ordinary urban life. It is hardly to be wondered at that Ansell's friends may have hesitated before trying to tackle him in his remote independence. I cannot think of any recommendation which, if implemented, would make it any easier for those who find themselves faced with these delicate decisions.

*Findings of the Inquest into the Deaths of Glen Anthony*
*Huitson and Rodney William Ansell,* page 50

The events of 3 August 1999 impacted on many, many people. Lisa Huitson lost her husband and her two little children will never know their father. Senior Constable Jamie O'Brien saw his mate die, and was forced to kill another human being, a position no one should have to be in. Dave Hobden, Jonathan Anthonyszz and Brian Williams suffered gunshot wounds from which they all suffer long-term effects. Although not physically injured, Jamie O'Brien, Anthony Hobden, Gary and Meg, and Brian Williams' partner and her young daughter went through the terror of being fired upon and believing they might be killed.

My two sons lost their father; George and Eve Ansell their second born son; Jennifer, Malcolm and Christine their brother. When someone dies in such a way, mixed up with the grief for their death is a terrible feeling of guilt. It's as if the surviving family takes up the burden of the blame for what was done. Their grieving has had to be hidden and private, and unacknowledged. Rod Ansell was from a good family, and his sons are good people. For whatever reasons he had, he took a bad turning in his life, and paid the ultimate price.

This book has been difficult to write. Writers often refer to their efforts as a labour of love, but that's not how I feel about this book, unless I think about my two sons Callum and Shaun. They are the reason I have put these words on paper. Since 1999, we have consistently refused to speak to the media, or to people wanting to write books about what happened. Then when it became clear that the attention was not just going to disappear if we ignored it, I decided that it was better to face it head on. If we said nothing, and someone went ahead and wrote a book, or made a movie, they would only have the testimony of drunks in pubs, vague acquaintances and the often sensationalised accounts in the newspapers on which to base their work. I have written it the only way I could, as my own memoir of those years.

Rod Ansell committed a terrible crime, and there is no excusing what he did. But the way he ended up was not the way he had lived, and it's not the way he is remembered by those who loved and admired him.

The last word should go to Luke McCall, who found Rod Ansell on the banks of the Fitzmaurice River all those long years ago, and who answered, when someone said to him that he 'should have just left that bastard Ansell out on the river': 'Well, the man I brought back wasn't like that. He was a different bloke, and there's no knowing how many dry gullies a man might have had to cross in his life.'

# Postscript:
# Where are they now?

Bull catching as a way of life has disappeared from the Northern Territory. Stations and stock are more tightly managed and there are no longer mobs of uncontrolled scrub bulls wandering the outback. So where do old bull catchers go?

Greg Keogh and Josie Coleman own a busy plumbing business in Humpty Doo. When they aren't exploring out-of-the-way places in foreign countries, they take their three children exploring the Territory. Greg has infused them with his passion for chasing pigs, fishing, and just being in the bush, preferring swags to beds as often as possible. Chris Penhall also prefers the bush to town, continuing to live and work in remote places in northern Australia, with his partner Roseanne. He and Greg are still great mates. After returning to Darwin to study, Felicity Butler graduated with an Associate Diploma of Applied Science, a Bachelor of Science degree and the University medal. She still loves living in isolated places, and is currently a weather observer at Giles meteorological station in central Australia.

Duane and Jane Fishlock and their three children own Sturt Creek Downs, a cattle station near Mataranka. Jane also runs her own travel agency in Katherine. As well as cattle, they breed rodeo bulls and operate a popular bull-riding rodeo around the Top End in their spare time. Geoffrey Reemeijer is a successful artist with several exhibitions and international sales to his credit, and lives in Darwin with his partner, gallery owner Karen Brown. Luke McCall has retired to a little town in the southern highlands of NSW, and keeps in touch with many old friends from the north. Dick Gill has a property in the mountains of the southern highlands of NSW, having swapped tropical heat and wild cattle for winter snow and deer. Bluey Lewis and his wife Anne own a hotel in Katherine, which keeps Bluey busier than inspecting stock ever did. The old station cook and fencer, Bob Thomas, retired to Katherine and took up oil painting. He also had several exhibitions and sold some of his works. Bob wrote me the most wonderful letters for a few years, but I don't know where he is now. Leonie and Craig Hemsworth live at Phillip Island, Victoria. Leonie is now a high school teacher, and Craig a regional manager for the Victorian Child Protection service, when he's not surfing with their three sons.

As for my family, Callum has been studying architecture and drafting, and presently works for a surveying company. Shaun graduated with a Bachelor of Environmental Science in 2004, works in land management, and also gets out bush as often as he can. They both still go fishing a lot. Lex continues to practice as a barrister in Darwin, but would rather be fishing. We were married in December 2004, at Leonie and Craig's house. Our daughter Ali is in her last year at primary school. Sophie is a lawyer, married with two gorgeous boys and another on the way, and lives with her husband Jim, also a lawyer, in Adelaide. Tom works for an advertising firm in Adelaide. I was a freelance illustrator and cartoonist for several years, and then worked as electorate officer for Gerry Wood Independent MLA out at Howard Springs after I helped with his election campaign. I owe Gerry a thank you for letting me take six months' leave to write this book, and for being so gracious when I finally resigned to finish it. I hope to be able to continue writing, but I think my next book will be fiction.

# Glossary

**barrage:** a barrier constructed across a river to prevent or impede the flow of salt water upstream. Salt water intrusion is a major issue in the Mary River system. Several barrages were constructed, including a major one at Shady Camp which vehicles could drive across.

**barramundi, barra:** popular game fish in northern Australia – great eating.

**Bedourie oven:** a rolled steel baking dish with a fitted lid that comes halfway down the sides of the dish, used for cooking in coals; also called a 'dourie.

**billy:** a metal tin used for boiling water; tea leaves are added to it to make tea.

**bogey:** a bath or a wash.

**breakaways:** animals which break away from the mob.

**brownie:** a solid kind of cake, flavoured with ginger and currants, cooked in a camp oven.

**BTEC:** Bovine Tuberculosis Eradication Campaign.

**bull catcher:** a cut down, highly modified four wheel drive vehicle used for catching cattle bulls and buffalo; the driver of a bull catcher.

**camp oven:** often known as a Dutch oven – a cast iron baking dish with a well fitted lid.

**coachers:** a quiet mob of cattle taken out on a muster, into which the new, fresh cattle are run.

**damper:** a solid kind of bread made from flour, risings, salt and water.

**donga:** a rough house or shelter.

**drover:** person taking cattle or sheep overland, usually long distances.

**esky:** an insulated ice box for carrying cold food and drinks.

**fire unit:** a portable water pump used for fire fighting as well as spraying weeds.

**flash:** smart, fancy.

**flogging:** a beating, or to beat someone at a game.

**gen-set:** a engine which generates electricity.

**hot water donkey:** a bush hot water system, made from a 44-gallon drum.

**jump-up:** a rough access up a steep escarpment.

**killer:** a cattle beast or buffalo butchered for meat. You 'get a killer'.

**long drop:** an outside toilet – a deep hole in the ground, with or without a toilet bowl fixed over it.

**mickey bull:** a young cattle bull.

**muster:** the action of gathering cattle or sheep together; called 'round up' in the US.

**pandanus:** a type of screw palm common in the north of Australia; has long narrow leaves with small thorns along the edges, and grows in a spiral fashion.

**pannikin:** an enamelled metal cup.

**punkah:** a large swinging fan, fixed to the ceiling. Modern versions are electrically operated, but in nineteenth century India they were moved by the 'punkah-wallah', who pulled a rope.

**rushing:** when a mob of cattle suddenly gallop off together – called 'stampeding' in the US.

**scrub bull:** an unbranded, wild cattle bull.

**smoko:** morning tea.

**station:** a large pastoral property running cattle or sheep; a 'ranch' in the US.

**stock camp:** a group of stockmen, or 'ringers', who go out on horseback mustering cattle, staying out for weeks or months at a time and sleeping in swags on the ground.

**swag:** a bedroll; a canvas groundsheet that encloses a thin mattress, sheets and blankets, is rolled up and tied with (usually) leather straps.

**tail out:** to walk mustered stock out and keep them quiet, usually on horseback.

**to be cactus:** to be finished, ruined, even dead. 'He's cactus' means he's dead.

**ute:** short for 'utility vehicle'.

**VJY:** the Out Post Radio network based in Darwin. It was the public communications system for remote regions in the Top End, and operated by Telecom Australia.

**yabbies:** a type of freshwater crayfish.

# Acknowledgements

One of the pleasant aspects of writing this memoir was the opportunity it provided to catch up with old friends. In particular, I am indebted to the following for their long and accurate memories, and their generosity in taking the time to share a few cuppas and get the memory cells working overtime: Greg Keogh and Josie Coleman, Chris Penhall, Felicity Butler, Sabrina Lethbridge, Duane and Jane Fishlock, Geoffrey Reemeijer, Dick Gill, Luke McCall, Rachel Percy, Gavin Perry, Bluey Lewis, John Humphreys, Lenore Humphreys, Julie Carr, Rina Madden, Richard Ledgar and Lyn Allen, Paul Josif, Graham Michell, Wayne Miles, Patrick Loftus, Geoff Stewart and Mary Willem, Dwyn Delaney, and Leonie and Craig Hemsworth. Also Max Finlayson from ERISS, for information on the Waler Expedition, Frank Geddes from the Darwin RSL, for information about Waler horses, and John Mitchell for the use of his great photos. Patrick Loftus also represented the family pro bono at the Coronial inquest.

For their unstinting support while I was writing: Jane Miles, Julia Christensen, Elizabeth Desailley, Terry Robson, Helen Thistlethwaite, Sue Dengate, Les and Annette Woodbridge, Mac Cocker and Patty Ring. Territory author and editor Kim Caraher read a very early first draft, and put me on the right track. I would also like to thank Patty Ring and Paul Costigan of the Roma Bar in Cavenagh Street for great coffee and a table when I was sick of my own space at home. In Sydney, Wendy Day for her wisdom and good advice when I needed it, and Carolyn Beaumont for assistance and an introduction to my agent Selwa Anthony.

Two special women in my life encouraged me for years to write this account, but sadly died before it was completed: Barbara James and Elizabeth Loftus. One or the other was hovering at my shoulder whenever I felt like it was all too hard.

I had the benefit of a fine publishing team – in particular, Jude McGee and Roberta Ivers of Random House were a delight to work with, and made the task of putting this book together much more enjoyable than it might have been. My editor Jo Jarrah was brilliant, and I fervently hope I get to work with her again. I am also very fortunate to have the wonderful Selwa Anthony as my agent, and thank her for her generosity and advice.

I owe an enormous thank you to my great friend Sabrina Lethbridge, who kept twenty-five years' of my letters and gave them all back to me when I began to write; my beautiful and sensible sister Leonie Hemsworth who is both my staunchest defender and my best critic; my marvellous parents Martin and Therese van Os for their love and support all my life; and to all of my family in Melbourne – Peter, Craig, Rob, Ali and Danielle and their families for cheering me on.

Most of all, to my family here in Darwin and Adelaide I owe a huge debt of gratitude – to my husband Lex Silvester for his unflagging faith in my ability to do this, for living with my past for the last two and a half years, and for always being willing to listen and give me his opinion; to Ali for being proud of me for writing a book and for being such a lovely daughter; and to Sophie, Jim and Tom in Adelaide for their love and support. To my two special, brilliant sons Callum and Shaun, who gave me permission to write this account: I wrote this book for you, and I thank you for the being the best sons any mother could wish for.